Selected Sites in the Hill Lake Locality

AMERICAN BOTTOM ARCHAEOLOGY
FAI-270 Site Reports
Volume 13

Series Editors:

Charles J. Bareis (Principal Investigator and Program Coordinator)
and
James W. Porter (Project Director)

Technical Editor:
Carolyn L. Handell-McElrath

Investigations conducted under the auspices of
the Illinois Archaeological Survey in
cooperation with:

The United States Department of Transportation
Federal Highway Administration

The United States Department of the Interior
National Park Service

The State of Illinois
Department of Transportation

J. Paul Biggers (Chief of Environment)
John A. Walthall, Ph.D. (Chief Archaeologist)

Selected Sites in the Hill Lake Locality

Andrew C. Fortier

with a contribution by
Sissel Johannessen

Published for the Illinois Department of Transportation
by the University of Illinois Press
Urbana and Chicago
1985

Library of Congress Cataloging-in-Publication Data

Fortier, Andrew C., 1947-
    Selected sites in the Hill Lake locality.

    (American Bottom archaeology ; v. 13)
    "Represents revised versions of reports 5 (Fiege
Site), 18 (Truck #4 Site), 27 (Carbon Monoxide Site),
and 30 (Truck #7 and Go-Kart South sites)" — Pref.
    Bibliography: p.
    1. Indians of North America — Illinois — American
Bottom — Antiquities. 2. American Bottom (Ill.) — An-
tiquities. 3. Illinois — Antiquities. I. Johannessen,
Sissel. II. Illinois. Dept. of Transportation.
III. Title. IV. Series.
E78.I3A58 1985   vol. 13   970 s   [977.3'8]   85-16458
[E78.I3]
ISBN 0-252-01075-2 (vol. 13)
ISBN 0-252-01061-2 (set)

CONTENTS

PREFACE

In June of 1977, the University of Illinois at Urbana-Champaign signed an agreement with the Illinois Department of Transportation for the mitigation of archaeological resources within the right-of-way of Federal Aid Interstate 270 (redesignated 255) in the American Bottom in Monroe, St. Clair, and Madison Counties, Illinois. As part of this agreement, the University, in cooperation with the state and the Illinois Archaeological Survey, has the right to publish the results of these archaeological investigations. This volume represents revised versions of Reports 5 (Fiege Site), 18 (Truck #4 Site), 27 (Carbon Monoxide Site), and 30 (Truck #7 and Go-Kart South Sites), all by Andrew C. Fortier, which were originally submitted by the FAI-270 Archaeological Mitigation Project to the Illinois Department of Transportation in partial fulfillment of contractual obligations of the agreement. This volume also represents one of a series of major site reports that have been selected by the Project for publication by the University of Illinois Press. Each of the descriptive site reports will present a detailed summary of the archaeography of particular sites investigated by the Project. These volumes will not attempt to make regional comparisons or interpretations, since such syntheses are presented in a summary volume of the FAI-270 Archaeological Mitigation Project entitled "American Bottom Archaeology," edited by Charles J. Bareis and James W. Porter, and published by the University of Illinois Press (March, 1984).

For the Department of Anthropology, University of Illinois at Urbana-Champaign, I would like to acknowledge the support and cooperation of the United States Department of Transportation, Federal Highway Administration; the State of Illinois, Illinois Department of Transportation; the Illinois Archaeological Survey; and the University of Illinois Press.

Charles J. Bareis
Principal Investigator
and
Program Coordinator

ACKNOWLEDGMENTS

A number of individuals have contributed significantly to the completion of the individual reports and to the production of this volume. The FAI-270 Program Coordinator, Charles J. Bareis, and the Project Director, James W. Porter, have made invaluable criticisms of each report and, of course, provided the primary impetus and organizational framework for the excavation, analysis, and report writing stages involved in the completion of this work. The senior author was assisted in the field by two chief supervisors, Fred A. Finney and Michael Morelock. Supervisors George Milner and Dale McElrath also lent assistance at the Go-Kart South and Carbon Monoxide sites, respectively. A list of crew members who worked at the various sites is provided below. This list does not include the many laboratory personnel who washed, processed, and labeled the artifacts from these sites, but special thanks are extended to Connie Bodner, who organized and oversaw those activities. The senior author would also like to acknowledge John Kelly, who organized and supervised much of the 1975-1977 survey and testing conducted in the Hill Lake locality, and who provided valuable input on ceramic and lithic identifications, excavation strategy, and general site interpretation. The analysis and write-up benefitted from the interaction and discussions between the authors and several other members of the FAI-270 Project, including James Porter, Mark Mehrer, Dale McElrath, Tom Emerson, and George Milner. A special acknowledgment is given to Drs. James B. Griffin and John Walthall for making useful comments concerning the ceramic and lithic materials recovered from the Hill Lake sites. Thanks are also extended to Bill White, Lawson Smith, Linda Bonnell, and Dr. Charles Alexander for the analysis and identification of geomorphic environments within the Hill Lake locality.

The contributions of the following people are gratefully acknowledged by Sissel Johannessen, who served as the project ethnobotanist: Debby Pearsall, who established the paleoethnobotany lab and served as consultant; Lucy Whalley, who developed the sampling strategy for floral remains, and the following people who sorted the flotation samples: Lisa Carlson, Alvin Hishinuma, Guinivere Joy, Mike Lawrence, Steve Means, Arne Price, Eric Voigt, and Gerry Wait.

Faunal remains were identified and tabulated by Paula Cross and Lucretia Kelly. Flotation and sorting of samples was initially organized and conducted by Denise Steele and later by Michael Morelock. The individual faunal sections were organized and written by the senior author.

Site and feature maps along with all graphs were prepared by Guy Prentice, assisted by Mary Engbring, Ruth Krochock, Richard Lacampagne,

Scott Wade, and Chris Dunbar. Artifact illustrations were accomplished
by Rusty Smith, Alison Towers, Mary Weismantel, and Marilyn Weiss.
Computer programs were devised and run by Merrily Shaw and Richard
Lacampagne. Richard Lacampagne was also responsible for the tabulation,
computerization, and initial write-up of the lithic assemblages at the
Truck #7 and Go-Kart South sites. He also helped in the formatting of
many of the figures and tables included in this volume. Fred Finney
also prepared the initial ceramic descriptions for the Truck #7 report.
Acknowledgment is given to Jeff Abrams and Dean Meador for formatting
and photographing the plates and printing the numerous maps and figures
included in this volume. The maps were prepared by Guy Prentice and
Scott Wade. The block map of the Hill Lake locality was produced by
Linda Alexander.

Overall production and editoral supervision of this volume were
provided by the Project Editor, Carolyn McElrath. Jennifer Eleveld and
Cornelia Bos assisted with grammatical and stylistic editing. Computer
editing and formatting of this volume were performed by Luann White,
Helen Sullivan, Anna Fernyhough, Roland Stone, Ellen O'Callaghan, Tom
Aleto, and Mary Weismantel. The author gratefully acknowledges the
contributions of these individuals to the completion of this volume.

The contents of this volume reflect the authors' views, who are
solely responsible for the facts and the accuracy of the data presented
herein. The contents do not necessarily reflect the official views or
policies of the Illinois Department of Transportation and/or the Federal
Government.

Site Supervisors

Fred Finney
Michael Morelock
Dale McElrath
George Milner

1978-1979 Crew Members	Sites (11-Mo-)
Pat Anderson	593, 609, 200
Kevin Andres	593, 609, 200
John Arnold	593, 609, 200, 552S
Andrea Berlin	593, 200
Jane Bouchard	593, 200
Caven Clark	593, 200, 552S
Kelly Cox	593, 609, 195, 200
Paula Cross	593, 609
Patricia Daley	593, 200, 552S
Helen Deluga	593, 609, 200, 552S
Tom Emerson	609
Sheryl Goodnick	200
Lisa Gruber	609
Nick Hakiel	593, 195, 200, 552S
Edward Hayden	593, 195, 200
Kathy Hesterberg	593, 609, 195
Doug Jackson	593, 200
Jill Jefferson	195
Susan Jelly	593
Denise Knight	593, 200
Don Koelb	195
Ruth Krochock	593, 200
Richard Lacampagne	593, 609, 200
Ellen Lefferts	593, 552S
Eric Markman	593, 195
Melissa Marshall	195
Lise Marx	593, 200
Gareth McNair-Lewis	593, 200
Mark Mehrer	609
Mary Mruzik	609
Steve Ozuk	609
Guy Prentice	609, 200, 552S
Don Reinhold	593, 200
Sandy Riebling	593
Jackie Riechmann	593, 195
Susan Salach	593
Becky Schaefer	593, 609, 200
Debra Schindler	609, 200
Cora St Martin (Bentz)	593, 195, 200
Marilyn Stachle	593
Ann Stahl	593

Jim Sterbenz   593, 200
Sharon Taube   593, 200
Mark Thurner   195
Allison Towers   593
Craig Volkert   593, 609,
Roger Williamson   593, 609, 200
Charles Witty   593, 609, 200
Michael Zdanovich   195

American Bottom Chronology

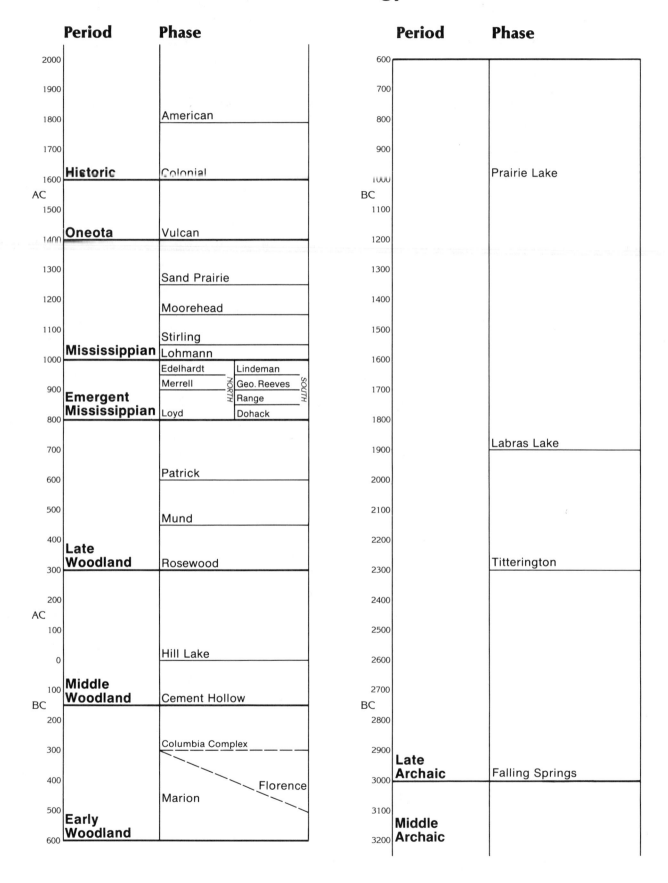

	Period	Phase
2000		
1900		
1800		American
1700		
1600	**Historic**	Colonial
AC 1500		
1400	**Oneota**	Vulcan
1300		Sand Prairie
1200		Moorehead
1100		Stirling
1000	**Mississippian**	Lohmann
900	**Emergent Mississippian**	Edelhardt / Lindeman; Merrell / Geo. Reeves (NORTH / SOUTH); Range; Loyd / Dohack
800		
700		
600	**Late Woodland**	Patrick
500		Mund
400		Rosewood
300		
200		
AC 100		
0		Hill Lake
100	**Middle Woodland**	Cement Hollow
BC 200		
300		Columbia Complex
400		Florence
500		Marion
600	**Early Woodland**	

	Period	Phase
600		
700		
800		
900		
1000		Prairie Lake
BC 1100		
1200		
1300		
1400		
1500		
1600		
1700		
1800		
1900		Labras Lake
2000		
2100		
2200		Titterington
2300		
2400		
2500		
2600		
2700		
BC 2800		
2900	**Late Archaic**	Falling Springs
3000		
3100	**Middle Archaic**	
3200		

CHAPTER 1. INTRODUCTION

The chapters in this volume present the results obtained from five
sites excavated by the University of Illinois at Urbana-Champaign (UIUC)
FAI-270 Archaeological Mitigation Project during the period 1978-1979.
These chapters present a set of discrete sites located at the southern
end of the Hill Lake meander locality, which is situated in the American
Bottom floodplain of southwestern Illinois. Analysis and report writing
were accomplished at the University of Illinois at Urbana-Champaign
FAI-270 laboratory during 1979-1981.   The reports presented in this
volume represent slightly revised editions of contractual reports
previously submitted to the Illinois Department of Transportation
(IDOT).

For the most part, the order of report presentation is organized on
the basis of the south to north positioning of the sites along the
FAI-270 alignment. The length of individual reports, of course, varies
according to the amount and diversity of recovered materials and
features from a site. The Truck #7 and Go-Kart South sites are combined
here into a single report although they were excavated as separate
entities. Originally, a volume was planned to cover all of the sites
excavated in the Hill Lake locality. However, a decision was made to
exclude three sites from this volume because of size limitations.   The
results from those sites, including the Go-Kart North (11-Mo-552N), Mund
(11-S-435) and Carbon Dioxide (11-Mo-594) sites, are presented in other
FAI-270 volumes (Fortier and Emerson 1984; Fortier et al. 1983; and
Finney and Fortier 1985).

PHYSIOGRAPHIC SETTING

The American Bottom, situated between Alton and Chester, Illinois,
extends for nearly 130 km in a north-south direction and constitutes a
level-to-gently undulating floodplain that contains a variety of complex
geomorphological features.   These include modern river and stream
meanders, abandoned meander scars and banks, oxbow lakes, sloughs,
marshes, natural levees, stream and lake terraces, point bar deposits,
inner channel ridges and swales, and alluvial and colluvial outwash
slopes, which emanate from the loess-covered limestone bluffs that mark
the eastern border of the American Bottom. Much of the physiographic
diversity in the American Bottom can be attributed directly to the
meandering of the Mississippi River, most of which occurred prior to
1500 B.C.

Five archaeological sites are discussed in this volume, which are located at the southern end of the FAI-270 alignment and situated specifically within the southern portion of the Hill Lake meander scar locality (Figure 1 and Plate 1). Included from south to north are the Fiege site (11-Mo-609), the Carbon Monoxide site (11-Mo-593), the Truck #4 site (11-Mo-195), the Truck #7 site (11-Mo-200), and the Go-Kart South site (11-Mo-552S). These sites represent a cultural continuum which extends from Early Woodland (ca. 500 B.C.) through early Mississippian (ca. 1000 A.C.) times. A number of undated historic materials, including slag, glass, musket balls, etc., were also recovered from the sites.

The Hill Lake meander scar represents one of several clearly defined cut-off Mississippi River channel scar localities in the American Bottom. The FAI-270 alignment in this locality extends for nearly 4 km in a north-south direction between U.S. Bypass 50 in northern Monroe County to Cement Hollow in southern St. Clair County. The alignment transect in this area varies in width from 600 m at the southern end to 100 m at the central and northern limits and comprises an area of ca. 0.45 km2. The area within the southern portion of the Hill Lake locality represents slightly more than 50% of the total area of the Hill Lake locality, or 0.25 km2 (Figure 2).

The alignment includes the east bank of the old Hill Lake meander channel as well as various inner channel ridges, sand bars, swales, and alluvial fans extending out from the bluffline, which is located ca. 200 m to 400 m east of the highway corridor. The bluffline above the corridor maintains a relatively gradual slope, with elevations ranging from 30 m to 45 m above the floodplain. Hill Creek, which flows from Cement Hollow, and Hill Lake Creek, located several kilometers to the south, drain into the floodplain from the surrounding bluffs. Both creeks have deposited upland sediments over the floodplain and have covered the old channel depression with a thick, silty loess overburden. Many of the sites in the Hill Lake locality, therefore, have been buried and thus protected from extensive plowing and erosion. It should be noted, however, that even within this century much of the Hill Lake locality was still characterized as a low-lying marsh and lake, and it was not until the early 1950s that this area was completely drained and filled by bluff deposits. Several of the sites excavated in the alignment exhibit old, buried plowzones, which are situated nearly 1 m below the present surface.

Ecological resources within the Hill Lake locality are best described as intermittent, following cut-off from the main channel. Water levels within the channel scar were probably never greater than 1 m to 2 m in depth, and both vegetational and fish resources occurred in abundance only during optimal, high water periods (Greenup 1838; Coulter 1904: 39-71; Parmalee et al. 1972: 18-20). For example, the lake or marsh would have had renewed fish resources each spring with the

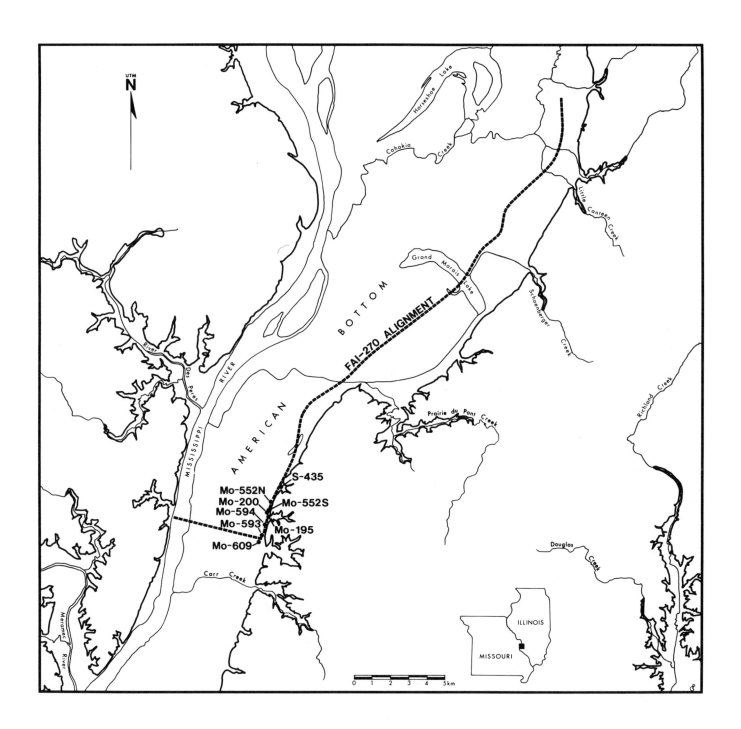

Figure 1. Distribution of Hill Lake Locality Sites
within the FAI-270 Alignment

Plate 1.   Aerial View of Sites in the Southern Portion of the Hill Lake
Locality: a, Fiege; b, Carbon Monoxide; c, Carbon Dioxide; d, Truck #4;
e, Truck #7; f, Go-Kart South

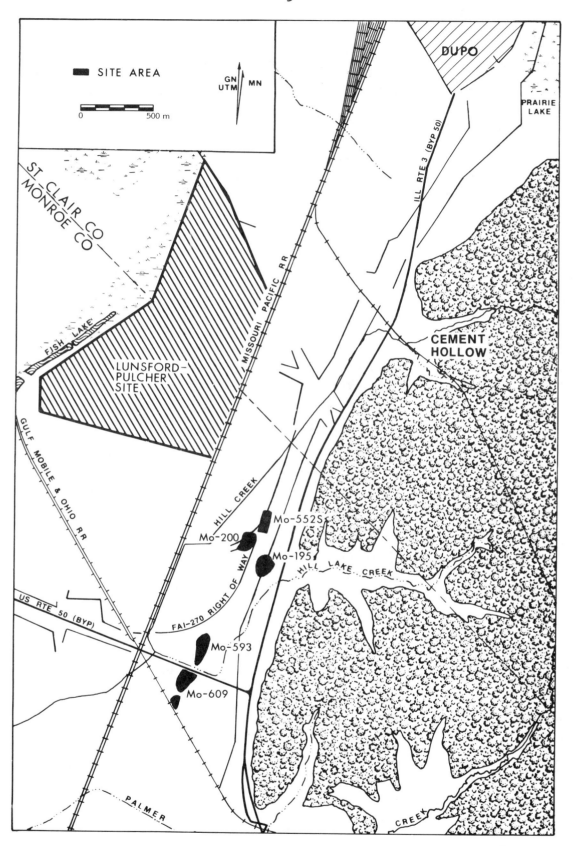

Figure 2. Distribution of Hill Lake Locality Sites in Relation
to the Lunsford-Pulcher Site Area

higher water stage. A general absence of mussel shell in prehistoric occupations in the Hill Lake locality also suggests that prehistorically, Hill Lake constituted a seasonal body of water capable of supporting only a limited variety of aquatic resources (Finney and Fortier 1985).

The geomorphic history of the southern sector of the Hill Lake locality can be summarized within the context of two primary geomorphic influences: 1) fluvial processes within the channel, and 2) depositional fan-building processes originating from the adjacent bluffs. The formation of inner channel ridges and the build-up of an alluvial fan extending out of Hill Lake Creek represent the two most significant geomorphic events with regard to the prehistoric occupation of this area.

The dominant physiographic feature of this locality was the Hill Lake meander channel itself (Figure 3). Radiocarbon determinations extracted from geomorphological cores taken within the channel fill indicate that the Hill Lake channel was still active at 2400 B.C. and had not yet begun to fill. However, by 1300 B.C., the channel had become cut off and had already been filled with nearly 2.5 m of fluvial sediments. Subsequently, between this period and ca. 500 B.C., an additional 13.4 m of deposition accumulated in the channel, and in various places inner channel sandy and silty ridges were formed. By this time, the channel area essentially consisted of a series of shallow lakes and/or marshes. After ca. 500 B.C., these inner channel fluvial sedimentary processes, with the exception of minor depositional episodes resulting from fluctuations in water levels, ceased to be a major geomorphic factor in the Hill Lake locality. As a result of the marshy environment a relatively thick humus horizon has developed over the fluvial deposits within the inner channel area. Overlying these deposits in most places are fan sediments originating from the adjacent bluffs.

The geomorphic fan-building processes at the outlet of Hill Lake Creek were relatively complex. Fan deposition may have occurred while the channel was still active, but significant fan development was apparently truncated by the moving waters of the channel. Fan development in the channel itself was only made possible as a result of the cut-off and stabilization of the Hill Lake channel. Evidence suggests that this fan, which is oriented primarily to the northwest, was formed prior to 1000 A.C. but probably after 200 A.C. to 300 A.C. This silty loess fan, the sediments of which are derived from the adjacent uplands, was built directly over the eastern clay cut bank of the Hill Lake channel. Approximately 2 m of fan sediments overlay this bank surface. The suggested date of fan formation is based on two archaeological observations. The early Mississippian Truck #4 site occupied the uppermost portion of the Hill Lake Creek alluvial fan;

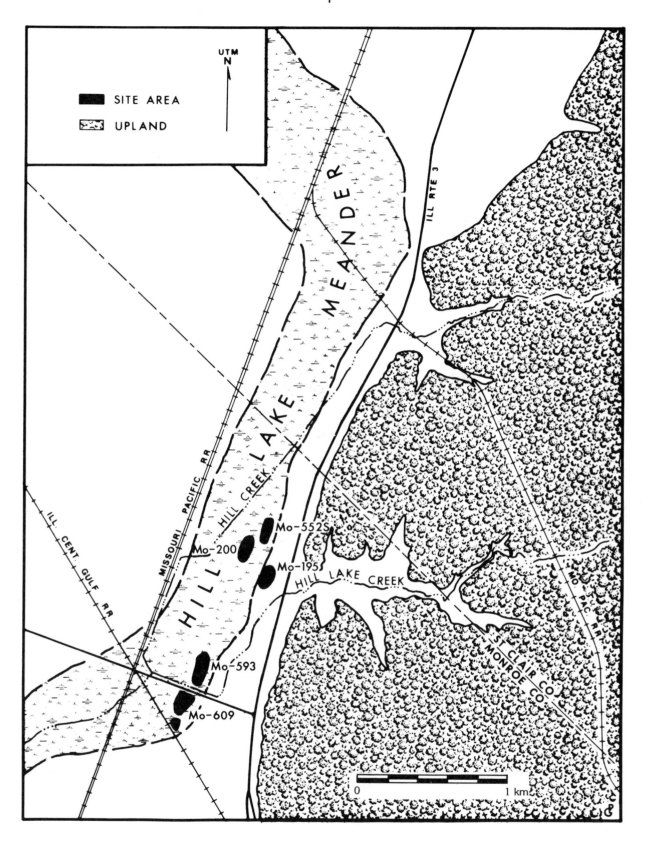

Figure 3. Distribution of Hill Lake Locality Sites in Relation to the Hill Lake Meander

2000 BC
Archaic
Mississippi River Channel

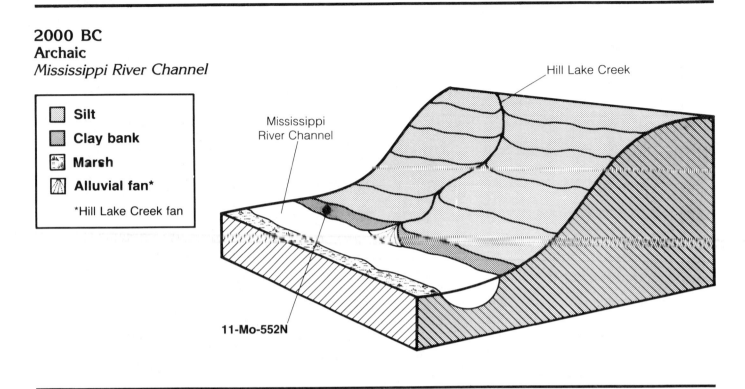

Silt	
Clay bank	
Marsh	
Alluvial fan*	

*Hill Lake Creek fan

Hill Lake Creek

Mississippi River Channel

11-Mo-552N

500 BC–300 AC
Early and Middle Woodland
*Channel cut-off, initial filling,
and initial Hill Lake fan formation*

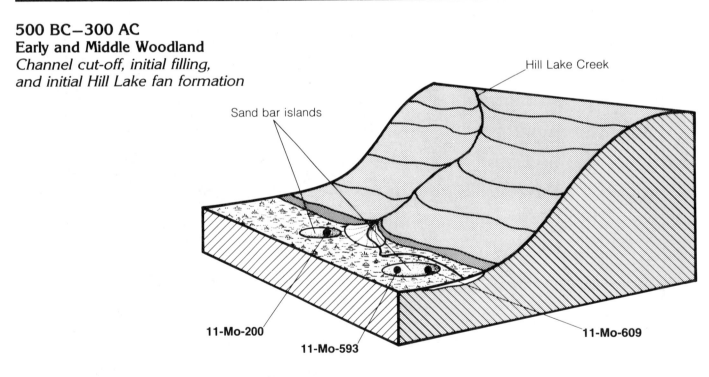

Sand bar islands

Hill Lake Creek

11-Mo-200

11-Mo-593

11-Mo-609

Figure 4. A Block Diagram Geomorphic History of the Southern Hill Lake Locality

9

300 AC – 1200 AC
Late Woodland/Mississippian
Channel filled and Hill Lake fan
extended

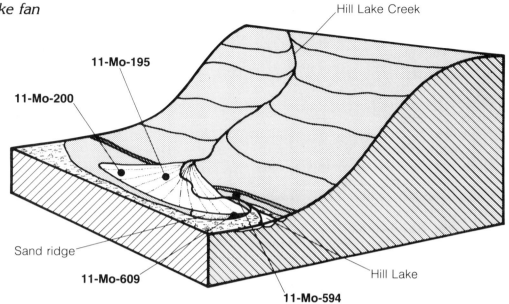

19th Century

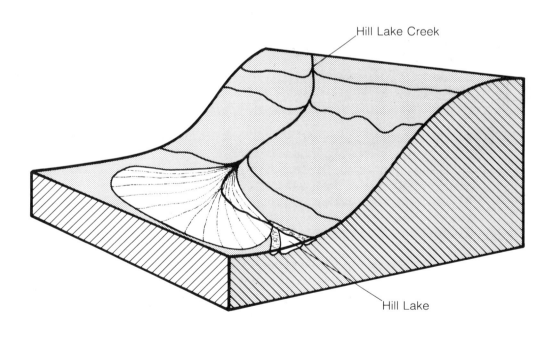

Figure 4. continued

therefore, the fan must have developed prior to 1000 A.C. Second, the Middle Woodland occupation at the Truck #7 site, which was located on a sandy inner channel ridge just 200 m northwest of the Hill Lake Creek fan, and which has been radiocarbon dated to ca. 160 A.C., was buried by the deposits of the Hill Lake Creek fan; therefore, fan development could not have been particularly active prior to 160 A.C. Overall, the fan does not appear to have been completely developed until sometime between 200 A.C. and 1000 A.C. (Figure 4).

The orientation of the fan and of Hill Lake Creek were to the northwest. Bluff sediments were apparently not deposited to any appreciable degree in the inner channel area to the southwest. In fact, the southwest area appears to have been a relatively stable marsh or low-lying lake. The silty clay bank of the eastern cut-bank of the meander was likewise not influenced by depositional episodes emanating from the bluffs in the southwest area. Evidence of bank stability in this area was derived from excavations at the Carbon Dioxide site, which was located ca. 250 m south of the Hill Lake Creek fan (Finney and Fortier 1985).

The Carbon Dioxide site was located on a bifurcated, silty clay cut bank portion of the meander scar and contained early Late Woodland (ca. 250 A.C.) and early Mississippian (ca. 1000 A.C.) occupations (Finney and Fortier 1985). Both occupations were situated on the same bank surface despite a temporal interval of ca. 700 years. Silty loess deposits up to 1 m in depth, in places, had buried both occupations, but these deposits were laid down after the prehistoric occupations (i.e., after 1000 A.C.). Based on the varied site data, it is obvious that portions of the Hill Lake locality remained stable for long periods of time while other portions were quite dynamic.

The final stage of geomorphic activity in the southern part of the Hill Lake locality has occurred within the past 50 years. Due to poor soil management policies in the uplands during the early 1900s, bluff erosion became increasingly severe, especially during the 1930s and 1940s. By the early 1950s, the remnant marshes and shallow lakes in this area had been completely filled in by loess deposits from the bluffs.

> Many small streams that drain the upland basins and the floodplain lakes and marshes have been canalized in the past 150 years (cf. Greenup 1838; Helm 1905:91-116). This canalization coincides with a period of levee building and draining of lakes and marshes on the American Bottom (Helm 1905). At least 40 years ago a canalized Hill Lake Creek traversed the Hill Lake Meander Scar immediately west of the site [i.e., the Carbon Dioxide site]. This diversion

appears on a 1940 United States Army Corps of
Engineers map of the American Bottom compiled from
aerial photographs taken between 1935 and 1937. At
that time the stream drained a marsh south of the
Carbon Dioxide site and east of the Carbon Monoxide
and Fiege (11-Mo-609) sites. Sometime between 1937
and 1955, Hill Lake Creek was recanalized east of the
site to the eastern edge of the modern agricultural
field. The present location of Hill Lake Creek can
be found on the 1955 United States Geological Survey
15´ Waterloo Quadrangle map (Finney and
Fortier 1985:11).

Prior to the final canalization of Hill Lake Creek (sometime between
1937 and 1955), the marsh, the old inner channel ridges, and the bank
portions of the meander scar were already covered with varying
thicknesses of silt, measuring up to 2 m in depth. The old prehistoric
surfaces, some of which had subsequently been plowed by early twentieth
century farmers in this area, were consequently buried beneath this deep
mantle of soil. This overburden subsequently protected the sites in
this area from modern cultivation practices that became particularly
intensified following the disappearance of the marsh. In addition, with
improved upland soil management and the canalization of Hill Lake Creek,
massive erosional deposition during the past 20 years has been
effectively eliminated.

RESEARCH DESIGN

The Fiege, Carbon Monoxide, Truck #7, and Go-Kart South sites were
all situated on buried inner channel ridges within the old Hill Lake
meander scar. The Truck #4 site was located in the upper portion of an
alluvial fan extending out from Hill Lake Creek.

The Fiege and Carbon Monoxide sites were both buried as a direct
result of depositional episodes occurring within this century. The
buried nature of these sites made their initial discovery and subsequent
exposure a difficult task. More specifically, it required a sampling
approach broad enough to detect not only the buried resources themselves
but one that could expose a large enough area to permit determinations
of the size and extent of these occupations as well as their precise
environmental setting.

The excavated sites within the Hill Lake locality provide a unique
opportunity to study the utilization of a single physiographic unit of

the Mississippi River floodplain by various cultural groups through time
(Bareis et al. 1977). The Hill Lake locality represents a discrete
physioecological zone where prehistoric occupants had ready access for
over 3000 years to a variety of aquatic resources associated with the
Hill Lake channel and to a variety of upland resources located in the
oak-hickory forest environs of the adjacent bluffs. Prehistoric groups
occupying the bank of the Hill Lake meander or its inner channel point
bar ridges could have exploited a variety of ecological niches with only
a minimal amount of settlement dispersion.

Sites in the Hill Lake locality, particularly at the southern end,
were generally small and of short duration. Most of the sites appear to
represent seasonal extractive camps. That this locality did not support
large, permanent settlements may be attributed to the dynamic nature of
its physiographic position in the American Bottom where it was subject
to the influences of both a fluctuating fluvial environment,
characterized by the seasonal rise and fall of water levels, and to the
effects of periodic, depositional episodes emanating from the
surrounding uplands. The dynamic aspect of the physical environment
affected not only the duration of settlements in this locality but also
their location.

The variation exhibited in location of occupation in the Hill Lake
locality from 500 B.C. to 1000 A.C. appears to have resulted primarily
from group adaptations to the geomorphic and ecological dynamics of this
locality. A research design for the Hill Lake locality as a unit was,
therefore, created to address six broad questions concerning the nature
and extent of these adaptations through time.

1) A determination of the nature and extent of all
   subsurface prehistoric occupations and their
   relationship to specific physiographic units
   within the Hill Lake locality. Particularly
   important is the recognition of prehistoric site
   selection factors within the context of dynamic
   geomorphic processes.
2) A determination of the chronological and cultural
   affiliations of individual components and their
   placement within the American Bottom prehistoric
   cultural continuum.
3) A determination of the temporal relationships
   between cultural components at individual sites.
4) A determination of site function and intrasite
   variability. This includes the recognition of
   activity areas and the determination of feature
   functions where possible.
5) A determination of subsistence practices
   associated with each cultural component at each
   site with a view toward interpreting the various

functions of settlements within the Hill Lake meander scar. The observation of seasonal patterns of settlement may contribute to our understanding of the mobility and organization of social systems within the Hill Lake locality and within the American Bottom area as a whole.

6) A determination of major subsistence shifts through time, especially in relationship to the physiographic dynamics of the Hill Lake locality and to concurrent shifts occurring in the American Bottom area as a whole. In other words, do the subsistence trends observed at sites in the Hill Lake locality coincide with similar trends within the greater American Bottom area?

The reports in this volume are individually focused on site-specific data. However, an attempt is made in the concluding chapter of this volume to relate this site specific information to the broader Hill Lake research problem orientation.

The data presented in this volume represent a significant contribution to American Bottom prehistory. Extensive data from a single locality encompassing a variety of cultural components has never before been assembled for the American Bottom. The artifact assemblages, including pit, structure, and material types recovered from the various sites represent unique data for this area. The floral and faunal information recovered from these sites have provided the first extensive subsistence data for this portion of the American Bottom. The reader should regard as relevant three other sites from this locality, namely the Mund, Go-Kart North, and Carbon Dioxide sites, which are not included in this volume but which have been described in previous volumes in this FAI-270 site report series (Fortier and Emerson 1984; Fortier et al. 1983; and Finney and Fortier 1985). These three sites yielded occupations dating to the Late Archaic, Early Woodland, and Late Woodland periods, and for this reason the complete settlement history of the Hill Lake locality cannot be understood without reference to those site reports. In particular the Mund site report presents critical information with regard to the life history of the Hill Lake locality and to fan-forming processes on the northern edge of this locality.

In summary, the information recovered from the Hill Lake locality is significant because 1) it is unique in the sense that material assemblages from well-defined contexts as well as entire community plans have been defined; 2) this information can be related as a unit to a single physiographic locality; and 3) this information covers a cultural continuum from the Early Woodland to early Mississippian time periods. The question of significance and the degree to which individual objectives of the Hill Lake research design were resolved will be further detailed in the concluding chapter of this volume.

EXCAVATION STRATEGIES AND PROCEDURES

> . . . it was made clear early in the Project that the
> University of Illinois-Urbana position regarded the
> FAI-270 alignment as a narrow strip imposed across an
> archaeologically rich American Bottom, and that the
> strip itself constituted only a sample of the
> totality of past human behavior...it was decided and
> agreed upon by all parties concerned that total
> excavation of archaeological sites should form the
> basis of the excavation strategies on most site
> areas. In addition, the archaeological need for
> total community plans for any time period would
> necessitate large scale plowzone removals (Porter
> 1980:2).

The total impacted area within the Hill Lake portion of the FAI-270 corridor between the Go-Kart South and Fiege sites comprised ca. 0.25 km2. The five sites identified in this corridor contained surface materials covering an area of 5.94 ha. Just over 25,200 m2 (2.52 ha) of plowzone were eventually removed by heavy machinery within these site areas (Figure 5). The excavated sample from the corridor amounted to about 10% (0.025 km2) of the total impacted area and just under 50% of the surface-defined site areas. Sampling, therefore, played an important role in the excavation strategies employed at each site within the impacted area. Sampling strategies, however, were always oriented toward the complete delineation of all subsurface occupations, a fact that appears contradictory given the excavation of only one-half of the surface-defined site area; however, this apparent contradiction is resolved by taking into account the fact that buried occupations often comprised an area less than one-half of their corresponding surface distribution (Table 1).

To remove the plowzone or deep silty overburdens covering the sites of this locality, a variety of heavy machinery, including large paddlewheel scrapers, backhoes, and bulldozers, were employed, often in tandem. Paddlewheel scrapers were the major piece of heavy equipment employed for removal of plowzone and overburden at all sites. These scrapers averaged between 1500 m2 and 5000 m2 of plowzone removal per day and were most effective at the Carbon Monoxide site where a thick overburden, measuring nearly 2 m deep in places, was encountered. Backhoes were used for more limited scraping following the removal of plowzone, and were also employed to excavate deep trenches for geomorphological studies. Backhoe scraping (with a modified, broad, shallow blade) allowed for a rapid assessment of feature configurations and had the added advantage of not compacting the soil around features. Bulldozers were employed to remove piles of backdirt or to backfill deep trenches. Bulldozers proved to be less effective than backhoes or

15

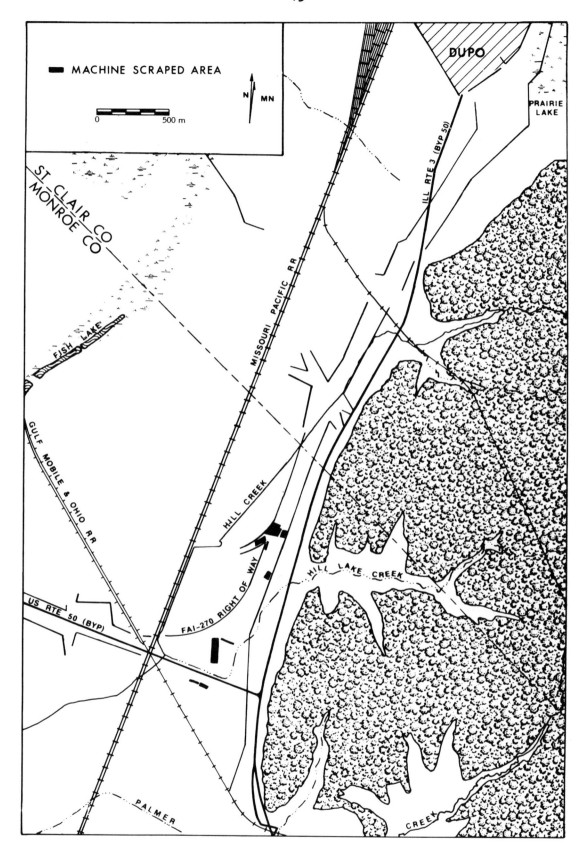

Figure 5. Machine Scraped Site Areas

Table 1. Summary of Excavation Results at Hill
Lake Locality Sites

Site	Estimated Site Area (ha)	% of Site Impacted by FAI-270	Total Plowzone Removal (m2)	% of Impacted Site Area Excavated	N of Excavated Features	Total Work Hours	Subsurface Cultural Components*
Carbon Monoxide	1.40	100	11775	84	50	2996	A
Fiege	2.30	60	1880	14	12	203	A,C**
Truck#4	0.59	45	1635	36	27	252	C
Truck#7	0.85	30	2348	92	25	1060	A**,B,C
Go-Kart South	0.80	60	7688	90	1	444	A**,B,C**
Total	5.94		25326		115	4955	

*Cultural Components
A Early Woodland
B Middle Woodland
C Mississippian

** Isolated finds

paddlewheel scrapers for archaeological scraping, since they tended to
create an uneven surface and to compact the soil through repeated
forward and backward movements.

The removal of plowzone from sites was normally accomplished in
stages. The size of excavation blocks varied according to the extent of
recognized subsurface features, and often was dependent on the
particular physiographic setting of the prehistoric occupation.
Preliminary geomorphic evaluation of a site area played a critical role
in determining where the initial excavation blocks would be placed,
although in several cases (i.e., the Fiege and Truck #7 sites),
excavation was initially focused on areas producing the densest surface
concentrations. The expansion and orientation (size and shape) of
excavation blocks were subsequently dictated by the nature and extent of
the subsurface occupation. The excavation strategy employed at any
given site in terms of the eventual expansion of specific block units
was developed during the course of excavations and varied according to
the specific problems which emerged at the site.

Once an area had been exposed by heavy machinery, it was
subsequently shovel scraped, and features, if present, were defined and
mapped within the established grid system. All features were completely
excavated. Pit features were excavated in halves and by natural levels
or fill zones. Generally, one ten-liter sample of soil per zone was
recovered from each pit half and submitted to the field laboratory for

water-screening and flotation. Soil samples were also taken from the profile wall following completion of the profile map. Nonpit lithics and ceramic concentrations were piece-plotted item by item with both vertical and horizontal proveniences recorded. Basin and post structures were also encountered, and the procedures used in their excavation are presented within the individual site reports.

The utilization of heavy machinery to remove soil overburdens immediately above subsurface prehistoric occupations inevitably resulted in the loss of some cultural materials. On the other hand, the successful achievement of the research design, which was structured to study community size and function rather than noncontextual or disturbed artifacts, could not have been accomplished without heavy machinery. The reader will have to judge the merits of this approach on the basis of the results presented in each of the following site reports. Since many of the artifacts in plowzone or erosional overburden contexts in the Hill Lake locality were not associated with the underlying occupations, the recovery of such artifacts at the expense of wide-scale machine excavation would have been too time-consuming and expensive and, more significantly, would only have augmented existing surface collections, while hindering, if not rendering impossible, the resolution of the research objectives proposed for sites in this locality. It should be added, however, that all artifacts that were observed during machine excavation were collected and, in many cases, were given precise provenience. Nonfeature context subplowzone materials were always collected in a systematic manner.

ARCHAEOLOGICAL BACKGROUND

The history of site investigations in the Hill Lake locality is directly associated with the overall history of the FAI-270 Archaeological Mitigation Project, which has been detailed elsewhere (Kelly et al. 1979; Bareis et al. 1977, Bareis and Porter 1984). Various formal agreements established between the IDOT and the Illinois Archaeological Survey (IAS) since 1959 constitute part of a long history of cooperation between highway planners and the Illinois archaeological community. Without this cooperation, the FAI-270 Archaeological Mitigation Project could not have been accomplished.

During 1975, the IAS was asked by the IDOT to undertake an intensive site survey of the proposed FAI-270 alignment between Jefferson Barrack's Bridge and FAI-55/70. The results of that work have been presented in Kelly et al. (1979). It was determined that 59 sites would be directly impacted by the FAI-270 right-of-way. An IAS FAI-270 committee was formed, and planning for the mitigation of the impact on those 59 sites was initiated. The UIUC was to serve as the prime contractor, with work also subcontracted to Western Illinois University- Macomb (WIU), Southern Illinois University- Edwardsville (SIU-E), and the University of Illinois- Chicago Circle (UICC). All of the sites located within the Hill Lake locality were excavated by the prime contractor, UIUC. The Fiege site had originally been subcontracted to SIU-E, but in order to fulfill contract obligations, the prime contractor was compelled in 1979 to initiate and complete mitigation of the impact on that site.

The surface reconnaissance of the alignment in the Hill Lake locality was conducted from 1975 to 1977, and it produced a variety of cultural materials from different time periods. However, even at that time, the surveyors were aware of the dangers involved in evaluating the extent or nature of sites in an environment subjected to heavy alluvial and fluvial deposition, and they realized that extensive subsurface testing would be necessary to substantiate the presence of subsurface archaeological resources.

During 1977, a testing program was initiated at the Carbon Monoxide, Truck #4, Truck #7, and Go-Kart South sites to evaluate the need for more extensive archaeological investigations. The results of testing at these sites and at three others (11-Mo-603, 11-Mo-604, and 11-Mo-608), which were eventually dropped from the Hill Lake site package, are presented in the testing report for the Hill Lake locality (Bareis et al. 1977). The following discussion provides both a summary of the survey and testing results obtained from each site and a rationale for the further mitigation of the impact on these sites. In order to maintain the organizational framework of presentation of sites in this volume, the Fiege site will also be included in this testing summary even though it was originally subcontracted to SIU-E and was, therefore, not actually tested by UIUC until 1978 for reasons cited above.

Carbon Monoxide Site (11-Mo-593)

The Carbon Monoxide site was first located in November 1975 by archaeological survey crews employed by the IDOT. A light scatter of surface material, oriented in a north-south direction, was observed over an area of ca. 1.4 ha. Surface materials indicated Middle Woodland and Late Bluff (Emergent Mississippian) components; however, it was recognized that these materials were associated with recent depositional sediments and were not related to an actual prehistoric occupation in this specific location. During 1976, soil probe tests to depths exceeding 1 m revealed the presence of a buried Early Woodland component, evidenced by the occurrence of a single Marion Thick sherd in one of the probe samples. The recovery of this sherd from subsurface contexts suggested the need for more extensive subsurface testing.

The 1977 testing of the Carbon Monoxide site was accomplished by UIUC archaeological crews during a six-day period in October. A contour map was prepared, and a Universal Transverse Mercator grid (UTM) was established. Eight machine-power trenches were placed in two separate areas that appeared to have high potential for subsurface remains, including the area from which the Marion Thick sherd had been recovered. A total of 370 m2 of surface area was stripped of its plowzone by heavy machinery. The 1977 test units confirmed the presence of a buried Early Woodland component at this site. Although no feature numbers were assigned, a scatter of Marion Thick pottery, sandstone, and chert was identified in precisely the same area that had yielded the Marion Thick sherd during the 1976 probe tests. During 1977, a portion of this Early Woodland scatter, located just over 1 m below the surface, was piece-plotted with precise vertical and horizontal dimensions recorded for each item. The recognition of a buried Early Woodland occupation during 1977 provided the impetus for further investigation of this site during 1978-1979.

Fiege Site (11-Mo-609)

The Fiege site was first surveyed on 30 March 1976 by an IDOT archaeological survey crew consisting of two persons. Three nondiagnostic chert flakes were recovered. Field visibility was poor at the time (15% to 20%), and it was suggested that the field be resurveyed at a later date (Kelly et al. 1979:108).

Further survey and testing was contracted to SIU-E. However, during 1978, the UIUC reassumed responsibility for this site when the subcontractor was not able to complete its obligations. On 21 April 1978, UIUC crews resurveyed and tested the site. The surface survey covered the area within the proposed FAI-270 right-of-way. Ground visibility was excellent, resulting in the recovery of 213 lithic items and 1 diagnostic sherd. Recovered artifacts indicated possible Early and Middle Woodland components at the site. The site boundaries were considerably expanded to include ca. 2.3 ha. Only a small portion of the materials collected were located within the existing FAI-270 right-of-way at that time. The main concentration occurred ca. 30 m to 50 m southeast of the highway right-of-way.

Two 2 m x 2 m test units (Test Units A and B) were placed within the right-of-way limits and were hand-excavated to a depth of ca. 40 cm.

Two chert flakes and one piece of sandstone were recovered below the plowzone in Test Unit A, and several small sandstone pieces were found at the base of the plowzone in Test Unit B. Also, a total of 107 soil probes were taken along four transects, which revealed six possible fill areas that were interpreted as modern soil disturbances originating from the construction of Bypass 50, located only 30 m north of the soil probe lines.

In summary, the 1978 tests provided no solid evidence for the presence of subsurface features within the highway right-of-way. The main surface concentration lay outside of the right-of-way to the south. Because of the small site area inside the right-of-way and its proximity to previous soil disturbances, it was recommended that further excavation at the Fiege site was not warranted.

During the winter of 1979, however, the prime contractor was informed that plans were being formulated to rechannelize Hill Lake Creek through the center of the main surface material concentration at the Fiege site. After IDOT surveyors had staked the proposed channel right-of-way, a systematic survey was conducted on 28 March 1979. The surface collection conducted in March produced a definable concentration of materials both within the right-of-way and immediately adjacent to it on the north and south.

Twenty-two survey collection blocks, averaging 15 m x 8 m in size, were staked out within the proposed channel, and all materials encountered within these blocks were collected. In addition, a general surface collection from areas south and north of the channel right-of-way was also accomplished. All diagnostic artifacts were piece-plotted.

A total of 214 lithic items and 4 ceramic sherds were collected within the channel right-of-way area. Nearly 60% of this material was recovered from the easternmost portion of the right-of-way. Density of material within the channel unit was calculated at 1 item per 7 m2.

Diagnostic materials recovered from the surface collection within the channel right-of-way indicated possible subsurface Early and Middle Woodland components. The occurrence of both Marion Thick pottery and a possible Kramer projectile point suggested that the main component was probably Early Woodland. It was decided, therefore, that the impact of the proposed channel on the Fiege site should be mitigated.

Truck #4 Site (11-Mo-195)

The Truck #4 site was surveyed during the winter of 1975-1976 by IDOT survey crews although the site had first been reported in conjunction with the 1971 Historic Sites Survey (Porter 1971). The extent of the Truck #4 site was 0.59 ha within the limits of the right-of-way. The material obtained from the 1975 survey indicated a Late Bluff (Emergent Mississippian) occupation. Two limestone-tempered sherds and a single grog-tempered sherd were recovered, as were 2 biface fragments, 4 chert edge tools, 1 chert core, 54 chert flakes, and 22 nonchert items, including 16 pieces of sandstone.

During 1977, a controlled surface collection was conducted over an area of ca. 0.38 ha. Materials were most heavily concentrated at the southern end of the site, as well as along and outside the eastern portion of the right-of-way. In addition to 370 lithic items (including 12 nondiagnostic worked chert tools), 53 pieces of pottery were recovered, 75% of which were limestone-tempered. Approximately 10% of the limestone-tempered ceramics were red-slipped, (e.g., Monks Mound Red variety), and 35% were plain (Pulcher Plain). The ceramics from the surface indicated a "Late Fairmount" (Lohmann) phase Mississippian occupation.

Test excavations were carried out at this site during a six-day period from 29 July to 3 August 1977. The site was tested with soil probes, and five 2 m x 2 m test units were excavated. The soil-probe technique resulted in the discovery of a single subsurface pit feature (Feature 1) initially identified by abundant charcoal flecking in the probe. An area of 10 m2 was subsequently removed by a combination of hand and machine excavation in this location, revealing a pit which was irregular in plan view (97 cm by 75 cm), 16.5 cm deep, and basin-shaped in profile. No diagnostic cultural materials were recovered from the pit. In addition to the pit feature exposed in this area, sandstone fragments were found at a depth of 100 cm to 120 cm below the surface, providing evidence of a possible buried cultural horizon.

Based on the surface collection and testing carried out during 1975 and 1977, it was recommended that the impact on the Truck #4 site be mitigated. Although it was apparent from the surface distribution that the major portion of this site lay outside the right-of-way to the east, the presence of a subsurface pit and a small number of Late Bluff (Emergent Mississippian) surface ceramics suggested that at least a portion of a possible Emergent Mississippian or early Mississippian (Lohmann phase) period occupation might lie within the right-of-way. It was anticipated that a small early Mississippian farmstead or hamlet would be exposed.

Truck #7 Site (11-Mo-200)

The Truck #7 site was initially located in 1971 during the Historic Sites Survey of this area (Porter 1971). A small collection of nondiagnostic chert and a single, dentate-stamped body sherd were recovered. The multicolored chert types recovered were similar to those recovered from the Middle Woodland Dash Reeves site (11-Mo-80), located ca. 2 km to the south. The Truck #7 site was, therefore, assigned a Middle Woodland cultural affiliation.

During 1975, IDOT survey teams relocated the Truck #7 site and defined a site area of 0.42 ha. In addition to the recovery of an expanding-stemmed, Middle Woodland point base, three shell/grog-tempered body sherds were identified, providing evidence for a small Mississippian or "Late Bluff" (Emergent Mississippian) component (Kelly et al. 1979:101).

Additional information was obtained in 1977 by UIUC survey and testing crews. From 15 to 17 August 1977, a site contour map, a controlled surface collection, soil probing, and subsurface test excavations were accomplished. The surface collection, covering ca. 1 ha, confirmed the presence of Middle Woodland and Emergent Mississippian surface materials, expanded the original site area to ca. 0.85 ha, and identified an extremely dense concentration of chert and ceramic debris in a 1600 m2 area.

Preliminary testing (8 m2) and soil probing revealed the presence of subsurface materials and a single postmold. The subsurface materials were not generally diagnostic, but the surface collection contained Middle Woodland ceramics, including a "Hopewell" rocker-stamped rim, as well as Emergent Mississippian/Mississippian ceramics (numerous limestone-tempered and shell-tempered sherds). Based on this information, it was expected that the Truck #7 site would contain buried Emergent Mississippian/Mississippian and Middle Woodland occupations. Since very few Middle Woodland occupations had been investigated in the American Bottom, further investigations at this site were deemed necessary.

The Go-Kart South Site (11-Mo-552S)

The Go-Kart South site was originally included within the limits of a larger site area called the Go-Kart site which was arbitrarily divided into three sectors: Go Kart North, Central, and South. The North sector of the Go-Kart site was excavated separately in 1978-1979, exposing an extensive subsurface Late Archaic occupation consisting of numerous pits and lithic artifacts (Fortier and Emerson 1984). The Central sector produced only a limited quantity of surface materials mixed with dense historic debris and modern structural disturbances and did not warrant further investigation. The South sector extended from a horse corral, marking the southern boundary of the Central sector, to a slightly raised levee and field road marking the northern boundary of the Truck #7 site. Thus, the Truck #7 and Go-Kart South sites were only separated arbitrarily by a field road and not on the basis of archaeological surface materials.

During the summer of 1976, IDOT survey crews conducted probe and phosphate tests in the South sector of the Go-Kart site, and a contour map was made of the site area. A controlled surface collection was restricted to the North sector. The site limits, as defined by the surface collection in the South sector, encompassed an area of ca. 0.80 ha, ca. 60% of which was to be impacted by the proposed FAI-270 highway corridor.

Because of several high phosphate readings, test excavations were undertaken at the Go-Kart South site during 1976. Three test units were placed in various areas of the South sector. Units 1 and 3, each 1 m x 1 m, contained a very dark to dark grayish-brown (10YR 3/2) to black (10YR 2/1) clay gumbo soil. Subsurface cultural material consisted of nondiagnostic sherds, chert, and limestone (Bareis et al. 1977:61). Excavation Unit 2 was a 1 m x 5 m unit that also yielded subsurface materials. The recovered ceramics consisted primarily of plain, limestone-tempered body sherds similar to the Emergent Mississippian/Mississippian materials recovered from the adjacent Truck #7 site.

Based on the presence of subsurface materials, mitigation procedures were recommended for the Go-Kart South site. Mitigation phase strategies were independently designed for the Truck #7, Go-Kart South, and Go-Kart North sites. In this volume, the Go-Kart South and Truck #7 sites have been combined in a single chapter since they are viewed as constituting, in fact, a single site.

Summary

From the above accounts of the preliminary survey and testing of sites in the Hill Lake locality, the reader may observe that a variety of techniques were used to evaluate the need for further mitigation efforts. At some sites, controlled systematic block surveys were carried out, while at others only generalized recovery techniques were employed. Numerous soil probes were taken at some sites, while none were taken at others. Machine test excavation units were undertaken extensively at the Carbon Monoxide site (which had a deep silty overburden); however, machine testing was minimal at the Truck #4 site and not used at all at the Truck #7, Go-Kart South, and Fiege sites.

Accurate evaluations of deeply buried prehistoric occupations based solely on surface material distributions in floodplain environments such as the American Bottom, are clearly impossible regardless of the surface sampling techniques utilized. At the nearby Carbon Dioxide site, for example, an entire subsurface Mississippian occupation lay directly beneath a surface devoid of prehistoric cultural materials (Finney and Fortier 1985). The Carbon Monoxide and Go-Kart South subsurface occupational materials were likewise unassociated with their surface materials. Knowledge of an area's geomorphic history, therefore, is a critical initial step in ascertaining the potential that a specific prehistoric environment, which may be very dissimilar to the modern surface environment, may have had for containing prehistoric occupations. This also means that testing strategies should be adapted to site-specific problems. Such testing strategies should seek to provide preliminary information not only in regard to the presence or absence of buried prehistoric remains but also to ascertaining the physiographic constitution of the surrounding landscape.

CHAPTER 2. EARLY WOODLAND OCCUPATIONS AT THE CARBON MONOXIDE SITE

by Andrew C. Fortier

This chapter presents the results obtained from archaeological investigations at the Carbon Monoxide site (11-Mo-593) conducted from 1977 to 1979. A surface reconnaissance during November 1975, by an IDOT survey team, produced isolated materials indicative of Early Woodland (Marion), Middle Woodland (Havana), and "Late Bluff" (Emergent Mississippian) components. Subsequent testing in 1977 provided evidence of a deeply buried Early Woodland Marion phase component. During 1978 and 1979, two buried and stratified Early Woodland occupations were exposed, yielding a total of 49 features. The more deeply buried occupation dated to the Marion phase of the Early Woodland period. Above this occupation were features dating to a later phase of the Early Woodland period. This occupation is designated as the Columbia Complex and may be most closely associated with the Florence phase in this area. This occupation is designated as a complex, rather than a phase, because of the small size of the assemblage and its unique materials. The name "Columbia" is derived from a nearby town and from the interchange area built over the Carbon Monoxide site, referred to as the Columbia interchange. The site name originated following the survey and was derived from the fact that this was the first site recorded on the USGS 7 1/2´ Columbia quadrangle. Hence, its initial field number was CO-1. A nearby site, CO-2, was referred to as the Carbon Dioxide site, which has been reported in another volume (Finney and Fortier 1985).

PHYSIOGRAPHIC AND GEOMORPHOLOGICAL BACKGROUND

The Carbon Monoxide site (11-Mo-593) represents a multicomponent occupation situated on an inner channel sand ridge of the Hill Lake meander scar (Figure 6). The Hill Lake channel exhibits a number of such ridges formed by fluvial processes within the channel at the time during which the channel was cut off from the Mississippi River (ca. 1300 B.C.). The ridge at Carbon Monoxide, ca. 350 m in length, was oriented in a north-south direction parallel to the Hill Lake meander channel. The Carbon Monoxide site was situated on the northern and central crest portions of the ridge. The Fiege site (11-Mo-609), which also contained an Early Woodland occupation, was located on the southernmost portion of this ridge.

This inner channel ridge constitutes an old sand bar which has been overlain with a thin, silty clay deposit measuring 15 cm to 20 cm in thickness. The base of this silty clay cap, at ca. 1 m below the

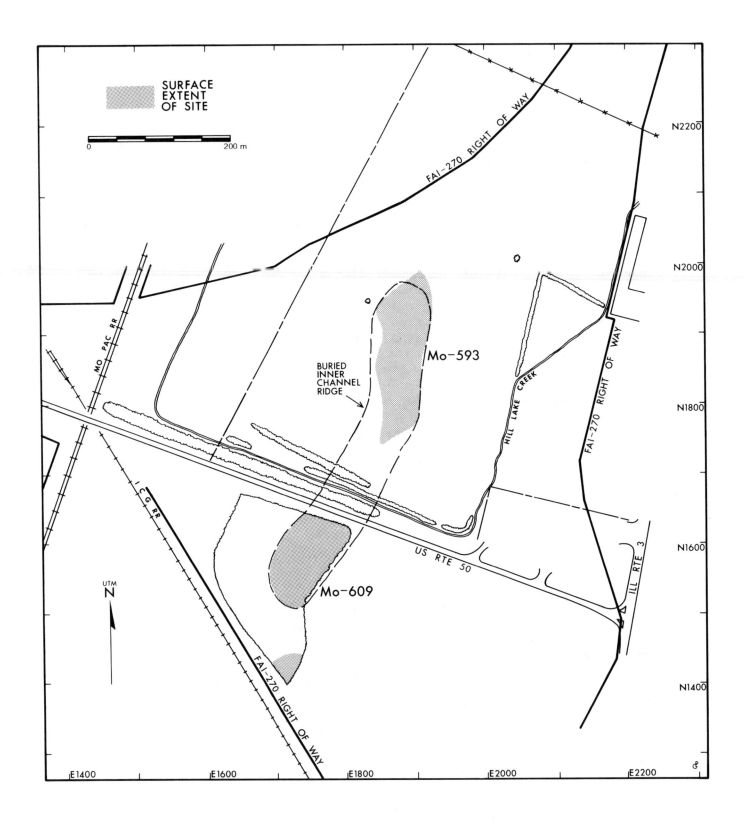

Figure 6. Extent of Buried Inner Channel Sand Ridge at the
Carbon Monoxide and Fiege Sites

present surface, contained no cultural material. Above this deposit was a dark gray humus silty clay horizon ca. 20 cm to 30 cm thick. Presumably, this humus horizon, which contained both the Early Woodland occupations, was formed gradually. This humus horizon had formed under paludal conditions. The upper portions (15 cm to 20 cm) had been disturbed by modern plowing. Confirmation of this plowing activity was provided by the occasional occurrence of historic materials in features. Above this was deposited a thick, undifferentiated, silty loess alluvium varying in depth from 40 cm to 100 cm. This loess overburden, of modern origin, was derived from erosional deposition from the adjacent bluffs located ca. 500 m to the east. It effectively buried both the inner channel ridge and its associated prehistoric occupations.

The inner channel ridge was first occupied during the Marion phase of the Early Woodland period at a time when the humus soil above the sandy ridge was only weakly developed. It is probable that this ridge first became exposed in the channel during the terminal Late Archaic to Early Woodland transitional period, around 700 B.C. to 600 B.C. Project geomorphologists have indicated that the Hill Lake channel may have been active until as late as 1000 B.C. A date of 960 $\pm$ 75 B.C. was obtained from the Carbon Monoxide site locality for a secondary, post cut-off fill level just above the Hill Lake channel fill (Bonnell and White 1981a). The occupation of this ridge by Early Woodland Marion groups indicates that the inner channel area was stable enough to have supported at least short-term occupation. The inner channel ridge increases in elevation to the south and, presumably, Early Woodland groups had access to the main ridge from the south. Both occupations were confined to the upper crest portions of the ridge.

The Columbia Complex occupation, located ca. 5 cm to 10 cm above the previous Marion occupation, occurred in both the plowed and unplowed portions of the buried humus. Early Woodland Marion phase materials were found exclusively at the base of the undisturbed humus horizon. The Columbia Complex occupation apparently occurred after the humus horizon was relatively well developed and presumably when the marshlands around the ridge were well defined. The occurrence of Early Woodland occupations within the humus horizon indicates that both groups occupied an elevated ridge within a relatively stable inner channel marsh.

The cultural materials on the ridge were stratified, particularly in the central and northern portions. The Columbia Complex occupational surface occurred somewhere in the upper portion of the buried humus horizon, but because this horizon had been plowed, it was impossible to detect the original occupational surface. It is significant that nearly 70% of the chert tools associated with the Columbia Complex component were recovered from the plowed portion of the humus horizon. This suggests that the occupational surface lay somewhere within this plowed portion. However, plowing had resulted in such disturbances of pit features that they could not be recognized at this level. Pits were not actually recognized until the plowed portion had been removed.

As stated above, specific occupational surfaces were difficult to identify due to the dark color of the soil and the translocation of materials within horizons. The Columbia Complex horizon, for example, was ca. 25 cm thick. The vertical extent of these occupational materials did not result from midden accumulation, but from vertical transportation of materials within a relatively moist, spongy soil. It is probable that the inner channel ridge within the Hill Lake marsh was periodically inundated by floods, providing relatively permeable soil conditions on the ridge. Periodic flooding of the ridge may have prohibited permanent occupation by Early Woodland peoples.

The relationship between the various soil horizons defined above and the cultural components at the site is exhibited in Soil Profile 3 from Excavation Block IV (Figure 7 and Plate 2). It is important to mention, however, that this stratigraphy was only apparent in isolated portions of the ridge. The best example of stratigraphy was actually obtained during excavation of a Marion ceramic scatter (Feature 17), which was superimposed by a Columbia Complex activity area. The two components were separated by only 5 cm to 10 cm of soil that contained no Marion materials and only occasional Columbia Complex remains. This feature as well as the other features and remains comprising the Early Woodland occupations will be discussed in greater detail below.

The loess overburden that covered the prehistoric occupations and the ridge was apparently deposited in recent times, i.e., post 1900 A.C. The location of the plowed upper portion of the humus horizon, at 50 cm to 80 cm below the present surface, strongly supports this. In addition, local farmers and residents in this area have indicated that the bulk of the alluvial deposits in this locality were deposited relatively rapidly during the late 1930s. Apparently, poor soil management policies in the adjacent bluffs precipitated a major erosional episode during this period. However, the marsh remained extant, even at that time. Maps of this area as late as 1955 still exhibited marshes, particularly in the vicinity of the Fiege and Carbon Monoxide sites (Board on Examination and Survey of Mississippi River 1908 - Chart No. 2; United States Army Corps of Engineers 1940 - Sheet No. 34; USGS Waterloo Quadrangle 15´ Map, 1955).

It is obvious that the marsh and ridge served as an important locus for Early Woodland occupation in the Hill Lake locality. Aquatic resources, including various marsh flora, fish, and birds, apparently attracted early post-Archaic groups into such inner-channel environments. The apparent lack of occupation of this ridge following the Early Woodland period is curious. Theoretically, the ridge

— 124.5 m

SURFACE

PLOW ZONE

ZONE A

— 124.0

Plow Scar   Plow Scars

Columbia
Complex
level

ZONE B₁

ZONE B₂

— 123.5

Marion
Phase
level

ZONE C

ZONE D

— 123.0

Limit of Excavation

11-Mo-593

SOIL PROFILE 3
BLOCK IV

0   25 cm

Zone A – Alluvial silty loess overburden (10YR $5/4$)

Zone B₁ – Plowed buried silty clay humus (10YR $3/2$)

Zone B₂ – Unplowed buried silty clay humus (10YR $3/2$)

Zone C – Silty clay (10YR $5/4$) cap over sand bar deposit

Zone D – Sterile sand bar deposit (10YR $6/4$)

– Silt bands (10YR $5/4$)

Figure 7. Soil Horizons and Occupational Levels at the
Carbon Monoxide Site

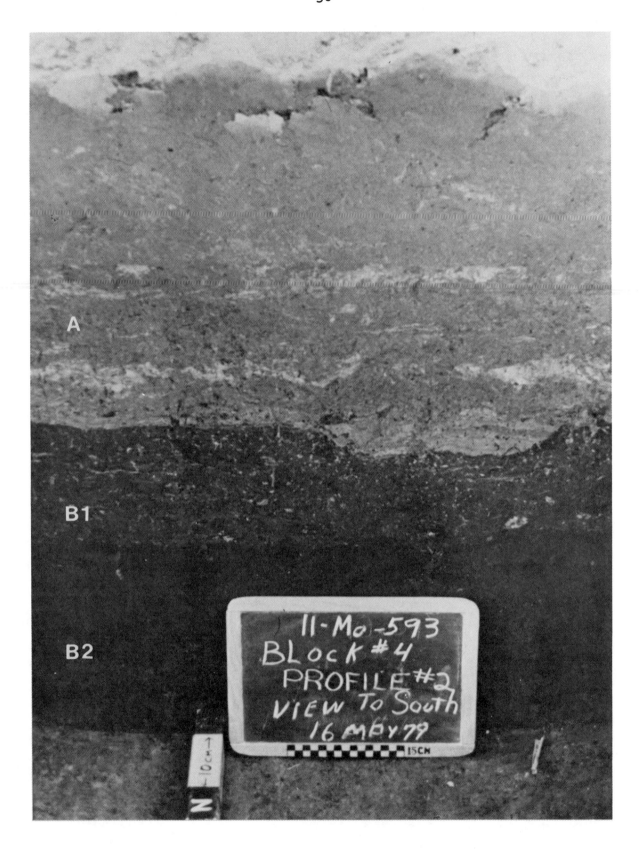

Plate 2. Soil Horizons at the Carbon Monoxide Site: A, alluvial overburden; B1, plowed humus; B2, unplowed humus

continued to be accessible. The probable reason for avoidance of this area following the Early Woodland period may have been the gradual dwindling of water resources in the channel area. It may be assumed that the gradual contraction of water resources would have led to the disappearance of a major portion of the aquatic resources supplied by the channel area.

HISTORY OF SITE INVESTIGATIONS

The surface extent of the Carbon Monoxide site was 1.4 ha, of which 370 m2 were tested in 1977, revealing the presence of a buried Early Woodland Marion phase occupation (Figure 8). This occupation had been buried by nearly 1 m of silty loess. There was, therefore, no relationship between the surface materials and subsurface components at this site. The nature and extent of the subsurface Early Woodland component were unknown, although testing had clearly indicated its presence as well as that of the ridge on which it was situated. Further excavation was deemed necessary over a broader area (coinciding with the extent of the buried ridge) to expose what appeared to be a unique occupation.

Therefore, during 1978, UIUC crews returned to the Carbon Monoxide site to undertake broad-scale excavations (Figure 9). A paddlewheel earth scraper was employed to strip off the 40 cm to 100 cm deep alluvial overburden covering the ridge. The following is a brief summary of the excavation blocks and the excavation strategies utilized during the 1978 and 1979 seasons.

The first block to be stripped in 1978 was Block I, which encompassed an area of 3000 m2 that coincided with the northern apex of the buried ridge. The northern end of Block I contained the partially excavated Marion Thick ceramic scatter exposed during 1977. After the paddlewheel had cut into the buried humus horizon, excavation by machine was terminated in that area. Preliminary stripping of this horizon revealed the following: a dense concentration of chert at the southern end of Block I; numerous chert tools; two pits (Features 3 and 4); a structure (Feature 6); and the Marion scatter previously defined and now redesignated as Feature 1 (this scatter was fully exposed and excavated in 1978). The occurrence of both Marion and Columbia Complex ceramics in Excavation Block 1 indicated that the occupation was multicomponent.

The presence of dense areas of material debris, (including ceramics, as well as chert and nonchert lithics) dictated an excavation strategy which included the piece-plotting of individual items to determine the

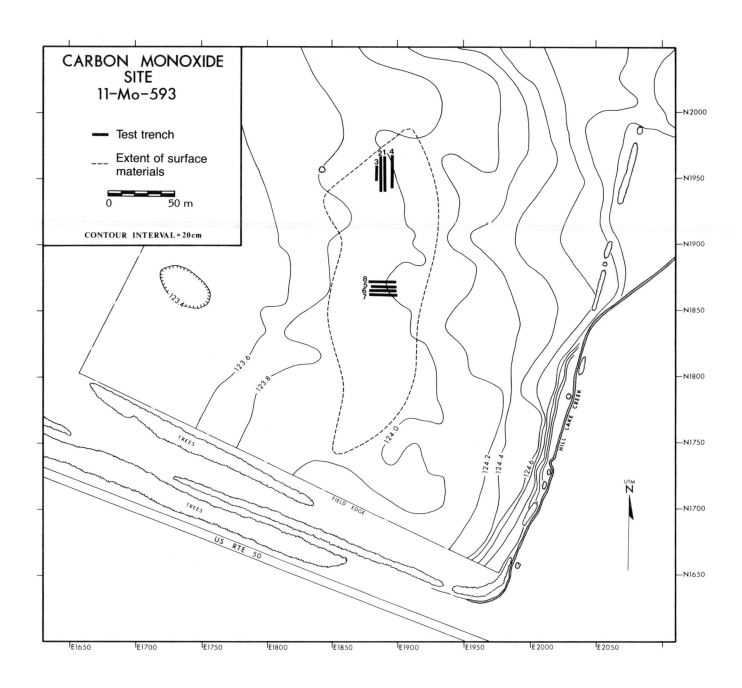

Figure 8.   Extent of Surface Materials and 1977 Test Trenches

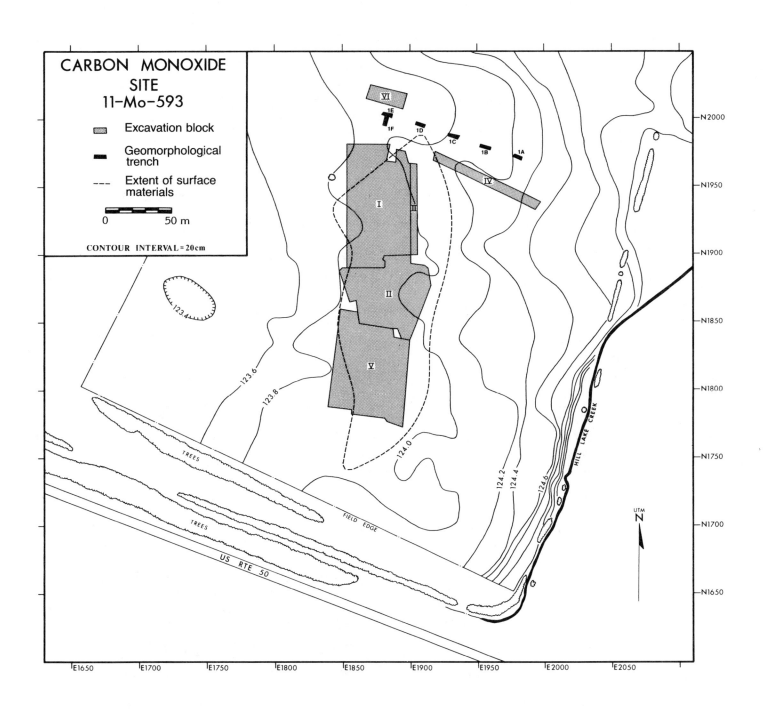

Figure 9. Excavation Blocks I-VI and Geomorphological Trenches 1A-1F

vertical range of material density and the horizontal extent of the
debris. Initially, it was difficult to determine whether these areas of
material represented circumscribed activity areas or randomly
distributed middens. For this reason, extensive piece-plotting was
necessary. This technique eventually allowed us to establish 1) that
these material scatters were circumscribed and were, therefore, activity
areas; 2) that they were stratigraphically superimposed above the Marion
Thick ceramic scatters; and 3) the direction and degree of the slope of
the ridge on which both occupations were situated.

One of the excavation techniques utilized in Block I was a
systematic, random block and test-square approach to establish the
extent of the material debris, the circumscribed nature of which still
remained unknown in 1978. A 30 m x 30 m unit was selected in the
southeastern portion of Block I because of the higher density of
materials exposed in that area by machine stripping. This 900 m2 unit
was subdivided into nine blocks of 100 m2 each (labeled Blocks A-J). A
10% sample was chosen from each block for excavation, i.e., ten 1 m x 1
m squares were selected in each block from a table of random numbers to
minimize bias on the part of the selector. Thus, a total of ninety 1 m
x 1 m squares were placed between UTM N1900-1930 and E1870-1900
(Figure 10).

The results of this random test-square strategy confirmed that the
material scatters previously observed were, in fact, discrete activity
areas and not general midden deposits distributed over the entire area.
For example, many of the squares produced no material at all,
particularly in the western area of the test block. The effort expended
on this operation was minimal, especially considering that about 600 m2
of the remaining portion of this block did not have to be shovel-scraped
or further excavated since the random-block approach described above had
revealed no new features or activity areas.

It became obvious in 1978 that the Carbon Monoxide site encompassed
a greater areal extent than was previously recognized and contained
minimally two distinct components. Excavations were expanded south from
Block I in 1978 and 1979 to incorporate the remaining portion of the
ridge. Block II was opened during the fall of 1978, and additional pit
features were located. Block V was exposed during 1979 and, again,
additional features were found. Also in 1979, Blocks III, IV, and VI
were placed in various areas of the ridge to determine the extent of
prehistoric occupation in the ridge area. Various geomorphic trenches
and test pits were placed in strategic areas of the site to determine
the physiographic character of the inner channel ridge and surrounding
area.

A total of 2996 man hours were expended at this site, and a total of

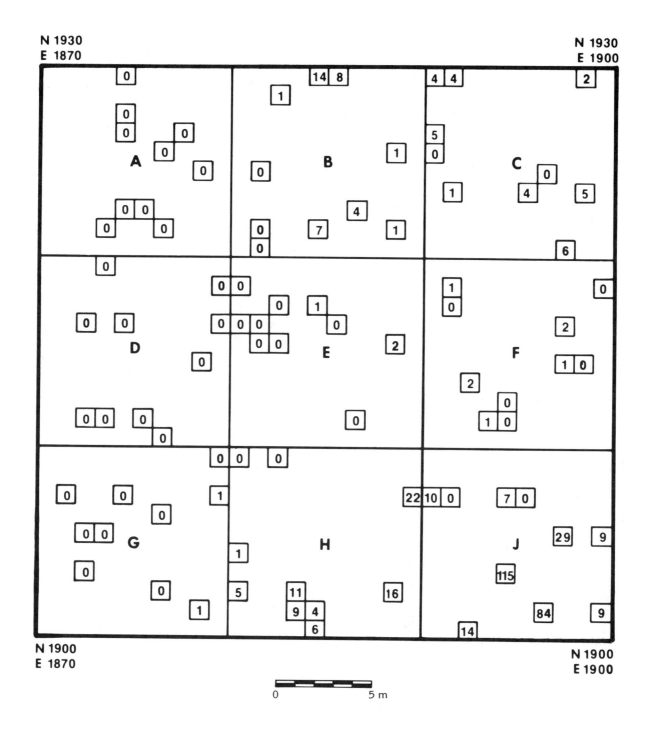

Figure 10. Distribution of Chert Flakes within Random Test Squares of Test Blocks A–J in the Central Excavation Area of the Carbon Monoxide Site

11,775 m2 of soil were stripped over a period of two years. The Carbon Monoxide site was a significant site in the alignment because of the presence of two buried Early Woodland components. The wide-scale stripping of this site represents the first systematic attempt to expose community patterns for these phases in the American Bottom. The results obtained from the 1975 survey, the 1976 through 1977 testing phase, and the 1978 through 1979 excavation period are presented in the following sections.

RESULTS OF SURVEY AND TESTING

The site was located in November 1975 by the IDOT archaeological survey of the FAI-270 alignment (Bareis et al. 1977 and Kelly et al. 1979) and, based on the surface distribution of cultural material, the site area was believed to encompass 1.4 ha. This survey established the presence of both Middle Woodland and "Late Bluff" (Emergent Mississippian) components by the recovery of three diagnostic sherds and various lithic artifacts. It was not, however, until 1976 when probe and phosphate testing were conducted that the buried Early Woodland Marion occupation was discovered.

Testing Results

Probe and phosphate tests were undertaken in March 1976 by an IDOT crew. One thousand one hundred nine probe samples were taken along a grid pattern at 4 m intervals and subsequently examined for phosphate content and indications of subsurface occupation. The results of the phosphate testing showed "high" phosphate values in the southern portion of the site (UTM N1750-1800, E1870-1920). As at other sites in the alignment, these results showed that there was little if any correlation between "high" phosphate values and the presence of subsurface features. The southern portion of the Carbon Monoxide site, which had produced high phosphate values, yielded neither features nor cultural debris during the 1978 and 1979 investigations. One positive result of the probe testing was the recovery of a Marion Thick sherd from a deep probe taken in the northern area of the site.

In October 1977, the UIUC established a grid at the site based on the UTM system and also made a contour map of the site area. Ten test units were excavated, including two hand-excavated units (Test Units 9 and 10) representing 5 m2, and eight machine-excavated units (Test Units 1-8) representing 369.8 m2. Each unit was taken down 50 cm to 75 cm below the present surface. The test units were placed in two areas: the "Northern Area", which included Test Units 1-4, 9 and 10; and the "Southern Area", which included Test Units 5-8.

Test Unit 9, a 2 m x 2 m square, was opened by hand in the area where the 1976 testing had unearthed the Marion Thick sherd. More sherds were found 50 cm to 60 cm below the surface in Test Unit 9. Test Units 1 and 2 were excavated on either side (running north-south) of Test Unit 9 to ascertain the limits of the Marion Thick concentration. At the time of the subsurface testing, the intent was to locate definable feature fill limits although the possibility of designating the area either as an activity area or as a midden was also recognized (Bareis et al. 1977:85). Test Units 1 and 2 were cut by machine through the overburden and humus until the Marion Thick pottery scatter was observed; this level was then shovel scraped and hand excavated. All cultural material larger than 2 cm in size was piece plotted, and smaller material was collected by 1 m squares. A total of 196 Marion Thick sherds, along with sandstone and chert, were recovered between 123.53 m and 123.37 m amsl. This area of ceramic material was eventually designated as Feature 1 in 1978 and was expanded at that time to expose the actual limits of the scatter.

Test Unit 10 was a hand-excavated 1 m x 1 m square devoid of cultural material. Test Units 3 and 4 were machine-cut trenches parallel to Test Units 1 and 2, containing only a few pieces of sandstone each (Tables 2 and 3).

The Southern Area test units were machine-cut trenches oriented in an east-west direction. No ceramics were recovered from Test Units 5-8; however, occasional chert debris, sandstone, and rough rock were recovered. Test Unit 5 contained a small area (ca. 1 m x 2 m) of concentrated chert debris along with some burned clay and charred nutshell. The limits of this concentration were not exposed. A distinct stratigraphy was recognized in the profiles of the Southern Area trenches. Testing revealed a complex stratigraphic situation, which included an alluvial overburden 40 cm to 100 cm deep; a buried humus horizon ca. 20 cm to 26 cm thick; and the presence of sand bar deposits, which represented the original inner channel ridge of the Hill Lake meander scar.

The most significant result obtained from the 1977 testing was the recognition of an Early Woodland Marion cultural horizon in the buried humus at the Carbon Monoxide site. The 1977 subsurface testing provided no confirmation for either the Middle Woodland or Late Bluff occupations indicated by the previous surface collections. However, the discovery of a buried humus horizon containing various cultural materials, including the Early Woodland component, indicated the need for

Table 2. Surface Collection and Test Excavation Material (1975-1977)

Cultural Materials	Power Units					Surface Collection	Total
	1	2	4	5	8		
Marion Thick Body Sherds	52	129	-	-	-	-	181
Marion Thick Rims	4	8	-	-	-	-	12
Marion Thick Base Sherds	1	2	-	-	-	-	3
Miscellaneous Ceramics*	-	-	-	-	-	3	3
Chert Flakes/ Pieces	7	14	-	87	8	128	244
Utilized/Retouched Flakes	-	-	-	-	1	6	7
Projectile Point Fragments	-	-	-	-	-	1	1
Chert Cores	-	-	-	-	-	2	2
Sandstone	23	13	3	1	-	-	40
Rough Rock	-	3	-	2	-	-	5

* Includes 1 Havana Cordmarked sherd; 1 Monks Mound Red sherd; 1 Havana Plain (?) sherd

Note: Materials in Power Units 1, 2, and 4 were all derived from Feature 1. (Adapted from Bareis et al. 1977:81, Table 18)

Table 3. 1977 Test Units from the Carbon Monoxide Site

Excavation Unit	UTM Coordinates of Excavation Units	Method of Excavation	PZ Cleared (m2)	Material Found
Northern Area				
1	N1939.00-1967.20, E1889.64-1891.76	Machine/Hand	56.40	Marion Thick, Chert, Sandstone
2	N1938.80-1966.90, E1886.76-1888.68	Machine/Hand	56.20	Marion Thick, Chert, Sandstone, Rough Rock
3	N1947.20-1961.30, E1883.48-1885.34	Machine	28.20	Sterile
4	N1941.30-1968.40, E1895.20-1897.40	Machine	54.20	Sandstone
9	N1958.00-1960.00, E1892.00-1894.00	Hand	4.00	Marion Thick, Chert, Sandstone
10	N1948.00-1949.00, E1893.00-1894.00	Hand	1.00	Sterile
Southern Area*				
5	N1867.80-1869.60, E1879.40-1900.00	Machine	41.20	Chert
6	N1864.60-1866.50, E1878.60-1900.00	Machine	43.60	Sterile
7	N1861.80-1863.70, E1877.40-1900.00	Machine	46.80	Sterile
8	N1871.20-1872.80, E1877.40-1900.00	Machine	43.20	Chert

* The UTM coordinates for these trenches are corrected from those presented in the 1977 report (Bareis et al. 1977:83).

large-scale stripping. On this basis, further investigation of the site was recommended.

Excavation Results

Archaeological excavations at the Carbon Monoxide site were accomplished between 29 September and 6 December 1978 and between 5 April and 4 June 1979. Fifty feature numbers were assigned to the following: 4 Marion Thick ceramic scatters, 6 Columbia Complex activity areas, 27 pits, 1 structure, 4 postmolds, and 12 stains. One postmold was initially assigned a feature number (Feature 47), but this number was subsequently dropped and the postmold was given a postmold number (PM 4). Therefore, the total number of features excavated at this site was 49 (Figure 11).

Machine excavation was utilized for the initial removal of the silty loess overburden. The first excavation unit coincided with the area in which testing in 1977 had exposed the Marion Thick scatter. This unit was designated Block I and encompassed an area of about 2700 m2. Approximately 40 cm to 60 cm of overburden were removed from the area, revealing a concentration of materials and features at the southern end of Block I and two Marion Thick ceramic scatters in the northern portion of Block I (Plate 3).

Once it had been established that subsurface features were present in Block I, an additional area (Block II), directly south of Block I, was opened in 1978. This area encompassed ca. 2400 m2, and it produced additional features. A total of 5180 m2 were eventually opened up during 1978, encompassing Blocks I and II (Figure 9).

After elevations and a UTM grid were established at the Carbon Monoxide site (from an established datum and grid at the Carbon Dioxide site), excavations were undertaken on the defined features (Features 1-17). Excavations were completed on all of these features except Features 9, 10, and 17 during 1978.

During the 1978 season a random block and test-square sampling strategy (described above) was used to determine the density and extent of material debris in the southern portion of Block I. This area had already been stripped of its alluvial overburden when sampling was undertaken. Each square was excavated into the sterile sandy ridge deposits. In each block, one square was excavated deeper than the others to provide information about the geomorphology of the ridge.

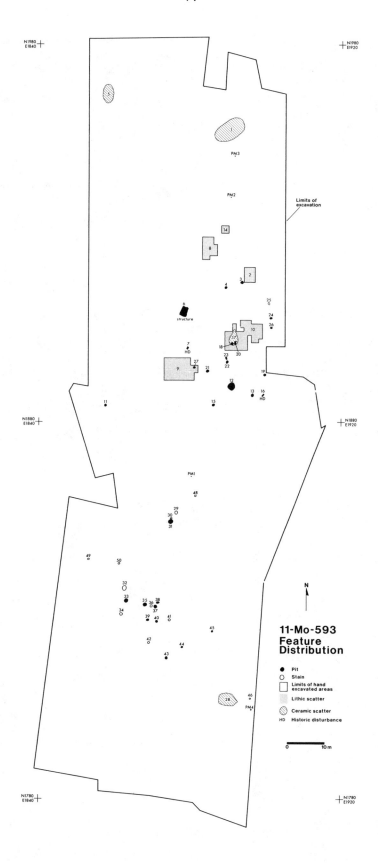

Figure 11. Distribution of Features at the Carbon Monoxide Site

42

Plate 3. Excavation at the Carbon Monoxide Site: upper left, Block I, view to the west; upper right, machine excavation in Block V, view to the south; lower left, excavation in Feature 17; lower right, random sample test units in Block I, view to the northeast

Figure 10 and Table 4 present the results of this sampling operation. It essentially confirmed the presence of discrete scatters of material and negated the alternative contention that these scatters were distributed randomly over the entire occupation area.

During 1979, the remaining portion of the buried ridge was exposed (designated as Blocks III and V). Block III (335 m2) represented an eastern extension of Block I. It was scraped with a backhoe adapted with a modified, flat, wide blade. Three features (Features 24-26) were found in this block. This modified backhoe was also utilized in Block II, resulting in the discovery of Features 19, 21, 22, 23, and 27.

Block V was a southern extension of Block II, encompassing an area of 3680 m2 and revealing Features 28 through 50. Except for Feature 28, which was a Marion Thick scatter, the features were all pits which contained no diagnostic material and could not be associated with a particular component.

Two additional blocks (Block IV, covering 600 m2, and Block VI, covering 350 m2) were excavated by heavy machinery north and east of Block I to examine soil profiles off the ridge area. No material was recovered from Block VI, and very little was recovered from Block IV. Features 1 and 5, therefore, in Excavation Block I appear to represent the northernmost extent of the prehistoric occupation of this ridge.

A total of 11,775 m2 of area were exposed to varying depths during the course of the 1978 and 1979 seasons. Feature excavation was completed on 4 June 1979. Wide-scale stripping revealed a dispersed pattern of feature occurrence along the buried ridge although the Columbia Complex component was primarily concentrated in the southern portion of Block I. The Early Woodland components on this ridge represent relatively distinct occupations with feature superpositioning or mixing observed in only a few cases (e.g., Features 10, 17, and 19).

Tables 5-7 summarize the materials, components, and feature classes recovered during UIUC investigations at the Carbon Monoxide site. Organized by component, the following sections will describe the nature and distribution of the features and material remains recovered during the 1978 and 1979 seasons.

Table 4. Materials Recovered
from Random Test Units within Block I

	N	Wt(g)
Chert Flakes	411	346.5
Chert Block Fragments	27	77.7
Chert Tools	11	127.7
Sandstone	44	328.1
Limestone	2	16.9
Other Lithics*	18	11.6
Burned Clay	10	4.6
Ceramics	19	56.6
Total	542	969.7

*Includes hematite, rough rock
 and waterworn pebbles

Table 5. Total Material Remains* Recovered
from the Carbon Monoxide Site

	N	Wt(g)	% Wt
Nonutilized Chert	5748	5694.4	29.7
Utilized Chert	173	1696.8	8.9
Nonchert Lithics**	460	4358.1	22.7
Ceramics	4010	6876.3	35.8
Burned Silt/Cinder/Bone	687	556.8	2.9
Total	11,078	19,182.4	

 * Includes both Marion and Columbia Complex
   materials.

** Includes sandstone, limestone, igneous rock,
   hematite, rough rock, silicified sediment,
   Missouri River clinker, and tools made of
   igneous rock and sandstone.

Table 6. Feature Classes by Cultural Component

Feature Class	Component				Total
	Marion Phase	Columbia Complex	Historic	Unassociated	
Pits	2?	11	2	12	27
Activity Areas	-	6	-	-	6
Ceramic Scatters	4	-	-	-	4
Postmolds	1	-	-	3	4
Structures	-	1	-	-	1
Stains	-	-	-	12	12
Total	7	18	2	24	50*

*Feature 17 is counted twice, once as a Marion phase ceramic scatter
 and again as a Columbia Complex activity area. Postmolds are not included
 in the feature total.

Table 7. Feature Classes by Component and Feature Number

Feature Class	Component			
	Marion Phase	Columbia Complex	Historic	Unassociated
Pits	18?, 20?	3, 4, 12, 13, 15, 19, 21, 22, 23, 26, 27	7, 16	11, 24, 31, 33, 35, 37, 38, 39, 40, 43, 44, 45
Activity Areas	-	2, 8, 9, 10, 14, 17	-	-
Ceramic Scatters	1, 5, 17, 28	-	-	-
Postmolds	PM 4	-	-	PM 1, PM 2, PM 3
Structures	-	6	-	-
Stains	-	-	-	25, 29, 30, 32, 34, 36, 41, 42, 46, 48, 49, 50

EARLY WOODLAND MARION COMPONENT

The Early Woodland Marion component consisted of four discrete areas
of material scatter (Features 1, 5, 17, and 28); two small, shallow
basin cooking/processing pits (Features 18 and 20); and a single
postmold (PM 4) associated with Feature 28. Features 1 and 5 were
located at the northern end of Excavation Block 1. Features 17, 18, and
20 were located at the southern end of Block 1, ca. 60 m south of
Feature 1. Feature 28 and its associated postmold were situated in the
southeastern portion of Block V, ca. 95 m south of Feature 17 and 150 m
south of Feature 1. Based on the Marion Thick ceramic types recovered
from the material scatters, this occupation was dated to the Marion
phase of the Early Woodland period.

During the 1978 investigations, one of the first areas exposed at
the site was the Early Woodland Marion scatter that had been initially
uncovered in 1977. This scatter marked the northern limits of
Excavation Block I. The remaining portion of this feature, which was
designated Feature 1, was excavated during the fall of 1978. A more
detailed description of this feature is provided below.

After the remaining portion of Block I had been exposed, another
Marion Thick scatter was uncovered ca. 30 m west of Feature 1. This
scatter was designated as Feature 5.

A third scatter of Marion Thick pottery was identified at the
southern edge of Block I, ca. 60 m south of Features 1 and 5. This
feature, which was not completely excavated until 1979, was designated
as Feature 17.

Unlike Features 1 and 5, Feature 17 yielded mixed materials,
consisting of a Columbia Complex component lithic activity area
overlying a Marion Thick pottery concentration. The Marion scatter
occurred at the base of the lower, unmixed humus horizon. The Columbia
Complex materials occurred above this Marion scatter in the upper
portions of the unmixed humus and in the mixed or plowed humus.
Although chert flake material and Columbia Complex pottery extended for
nearly 30 cm above the Marion pottery concentration, no material was
found below the Marion scatter. The Columbia Complex component of this
feature was apparently related to Feature 10, an adjacent lithic
activity area.

Two shallow pit features were defined at the southern end of
Feature 17 (Features 18 and 20). No diagnostics were recovered from
these pits. Their uppermost elevations indicate, however, that they

were associated with the Feature 17 Marion Thick scatter and not with the upper Columbia Complex component. Both features probably served as shallow processing/cooking pits.

Nearly 95 m to the south of Feature 17, another Marion scatter was identified during 1979 while excavating Block V. This scatter was designated as Feature 28. Feature 28 consisted of an irregular scatter of Marion Thick pottery. Approximately 4 m to the east, a postmold was identified and excavated which contained a Marion Thick sherd; on this basis, this postmold was considered to be associated with the Feature 28 Marion Thick scatter.

Feature Descriptions

Feature 1

Feature 1 was an oval scatter (ca. 7.80 m x 5.60 m) of Early Woodland Marion material situated in the northeastern portion of Block I. The scatter was oriented in a northeast-southwest direction. Excavations were initiated on this feature during 1977 and completed during 1978. All items were piece plotted both vertically and horizontally. This feature was buried beneath ca. 40 cm of silty alluvium and ca. 10 cm to 15 cm of mixed and unmixed humus. The scatter itself ranged in elevation from 123.44 to 123.32 m amsl and averaged 10 cm in thickness. It was situated within the lower portion of a dark gray, unmixed humus horizon that capped the original sand bar ridge. These materials were recovered from elevations nearly 10 cm below those recorded during the 1977 testing of this feature. It is probable, therefore, that excavations during that period were not carried deep enough to define the vertical extent of this material concentration. This was accomplished during the 1978 excavations.

Cultural remains were piece plotted within 1 m x 1 m squares following the removal of the alluvial overburden by heavy machinery. No materials were observed in the alluvium during machine or hand excavation. Each recovered item was recorded and eventually computer coded. A total of 359 ceramic items and 209 nonceramic items were plotted. Some items were not plotted and were simply recorded on 1 m by 1 m squares.

The piece plot map revealed that the scatter of pottery, initially thought in the field to be randomly distributed, actually comprised two distinct clusters of broken pottery, each representing a separate vessel (Figure 12). The presence of these two vessels in mutually exclusive contexts suggests that this scatter had not been disturbed by plowing, erosion, or any form of mixing. This also indicates the relatively stable nature of this inner channel ridge, at least during the formative period of humus development over the ridge.

The scatter also contained various chert and nonchert lithic debris, including a large number of burned sandstone fragments (Figure 13). For this reason, Feature 1 was not regarded as merely a ceramic scatter. It represents, in all probability, a circumscribed activity area, perhaps focused on the processing of plants obtained from the nearby marsh.

The remains of two Marion Thick vessels were recovered from Feature 1 (Figure 12). Vessel 1 was distributed throughout the western portion of the scatter, although sherds were also found mixed with Vessel 2 in the eastern portion of the scatter. A description of each vessel is given below.

Vessel 1. Vessel 1 represents a flat-based, deep bowl. The orifice diameter ranged from 32 cm to 34 cm, an estimate based on the recovery of ca. 45% of the rim/orifice area. The lip was flat, broad (11 mm to 12 mm), and cordmarked. The interior rim portion was slightly demarcated at ca. 6 mm below the top of the lip. The vessel walls were thick, ranging from 8 mm below the lip to 16 mm along the midportion of the vessel. Both the exterior and interior surfaces were cordmarked but also highly eroded. Both surfaces were hard but very crumbly. The vessel walls in cross section were extremely compact. The vessel was tempered with coarse grit, consisting of relatively large, crushed granitic igneous and quartz inclusions (ranging in size from 2 mm to 6 mm). Most of the vessel was fired red (10 YR 6/8 to 10 YR 5/6), but a portion of the interior had been scorched black, either during firing or through use. The total weight of the vessel remains was 1512.2 g, but this did not represent the entire vessel. Fifty-five percent of the rim was missing, as was most of the base. The crumbly nature of this pottery indicated that the remaining portion of the vessel had probably disintegrated in situ.

Vessel 2. Vessel 2 was a deep bowl or jar with an orifice diameter ranging from 22 cm to 26 cm, an estimate obtained from the recovery of ca. 20% of the rim/orifice area. The base type was unknown. The lip was flat and relatively thin (5 mm wide). The vessel walls varied from 5 mm to 9 mm in thickness. The exterior and interior surfaces were highly eroded, but thin cordmarking was present on both surfaces. The cordmarks appeared to be overlapping and irregular in direction. The vessel was cordmarked up to the exterior lip, but not on the lip itself.

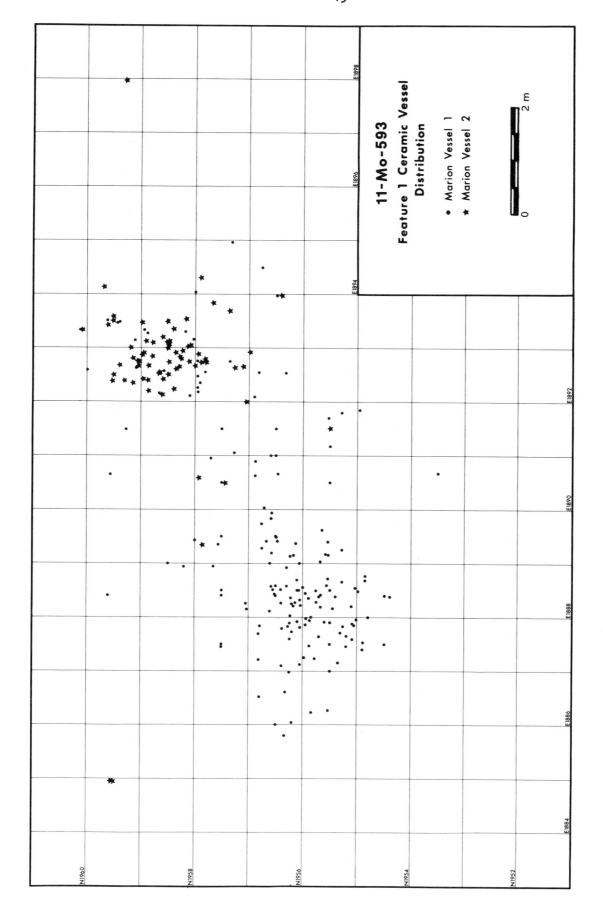

Figure 12. Piece-Plot Distribution of Marion Thick Vessels 1 and 2 in Feature 1

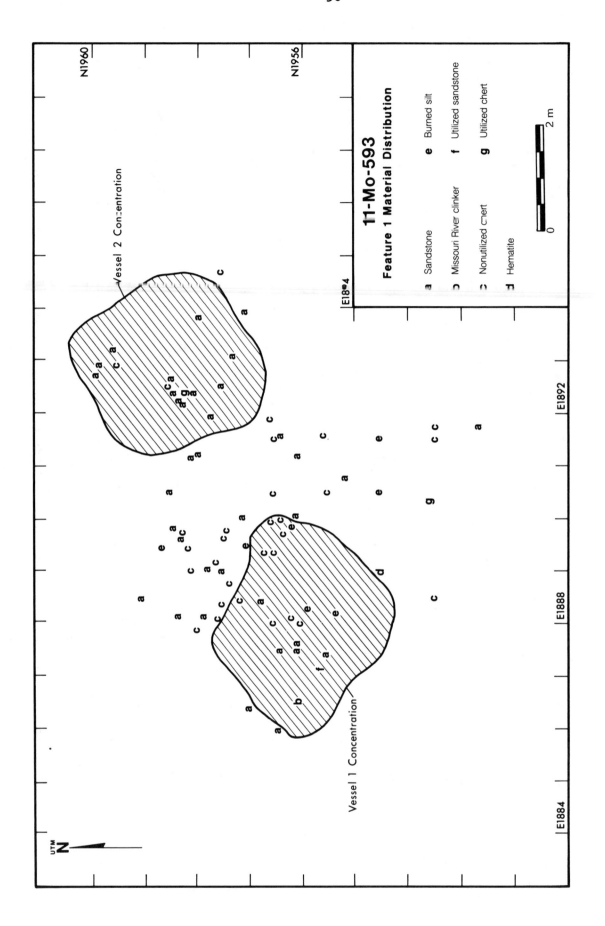

Figure 13. Piece-Plot Distribution of Nonceramic Materials in Feature 1

Unlike Vessel 1, the paste in Vessel 2 was fine and "creamy-textured". This vessel was primarily grit-tempered with black feldsparic rock inclusions. It is possible that the "creamy" texture of the paste resulted from a crushed grog-temper, but distinct grog inclusions were not observed. Exterior and interior surface color ranged from 7.5 YR 7/6 to 7.5 YR 6/6 (reddish yellow). A total of 66 pieces, weighing 469.6 g, were recovered. The highly eroded nature of this vessel suggested that most of the vessel had disintegrated in situ.

Vessel Summary

Vessels 1 and 2 both represent Marion Thick type pottery, but they differed from one another in several respects, including temper type, paste texture, wall thickness, surface color, and lip width. Vessel 2, if it had been recovered from isolated contexts, would probably not have been identified as Marion Thick because of its thin vessel walls and thin lip. However, vessel wall thickness variation in Marion Thick assemblages has also been observed at the Jean Rita (Linder 1974) and Schultz (Fitting 1972) sites. The term Marion "Thick" does not accurately define the range of variation in vessel wall thickness found in Marion ceramic assemblages, and certainly cannot constitute the sole criterion for type definition. Generally, the attributes that characterize Marion Thick ceramics include 1) flat lip treatment; 2) coarse grit-tempering, usually with crushed igneous rock; 3) flat bases; 4) thick vessel walls; and 5) interior-exterior depression cordmarking. Of these traits, flattened lips and thick vessel walls are not really the key indicators of the Marion Thick pottery type (Plate 4).

One hundred fifty-seven lithic items were recovered from Feature 1 (Table 8). No diagnostic artifacts were present. Recovered artifacts included a single fragment of a smoothed sandstone grinder; one piece of modified, rubbed, multifaceted hematite; and a single retouched flake. Chert flakes, a single chert blade, and several chert pieces indicated that secondary reduction activities were associated with this feature. Cortical flakes or pieces were not recovered. The chert types were of local origin, including a fine-grained, oolitic chert and a bluish-gray chert with crystalline quartz inclusions. This bluish-gray chert may derive from nearby Ste. Genevieve formations; it has been referred to as Ste. Genevieve purple in previous reports (McElrath and Fortier 1983). This chert type occurred exclusively in Feature 1 at the Carbon Monoxide site. The oolitic chert appeared to have been thermally altered, but it lacked luster. Many of the chert flakes were concentrated in one area adjacent to the Vessel 1 concentration, supporting the contention that the debris in these scatters represents specific activities rather than randomly mixed midden.

Just over 530 g (89 pieces) of sandstone were found throughout the

52

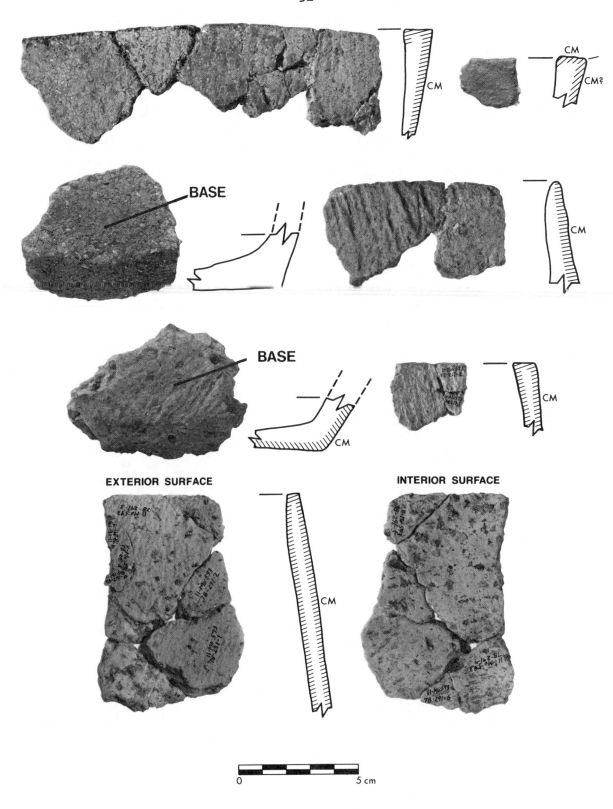

Plate 4. Marion Thick Ceramics from the Carbon Monoxide Site

Table 8. Lithics from Feature 1

	N	Wt(g)	Mean Wt(g)
Chert Flakes	30	80.2	2.67
Chert Pieces	7	36.7	5.24
Chert Blade	1	2.9	2.90
Retouched Chert Flake	1	6.3	6.30
Sandstone	89	531.5	5.97
Silicified Sediment	3	54.1	18.03
Rough Rock	22	2.4	0.11
Hematite	1	0.1	0.10
Missouri River Clinker	1	0.3	0.30
Utilized Sandstone	1	12.9	12.90
Utilized Hematite	1	26.9	26.90
Total	157	754.3	

feature although a concentration of fragments appeared between the two vessel scatters. The high occurrence of sandstone at Early Woodland sites has been noted elsewhere (Linder 1974) and has been observed in scatters of Marion Thick pottery at the Mund (11-S-435) [Fortier et al. 1983], Go-Kart South, and Fiege sites (see this volume). The presence of 52 burned silt fragments (24.2) in this feature, as well as some fragments of burned sandstone, indicated that one or more fires had existed within the feature area. Rough rock amounted to only 2.4 g, but totaled 22 pieces. These pieces appeared to represent temper fragments from disintegrated Marion Thick sherds. Finally, a single piece of Missouri River clinker was found. This may have been washed naturally onto the sand bar ridge, but it is more likely that its occurrence was the result of human selection. Missouri River clinker represents a buoyant scoria originating in the Upper Missouri River valley. It occurs infrequently at Late Archaic through Mississippian occupations in the American Bottom, and it was generally utilized for abraders and as a temper for ceramic vessels.

Feature 5

Excavated in 1978, Feature 5 was an oval scatter (5.00 m x 2.70 m) of Early Woodland Marion Thick pottery located 30 m west of Feature 1 (Figure 14). This scatter was oriented in a north-south direction and had well-defined boundaries. Situated in the unplowed lower humus horizon (B2), it averaged 14 cm in depth, between 123.22 m and 123.08 m amsl.

54

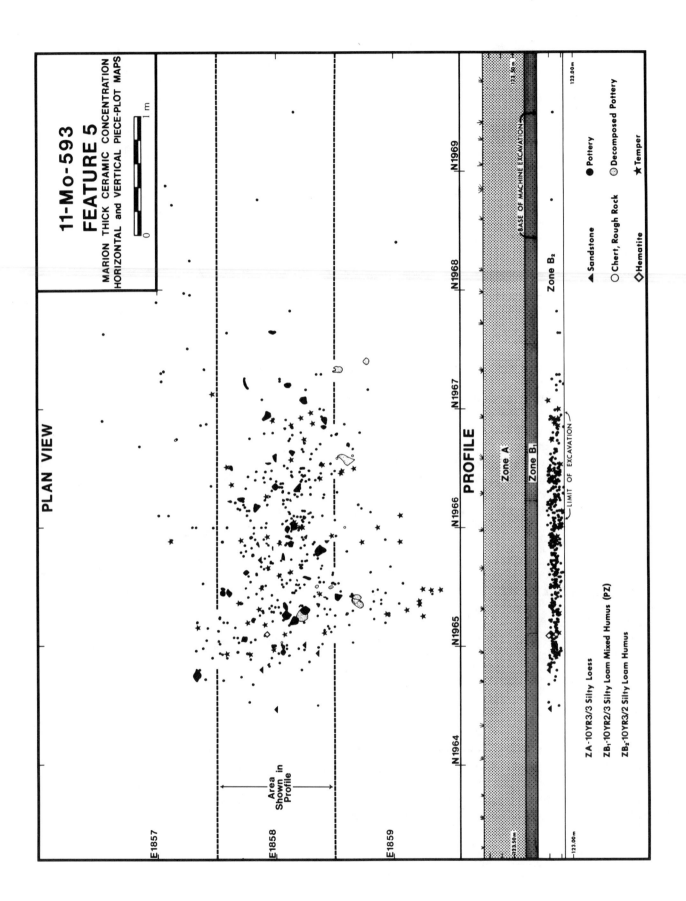

Figure 14. Plan and Profile Views of Feature 5

Feature 5 was exposed during machine scraping and was subsequently troweled within a 7 m x 5 m area. All items, including temper fragments, were piece plotted. A total of 2251 pieces of pottery and temper fragments, weighing 1544.3 g, were eventually recovered. Several chert pieces (local chert) and fragments of hematite, rough rock, and burned clay also occurred in this scatter. The soil was stained with red ochre fragments, although only a few well-preserved pieces were actually recovered (Table 9). Feature 5 probably represents an activity area similar to Feature 1.

The remains of only one vessel (Vessel 4) were identified in Feature 5. These remains were extremely fragmented. The exterior and interior surfaces of the sherds were almost completely eroded although faint cordmarking could be detected on both surfaces of several sherds. Rims were not present in this scatter, but one basal sherd, flat and cordmarked on the base, indicated that Vessel 4 represents a "classic" Marion Thick, flat-bottomed jar.

Vessel 4 was tempered with extremely coarse and angular grit pieces, with inclusions measuring as much as 15 mm to 20 mm in length. The grit appeared to be primarily a crushed form of low grade and possibly heat-altered chert although granitic or dioritic fragments were present as well. The vessel appeared to have disintegrated in situ as evidenced by the numerous temper fragments (initially misidentified in the field as chert flakes and pieces) recovered from this scatter. Because of the high density of temper inclusions, the pottery fragments were very compact. The vessel walls averaged about 13 mm to 16 mm in thickness.

Feature 17

Feature 17 was an irregular scatter of Marion Thick pottery measuring ca. 5.20 m x 3.30 m in extent. It consisted exclusively of broken fragments of Marion Thick pottery scattered through ca. 15 cm of soil between 123.50 m and 123.35 m amsl. A determination of the nature of Feature 17 was made difficult by dense Columbia Complex chert flake debris that overlay the Marion Thick scatter. Some of the chert and sandstone debris had filtered down into the Early Woodland Marion materials, making it impossible to clearly associate any of the chert with the Marion Thick scatter. However, all of the chert types found with the Marion scatter represent types found generally in the Columbia Complex features. It is believed that the sandstone was associated with the Marion scatter, since the sandstone generally was recovered from lower levels than the chert debris.

The Feature 17 Marion scatter represents a single vessel (Vessel 3) consisting of only 1 rim, 267 body sherds, and 73 fragments, weighing

Table 9. Summary of Excavated Remains
from Feature 5

Ceramics	N	Wt(g)	Mean Wt(g)
Body Sherds*	1043	1289.00	1.24
Base Sherds*	1	69.30	-
Grit Temper Pieces	446	79.90	0.18
Misc. Fragment	761	106.10	0.14
Total	2251	1544.30	
Lithics			
Chert Pieces	2	4.7	2.35
Rough Rock	1	0.4	0.40
Hematite	2	0.4	0.20
Red Ochre	6	8.6	1.43
Total	11	14.1	

* Marion Thick

Table 10. Vessel 3 from Feature 17

Sherd Type	N	Wt(g)	Exterior Decoration	Interior Decoration
Rim	1	37.1	Cordmarked	Plain
Body	123	542.6	Cordmarked	Plain
Body	1	3.7	Cordmarked	Cordmarked
Body	31	78.5	Cordmarked	Indeterminate
Body	9	11.7	Indeterminate	Plain
Body	103	182.5	Indeterminate	Indeterminate
Misc. Fragments	73	41.5	-	-
Total	341	897.6		

897.6 g. Vessel 3 was characterized as a coarse, grit-tempered (crushed igneous rock and quartz) jar with a rounded lip and with an orifice diameter of 22 cm to 26 cm (estimated from the single recovered rim that represents only 10% of the rim portion of the vessel). Rounded lips have been only infrequently observed in Marion Thick assemblages in this area although they were present at both the Jean Rita site (Linder 1974:124) in Illinois and at the Schultz site in Michigan where 40% of the Schultz Thick rims possessed rounded lips (Fitting 1972:142). Vessel walls measured 6 mm to 12 mm in thickness, with thinning toward the lip portion of the vessel. The vessel was coarsely cordmarked on both the interior and exterior surfaces and over the lip; however, ca. 50% of the body sherds lacked cordmarking on the interior (Table 10).

The chert debris that overlay the Marion pottery scatter extended from 123.72 m down to the Marion Tick scatter, and included with it were Columbia Complex type ceramics. Two projectile points, a Waubesa-like, contracting-stemmed point and a broken point similar to a Liverpool-stemmed type were found at the southern end of the Marion scatter, but at an elevation that associated them with the Columbia Complex occupation. Feature 17 (the Marion component) appeared to represent an activity area similar to Features 1 and 5.

Features 18 and 20

Two small, shallow, basin-shaped pit features (Features 18 and 20) were defined and excavated at the southern end of Feature 17 at about the same elevations as the Marion scatter (Figure 15). These pits exhibited evidence of burning throughout their fills although the charcoal was poorly preserved. No diagnostics were recovered from these pits. Their uppermost elevations indicated, however, that they were associated with the Feature 17 Marion Thick scatter and not with the upper Columbia Complex component. Both features probably served as processing pits. Feature 18 contained remains of American lotus, a marsh plant that was probably ground and utilized for food.

Feature 28

Feature 28 was a Marion Thick scatter located along the eastern portion of Block V, which measured ca. 5.16 m x 3.14 m in extent and was oriented in an east-west direction. Only one chert flake occurred in this Marion Thick scatter; in this respect, it differed from the Feature 1 and 5 scatters, which yielded relatively high quantities of lithic materials. The Feature 28 scatter extended 10 cm in elevation from 123.58 m to 123.48 m amsl.

58

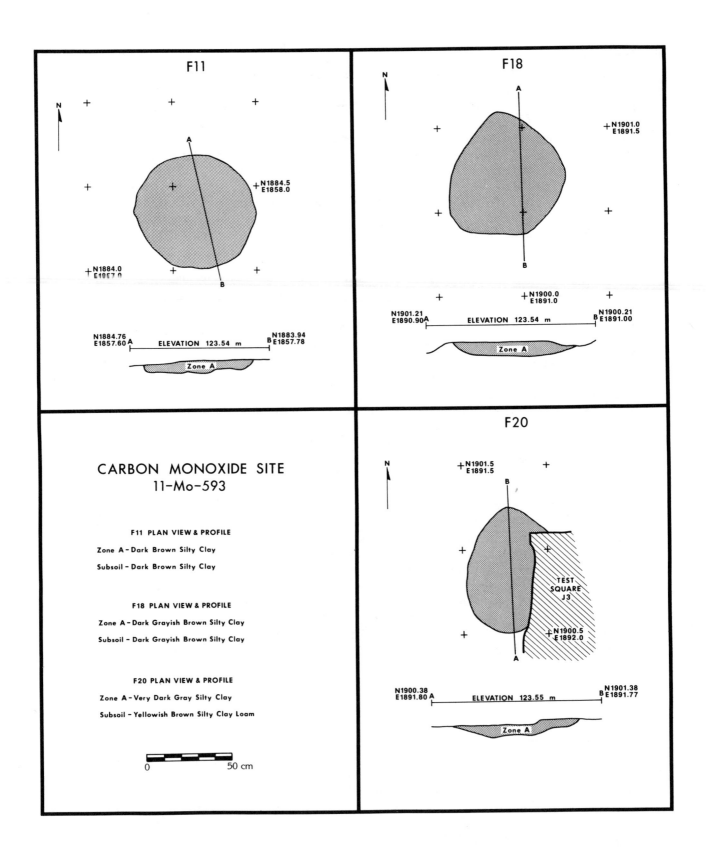

Figure 15. Plan and Profile Views of Marion Pits (Features 18 and 20) and Unassociated Pit (Feature 11)

The area in which the Feature 28 ceramic scatter occurred contained little or no evidence of a humus horizon. The alluvial overburden in this area measured only 30 cm to 40 cm, and the scatter was found at an elevation of nearly 20 cm above the northern Marion scatters (Features 1, 5, and 17). The ridge was apparently more elevated in this locality.

This scatter, although possessing well-defined limits, may represent an activity area as has been postulated for Features 1, 5, and 17. However, in the absence of other kinds of debris such as sandstone or burned clay it appears that the Feature 28 scatter merely represents the remains of a discarded Marion Thick vessel.

A single postmold (PM 4) was found 1 m south and 4 m east of Feature 28. It contained burned charcoal and four Marion Thick body sherds (5.0 g). The maximum diameter of this post was 20 cm, and its maximum depth was 21.5 cm. The sides were vertical; the bottom was rounded. Presumably, this post was related to the Feature 28 scatter although its function is unknown.

The fragments of a single vessel (Vessel 5) comprised the ceramic material from Feature 28. Vessel 5 consisted of only 1 rim, 254 body sherds, and 206 fragments, weighing a total of 757.6 g. The vessel was cordmarked on the interior and exterior surfaces up to the lip, which was flat, 11 mm to 12 mm wide. It was tempered with coarse grit (crushed igneous rock), and the paste was extremely compact. The vessel walls varied in thickness from 10 mm to 13 mm. Vessel 5 most closely resembled Vessel 3 from Feature 17 in terms of paste, temper, and cordmarking (thick and depressed), but it possessed a flattened lip like Vessel 1 in Feature 1 (Table 11).

Summary

The distribution of Marion phase features at the Carbon Monoxide site indicated an extremely dispersed pattern of occupation along the inner channel ridge. Ceramic scatters typified the features of this component. Whether or not these scatters were produced during a single occupation remains unclear, but the paucity of material in these scatters indicates that the occupation or occupations were not intensive and were of relatively short duration. Each scatter contained a slightly different variety of Marion Thick pottery, as defined by lip type, temper, and decoration. While ceramic variation existed within the Marion Thick assemblage, this does not necessarily indicate chronological differentiation among the scatters (Features 1, 5, 17, and

Table 11. Vessel 5 from Feature 28

Ceramics	N	Wt(g)	Mean Wt(g)
Rim Sherd	1	7.2	7.20
Body Sherd	254	678.9	2.67
Misc. Fragments	190	68.0	0.36
Granitic Temper Pieces	16	3.5	0.22
Total	461	757.6	

Table 12. Marion Thick Vessels from
Features 1, 5, 17, and 28

Feature	Vessel	Sherds	Wt (g)	Mean Wt(g)
1	1	197	1512.2	7.68
	2	66	469.6	7.12
17	3	341	897.6	2.65
5	4	2251*	1544.3	0.69
28	5	461	757.6	1.65
Total		3316	5181.3	1.56

* Includes 446 (79.9 g) fragments of grit temper

28).   There is simply no basis at this time for arguing for or against contemporaneity of these scatters (Table 12).

The nature and function of these scatters is also difficult to resolve.   Such scatters appear to constitute a feature type representative of the Marion culture in the Midwest, also occurring at both the Jean Rita (Linder 1974) and Mund (Fortier et al. 1983) sites in the American Bottom.   Nowhere, however, have such scatters been as clearly demarcated as at the Carbon Monoxide site.

Most of these scatters do not merely represent the remains of isolated, randomly abandoned vessels. In each of the scatters at the Carbon Monoxide site, with the exception of Feature 28, the ceramic fragments were found mixed together with chert flakes, burned silt, rough rock, and sandstone. In Feature 1, a utilized, ground piece of sandstone and a piece of utilized hematite were also recovered. Hematite was also found in Feature 5. In addition, Feature 1 contained the remains of two vessels, each broken in a different portion of the scatter. In short, these scatters were the result of specific activities carried out within well-defined areas.

Each of the scatters had well-defined boundaries and was usually oval shaped.   Lithic and/or processing activities could have produced oval scatters of debris but, in the author's opinion, the consistency in shape of these circumscribed scatters at the Carbon Monoxide site is indicative of possible temporary shelters. Although postmolds were not observed along the edges of any of these scatters, the black or dark gray humus nature of the soil at this site rendered the identification of postmolds extremely difficult. In addition, the postulated shelters may only have consisted of lean-to covers, which utilized small posts, sticks, or reeds. A single post was found near Feature 28, but the function of this post could not be determined. Isolated posts were also found south of Feature 1, but these were nearly 15 m away from the scatter. Similar isolated posts have also been identified at the Jean Rita and Schultz sites (Linder 1974; Fitting 1972). At the Schultz site, posts occurred in the midst of a concentration of pits, and the excavator interpreted this configuration as possibly constituting a shelter.

In summary, the Early Woodland occupation at the Carbon Monoxide site was characterized by the occurrence of four scatters of Marion Thick pottery, two shallow basin processing pits, and a single postmold located near one of the scatters. The circumscribed nature of these scatters indicated that these were well-defined habitation and activity areas.   Burned silt, sandstone, and calcined bone were apparent in Feature 1 and suggest that cooking or roasting activities were carried out in that area. The ground sandstone fragment in Feature 1 probably represents a plant-grinding implement, and the small chert flakes in the scatters are indicative of tool maintenance or sharpening activities. All of the scatters were identified as Early Woodland on the basis of associated broken Marion vessels.

Each of the Early Woodland scatters appears to represent a family habitation and work area. The relationship between these activity areas is unclear, given the absence of Marion materials and pits between the various units. It is possible that the four identified scatters represent a single occupation by multiple families. Such an occupation would have been of a short-term, seasonal nature and would have functioned essentially as a temporary campsite established to procure the local plant (e.g., American lotus) and animal resources of this inner channel marsh zone. Alternatively, these scatters may represent isolated occupations by individual family units or by a single family unit over a period of time.

EARLY WOODLAND COLUMBIA COMPLEX COMPONENT

A total of 18 features comprised the Columbia Complex component. These features represent a discrete community plan at the Carbon Monoxide site. They include 11 pits, one structure, and 6 activity areas. This occupation was located in Blocks I, II, and III and was particularly focused at the southern end of Block I in the central excavation area (Figure 16).

The Columbia Complex occupation was identified on the basis of recovered plain and cordmarked sherds for which there are no known analogous types in the American Bottom, and a chert assemblage dominated by thermally altered, gray and tan cherts, probably derived from local Salem formations. Many of the features lacked diagnostic pottery and were cross dated on the basis of their chert types to features containing both Columbia Complex pottery and local gray and tan chert types.

The late Early Woodland affiliation of this occupation is somewhat tenuous and is based on ceramics which have few analogues in Illinois. The plain and cordmarked, grog-tempered ceramics, designated here as Columbia Plain and Columbia Cordmarked, are most similar to the plain and cordmarked Crab Orchard varieties known from sites from the floodplain of Jackson County, Illinois. The lithic assemblage and the Columbia Plain ceramics, however, also bear a close resemblance to the lithic and ceramic assemblages (some of the plain, grog-tempered ceramics) recovered at the Early Woodland, Florence Street (11-S-458) site (Emerson et al. 1983).

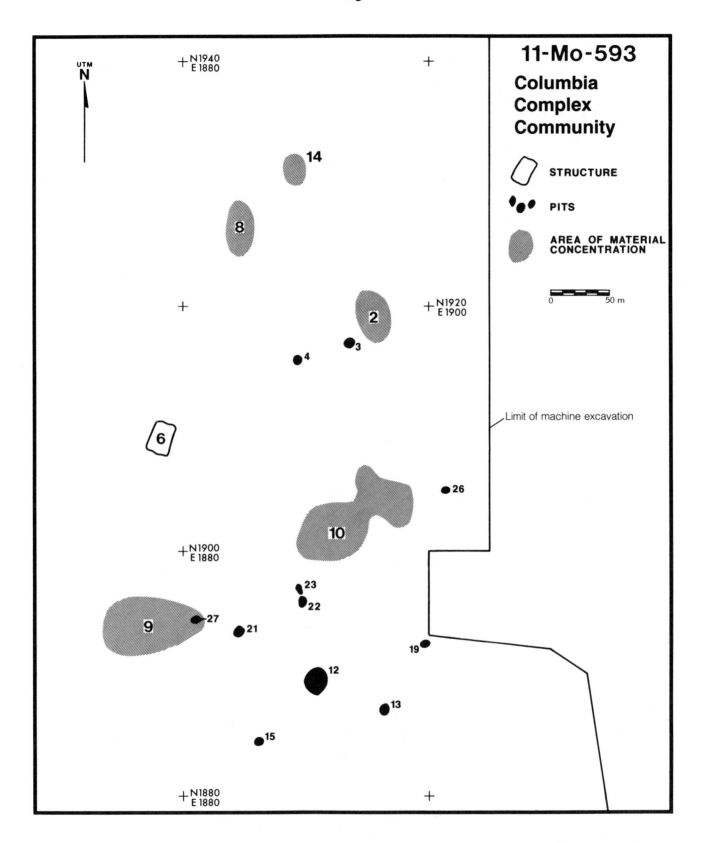

Figure 16. Columbia Complex Community Plan

Because of the tenuous typing of the ceramics from this component at the Carbon Monoxide site, it was impossible to assign this occupation to a particular phase. For this reason, the assemblage and occupation have been designated as the Columbia Complex. This complex probably dates from about 170 B.C. to about 150 B.C. and fills a temporal gap between the preceding Early Woodland period and the subsequent appearance of Havana tradition complexes in the American Bottom. The Columbia Complex will be referred to in this volume as a late Early Woodland complex. Clarification of the cultural status of this complex must, however, await further work in this area.

The chert types recovered from the Columbia Complex had been obtained exclusively from American Bottom sources. They included oolitic and glossy white Burlington varieties from the local Keokuk-Burlington formation, as well as the gray and tan cherts mentioned above, which most probably were derived from local Salem formations outcropping along the bluff edge of the Hill Lake locality. A gray-banded chert of local Salem derivation also occurred commonly in this assemblage. Additional chert types in the assemblage, represented by only small quantities of material, were a red variety from the Ste. Genevieve formation and a Fern Glen variety from the Burlington formation.

The Columbia Complex occupation was identified initially in 1978 during machine scraping of Block I. When a large quantity of chert debitage was observed at the southern end of Block I, machine excavation was halted, and the area was shovel scraped (Figure 17; Tables 13 and 14). Shovel-scraping resulted in the discovery of several pits, including Features 3 and 4, and two relatively concentrated areas of chert debitage just south of these features. Both Features 3 and 4 were subsequently excavated. Feature 4 produced a large number of ceramic sherds from a single broken vessel (Vessel 6), a grog-tempered, plain jar. Also recovered from these features were thermally-altered gray and tan cherts similar to those observed in the lithic concentration areas to the south, which were designated as Features 9 and 10.

Because of the initially amorphous appearance of the Feature 9 and 10 scatters, systematic piece-plotting of items was undertaken in order to define both the vertical and horizontal distribution of materials. During excavation of these features, a number of plain, grog-tempered sherds, like those found in Feature 4, were recovered. Hence, Features 9 and 10 were associated with Feature 4. The limits of Features 9 and 10 were eventually established during the 1979 season. The Feature 10 scatter extended into and covered Feature 17, an Early Woodland Marion Thick pottery scatter. Features 9 and 10 had well-defined limits and were interpreted as activity areas. Eventually, three additional areas of lithic reduction were defined in Block I (Features 2, 8, and 14) [Figure 18].

Table 13. Total Machine Scraped Material from Plowed (B1) and Unplowed (B2) Humus Horizons

Type	Block I N	Block I Wt(g)	Block I Mean Wt(g)	Block II N	Block II Wt(g)	Block II Mean Wt(g)	Block V N	Block V Wt(g)	Block V Mean Wt(g)	Total N	Total Wt(g)	Total Mean Wt(g)
Nonutilized Chert												
Flakes	235	238.3	1.01	312	292.8	0.93	25	27.5	1.08	572	558.6	0.98
Pieces	17	367.6	21.62	53	780.3	14.72	4	88.0	22.00	74	1235.9	16.70
Preforms	2	175.3	87.65	-	-	-	-	-	-	2	175.3	87.65
Cores	4	366.1	91.52	1	8.3	8.30	-	-	-	5	374.4	74.88
Total	258	1147.3	4.45	366	1081.4	2.95	29	115.5	3.98	653	2344.2	3.59
Utilized Chert												
Blades	2	6.2	3.10	-	-	-	1	3.6	3.60	3	9.8	3.27
Retouched Flakes	46	201.0	4.37	55	250.1	4.54	4	21.5	5.37	105	472.6	4.50
Retouched Pieces	3	87.6	29.20	1	59.9	59.90	-	-	-	4	147.5	36.87
Biface Fragments	7	126.2	18.02	8	162.1	20.26	1	23.1	23.10	16	311.4	19.46
Spokeshaves	2	9.8	4.90	1	10.9	10.90	-	-	-	3	20.7	6.90
Core Scrapers	4	254.3	63.57	8	290.4	36.30	-	-	-	12	544.7	45.39
Knife	1	30.4	30.40	-	-	-	-	-	-	1	30.4	30.40
Projectile Point Fragments	2	25.6	12.80	-	-	-	-	-	-	2	25.6	12.80
Drill Fragment	1	8.8	8.80	-	-	-	-	-	-	1	8.8	8.80
Gouge	1	42.5	42.50	-	-	-	-	-	-	1	42.5	42.50
Total	69	792.4	11.48	73	773.4	10.59	6	48.2	8.03	148	1614.0	10.90
Nonchert Tools												
Hammerstone	-	-	-	1	201.8	201.80	-	-	-	1	201.8	201.80
Mano	1	417.1	417.10	-	-	-	-	-	-	1	417.1	417.10
Total	1	417.1	417.10	1	201.8	201.80	-	-	-	2	618.9	309.45
Nonutilized Lithics												
Hematite	1	0.1	0.10	-	-	-	1	0.4	0.40	2	0.5	0.25
Sandstone	67	251.8	3.75	38	373.7	9.83	7	30.4	4.34	112	655.9	5.86
Limestone	2	131.7	65.85	3	127.5	42.50	1	7.0	7.00	6	266.2	44.37
Igneous Rock	16	226.0	14.12	5	337.7	67.54	2	182.6	91.30	23	746.3	32.45
Missouri River Clinker	3	7.4	2.46	-	-	-	1	0.6	0.60	4	8.0	2.00
Waterworn Pebble	1	0.1	0.10	1	1.7	1.70	1	3.4	3.40	3	5.2	1.73
Cinder	4	1.1	0.27	4	7.7	1.92	-	-	-	8	8.8	1.10
Rough Rock	8	1.7	0.21	4	213.9	53.47	-	-	-	12	215.6	17.97
Quartzite	-	-	-	-	-	-	1	16.4	16.40	1	16.4	16.40
Limonite	-	-	-	-	-	-	11	2.5	0.22	11	2.5	0.22
Coal	1	0.6	0.60	2	2.7	1.35	-	-	-	3	3.3	1.10
Total	103	620.5	6.02	57	1064.9	18.68	25	243.3	9.73	185	1928.7	10.42

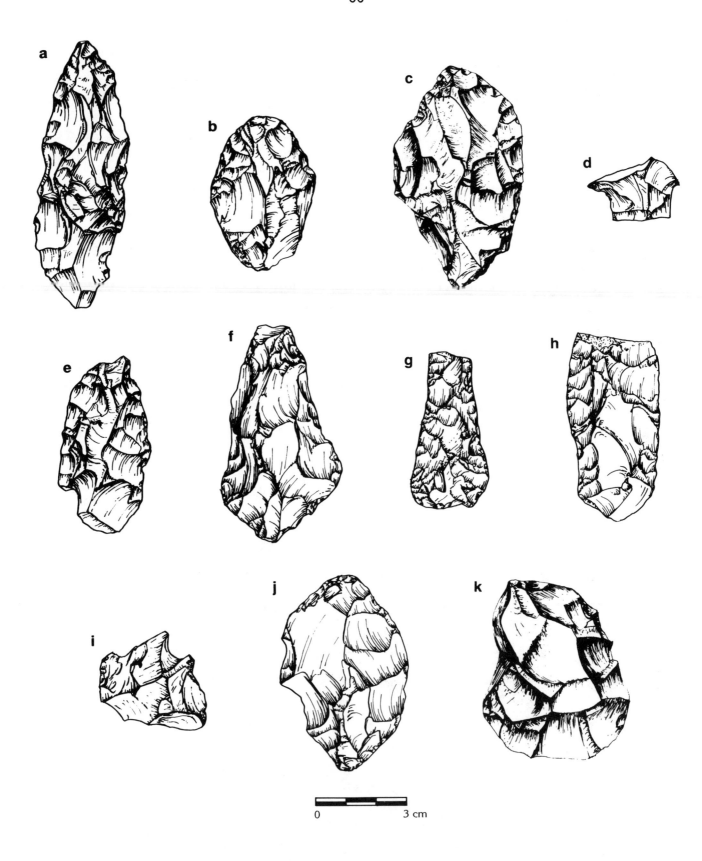

Figure 17. Columbia Complex Chert Artifacts Recovered During
the Machine Excavation of Block I

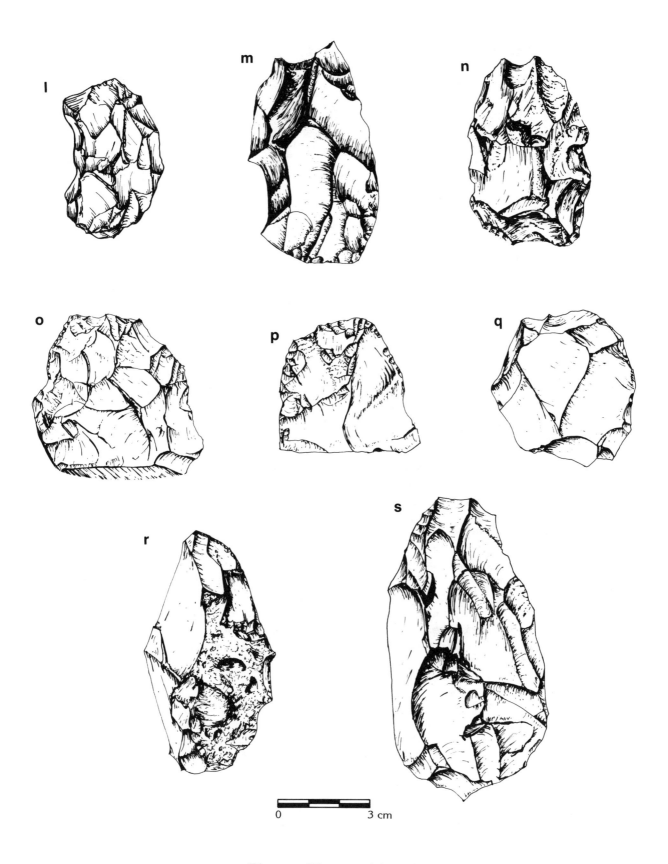

Figure 17. continued

Table 14. Total Nonfeature Remains Recovered from the
Plowed Humus Horizon (B1)

	N	Wt (g)	% Wt	% N
Nonutilized Chert	648	1798.9	31.6	11.3
Utilized Chert	125	1083.5	63.9	72.2
Nonchert Lithics	184	2652.0	60.9	40.0
Ceramics	133	325.5	4.7	3.3
Burned Silt/Cinder/Bone	62	163.6	29.4	9.0
Total	1152	6023.5	31.4	10.4

The pits associated with the Columbia Complex (Features 3, 4, 12, 13, 15, 19, 21, 22, 23, 26, and 27) generally contained very little material and were consistently similar to one another in profile shape, size, and depth. Of the 11 pits, 10 were shallow and basin shaped. Seven pits were oval and medium sized in plan view, three were circular and medium sized in plan view, and one was oval and large in plan view. Most appeared to represent either processing or cooking pits. Charcoal was very poorly preserved in these shallow basin pits, but burned clay and silt were generally present. Feature 12 was the largest pit, measuring 186 cm x 160 cm, but it contained only chert debitage. The function of this pit is unknown. Feature 15 was the deepest pit at this site (42 cm), and it contained evidence of burning in the form of a thin layer of orange, oxidized soil that coated the lower interior portion of the pit. This pit may have functioned as a shallow earth oven or sunken hearth, and it is unique at this site.

A single structure (Feature 6) was located ca. 15 m northwest of Features 10 and 17. This basin structure, which contained no posts, was associated with the Columbia Complex component on the basis of the chert flakes found in the basin fill. The uneven distribution of chert at the base of the structure (detailed below) suggests that the flakes were not just randomly deposited when the basin was filled, but had been deposited by the prehistoric occupants. The chert types were identical to those excavated in Features 4, 9, and 10, and above Feature 17.

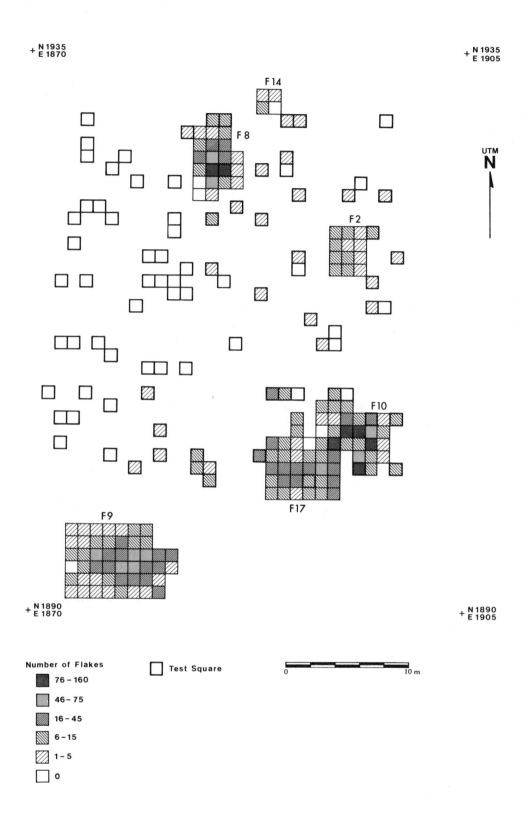

Figure 18. Chert Densities in Columbia Complex Activity Areas and Random Sample Squares

Feature Descriptions: Activity Areas

Features 2, 8, 9, 10, 14, and 17 represent circumscribed areas of concentrated chert flakes, ceramics, and nonchert lithic debris in the southern portion of Block I. Each of these areas was piece plotted separately to determine its horizontal extent. These scatters are interpreted as activity areas associated with the Columbia Complex component. They occurred in both the plowed and unplowed buried humus zones.

Feature 2

Feature 2 occupied an area of ca. 15 m2 and consisted of an irregular scatter of 70 chert and 26 nonchert lithic items, ceramics (11 sherds), small pieces of calcined bone (N=21), and pieces of fired, silty clay (N=13). The scatter was ca. 21 cm deep, varying in elevation from 123.55 m to 123.34 m amsl. It was located several meters northeast of Feature 3 (a pit). Feature 2 was dated to the Columbia Complex component primarily on the basis of the recovered chert. The ceramics were characteristically fine, grit-tempered plain and cordmarked body sherds. Two of the body sherds exhibited exterior cordmarked surfaces with small, elevated, "finger-pinched" areas (Tables 15 and 16).

Feature 8

Feature 8 occupied an area of ca. 18 m2. It represents a concentrated, irregular area of 492 chert and 5 nonchert lithic items, 4 pieces of burned, silty clay and 19 ceramic sherds. This feature was virtually identical to the Feature 2 and Feature 14 scatters, except for the occurrence in this feature of 19 early Mississippian (Lohmann phase) sherds, the only early Mississippian subsurface ceramics found at this site. The scatter was ca. 15 cm deep, ranging in elevation from 123.45 m to 123.33 m amsl (Tables 17 and 18).

Like the chert types in Features 2, 9, 10, 14, and 17 the types in this scatter consisted primarily of thermally altered, oolitic, white Burlington cherts as well as gray and tan Salem cherts. The northern portion of Feature 8 had been cut into by a silty, loess-bearing erosional rill or gully. The top of this rill was observed initially at the base of the uppermost modern plowzone, and it cut through the entire overburden situated above this feature (Figure 19). The rill was nearly 70 cm wide and ca. 60 cm deep at the point at which cultural materials were first observed in this feature. This rill was oriented in an east-to-west direction and extended across the entire portion of Excavation Block I. The early Mississippian ceramics in Feature 8

Table 15. Nonceramic Remains from Feature 2

	N	Wt(g)
Nonutilized Chert Flakes	58	71.3
Nonutilized Chert Pieces	12	182.2
Sandstone	10	51.5
Igneous Rock	15	11.4
Quartzite	1	3.0
Burned Silt/Clay	13	2.0
Unidentified Calcined Bone	21	0.6
Total	130	322.0

Table 16. Ceramics from Feature 2

Sherd Type	N	Wt(g)	Temper	Exterior Surface	Interior Surface	Type
Body	5	19.8	Grit	Cordmarked	Plain	Columbia Cordmarked
Body	2	2.9	Grit	Plain	Plain	Columbia Plain
Body	2	18.5	Grit	Cordmarked and pinched	Plain	Columbia Cordmarked
Body	1	10.7	Grit	Indeterminate	Plain	
Misc. Fragments	1	0.1	Grit	Indeterminate	Indeterminate	
Total	11	52.0				

Table 17. Nonceramic Remains From Feature 8

	N	Wt(g)
Nonutilized Chert Flakes	470	217.6
Nonutilized Chert Pieces	22	15.7
Sandstone	3	20.8
Rough Rock	1	0.1
Missouri River Clinker	1	1.2
Burned Silt/Clay	4	0.5
Total	501	255.9

Table 18. Ceramics from Feature 8

Sherd Type	N	Wt(g)	Temper	Exterior Surface	Interior Surface	Type
Rim	4	5.4	Limestone	Red-slipped	Red-slipped	Monk's Mound Red
Body	2	0.6	Limestone	Red-slipped	Red-slipped	Monk's Mound Red
Body	8	9.8	Limestone	Cordmarked	Plain	
Shoulder (Jar)	2	11.0	Limestone	Plain	Plain	
Misc. Fragments	3	0.2	Limestone	Indeterminate	Indeterminate	
Total	19	27.0				

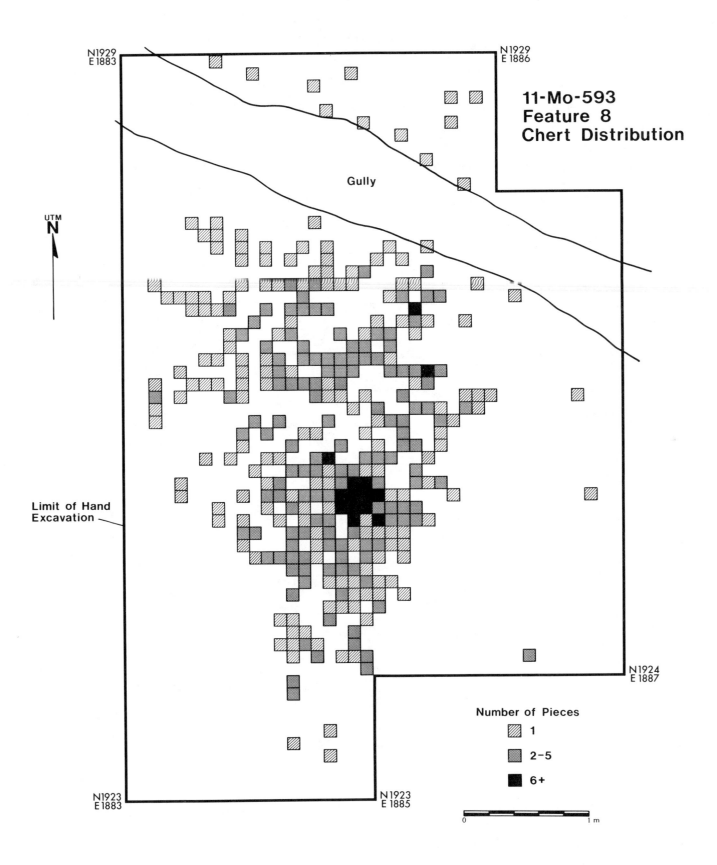

Figure 19. Chert Density in Feature 8

(including 4 red-slipped Monks Mound Red limestone-tempered rims too small to profile and 15 Pulcher Plain and Cordmarked limestone-tempered sherds), were probably deposited in this feature by the incised erosional rill. The sherds were all very small and highly eroded. Unfortunately, no attempt was made to excavate the rill outside of Feature 8. In all probability, additional cultural materials dating to the Lohmann phase would have been found. It is noteworthy that the surface surveys at the Carbon Monoxide site yielded similar early Mississippian ceramics, but machine excavation and extensive piece-plotting of subsurface material concentrations failed to yield a single early Mississippian sherd, except in this disturbed feature. Feature 8 was assigned to the Columbia Complex component primarily on the basis of its similarity to other Columbia Complex scatters of this occupation, and on the basis of its chert types, which were identical to those types associated with Early Woodland, Columbia Complex features at this site. The Mississippian materials associated with this site represent items alluvially transported from a site somewhere to the east of the Carbon Monoxide site. They may even be derived from the nearby Carbon Dioxide site Lohmann phase occupation, which lay ca. 300 m to the northeast.

Feature 9

Feature 9 was exposed while machine scraping the southern end of Block I. A large quantity of chert debitage was initially observed in a circumscribed area of about 10 m2. A grid of 1 m x 1 m squares was established over this area, and all materials exposed were subsequently piece plotted within each square. Feature 9 was excavated in this manner during both the 1978 and 1979 seasons. Excavation was expanded to eventually include 48 m2, and a dense activity area with definable limits was exposed. The scatter, which was irregular in shape, extended ca. 20 cm in depth, occurring within both the mixed and unmixed portions of the humus horizon.

The material recovered from Feature 9 (Table 19) consisted primarily of small chert reduction flakes (N=880), but also included 1 ground sandstone slab, 1 bifacial scraper, 3 biface fragments, 2 worked chert flakes, 1 worked chert tool, and 1 chert preform fragment (Table 20). In addition, a small piece of galena, several drilled sandstone beads, sandstone pieces, rough rock, silicified sediment, and 84 pieces of burned silty clay were recovered (Figure 20 and Table 21). The majority of the ceramics recovered were grog-tempered, Columbia Plain and Columbia Cordmarked sherds (N=20) including one cordmarked grog-tempered rim (Table 22); a single Marion Thick sherd was also recovered. A chert flake density map indicated a concentrated area of tool manufacture and maintenance activity in the central and eastern portions of the scatter. A shallow basin pit (Feature 27) was found at the eastern end of the scatter. Material was also found distributed around the pit.

Table 19. Chert Debitage from Feature 9

Chert Type	Reduction Flakes				Reduction Pieces				Blades			
	N	Wt(g)	Mean Wt(g)	% Wt	N	Wt(g)	Mean Wt(g)	% Wt	N	Wt(g)	Mean Wt(g)	% Wt
Dark Gray Local	424	242.6	0.57	46.0	38	29.0	0.76	34.4	4	6.6	1.65	89.2
Burlington Glossy	24	5.6	0.23	1.1	-	-	-	-	-	-	-	-
Burlington Fossiliferous	123	78.4	0.64	14.9	7	17.7	2.53	21.0	1	0.8	0.80	10.8
Tan/Brown Local	72	40.1	0.56	7.6	-	-	-	-	-	-	-	-
Gray Banded	37	23.0	0.62	4.4	-	-	-	-	-	-	-	-
Bluish-white Crystalline	28	13.2	0.47	2.5	-	-	-	-	-	-	-	-
Fern Glen	3	3.5	1.17	0.7	2	32.8	16.40	39.0	-	-	-	-
Kaolin?	1	0.1	0.10	0.1	-	-	-	-	-	-	-	-
Unknown	95	31.4	0.33	5.9	3	2.7	0.90	3.2	-	-	-	-
Cortical	73	89.3	1.22	16.9	8	2.0	0.25	2.4	-	-	-	-
Total	880	527.2	0.60		58	84.2	1.45		5	7.4	1.48	

Table 20. Lithic Tools from Feature 9

Tool Category	Rock/Chert Type	Heat Alteration	Wt(g)
Edge Tool/Graver	Gray Fossiliferous	Yes	55.7
Biface Fragment	Gray Fossiliferous	Yes	3.3
Gouge Fragment	Gray Fossiliferous	No	14.8
Biface Fragment	Gray Fossiliferous	No	6.5
Preform Fragment	Gray Fossiliferous	Yes	17.6
Biface (Scraper)	Gray Banded	No	39.9
Utilized Flake	Gray Fossiliferous	Yes	30.1
Utilized Piece	Gray Fossiliferous	No	8.3
Grinding Stone	Sandstone	-	484.7
Goose Lake Knife	Gray Banded	No	19.1
Flake Scraper	Gray Fossiliferous	No	9.1

Table 21. Nonceramic*
Remains from Feature 9

Category	N	Wt(g)
Igneous Rock	1	4.8
Rough Rock	2	0.4
Silicified Sediment	2	0.6
Waterworn Pebble	2	0.8
Missouri River Clinker	1	0.1
Galena Piece	1	0.1
Sandstone	2	33.4
Drilled Sandstone Beads	2	5.4
Burned Silty Clay	84	33.2
Total	97	78.8

*excluding chert

Table 22. Ceramics from Feature 9

Sherd Type	Temper	Exterior Decoration	Interior Decoration	N	Wt(g)	Mean Wt(g)	Comments
Body	Grog	Plain	Plain	11	46.1	4.19	Columbia Plain
Body	Indeterminate	Plain	Plain	3	1.8	0.60	Columbia Plain
Body	Grog	Indeterminate	Indeterminate	5	4.0	0.80	-
Body	Grog	Cordmarked	Plain	1	15.0	15.00	Columbia Cordmarked
Body	Grit	Cordmarked	Cordmarked	1	8.4	8.40	Marion Thick
Rim	Grog	Cordmarked	Plain	1	8.3	8.30	Columbia Cordmarked
Misc. Fragment	Grit/Grog?	Indeterminate	Indeterminate	-	4.8	-	-
Total				22	88.4	4.02	

Table 23. Nonceramic* Remains from
Feature 10

	N	Wt(g)
Sandstone	3	19.5
Silicified Sediment	6	4.1
Limestone	4	12.1
Quartz Pebble	1	0.1
Historic Cinder	13	10.4
Burned Silt	18	7.0
Total	45	53.2

*excluding chert

Table 24. Chert Debitage from Feature 10

Chert Type	Reduction Flakes				Reduction Pieces				Blades			
	N	Wt(g)	Mean Wt(g)	% Wt	N	Wt(g)	Mean Wt(g)	% Wt	N	Wt(g)	Mean Wt(g)	% Wt
Dark Gray Local	283	168.1	0.59	32.7	22	47.8	2.17	66.8	2	2.25	1.12	95.7
Burlington Glossy	13	1.4	0.11	0.3	-	-	-	-	-	-	-	-
Burlington Fossiliferous	57	41.4	0.73	8.1	-	-	-	-	-	-	-	-
Tan/Brown (10YR 7/3) Local	126	69.3	0.55	13.5	5	9.9	1.98	13.8	1	0.10	0.10	4.3
Gray Banded	59	105.2	1.78	20.5	1	0.3	0.30	0.4	-	-	-	-
Local Gray Fossiliferous	53	39.0	0.74	7.6	5	11.9	2.38	16.6	-	-	-	-
Ste. Genevieve Red	4	1.5	0.38	0.3	-	-	-	-	-	-	-	-
Fern Glen?	3	0.9	0.30	0.2	-	-	-	-	-	-	-	-
Unknown	102	51.3	0.50	9.9	5	1.0	0.20	1.4	-	-	-	-
Cortical	89	35.6	0.40	6.9	2	0.7	0.35	1.0	-	-	-	-
Total	789	513.7	0.65		40	71.6	1.79		3	2.35	0.78	

Table 25. Chert Tools from Feature 10

Tool Type	N	Wt(g)	Chert Type
Perforator	1	24.4	Gray Banded
Retouched Flakes	2	4.5	Pink/Gray Fossiliferous
Bifacial Flake	1	13.0	Pink/Gray Fossiliferous
Hafted Biface	1	4.8	Gray Fossiliferous
Gouge	1	34.6	Glossy Burlington
Graver	1	68.5	Pink/Gray Fossiliferous
Flake Scraper	1	20.4	Gray Banded
Biface Fragment (Tip)	1	3.9	Unknown
Retouched Flake	1	6.3	White, Fossiliferous Burlington
Retouched Flake	1	2.5	Unknown
Utilized Flake	1	27.0	Gray Fossiliferous
Retouched Flake	1	3.5	Tan/Brown Local
Goose Lake Knife	1	13.0	Gray Banded

Table 26. Ceramics from Feature 10

Sherd Type	N	Wt(g)	Mean Wt(g)	Temper	Exterior Decoration	Interior Decoration	Type
Body	21	38.0	1.81	Coarse Grit	Indeterminate	Indeterminate	Marion Thick
Body	1	5.8	5.8	Grog	Cordmarked	Plain	Columbia Cordmarked
Body	16	126.2	7.89	Grog	Plain	Plain	Columbia Plain?
Rim	1	9.5	9.50	Grog	Cordmarked	Plain	Columbia Cordmarked with interior lip impressions
Body	2	44.2	22.10	Grit	Plain	Plain	Columbia Plain
Body	5	6.8	1.36	Unknown	Unknown	Unknown	-
Misc. Fragment	11	2.0	0.18	-	-	-	-
Total	57	232.5	4.08				

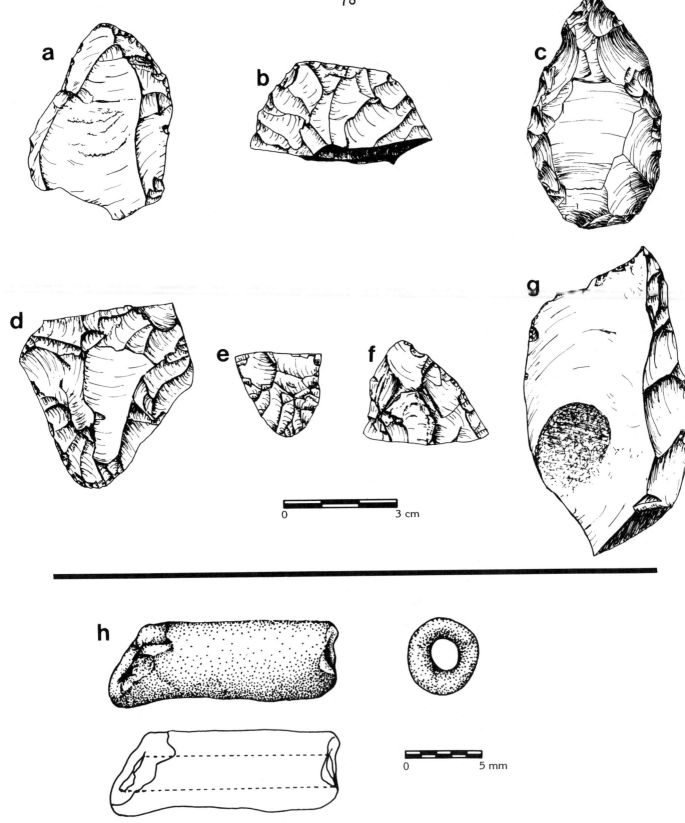

Figure 20. Miscellaneous Chert Artifacts (a-g) and Drilled Sandstone Bead (h) from Feature 9

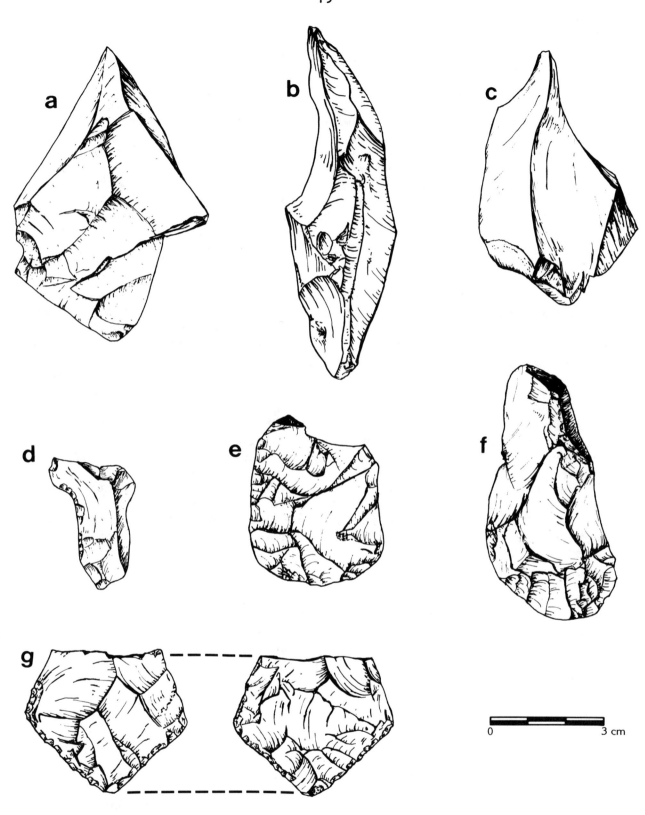

Figure 21. Chert Artifacts from Feature 10

Feature 10

    Feature 10 was situated in the southeast corner of Block I, and it represents an activity area similar to Feature 9. The main concentration of materials was oriented in a northwest-southeast direction and consisted primarily of chert debitage (N=832), although sandstone, silicified sediment, limestone, burned silt, and pottery were also recovered. The ceramics included 25 grog-tempered, plain and cordmarked sherds, including one grog-tempered, cordmarked rim with narrow, oblique, interior lip impressions; also recovered were 21 Marion Thick sherds, all from the lowest levels of the scatter (Tables 23-26).

    The upper portions of nearby Feature 17 were presumably associated with the Feature 10 activity area. The Marion Thick ceramics found in the lower portions of Feature 10 were probably related to the Marion scatter found nearby in Feature 17 since the sherds recovered from both features occurred at the same elevation.

    A variety of chert tools and fragments of broken tools were recovered from Feature 10 (Table 25, Figure 21). A chert gouge, perforator, and knife were found in relatively close proximity to one another within the high-density chert flake concentration in this feature. The abundant chert flakes, virtually all of which were small secondary reduction flakes, resulted from tool preparation and maintenance activities similar to those conducted in Feature 9. It was not possible to determine if the associated tools in this scatter had been utilized or had simply been discarded as byproducts of manufacturing activities.

    The chert types found in Feature 10 were analogous to the ones recovered from the other Columbia Complex lithic activity areas at the site. The plain and cordmarked sherds recovered from this scatter were similar to those recovered from several of the Columbia Complex features (Features 4, 9, 13, 17 and 19).

Feature 14

    Feature 14 represents an extremely small concentration of nonutilized chert flakes (N=24; Wt(g)=11.9) within an area slightly exceeding 2 m2 in size. It was the smallest activity scatter at the Carbon Monoxide site and probably resulted from reduction of a single chert nodule. The scatter extended only 4 cm in depth (123.475-123.435 m amsl). Feature 14 was the first lithic scatter excavated at the Carbon Monoxide site, and it represented the northernmost extent of the Columbia Complex community.

Feature 17

Feature 17 consisted of a scatter of both lithic and ceramic debris dating to the Columbia Complex component, and a concentration of Marion Thick pottery (described above) located ca. 5 cm to 10 cm below the Columbia Complex scatter. The Columbia Complex material in this scatter appeared to have been associated with Feature 10, located several meters to the east. There was, however, a gap in the chert distribution between Features 10 and 17, so the two scatters were determined to be independent activity areas.

The Columbia Complex material (Tables 27 and 28) extended in elevation from 123.72 m to 123.50 m amsl. The scatter consisted of over 800 small chert flakes and pieces, as well as sandstone, rough rock, burned silty clay, and several pieces of unidentified calcined bone. Three biface-tip fragments, a broken drill, and a worked core tool were also recovered from the scatter. Two projectile points, lying side by side, were recovered from an elevation that associated them with the Columbia Complex component; they consisted of a Waubesa-like contracting-stemmed point and a broken point similar to a Liverpool-stemmed type (Figure 22a and b). Twenty-nine Columbia Complex ceramic sherds were also found in association with this lithic debris.

Feature 17 represents a circumscribed activity area characterized by lithic reduction and cooking/processing activities. It was identical to the Feature 9 and 10 scatters found in this same area of the Columbia Complex occupation.

Feature Description: Structure

Feature 6 was initially identified in 1978 during machine stripping in Block I. It was observable as a rectangular, black stain within the unplowed portion of the humus horizon. This stain represented the fill of a relatively small, postless basin structure, which measured 2.44 m x 1.72 m. It was oriented along its long axis in a northeast-southwest direction. The basin fill was excavated in halves, the south half being removed first. The structure was profiled along its short axis, i.e., east to west (Figure 23 and Plate 5).

The basin fill contained two zones, an upper Zone A and a lower Zone B. The Zone A fill consisted of a very dark gray (10 YR 3/1), silty clay loam with occasional dark brown (10 YR 4/3) mottles. The Zone B fill was a dark brown (10 YR 3/3), silty clay with dark

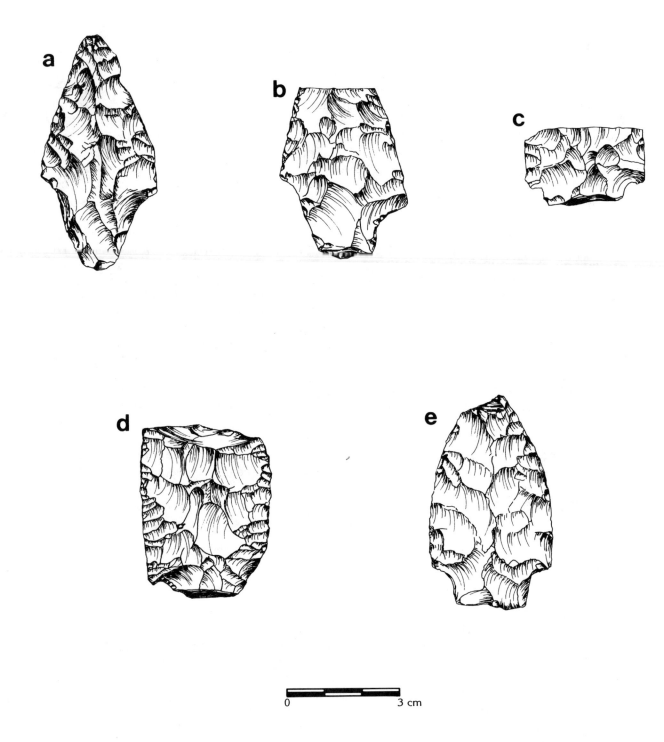

Figure 22. Hafted Bifaces: a-b, from Feature 17; c, from Feature 4; d-e, from Nonfeature Contexts

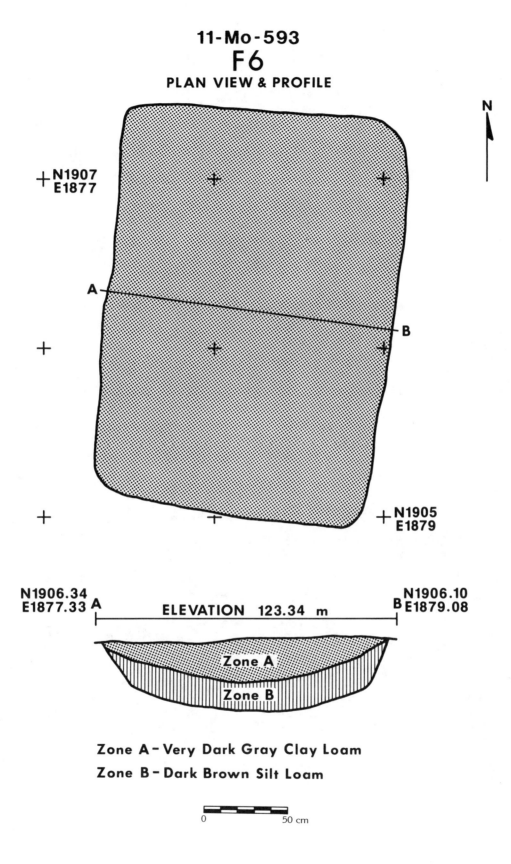

11-Mo-593
F6
PLAN VIEW & PROFILE

N

+ **N1907**
   E1877

A

B

+ **N1905**
   E1879

N1906.34
E1877.33 A

ELEVATION 123.34 m

N1906.10
B **E1879.08**

Zone A

Zone B

Zone A - Very Dark Gray Clay Loam

Zone B - Dark Brown Silt Loam

0   50 cm

Figure 23.   Plan and Profile Views of Feature 6 (Structure)

Plate 5.   Excavation of Columbia Complex Features: upper, Feature 17; lower, profile view of Feature 6

Table 27. Columbia Complex Remains from Feature 17

Lithics (Chert)	N	Wt(g)
Flakes	735	541.3
Pieces	128	184.3
Blades	6	4.8
Cores	1	13.8
Retouched Flakes	9	28.4
Cortical Flakes	1	1.3

Lithics (Nonchert)		
Sandstone	5	42.6
Hematite	1	0.3
Limonite	1	0.7
Silicified Sediment	1	5.3
Waterworn Pebble	1	0.1

Miscellaneous Material		
Burned Clay	55	32.6
Unident. Calcined Bone	5	1.0
Historic Cinder	8	0.9
Historic Bullet (.22)	1	1.8
Possible Clay Pipe Lip Fragments*	-	1.9

Chert Tools	Wt(g)	Chert Type
Drill Fragment (Tip)	1.0	Gray Banded
Biface Fragment (Tip)	1.5	Burlington (White Fossiliferous), Heat-altered
Biface Fragment (Tip)	0.8	Burlington (White Fossiliferous)
Biface Fragment (Tip)	3.8	Burlington (White Fossiliferous), Heat-altered
Edge Tool (Core)	14.5	Local Fossiliferous, Heat-altered

*Grog tempered, plain interior, rough exterior

Table 28. Columbia Complex Ceramics from Feature 17

Sherd Type	N	Wt(g)	Temper	Exterior Decoration	Interior Decoration	Comments
Rim	1	5.8	Grit	Cordmarked	Plain	Flat Lip
Rim	1	1.0	Grog	Indeterminate	Indeterminate	Cord impressions on interior lip
Body	2	16.9	Grog	Cordmarked	Cordmarked	
Body	12	33.0	Grog	Plain	Plain	
Body	3	6.0	Grog	Indeterminate	Plain	
Body	10	10.0	Grog	Indeterminate	Indeterminate	
Total	29	72.7				

Indeterminate ceramic fragments: N=195; wt(g)=42.5

Table 29. Chert Materials from Feature 6

	South Half			North Half			Total		
Chert	N	Wt(g)	Mean Wt(g)	N	Wt(g)	Mean Wt(g)	N	Wt(g)	Mean Wt(g)
Nonutilized Flakes	424	169.2	0.40	52	31.7	0.61	476	200.9	0.42
Nonutilized Pieces	69	63.0	0.91	8	7.6	0.95	77	70.6	0.61
Utilized/Retouched Flakes	1*	0.2	0.20	2	3.7	1.85	3	3.9	1.30

*Polished

grayish-brown mottles (10 YR 3/2). The boundary between the Zone A and B fills was clear and basin shaped. The Zone B fill, i.e., the base of the structure, rested on a sandy loam surface (10 YR 4/3) which represented the sandy portion of the inner-channel sand-bar ridge. The base of the structure was also basin shaped, with gently insloping walls. Due to the sandy and silty nature of the soil, however, it is probable that the original walls had collapsed or eroded downward into the basin. The basin measured 49 cm at the deepest point.

After both sides of the structure had been excavated, efforts were made to locate possible floor and wall posts. The base of the structure was trowelled down carefully, but posts could not be identified. Neither could the location of a structure floor be established although the excavator noted that chert flake orientations were flat near the base of the structure, as opposed to angled in the upper fill zones. The basin floor was riddled with rodent-run disturbances, which made the definition of an actual floor virtually impossible. The cultural remains recovered from Feature 6 consisted of 476 very small unretouched chert reduction flakes (50% of which were thermally altered), 3 retouched reduction flakes, and 77 shatter flakes. One of the small unretouched reduction flakes contained a silica polish. The chert types were restricted to varieties obtainable from local Salem formations. Neither pottery nor diagnostic lithic artifacts were recovered.

This structure may have been associated with the Columbia Complex component at the Carbon Monoxide site. This suggestion is based on analysis of the chert types, which were identical to the types of cherts recovered from the pits and activity areas comprising the Columbia Complex community. The majority of flakes recovered from this structure were restricted in occurrence to the lower Zone B portion of the fill. Moreover, 89% of the chert flakes and pieces (494 of 556) were restricted in occurrence to the southern half of the structure. It seems unlikely, therefore, that the materials found in Zone B had merely washed into the basin following its abandonment. Had this occurred, one would expect a random distribution of flakes throughout the structure and throughout both fill zones. The flakes appeared to have derived from lithic maintenance and resharpening activities, which were conducted within the structure itself (Table 29).

Feature 6 is not unlike the small, square, basin structures known from Emergent Mississippian and Mississippian contexts in the American Bottom. However, this similarity is based strictly on plan form. The absence of postmolds and diagnostic Emergent Mississippian or Mississippian ceramics in Feature 6, as well as the presence of local chert types similar to those recovered from other Columbia Complex features at this site, indicates that Feature 6 was likely associated with the Columbia Complex and not with an isolated Emergent Mississippian or Mississippian component. Feature 6 is interpreted as a temporary shelter.

An alternative interpretation of this feature is that it represents a large, basin-shaped processing pit. However, since no evidence of burning and only a few small seed (i.e., dock, Rumex sp.) fragments were observed within the basin fill, little support can be given to this interpretation.

Feature Descriptions: Pits

The Columbia Complex component contained 11 pits. The majority of these pits served as small processing or cooking facilities. Feature 15, however, probably represented a sunken hearth. The general characteristics of these pits are presented in Table 30. Materials recovered from these pits are described on a feature by feature basis below and are tabulated in Tables 31 and 32. The majority of the pits were small, shallow, and basin-shaped. Material contents were relatively sparse in most of them although Features 4, 12, and 13 yielded substantial amounts of chert, and Feature 4 also contained significant quantities of Columbia Complex pottery as well as floral and faunal materials.

Feature 3

Feature 3 was a shallow (7 cm), basin-shaped pit located near Features 2 (activity area) and 4 (pit) in the east-central portion of Block I. Feature 3 was initially recognized during machine-scraping of the plowed humus horizon. The fill matrix in Feature 3 was characterized by small calcined pieces of bone (1.35 g), burned silt/clay (25.2 g) and abundant but poorly preserved charcoal flecks. Forty-three small reduction flakes made of local dark-gray oolitic chert, all thermally altered, were recovered. Feature 3 is interpreted as a small processing/cooking pit (Figure 24).

Feature 4

Feature 4 was a shallow (19 cm), steep-sided, basin-shaped pit located south of Features 2 (activity area), 3 (pit), and 8 (activity area) in the east-central portion of Block I. It was one of the first pit features identified at the Carbon Monoxide site and contained the most abundant material of any pit at the site. The black silty clay fill of this pit contained abundant charcoal flecks and pieces, burned silt/clay (17.8 g), and a heavy concentration of small calcined bone fragments totaling 1203 pieces and weighing 40.7 g. A total of 236 unburned deer teeth fragments (2.9 g), and 6 unidentifiable burned fish

Table 30. Pit Attributes

Feature	Plan Shape	Plan Dimensions (cm)	Profile Shape	Maximum Depth (cm)	Top of Feature Elevation (mamsl)	Component
3	oval	84 x 75	basin	7	123.45	Columbia Complex
4	circular	63 x 60	basin	19	123.48	Columbia Complex (p)
7	rectangular	65 x 31	flat bottomed	9	123.44	Historic
11	circular	73 x 68	irregular	7	123.49	Unknown
12	oval	186 x 160	basin	16	123.67	Columbia Complex
13	oval	90 x 71	basin	15	123.65	Columbia Complex (p)
15	circular	60 x 60	basin	42	123.57	Columbia Complex
16	rectangular	75 x 25	basin	18	123.50	Historic
18	oval	74 x 67	basin	10	123.45	Marion phase
19	oval	72 x 63	basin	13	123.54	Columbia Complex
20	oval	73 x 39	basin	10	123.44	Marion phase
21	circular	87 x 82	basin	11	123.54	Columbia Complex
22	oval	75 x 51	basin	13	123.54	Columbia Complex (p)
23	oval	80 x 46	basin	10	123.56	Columbia Complex
24	oval	67 x 56	basin	8	123.52	Unknown
26	oval	63 x 55	basin	12	123.55	Columbia Complex
27	oval	72 x 56	basin	16	123.53	Columbia Complex
31	oval	134 x 123	irregular	12	123.42	Unknown
33	oval	88 x 77	flat bottomed	38	123.31	Unknown
35	circular	94 x 87	irregular	26	123.33	Unknown
37	oval	79 x 69	basin	31	123.36	Unknown
38	oval	65 x 48	basin	10	123.36	Unknown
39	oval	62 x 47	basin	10	123.38	Unknown
40	oval	52 x 44	basin	17	123.37	Unknown
43	circular	58 x 56	round	30	123.39	Unknown
44	oval	64 x 57	irregular	21	123.43	Unknown
45	oval	45 x 32	slanted	21	123.45	Unknown

Note: "p" indicates a feature which contains Columbia Complex ceramics

Table 31. Nonutilized Lithic Remains from Columbia Complex Pits

Features	Flakes		Pieces		Blades		Sandstone		Rough Rock		Missouri River Clinker		Burned Silt/Clay	
	N	Wt(g)	N	Wt(g)	N	Wt(g)	N	Wt(g)	N	Wt(g)	N	Wt(g)	N	Wt(g)
3	43	16.6	-	-	-	-	-	-	-	-	-	-	21	25.2
4	211	86.3	13	13.7	4	2.0	1	3.3	1	0.2	2	0.5	+	17.8
12	131	88.8	7	13.6	-	-	-	-	-	-	-	-	2	1.7
13	148	86.3	10	12.1	-	-	1	1.3	-	-	-	-	116	115.0
15	19	20.1	-	-	-	-	-	-	-	-	-	-	5	7.3
19	79	36.4	13	7.5	-	-	-	-	-	-	-	-	9	12.2
21	5	2.3	2	1.4	-	-	-	-	-	-	-	-	12	7.5
22	24	5.7	4	1.1	-	-	1	7.1	-	-	-	-	31	29.6
23	3	1.8	-	-	-	-	1	1.2	-	-	-	-	14	4.2
26	7	6.0	-	-	-	-	-	-	-	-	-	-	-	-
27	56	18.8	28	14.0	-	-	-	-	-	-	-	-	40	27.1
Total	126	369.1	77	63.4	4	2.0	4	12.9	1	0.2	2	0.5	250	247.6

+ = fragments

Table 32. Nonutilized/Nonretouched
Chert Flakes from Columbia Complex Features

Feature	N	Wt(g)	Mean Wt(g)
1	30	80.2	2.67
2	58	71.3	1.23
3	43	16.6	0.39
4	217	92.6	0.43
6	476	200.9	0.42
8	470	217.6	0.46
9	880	527.2	0.60
10	789	513.7	0.65
12	131	88.8	0.68
13	148	86.3	0.58
14	22	7.6	0.34
15	19	20.1	1.03
16	4	2.2	0.55
17	735	541.3	0.74
19	79	36.4	0.46
21	5	2.3	0.46
22	24	5.7	0.24
23	3	1.8	0.60
26	7	6.0	0.86
27	56	18.8	0.34
28	1	1.5	1.50
39	1	0.6	0.60
Total	4198	2539.5	0.60

92

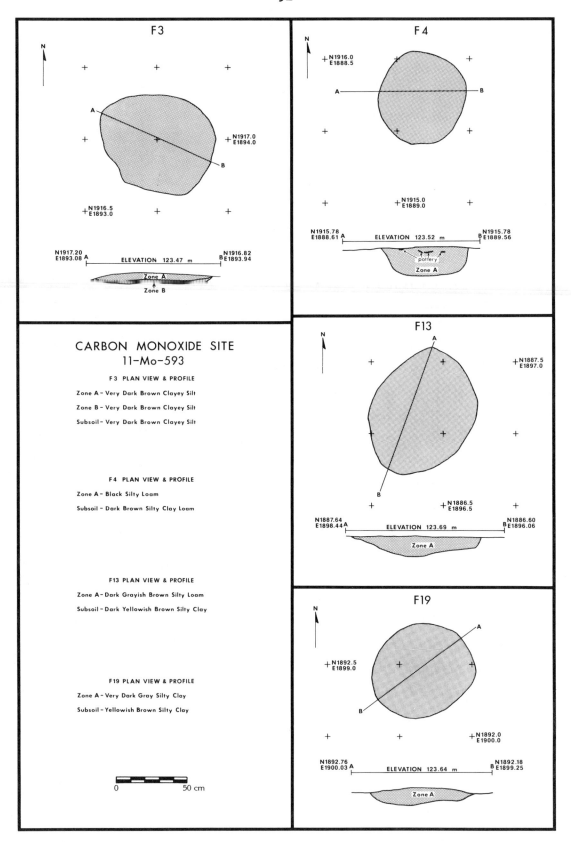

Figure 24. Plan and Profile Views of Columbia Complex Pits

vertebrae were recovered. By total weight, the Feature 4 bone material constituted 60% of the Columbia Complex faunal remains recovered from the Carbon Monoxide site. The deer teeth fragments were found in situ in a poorly preserved mandible. Feature 4 is interpreted as a cooking and processing pit, which served a secondary use as a refuse pit (Figure 24).

A total of 211 small reduction flakes (86.3 g), 13 chert pieces (13.7 g), and 4 blades (2.0 g) were recovered. The chert assemblage was composed of local gray, oolitic, and tan, fine-grained cherts. In addition, 1 piece of sandstone (3.3 g), 2 pieces of Missouri River clinker (0.5 g), and 1 small waterworn pebble (0.2 g) were recovered from this pit. Two retouched flakes, one made of thermally-altered, gray oolitic chert (4.2 g) and the other of a local, pink, fine-grained, thermally-altered chert (10.6 g) were also recovered. A fragment of a corner-notched, stemmed projectile point (6.1 g) made of thermally-altered, white, oolitic Burlington chert was also recovered from Feature 4. The lower midsection and base of this point had been snapped. Two barbs were apparent but not prominent. The blade portion was finely flaked. This point could not be assigned to a specific type. The stem of this point was broken, the blade width was 4.15 cm, and the blade thickness was 1.57 cm.

Remains of a grog-tempered, conoidal, flat-bottomed jar were recovered in Feature 4 and designated as Vessel 6. A total of 4 rims, 1 base sherd, and 113 body sherds were found in the fill of this feature. The total weight of the vessel fragments was 706 g. The exterior and interior surfaces were coated with clay (10 YR 5/4) and smoothed although much of the coating had eroded away. The paste was creamy-textured and tempered with finely crushed grog, the lip was undecorated and pinched, and the vessel walls varied from 6 mm to 8 mm in thickness. The orifice diameter was from 17 cm to 18 cm, an estimate based on the recovery of ca. 35% of the orifice. Portions of the exterior vessel wall and of the vessel base appeared scorched. This vessel has no equivalents in the American Bottom or Illinois River valley. In terms of its fine creamy paste and yellowish brown exterior, it most closely resembles plain Crab Orchard sherds from southern Illinois and plain sherds recovered from the Florence phase occupation at the Florence Street site (Emerson et al. 1983). It is designated here as Columbia Plain.

Feature 12

Feature 12 was a large, shallow (16 cm), basin-shaped pit located in the north-central portion of Block II, just south of Features 10 and 17 (activity areas). The dark gray-brown silty clay fill of this feature contained a small amount of burned silt/clay (1.7 g), 131 small reduction flakes (88.8 g), and 7 pieces of local dark-gray oolitic chert (13.6 g). Most of the chert was concentrated in the southern portion of the feature. Neither ceramics nor faunal materials were recovered from this pit. The function of this pit is problematical although it probably served as either a processing pit or a dumping area for chert debitage (Figure 25).

Feature 13

Feature 13 was a shallow (15 cm), irregularly shaped, basin pit located in the north-central portion of Block II. The dark grayish-brown silty clay loam fill of the feature contained a high concentration of burned, silty clay (115.0 g), 1 piece of sandstone (1.3 g), and calcined bone fragments (0.9 g). This pit is interpreted as a cooking facility based on the intensity of burning evidenced by the high concentration of burned clay/silt in the pit matrix. A total of 148 extremely small reduction flakes (86.3 g) and 10 chert pieces (12.1 g) made of local dark-gray oolitic chert were recovered from the feature. Over 50% of these flakes and pieces had been thermally altered (Figure 24).

In addition, a grit/grog-tempered, cordmarked rim sherd weighing 17.9 g and an associated body sherd weighing 1.6 g were recovered. Based on recovery of 10% of the orifice, the orifice diameter of this vessel is estimated to range from 14 cm to 16 cm. The vessel wall thickness varied from 8 mm to 10 mm. The exterior surface was cordmarked although it was very eroded and the cordmarks only appeared as shallow scratches. A very thin, pale-brown (10 YR 6/3) slip may have been applied to the surface prior to cordmarking, but most of it had eroded away. The cordmarked, grog-tempered sherds recovered from this occupation have been designated as Columbia Cordmarked.

Feature 15

Feature 15 was a medium-depth (41 cm), irregular-sided, round-bottomed, multizoned pit located in the north-central portion of Block II. The pit consisted of two zones, an upper A1 zone of dark brown, silty clay with a few small charcoal flecks and burned silt/clay fragments and a lower A2 zone of very dark gray silty clay with abundant charcoal flecks, burned silt/clay (7.3 g), and extremely small fragments of calcined bone (0.1 g). At the base of this pit, and coating the walls from 20 cm to 41 cm below the pit surface, there was a thin layer of orangish-brown, oxidized, silty clay, the result of intense burning. This burned layer contained abundant charcoal flecks. This layer did not show up in profile and was fragmented in the places in which it did occur (Figure 26).

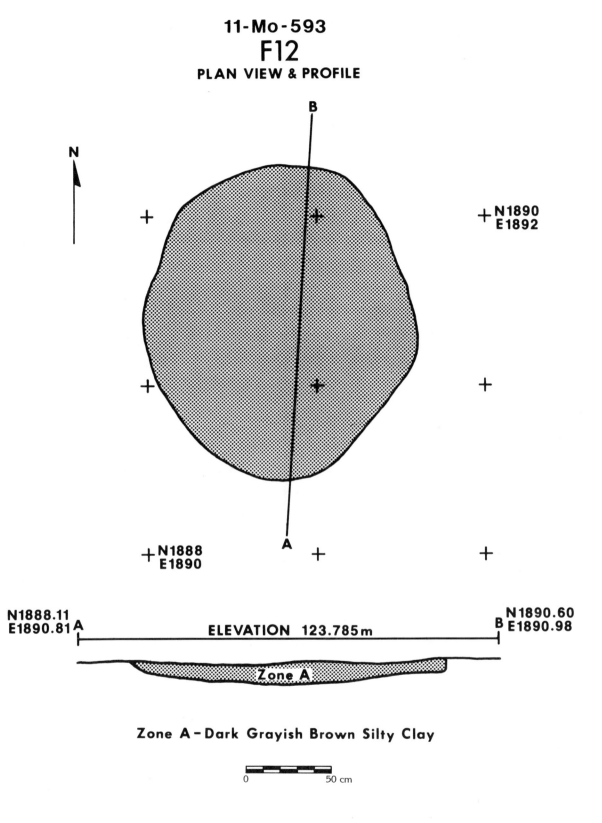

11-Mo-593
F12
PLAN VIEW & PROFILE

N

B

+ N1890
E1892

+ N1888
E1890

A

N1888.11
E1890.81 A   ELEVATION 123.785m   B N1890.60
E1890.98

Zone A

Zone A - Dark Grayish Brown Silty Clay

0   50 cm

Figure 25. Plan and Profile Views of Feature 12 (Pit)

96

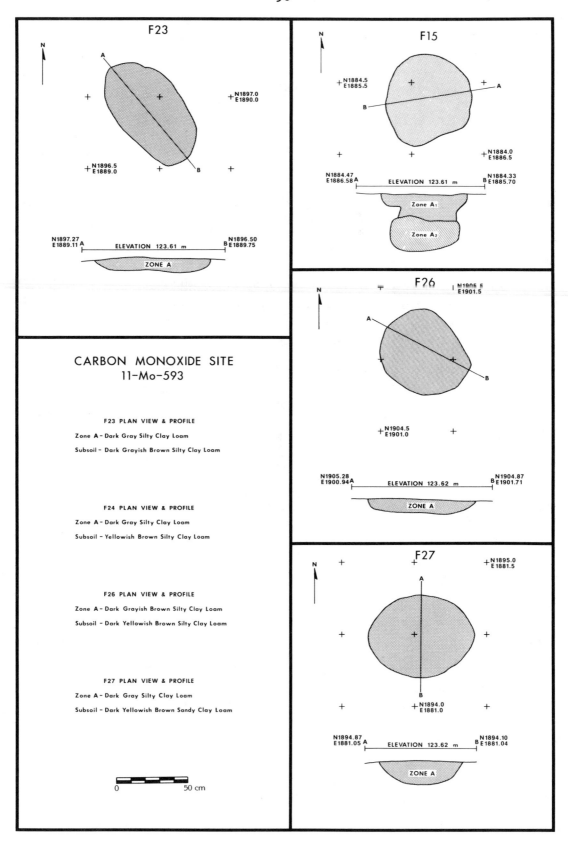

Figure 26. Plan and Profile Views of Columbia Complex Pits

97

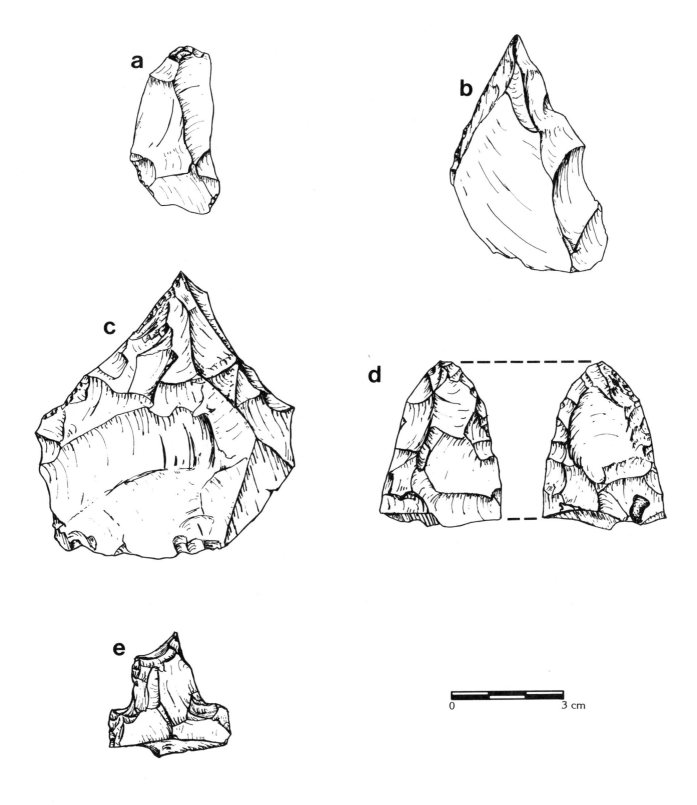

Figure 27. Chert Artifacts: a-b, from Feature 15; c, from Feature 8; d-e, from Feature 27

The excavator noted that about half of the chert flakes recovered from this feature occurred in the upper portion of Zone A1 and the other half in the lower portion of Zone A2. A sterile area of about 10 cm was observed between these zones. Zone A1, therefore, appears to represent a secondary fill which was deposited following the burning episode in Zone A2.

A total of 19 small reduction flakes made of dark-gray oolitic chert were recovered. In addition, two retouched flakes were found, both in the south half of the pit and both in Zone A2, one made of dark-gray oolitic chert (4.6 g), and the other of white fossiliferous chert (11.4 g) [Figure 27]. No ceramics were found. Feature 15 is interpreted as a fired sunken hearth or earth oven with secondary utilization as a refuse pit. The occurrence of oxidized pit walls in this feature was unique for this component.

Feature 19

Feature 19 was a shallow (13 cm), basin-shaped pit located north and east of Feature 13 (pit) in the northeastern portion of Block II. The very dark-gray, silty-clay fill of this feature contained charcoal pieces and flecks, burned silty-clay fragments (12.2 g), and 106 extremely small fragments of calcined bone (3.9 g). A total of 79 small reduction flakes (36.4 g) and 13 chert pieces (7.5 g), all made from local, dark-gray, oolitic chert, were recovered. One small retouched flake of the same material (0.8 g) was also found (Figure 24).

Two ceramic sherds were recovered from Feature 19. One was a grog-tempered, cordmarked (Columbia Cordmarked) body sherd (2.7 g) characteristic of the Columbia Complex ceramic assemblage at this site. The other was a coarse grit-tempered, Marion Thick body sherd intrusive to the pit. Based on both the recovered cherts and the recovered cordmarked sherd, this feature was assigned to the Columbia Complex component. A C14 sample was taken from this pit and a date of 170 $\pm$ 100 B.C. was obtained. The pit is interpreted as a cooking and processing facility.

Feature 21

Feature 21 was a shallow (11 cm), basin-shaped pit located in the north-central portion of Block II. The dark grayish-brown, silty clay loam fill of the feature contained several fragments of burned silty clay (7.5 g) and 72 pieces of calcined bone (3.6 g). Five small reduction flakes (2.3 g), two chert pieces (1.4 g), and one retouched chert flake (6.6 g), all manufactured from local white fossiliferous

Burlington chert, were also recovered from this feature. Retouch was present on the lateral edge of the dorsal side of the flake. No ceramics were recovered from this pit. Feature 21 is interpreted as a small cooking/processing pit.

Feature 22

Feature 22 was a shallow (13 cm), basin-shaped pit located next to Feature 23 (a pit) in the north-central portion of Block III. The dark gray, silty clay loam fill of this feature contained some charcoal flecks, burned clay (29.6 g), a piece of sandstone (7.1 g) and several small pieces of calcined bone (0.3 g). A total of 24 small reduction chert flakes (5.7 g) and 4 small pieces of chert (1.1 g) were also recovered. Local gray oolitic, white fossiliferous, and tan cherts were represented in this feature. A single plain, grog-tempered body sherd was also recovered (Columbia Plain). The sherd was similar to the vessel fragments (Vessel 6) found in Feature 4 and may be associated with that vessel. This feature is interpreted as a small processing/cooking pit.

Feature 23

Feature 23 was a shallow (10.5 cm), basin-shaped pit located near Feature 22 (a pit) in the north central portion of Block II. The dark gray silty clay loam fill of this feature contained a few small fragments of burned, silty clay (4.2 g) and calcined bone (1.0 g), one piece of sandstone (1.2 g), and three small reduction flakes (1.8 g) made from local gray oolitic chert. Feature 23 is interpreted as a cooking/processing pit (Figure 26).

Feature 26

Feature 26 was a shallow (12 cm), basin-shaped pit located just east of Feature 10 (activity area) in the southern portion of Block III. The dark grayish-brown, silty clay loam fill of this feature contained a few small charcoal flecks, but neither ceramics nor faunal materials were recovered. A total of seven small reduction flakes (6.0 g) made of dark gray oolitic chert and white fossiliferous Burlington chert were found. Feature 26 is interpreted as a small processing/cooking pit (Figure 26).

Feature 27

Feature 27 was a shallow (16.5 cm), basin-shaped pit located in the north-central portion of Block II. It was situated on the eastern edge of Feature 9 (activity area). The dark-gray, silty clay loam fill of this feature contained burned silt/clay (27.1 g), charcoal flecks, and just over 200 small calcined pieces of bone (6.2 g), including 1 mammal phalange (0.1 g) (Figure 26).

A total of 56 small chert reduction flakes (18.8 g) and 28 chert pieces (14.0 g) were recovered. In addition, 1 retouched chert flake (5.3 g), a biface fragment (tip and midsection) made of local, gray, oolitic chert (11.5 g), and a broken contracting-stemmed projectile point base (7.1 g), which had been remodified into a graver-like tool and was also made of local, gray, oolitic chert (Figure 27e), were recovered from this pit. No ceramics were recovered. Feature 27 is interpreted as a small cooking/processing pit, and it was probably associated with the Feature 9 activity area.

Columbia Complex Lithic Assemblage

In contrast to the Marion lithic assemblage at this site, that was both sparce and restricted in space, the Columbia Complex lithic assemblage was widely scattered over the community area and was characterized by a wide variety of tool types. The most predominant tool types were bifacial scrapers and knives (Plate 6). A relatively high percentage of the chert tools were broken. This probably resulted from use rather than manufacture since there was a notable absence of large debitage pieces or heavily modified cores. There was a relatively dense distribution of smaller debitage flakes, probably the result of tool maintenance or sharpening activities. A relatively low proportion of the flake debitage exhibited retouch or evidence of utilization and the debitage that did exhibit further modification consisted of larger secondary flakes.

The Columbia Complex chert lithic assemblage was predominantly made up of locally derived cherts, the majority of which probably came from nearby Salem formation outcrops located in the adjacent uplands. Various gray-banded, tan-colored or gray-oolitic types comprised the bulk of the chert assemblage. Other white cherts (glossy and oolitic varieties) probably came from nearby Burlington formations outcropping in Missouri.

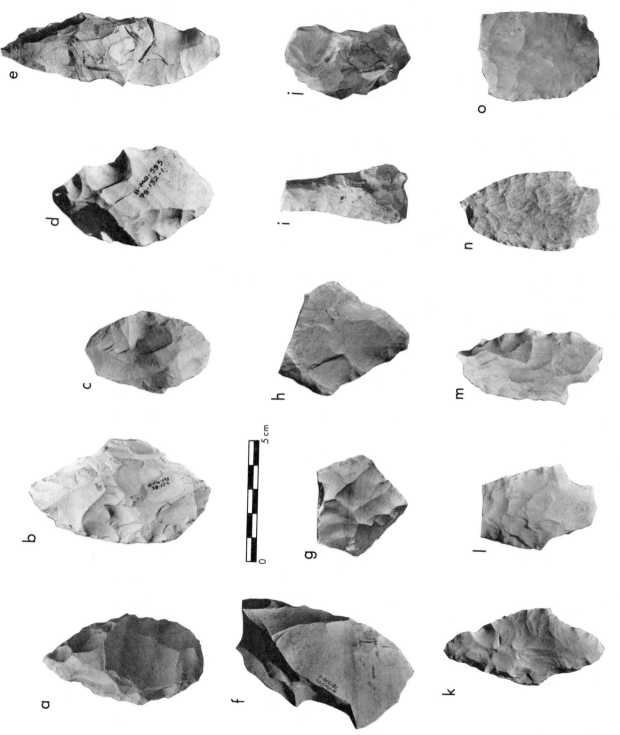

Plate 6. Columbia Complex Lithics: a-d, small core scrapers; e, knife; f-h, Goose Lake knifes; i, drill fragment; j, crescent-shaped scraper; k-l, Feature 17 projectile points; m-o, miscellaneous projectile points

There was a notable scarcity of nonchert tools in the Columbia Complex lithic assemblage. A small number of igneous grinding stone fragments and ground sandstone fragments comprised virtually the entire nonchert tool assemblage. Various sandstone, rough rock, and silicified sediment pieces made up the remaining portion of the assemblage.

Lithic tools were recovered from three contexts including pits, activity scatters, and generalized midden. The majority of the tools were found in the lower portion of the buried plowed humus horizon (B1) and the upper portion of the unplowed humus horizon (B2). It is obvious that these tools were scattered over an original occupation surface. However, this surface had been destroyed and mixed by historic plowing to the extent that the distribution of tools as they were discarded by the original inhabitants had been greatly altered. The author was unable to detect any significant clustering of tool types in the midden or in the main activity scatters (Tables 33 and 34).

The closest analogue of the Columbia Complex lithic assemblage can be found at the Florence Street site (Emerson et al. 1983). Contracting-stemmed points, Goose Lake knives, "humpback" scrapers, multidirectional core scrapers, and a broad-shouldered Adena-like point (Figure 22e) co-occurred at these two sites. It is primarily on the basis of these shared characteristics that the Columbia Complex occupation is dated to the latter portion of the Early Woodland period. It may specifically date to the end of the Florence phase, but this association is still debatable.

Table 33. Columbia Complex Hafted Biface Attributes

Artifact Type	Context	Chert Type	Max. Length (cm)	Max. Blade Width (cm)	Max. Thickness (cm)	Wt(g)	Comments	Figure
Waubesa Point	F-17	Dongola	6.75	3.50	1.40	17.0		22a
Projectile Point	F-17	Burlington	4.90	3.62	1.40	14.0	Broken (TA)	22b
Projectile Point	F-4	Burlington	-	4.15	1.57	6.1	Broken (TA)	22c
Projectile Point	Surface	Burlington	-	3.90	1.50	21.2	Broken (TA)	22d
Projectile Point	B2-humus*	Local Oolitic	6.10	3.61	1.53	19.4	Tip broken	22e
Goose Lake Knife	F-9	Salem	5.20	4.90	1.30	19.1	Broken (TA)	20d
Goose Lake Knife	F-10	Salem	3.51	4.10	1.10	13.0	Broken (TA)	21g

TA = Thermally Altered
* Recovered in Block IV in Soil Profile 1 at a Depth of 123.34 m. This point was found off of the main ridge in a thick black humus horizon.

Table 34. Chert Tools Associated with the Columbia Complex Occupation

Tool Type	Provenience	Wt(g)	Chert Type	Probable Formation	Comments
Projectile point	F-17	17.0	white oolitic	Burlington	Waubesa Type
Bifacial tool	F-17	14.0	Dongola	-	Goose Lake Knife
Projectile point fragment	surface	21.2	white oolitic	Burlington	reworked
Projectile point	B-1*	19.4	pink oolitic	Salem	heat-treated
Core scraper	B-1	47.2	tan/brown	Salem	-
Core scraper	B-1	53.9	white oolitic	Burlington	-
Preform	B-1	51.9	gray/tan oolitic	Salem	-
Core scraper	B-1	54.2	pink oolitic	Salem	heat-treated
Bifacial tool	B-1	30.4	gray/tan oolitic	Salem	-
Bifacial tool fragment	B-1	22.8	white oolitic	Burlington	-
Bifacial tool	B-1	21.4	tan/brown	Salem	-
Drill fragment	B-1	8.8	white oolitic	Burlington	-
Gouge fragment	B-1	42.3	gray/tan oolitic	Salem	polished distal end
Core scraper	B-1	71.4	gray banded	Salem	plano-convex
Edge tool	B-1	144.9	gray banded	Salem	-
End scraper	B-1	59.5	red jasper	glacial till	-
Flake scraper	B-1	20.7	gray banded	Salem	"humpback"
Flake scraper	B-1	19.1	tan/brown	Salem	crescent-shaped
End scraper	B-1	31.0	gray/brown oolitic	Salem	-
Core scraper	B-1	33.4	gray banded	Salem	-
Bifacial tool fragment	B-1	14.9	pink oolitic	Salem	heat-treated
Bifacial tool fragment	B-1	17.7	tan/brown	Salem	-
Bifacial tool fragment	B-1	14.3	white glossy	Burlington	-
Bifacial tool	B-1	27.7	pink oolitic	Salem	heat-treated
Flake scraper	B-1	64.0	gray/tan oolitic	Salem	-
Flake scraper	B-1	52.0	white oolitic	Burlington	-
Spokeshave	B-1	10.9	white oolitic	Burlington	-
Projectile point fragment	B-1	4.2	gray/tan oolitic	Salem	basal portion
Retouched flake	F-15	15.8	gray/tan oolitic	Salem	-
Retouched flake	F-15	4.6	dark gray oolitic	Salem	-
Projectile point fragment	F-4	6.1	white oolitic	Burlington	basal portion
Edge tool	F-8	81.2	gray/tan oolitic	Salem	-
Bifacial tool	F-27	11.5	gray/tan oolitic	Salem	-
Projectile point	F-27	7.1	dark gray oolitic	Salem	basal portion; reworked into graver
Gouge fragment	F-9	14.8	dark gray oolitic	Salem	-
Bifacial tool fragment	F-9	6.5	gray banded	Salem	tip
Bifacial tool fragment	F-9	3.3	pink oolitic	Salem	tip; heat-treated
Flake scraper	F-9	9.1	gray/tan oolitic	Salem	-
Bifacial tool	F-9	19.1	gray banded	Salem	Goose Lake knife
Knife/scraper	F-9	32.0	gray banded	Salem	-
Edge tool/graver	F-9	55.7	gray banded	Salem	-
Perforator	F-10	24.4	gray banded	Salem	-
Projectile point fragment	F-10	4.8	dark gray oolitic	Salem	reworked base
Graver	F-10	68.5	pink oolitic	Salem	-
Utilized flake	F-10	27.0	gray/tan oolitic	Salem	-
End scraper	F-10	34.6	white oolitic	Burlington	-

* Machine-scraped or piece-plotted materials within the plowed upper humus horizon (B-1)

Summary

The Columbia Complex occupation at the Carbon Monoxide site was relatively restricted spatially, unlike the Early Woodland Marion occupation which was much more dispersed. The Columbia Complex pits, activity areas, and the single structure were located along the central ridge portion of the site locality. Except for overlap with a single Marion Thick scatter (Feature 17) the Columbia Complex occupation was not spatially coincident with the Early Woodland Marion occupation at the site. Neither did it overlap with the 12 culturally unassociated pits and 12 stain areas located south of the Columbia Complex occupation. The Columbia Complex feature configuration at the site represents a clear community plan, one of only a few such community plans known at present for this time period in the American Bottom. An estimate of community size is problematical, but the community probably consisted of an extended kin group.

The Columbia Complex community appears to have been a short-term, seasonal occupation. In this sense, it did not differ functionally from the previous Marion occupation. Both components apparently occupied this area in order to exploit the plant and animal resources available in this marsh locality.

UNASSOCIATED FEATURES

There were a number of pits and stain areas which were located at the southern end of the site in Blocks II and IV, which contained either no diagnostic materials or no materials at all. It was not possible to associate these features (Features 11, 24, 31, 33, 35, 37-40, 43-45) with either of the Early Woodland components at the site (Figure 28). The majority of these features were shallow basin-shaped pits with charcoal flecking and occasional burned, silty-clay fragments. Feature 40 contained a large amount of fired, block-fractured, lowgrade chert (179.5 g) and heavy charcoal flecking throughout the matrix. Table 30 presents the dimensional attributes of these pits. Presumably, this feature configuration represents an area of cooking and/or processing activity.

105

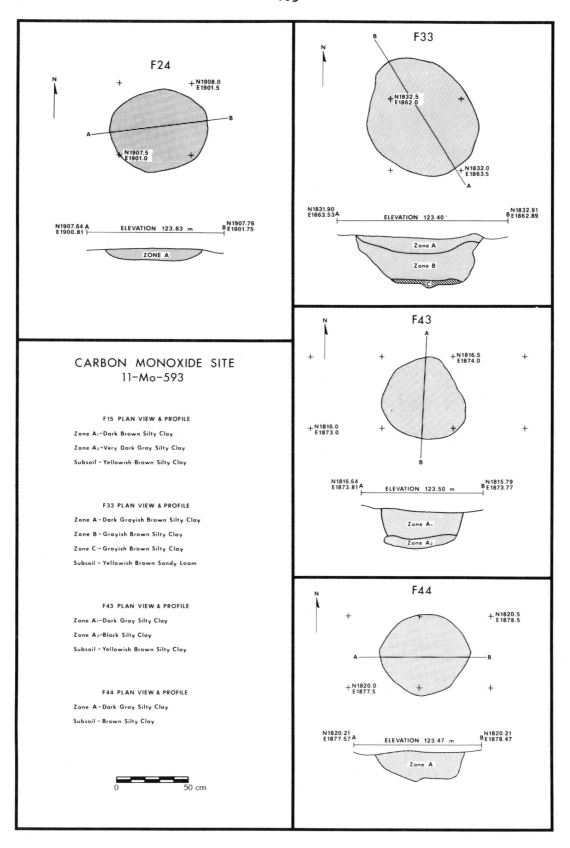

Figure 28. Plan and Profile Views of Unassociated Pits

SITE INTERPRETATION

The Carbon Monoxide site is interpreted as a multicomponent, stratified site containing an Early Woodland Marion occupation and a late Early Woodland occupation designated as the Columbia Complex. Both occupations were situated on a slightly elevated inner channel sand bar located in the old Hill Lake meander scar. The initial Early Woodland occupation occurred shortly after the Hill Lake channel became cut off from the main Mississippi River channel. Presumably, both occupations were situated in this locality in order to exploit the marsh resources that surrounded this inner channel ridge. A thick layer of recent alluvial deposition, nearly 1 m thick in places, covered the ridge and its associated prehistoric occupations.

Marion Phase Occupation

The Early Woodland Marion occupation at the Carbon Monoxide site consisted of four activity areas (circumscribed scatters of ceramic and lithic debris), two small shallow basin pits associated with Feature 17, and a single postmold associated with one of the activity areas (Feature 28). Each of the activity areas contained a slightly different variant (in terms of cordmarking, temper, and lip type) of Marion Thick pottery. Feature 1, at the north end of the occupation, contained a wide variety of materials, including two broken Marion vessels, chert flakes, sandstone fragments, burned silt, and hematite fragments, while Feature 28 at the far south end of the occupation contained the remains of only one broken Marion Thick vessel and a single chert flake.

These activity areas were spatially circumscribed. There was very little variation in either the horizontal or vertical extent of these activity areas. Similar scatters have been observed at the Jean Rita (Linder 1974), Mund (Fortier et al. 1983) and Adler Mound (Williams and Lacampagne 1982) sites. The Carbon Monoxide site, however, is the first Early Woodland occupation where the actual circumscribed nature of these scatters has been observed in subsurface contexts.

It is proposed here that the Marion scatters at the Carbon Monoxide site represent circumscribed activity areas and were not merely random midden debris or the remains of randomly discarded vessels (with the possible exception of Feature 28 which did in fact appear to represent the remains of a single discarded vessel). The circumscribed nature of these activity areas and their relative uniformity in size suggest that these areas may have resulted from activities carried out within an enclosure of some type. However, except for a single post near

Feature 28, posts were not observed in or around the scatters. If enclosures did in fact exist, they may have only consisted of small stick or reed windbreaks, which most likely would not be preserved.

Except for two pits (Features 18 and 20) at the Carbon Monoxide site, and several pits from the nearby Fiege site, pits have generally not been observed at Early Woodland, Marion phase sites in the American Bottom. [A single Marion Thick sherd had been previously reported from a refuse pit (Feature 101) "off the north feather edge of Mound I" at the Mitchell site (11-Ms-30) in Madison County (Porter 1974:346-347, 483)]. No Early Woodland pits were recognized at either the Jean Rita or Mund sites.

The general absence of pits during this period is puzzling, since extensive clusters of small, shallow, basin-shaped pits characterize the terminal Late Archaic occupation of this area. Sites such as Dyroff-Levin, Go-Kart North, and Missouri Pacific #2 have together yielded over 1500 Late Archaic pits, most of which appear to have been small processing or cooking pits. It should also be noted that circumscribed scatters of cultural materials, like those found at the Carbon Monoxide site, do not occur in Late Archaic contexts (Fortier and Emerson 1984; McElrath and Fortier 1983).

Late Archaic peoples apparently utilized pits for processing, cooking, and possibly for storing nut and wild seed resources. These kinds of non-portable natural containers (i.e., pits) utilized as facilities for processing, cooking, and possibly storing plant resources may have been replaced by the large Marion Thick jar forms characteristic of the Early Woodland Marion phase. This form of vessel may, in fact, have been developed as a portable substitute for the previous Late Archaic pits.

Generally, small quantities of lithic remains typify Early Woodland Marion assemblages in the American Bottom. At the Carbon Monoxide site the Marion lithic assemblage consisted of a small number of chert reduction flakes and pieces, a few utilized chert flakes, occasional broken ground stone fragments, a single piece of utilized hematite and numerous fragments of burned sandstone. No diagnostic projectile points could be associated with this component. Kramer points, usually found at Early Woodland sites on the American Bottom, did not occur at the Carbon Monoxide site. The Marion lithic assemblage at the Carbon Monoxide site appeared to be related to a number of activities including tool maintenance and resharpening (small reduction flakes), grinding (ground stone), and stone boiling (burned sandstone). However, the small numbers of materials within the discrete activity areas indicated that these activities were not extensive and were of only short duration.

Early Woodland Marion phase occupations in the American Bottom tend to occur most frequently at generally low elevations such as inner channel ridges or lake/marsh edges, and in localities that do not usually yield Late Archaic occupations. The majority of the Late Archaic sites in the American Bottom are located either on elevated channel banks or on the bluffs outlining the floodplain. This indicates that many of the low-lying inner channel ridges of the American Bottom may have initially become accessible to prehistoric inhabitants only during the Early Woodland period.

The Early Woodland occupants of the American Bottom appear to have focused primarily on marsh-edge resources in the floodplain. The subsistence base probably consisted of deer, fish, and fowl, but a heavy emphasis was also placed on plant utilization. Preservation at the Carbon Monoxide site was generally not good, and the activity areas, because they were open, were not particularly conducive to the preservation of either faunal or floral materials. Nonetheless, an exploitation of American lotus (Nelumbo lutea), various nuts, and wild seeds was indicated at the Carbon Monoxide site. The large Marion Thick jars may have functioned as containers for these wild plant resources. There was no evidence for cultivation of plants at this site but cultivation would not necessarily be expected at such a short-term camp.

Chronological Position of the Marion Phase Occupation

The chronological position of the Early Woodland Marion culture in the American Bottom was not clarified by the Carbon Monoxide excavations. Feature 19 (a pit) was originally regarded as an Early Woodland feature based on the occurrence of a single Marion Thick sherd. A date of 170 ± 100 B.C. was obtained from wood charcoal from this pit. During analysis, however, Feature 19 was reassigned to the Columbia Complex occupation based on the chert types and a single Columbia Complex sherd recovered from this pit. For these reasons, and because of the stratified nature of the components, it is presumed that the Early Woodland Marion occupation at the Carbon Monoxide site precedes the Feature 19 date and minimally precedes the date of 10 ± 110 B.C. obtained from Feature 4, also a Columbia Complex pit.

A date of 230 ± 90 B.C. was obtained from the Mund site (11-S-435), located several kilometers north of the Carbon Monoxide site, from a buried, burned-soil horizon directly overlying a Marion Thick ceramic scatter similar to those uncovered at the Carbon Monoxide site (Fortier et al. 1983). This again suggests that the Early Woodland period falls before 200 B.C. in the American Bottom. The initial dates for this period are unknown but have been postulated to range from 600 B.C. to 500 B.C. (Munson and Hall 1966). This latter date would coincide with the latest dates obtained from the terminal Late Archaic in this area, e.g., those obtained from the Missouri Pacific #2 site, which spans a period from 900 B.C. to 600 B.C. (McElrath and Fortier 1983).

Previous Historic Sites Surveys have suggested that northern Monroe County was not only a focus of Marion occupation but also the southern limit of this occupation in the Mississippi River valley. In particular the Hill Lake locality has produced more Marion remains than any other locality investigated by the FAI-270 Project. The occurrence of Marion materials east of this locality in the Richland Creek drainage, however, suggests that Marion peoples were not restricted to a specific locality nor exclusively to a floodplain habitat. Important questions concerning the duration of the Marion phase and its contribution to other Early Woodland and early Middle Woodland cultures in the American Bottom remain unresolved.

The Carbon Monoxide site excavations have revealed well-defined Marion material scatters, a general absence of pits, and an Early Woodland occupation focused on the exploitation of a marsh habitat which had probably not been accessible to Late Archaic peoples. The exact nature of Early Woodland Marion communities in the American Bottom must await further investigation.

Columbia Complex Occupation

The Columbia Complex was defined on the basis of the materials and features recovered from the Carbon Monoxide site. The Columbia Complex materials were stratified above the Marion remains and lay ca. 60 cm to 80 cm below the present surface. The Columbia Complex settlement was represented by 11 pit features, a possible basin structure, and 6 activity areas, characterized by well-defined scatters of lithic and ceramic debris.

The cultural affiliation of the Columbia Complex has still not been clearly established. The ceramics associated with this complex are unique in the American Bottom. They have no clear analogues with the previous Marion phase nor with the subsequent Havana tradition. The lithic assemblage, however, is more revealing and seems clearly related to the Florence phase. Radiocarbon dates of 10 and 170 B.C. clearly postdate the Florence phase but the chronological relationship to the subsequent Cement Hollow phase (initial Havana), which begins about 150 B.C., is not clear.

Columbia Complex Community Plan

The community defining the Columbia Complex occupied an area of ca. 1200 m2, and was situated on the apex of an innerchannel ridge within the Hill Lake Meander Scar. The community consisted of a dispersed pattern of pits, activity scatters, and a possible structure. The number of features comprising the settlement was not large and the total number of cultural remains was relatively small. This would indicate that the Columbia Complex occupation was short-term and probably seasonal in nature.

Activities at this settlement were focused on tool maintenance, animal and plant food processing, and cooking or roasting in pits. All of the pits at this occupation were single-zoned and very shallow (mean depth: 15.8 cm). Several of the pits contained dense concentrations of animal bone as well as lithic and ceramic debris. Most of the pits, however, produced few materials except burned silt fragments and small flecks of charcoal and calcified bone.

By far, most of the cultural material from this occupation was recovered from the activity areas. These areas varied in extent but usually did not exceed 25 m2. These areas were characterized by dense concentrations of lithic debitage, lithic tools, ceramics, burned silt, sandstone fragments, and occasional pieces of charcoal. The circumscribed nature of these debris scatters suggests that these were activity areas and not random midden accumulations. In addition, the small size range of the lithic debris recovered from these scatters indicated tool sharpening and maintenance activity. No cores or larger secondary flakes were recovered in these areas nor in the pits, suggesting that primary tool production was not undertaken at this occupation. Burned silt and charcoal within these scatters probably originated from surficial fires in the activity areas. Cooking and possibly thermal chert alteration (a high percentage of the cherts were heat altered) were conducted in these areas. Limestone and nonchert tools were notably absent from these scatters.

A small basin-shaped feature measuring only 2.44 m by 1.72 m may represent a structure. However, this unit, which was 49 cm in depth, contained no posts, and it is possible that it represents a specialized processing pit of some kind. Chert debris similar to that obtained from the activity areas and the pits was obtained from the fill of this feature. No ceramics were found in the fill.

Columbia Complex Ceramic Assemblage

The ceramic assemblage from this occupation was particularly
perplexing in that no directly identical types could be recognized
anywhere in the American Bottom nor for that matter in the Midwest. The
ceramics were characterized by a creamy, tan-colored paste which
appeared to contain finely crushed grog-temper. Exterior surfaces were
either plain (referred to as Columbia Plain) or roughly cordmarked
(Columbia Cordmarked). The lips were rounded or pinched and, except for
one isolated sherd, were undecorated. The single decorated rim
contained interior lip slashing. This slashing was very narrow,
shallow, and placed obliquely at 1-2 cm intervals along the interior
surface on and just below the lip. The interior surfaces appeared to
have been coated with a clay film and smoothed. Several of the plain
rims also exhibited burnished exterior surfaces although many of the
burnished portions had eroded off prior to excavation. One basal sherd
was recovered, which indicated a conoidal or subconoidal vessel
(Plate 7).

In the author's opinion, the Columbia Plain ceramic type from the
Carbon Monoxide site was somewhat similar though not identical to the
Florence Plain variety from the Florence site. They were similar in
terms of their grog tempers and creamy pastes. They were dissimilar in
that interior and exterior burnishing was found on the Columbia Plain
ceramics. The lip slashing found on one of the Columbia Complex sherds
also had no analogue in the Florence lip decorative pattern.
Exterior/interior burnishing is a trait that has been observed on Middle
Woodland, Havana ceramics in the American Bottom (i.e., Cement Hollow
and Hill Lake phases). However, burnishing is the only ceramic trait in
the Columbia Complex held in common with Middle Woodland ceramics in
this area.

The Columbia Complex plain and cordmarked varieties bear some
resemblance to the grog-tempered Crab Orchard ceramics from Jackson
county and particularly to ceramics from the Twenhafel site. It is
presumed that these ceramics date to the Middle Woodland period at the
Twenhafel site but their recovery in surface contexts makes this
association somewhat unreliable, since later component materials
occurred on the same surfaces. One could speculate, however, that the
grog-tempered Crab Orchard traditions of southern Illinois are
manifested in the northern American Bottom area in such complexes as
that observed at the Carbon Monoxide site. Such influences in the
American Bottom are still evidenced in subsequent early Middle Woodland
assemblages by fabric-impressed ceramics.

If the earlier Florence assemblage truly represents a southern
inspired tradition as Emerson has suggested (Emerson et al. 1983), then

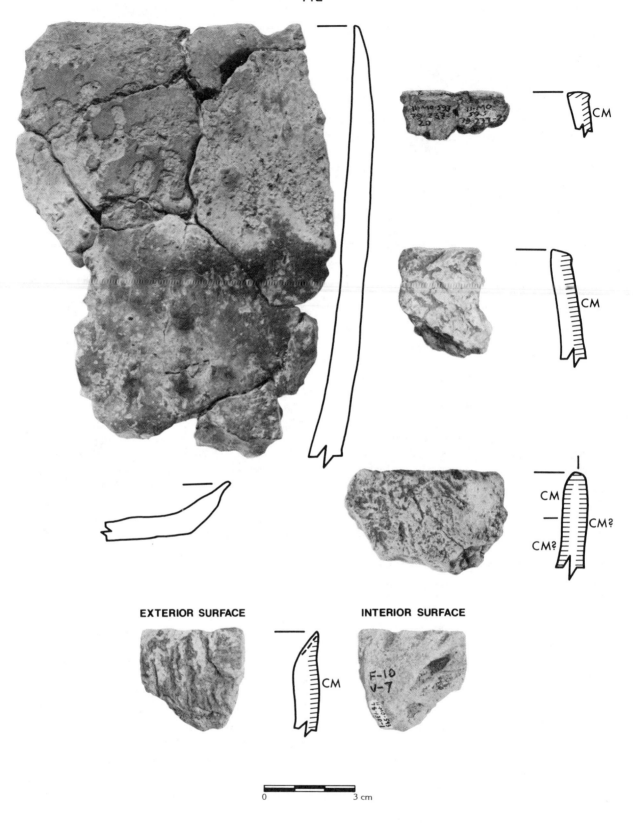

EXTERIOR SURFACE   INTERIOR SURFACE

0   3 cm

Plate 7. Columbia Complex Ceramics

it is reasonable that such influences may have persisted through the end
of the Early Woodland period and probably into the Middle Woodland
period as well. In any case, it is apparent that the Columbia Complex
ceramics bear a much closer resemblance to the Florence and southern
Crab Orchard traditions than to the subsequent Havana or American Bottom
Cement Hollow/Hill Lake phase ceramics.

Columbia Complex Lithic Assemblage

Like the ceramics, the lithic assemblage associated with the
Columbia Complex is relatively unique in the American Bottom. The
lithic tools consisted mostly of chert knives and scrapers. The
nonchert lithic assemblage included only a few fragments of ground
stone. All of the chert recovered from this occupation was of local
derivation. The most frequently utilized chert was a poor quality gray
and tan oolitic chert, probably obtained from local Salem formations
situated in the nearby uplands east of the site. However, the Ste.
Genevieve limestones located south of this area also contain dark gray
oolitic cherts, which are virtually indistinguishable from the gray
Salem cherts. Some of the low-grade cherts found at this site were also
virtually indistinguishable from the fine-grained limestone. As
immigrants into this portion of the American Bottom, the Columbia
Complex inhabitants may not have been aware of the better-quality chert
resources available in this locality.

The chert tool assemblage from this occupation very closely
resembled the Florence Street assemblage. Humpback scrapers, Goose Lake
knives and contracting-stemmed points occured in both assemblages.
However, the better quality of chert utilized as well as the overall
better workmanship applied to tools at the Florence Street site
contrasted with the generally poor quality of tools recovered from the
Carbon Monoxide site. However, this qualitative difference may have
simply resulted from the short-term nature of the Carbon Monoxide
occupation and, presumably, from the fact that a narrower range of
activities would have been conducted at such short-term camps.

Chronological Position of the Columbia Complex Component

Based on only a single assemblage and two divergent radiocarbon
dates the Columbia Complex is difficult to evaluate. In terms of the
American Bottom cultural continuum, we would place this complex
chronologically after the Florence phase, but prior to the Cement Hollow
(Early Havana) phase, i.e., between 300 B.C. and 150 B.C. Based on
similarities with the Florence Street assemblage, it is probable that
this complex represents a direct descendant of the Florence phase. The
complex may also represent an intrusive Crab Orchard assemblage from the

south, although so little is known about the chronological position of Crab Orchard assemblages in southern Illinois that a Columbia Complex-Crab Orchard association would be pure speculation at this time.

Interpretation of the Columbia Complex Occupation

The Columbia Complex represents a terminal Early Woodland culture in the American Bottom. It is clear that such a complex was not the precursor of the Havana tradition in the American Bottom. There was virtually nothing in the Columbia Complex assemblage that would indicate a Middle Woodland association. Both the ceramic and lithic assemblages of the subsequent Cement Hollow phase in the American Bottom radically differed from both the Florence phase and the Columbia Complex assemblage.

The Cement Hollow phase, which extended in time from 150 B.C.-0 B.C./A.C., was characterized by zoned, stamped (rocker and dentate) ceramics, broad-bladed Snyder's points, and increasing nonlocal chert utilization. The ceramics were mostly thick-walled and coarsely grit-tempered. These ceramics obviously represent a rapid departure from the grog-tempered, Early Woodland Florence-Columbia Complex continuum.

At this time an Early-Middle Woodland continuum is not apparent in the American Bottom. The Middle Woodland Havana tradition may well be derived from Morton or Black Sand assemblages, as Munson(1982) and Streuver(1968b) have suggested. Unfortunately, although Morton and Black Sand materials have been identified in the American Bottom, there is nothing approaching a complete or even partial Morton or Black Sand lithic or ceramic assemblage. Diagnostic ceramic remains always occur as isolated surface finds or in redeposited feature contexts (Kelly and Fortier 1983). Moreover, there are no specific diagnostic lithic artifacts associated with Morton and Black Sand so ceramics remain the sole criterion for identifying the presence of these Early Woodland materials.

Another candidate for an ancestor of the Cement Hollow phase is the Marion culture, pointing to the thick-walled, coarse, grit-tempered and flat-based attributes of Marion Thick ceramics. Some of the Cement Hollow phase vessel forms were barely distinguishable from the earlier Marion Thick ceramics of this area. In fact the Marion Thick ceramics and the Early Havana or Cement Hollow ceramics appeared to share a great many more attributes than Marion and Morton or Morton and Havana ceramics. In order to hypothesize the Marion culture as a direct Havana ancestor, however, the chronological range for the Marion culture would presumably occupy a 450-year period, i.e., from 600 B.C. to 150 B.C. It seems more likely that Marion occupied a narrower range, as suggested previously, and that another, as yet unknown, Early Woodland complex, possessing perhaps a mixture of Marion-like and Morton-like ceramic traits, and dating sometime between 300-150 B.C., served as a local precursor of the Havana-Cement Hollow tradition in this area.

It is, of course, popular to find antecedents and a continuum within every local sequence. It is possible, however, that the emergence of Havana in the American Bottom can simply be attributed to outside incursion. The earlier, stamped (rocker and dentate) traditions of the southeastern United States precede the Havana tradition in Illinois, and it seems likely that some influence from these traditions would eventually be felt in the upper courses of the Mississippi River valley. A blend of these new ceramic ideas with the local Marion-Morton and perhaps Florence traditions could easily have provided the building blocks of the Havana ceramic tradition in this area. If this scenario is correct, then we might well expect to find more complexes such as the Columbia Complex in the American Bottom with a mixture of ceramic traits.

Finally, in regard to the Early Woodland to Middle Woodland transition in the American Bottom it should be added that at this time we can see no perceptible differences between Early Woodland and early Middle Woodland groups in terms of settlement types, subsistence behavior, and site location preferences. There is an expressed preference throughout the Early and Middle Woodland periods for settlement within the floodplain and in localities not selected by either the previous Late Archaic or the subsequent Late Woodland peoples of the area. Low marsh edges, innerchannel ridges, and alluvial fan/floodplain edge environments were exclusively utilized during the Early to Middle Woodland periods and were avoided by Late Archaic and Late Woodland groups. There was heavy emphasis on aquatic and bottomland vegetation utilization and both Early and Middle Woodland sites appeared to represent almost exclusively small, seasonal, extractive camps. This pattern of life contrasts strongly with the more sedentary Late Woodland villages, and with the base locale settlements of the Late Archaic period. It suggests an Early to Middle Woodland continuum that may supercede in importance the various differences in ceramics and lithics exhibited by the Early and Middle Woodland phases and complexes.

SITE SIGNIFICANCE

The Carbon Monoxide site consisted of two separate, short-term occupations situated in the floodplain of the American Bottom. The exposure of this occupation required deep and extensive subsurface excavations.

The discovery at the Carbon Monoxide site of these deeply buried occupations which had not been indicated by surface collections, serves as a caution to archaeologists not to formulate elaborate settlement systems based solely on floodplain surface materials. The existence of these buried occupations at the Carbon Monoxide site and other Hill Lake sites suggests that such occupations may be more common in the American Bottom than was previously anticipated.

Early Woodland assemblages, prior to the Carbon Monoxide site excavations, have been known mostly from surface contexts and from isolated tests conducted in the American Bottom. The Carbon Monoxide site excavations, therefore, have not only provided new materials which were obtained from well-defined feature contexts for both these periods, but these excavations have also yielded two spatially and temporally distinct communities. These data have provided information concerning community patterning and resource exploitation for the floodplain inner channel localities of the American Bottom. The occurrence of Early Woodland and Middle Woodland occupations on sand bar localities within the Hill Lake meander, as evidenced by the Truck #7 (this volume) and Mund (Fortier et al. 1983) sites, as well as the Carbon Monoxide site indicates an occupational preference for low-lying aquatic zones during these time periods.

SUMMARY

Investigations at the Carbon Monoxide site revealed two Early Woodland occupations located along the higher portions of a deeply buried, inner channel sand ridge of the Hill Lake locality. The Early Woodland Marion occupation consisted of four activity areas dispersed over 150 m of the ridge in a north-south direction. The Columbia Complex occupation was more spatially restricted, occupying an area of ca. 1200 m2. Both occupations appear to represent short-term, seasonal camps situated in the locality in order to procure resources from the surrounding marsh.

CHAPTER 3.   AN EARLY WOODLAND OCCUPATION AT THE FIEGE SITE

by Andrew C. Fortier

This chapter presents the results obtained from archaeological investigations conducted at the Fiege site (11-Mo-609) by the UIUC during April 1978 and from April through May 1979.   Subsurface archaeological investigations were confined to a narrow corridor extending across the central portion of the site, which comprised an area of ca. 2450 m2.   About 70% of this area was exposed for archaeological investigation.   A total of 12 features were eventually defined and excavated, including 4 pits, 1 lithic chipping area, and 7 soil stains, which may represent surficial hearths.   No diagnostic materials were recovered from these features although Marion Thick ceramics were found at the same surface elevations and in close proximity to, some of the pits.   Based on the occurrence of Early Woodland Marion ceramics in both surface and subsurface contexts, the Fiege site occupation is considered to be Early Woodland in age.   It is probable that this occupation is related to the Early Woodland Marion occupational component at the Carbon Monoxide site, situated ca. 300 m to the north.

The Fiege site excavations exposed only a portion of what appears to have been a small, seasonal, Early Woodland settlement, with evidence for cooking, plant utilization, and tool maintenance activities.   The precise boundaries of this occupation could not be established due to excavation limitations imposed by the right-of-way.   However, the area excavated was adequate to establish the existence of an Early Woodland settlement with a feature configuration different from that found at other Early Woodland sites in the Hill Lake locality (e.g., Carbon Monoxide, Go-Kart South, and Mund).   Well-defined activity scatters, such as were recognized at these other sites, were not present at the Fiege site.   Rather, surficial hearths and isolated lithic chipping scatters were found, which are unique to the Fiege site for this time period.   Since settlement variation within the Marion phase is so poorly known at this time, a site such as Fiege, despite its small size and incompletely excavated community plan, represents a significant contribution to our knowledge concerning settlement function during this period.

The delineation of the range of activities present at Early Woodland occupations of this region, and of the variation present in feature configurations at these occupations constitutes one of the more significant contributions of these site excavations.   This analysis also provides additional support for the idea that Early Woodland groups in the American Bottom were primarily focused on lower, inner channel floodplain environments.

The Fiege site, as well as the Carbon Monoxide site, provide evidence that Early Woodland social systems operating in the floodplain were composed of relatively small groups. The kinds of isolated and sporadic feature remains found to be associated with Early Woodland groups in this area, stand in stark contrast to the dense pit feature concentrations and permanent settlements left by the preceding terminal Late Archaic communities. Such terminal Late Archaic remains are in evidence, for example, in the Prairie Lake locality, located north of the Hill Lake meander locality. Sites such as Fiege are significant since they indicate the occurrence of a rather sharp transition between the Late Archaic and Early Woodland periods in the American Bottom, at least in terms of a noticeable settlement shift from permanent base locales to temporary seasonal extractive settlements (Fortier and Emerson 1984; McElrath and Fortier 1983). The reasons for such a shift are presently unknown.

SITE DESCRIPTION

The Fiege site was located ca. 0.4 km west of the bluffline marking the eastern border of the American Bottom. Shallow alluvial loess deposits extended over most of the site area. The predominant soil was an alluvial silty clay. The site covered a triangular agricultural field, bounded by Bypass 50 to the north, by the Illinois Central and Gulf Railroad tracks to the west and south, and by woods and a remnant borrow pit to the east. The triangular field occupied an area of ca. 3.1 ha.

The Fiege site lay ca. 300 m south of the Carbon Monoxide site, and it was situated on the southern end of an inner channel ridge trending north-south within the old Hill Lake meander scar. The Carbon Monoxide site was situated on the northern and central portion of this ridge, which rises slightly in elevation in a southerly direction.

In addition to the alluvial silty clay characterizing the site, a sandy silt soil was found in the southeast corner of the triangular field in which the Fiege site was located. This soil appears to represent an exposed portion of the inner channel ridge fill. Since geomorphic investigations were not conducted at this site, the precise geomorphic character of soil units such as this could not be established with certainty. Of interest, however, was the absence of a deep silty alluvial overburden over the Early Woodland occupation. This portion of the ridge clearly lay outside of the influence of the Hill Lake Creek fan which covered the adjacent portion of this ridge at the Carbon Monoxide site just 300 m north of the Fiege site.

Excavations at the Fiege site were conducted across a proposed channel corridor that extended across the inner channel ridge in an east-west direction. An occupational surface was exposed at 20 cm to 40 cm below the present plowed surface. This surface dipped as much as 50 cm to the west. At the far western end of the channel corridor, the ridge dipped sharply, and a darker slough-like, clayey silt was encountered. No cultural materials or features were found in this area. The occupational surface along the ridge consisted of a silty clay soil, which presumably represents a soil cap deposited over the sandy inner channel ridge. This cap is identical to the one in which Early Woodland occupations at the Carbon Monoxide site were situated.

At the time of the Early Woodland Marion occupation of the Fiege site, the environment surrounding the inner channel ridge apparently consisted of a marsh. The ridge provided access to aquatic resources in the central portion of the marsh. The marsh itself represents a remnant of the recently cut off (ca. 1300 B.C.) Hill Lake channel and was essentially the product of a dying meander, which was gradually being filled in, even during the period of the Early Woodland occupation. Availability of aquatic resources thereafter declined in direct proportion to the gradual reduction of standing water in the shrinking channel. The shrinkage of the marsh and its associated resources through time represents a reasonable explanation of why this particular inner channel ridge was not heavily occupied after the Early Woodland period. The southeasternmost portion of this ridge, however, has produced evidence of Mississippian occupation although subsurface features have not been recognized.

HISTORY OF SITE INVESTIGATIONS

Survey and Testing

The Fiege site was surveyed for the first time during March 1976, by IDOT archaeological survey crews. At that time, only three nondiagnostic chert items were located. After the UIUC assumed contractual obligations for this site during the winter of 1978, an additional pedestrian survey was conducted within the confines of the triangular field. At that time (April 1979), the surface survey produced 213 lithic items, mostly chert flakes, and a single nondiagnostic sherd. Early and Middle Woodland components were recognized. The Early Woodland component was identified on the basis of several Marion Thick sherds and a single Kramer point. The Middle Woodland component affiliation was based on a single expanding-stemmed projectile point. In addition to the survey, 107 tube soil probes and two 2 m x 2 m test units were excavated in order to evaluate the

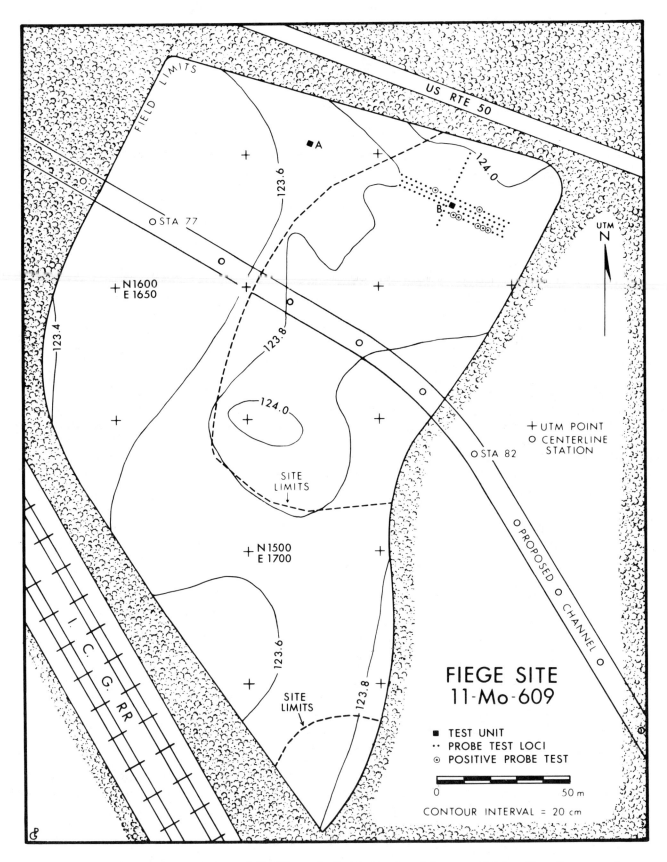

Figure 29. Test Units (1978) and Soil Probe Lines within the Proposed FAI-270 Alignment at the Fiege Site

potential for subsurface occupation. The tested areas, however, included only a narrow strip of right-of-way, located within 30 m of the adjacent Illinois Bypass 50 embankment (Figure 29). As a result, many of the probe units indicated disturbed fill from previous highway construction. Therefore, it was recommended that no further archaeological work was necessary within that specific area of the triangular field. The surface survey, however, indicated the possibility of subsurface occupation further south within the same field.

The subsequently proposed rechannelization of Hill Lake Creek through the triangular field, south of the previous right-of-way testing, led UIUC investigators back to the Fiege site in March 1979 to conduct additional and more systematic survey work within the confines of the proposed channel right-of-way (Tables 35 and 36).

Survey collection blocks subsequently produced a relatively dense concentration of material, particularly at the eastern end of the proposed channel. Early and Middle Woodland materials were again recognized in this area. Another survey of the entire triangular field also produced an early Mississippian component in the southeastern portion of the field. Limestone-tempered Monks Mound Red ceramics, a small ground celt, and several chert tools were recovered in this area. This material concentration was isolated from the proposed channel corridor material and lay nearly 200 m south of the proposed impact area (Figure 30). It was not directly affected by construction of either the highway or the rechannelized creek. However, it was recommended that archaeological investigations be undertaken in the proposed channel corridor, since there existed a strong possibility for exposing either a buried Early or Middle Woodland occupation.

Results of Excavations

The proposed channel corridor comprised an area of ca. 2450 m2, with the greatest density of surface material occurring in the eastern portion. Excavations were initiated during April 1979 and were completed in May 1979. A paddlewheel scraper was utilized to clear ca. 1880 m2 of plowzone within the right-of-way limits of the corridor. This total included 1100 m2 of stripped area in the eastern half of the corridor and 780 m2 in the western half. A total of only 203 field hours were expended on supervising the machine removal of plowzone, on subsequent shovel-scraping of the exposed occupation surface, on feature definition, and on feature excavation. Although only minimal amounts of material had been recovered from the surface in the western portion of the channel corridor, machine excavations were also undertaken in that

Table 35. Surface Collection Material (1978-1979): General

Ceramics

Temper	Exterior Surface	N	Wt(g)	Comments
Grit/grog	Plain	1	0.8	
Grit/grog	Indeterminate	2	2.4	
Grog	Indeterminate	3	3.3	
Grog	Plain	1	2.3	
Grog	Cordmarked	1	3.9	
Grit	Cordmarked	3	14.1	including 2 rims (13.5 g)
Grit	Indeterminate	2	5.5	
Grit	Plain	1	14.3	
Limestone	Plain	1	1.6	
Limestone	Red-film	1	5.4	Monks Mound red
Limestone	Cordmarked	1	3.4	
		17	57.0	

Lithics	N	Wt(g)	Mean	Comments
Chert Flakes	534	656.3	1.23	Nonutilized
Chert Pieces	22	123.2	5.60	
Chert Core	1	35.8	35.80	
Chert Flakes	9	35.9	3.99	Utilized
Chert Blades	7	2.9	0.40	
Sandstone	13	618.1	47.50	
Limestone	6	56.3	9.40	
Igneous Rocks	3	168.8	56.30	
Quartz Nodules	2	203.6	101.80	
Silicified Sediment	1	16.7	16.70	
Silicious Cobble	1	69.8	69.80	
	599	1987.4		

Table 36. Surface Collection Material (1978-1979): Chert Flakes and Pieces

Chert Type	Flakes			Heat-altered Flakes			Chert Pieces			Heat-altered Chert Pieces			Utilized Flakes			Heat-altered Utilized Flakes		
	N	Wt(g)	Mean	N	Wt(g)	Mean	N	Wt(g)	Mean	N	Wt(g)	Mean	N	Wt(g)	Mean	N	Wt(g)	Mean
Burlington	260	268	1.03	123	73	0.59	2	29	14.50	2	2	1.0	5	27	5.40	1	3	3.0
Gray Fossiliferous	21	25	1.19	11	79	7.18	1	13	13.00	-	-	-	-	-	-	-	-	-
White Fossiliferous	30	30	1.00	4	89	22.25	-	-	-	-	-	-	2	5	2.50	-	-	-
Fossiliferous	2	23	11.50	11	9	0.82	4	35	8.75	1	11	11.0	-	-	-	-	-	-
Root Beer (?)	1	2	2.00	-	-	-	-	-	-	-	-	-	-	-	-	-	-	-
Kaolin	3	1	0.33	-	-	-	-	-	-	-	-	-	-	-	-	-	-	-
Brown Banded	3	5	1.66	-	-	-	-	-	-	-	-	-	-	-	-	-	-	-
Unidentified	24	25	1.04	14	10	0.71	10	21	2.10	2	13	6.5	1	2	2.00	-	-	-
Cortical	27	19	0.70	-	-	-	-	-	-	-	-	-	-	-	-	-	-	-
Total	371	398	1.07	163	260	1.60	17	98	5.76	5	26	5.2	8	34	4.25	1	3	3.0

124

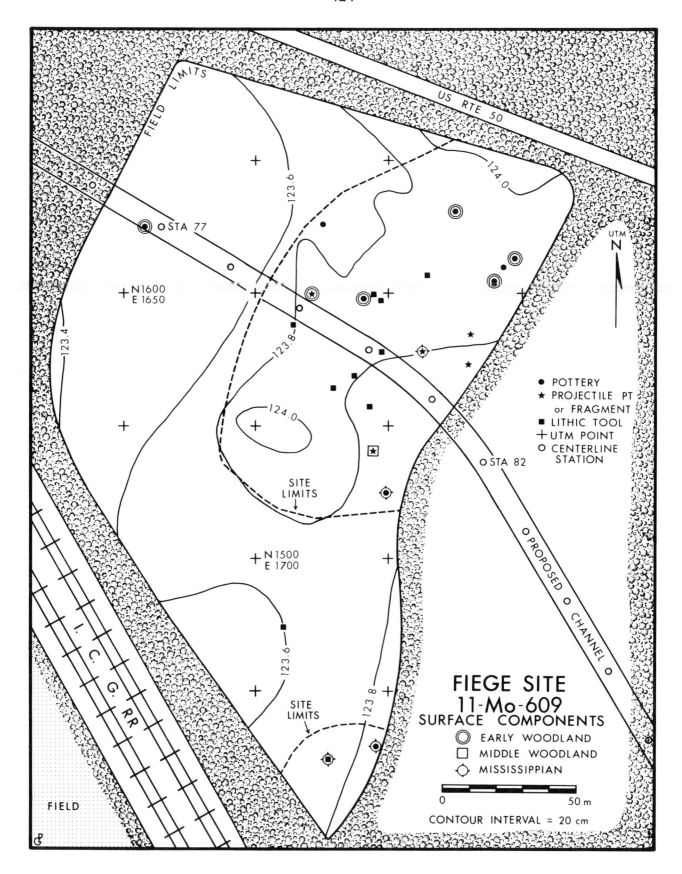

Figure 30. Surface Extent of the Fiege Site and Piece-Plotted Diagnostics

area. Initially, only a 3 m wide strip (i.e., the width of a single paddlewheel blade cut) was cut from east to west in the western half, but following observation of several dark feature stains, the western corridor portion was also expanded to include the entire right-of-way area (Figure 31 and Plate 8).

The excavation strategy at the Fiege site was initially focused on the removal of plowzone within the corridor limits, with the intention of exposing a possible subsurface occupational level. Once this occupational level was observed, the areas around feature surfaces as well as any areas where material concentrations occurred were shovel scraped. Pit features, soil stains, and possible hearths were defined, mapped, and excavated.

Recovered Materials

The amount of material recovered from machine excavation and shovel scraping was small in comparison with that recovered from the general surface collection previously conducted in the corridor area. Chert items, including worked tools and utilized flakes, numbered only 43, while over 200 chert items had been recovered during the surface collection (Figure 32). A total of 60 ceramic items, including 6 rims, were also recovered during machine stripping operations. All of these ceramic items have been identified as Marion Thick sherds. Five of the rims probably came from a single vessel, which exhibited smoothed-over exterior cordmarking. The interiors of these sherds were plain, with occasional finger impressing. All of the sherds were tempered with coarse grit inclusions. Two of the Marion sherds, including one rim, were found less than 2 m away from Pit Feature 11. The majority of items recovered were associated with the occupational level located below the plowzone. All of the Marion Thick sherds were found at this level, and most occurred within the central portion of the corridor, particularly at the eastern end of the western excavation area (Tables 37-39).

FEATURE DESCRIPTIONS

A total of 12 features were defined within the right-of-way corridor, but only 5 of these contained discernible fill and/or definable limits (Figures 33 and 34). Features 2, 4, 7, and 11 were small to medium-sized, shallow basin pits containing chert flakes, burned clay, sandstone, and occasional charcoal flecks. Feature 1 was

126

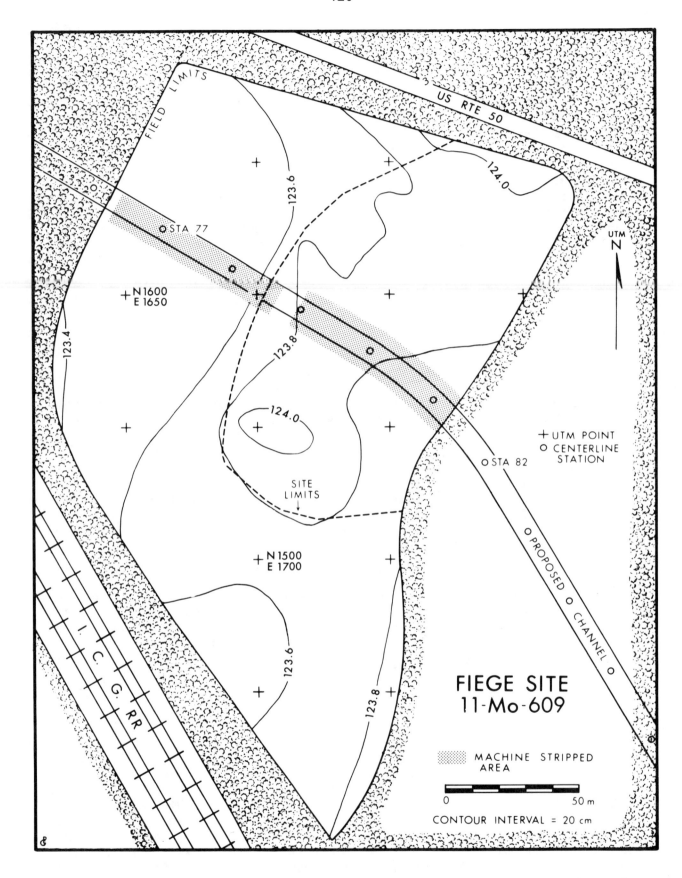

Figure 31. Limits of Machine Excavation and Proposed Diversion Channel

Plate 8. Excavation at the Fiege Site: upper left, machine excavation in the eastern portion of the diversion canal corridor; upper right, excavation of Feature 1 lithic concentration; lower left, exposed features in the western portion of the diversion canal corridor; lower right, excavation block following spring rainstorm

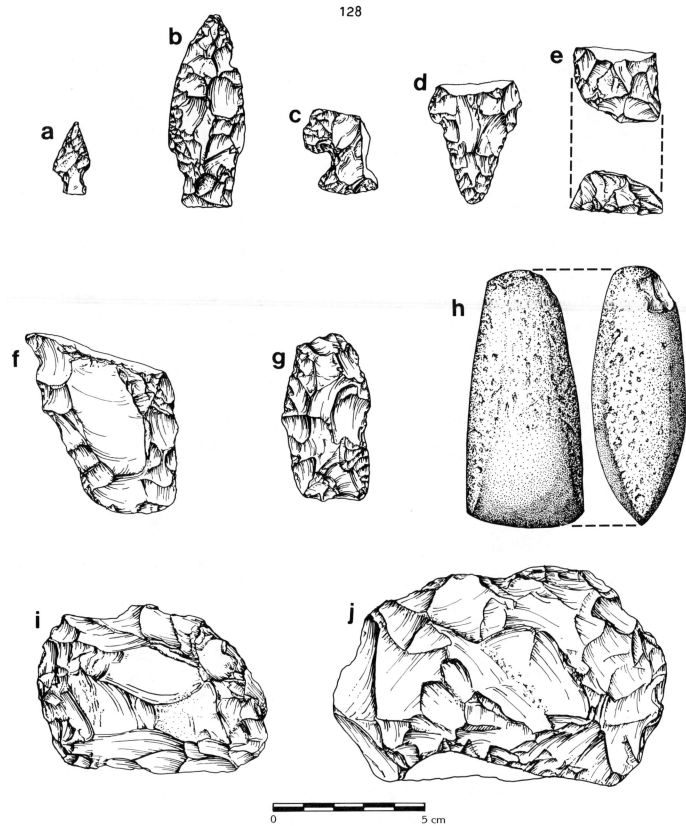

Figure 32. Lithic Artifacts: a–d, h, from surface;
e–g, i–j, from subplowzone contexts

Table 37. Materials Recovered from 1979 Machine Stripping

Ceramics

Temper	Exterior	Interior	N	Wt(g)	Comments
Grit	Cordmarked	Plain	13	55.1	Marion Thick (1 rim 10.7 g)
Grit	Smoothed over cordmarked	Plain	5	29.4	Interior fingermarks (all rims), same vessel
Grit	Indeterminate	Plain	36	64.6	Marion Thick
Grit	Plain	Plain	6	12.5	Marion Thick (?)
			60	161.6	

Lithics

	N	Wt(g)	Mean
Chert flakes	31	174.7	5.64
Utilized chert flakes	3	11.6	3.86
Chert pieces	3	151.8	50.60
Chert core	1	18.0	18.00
Chert blades	5	5.1	1.02
Sandstone	3	198.0	66.00
Igneous rock	1	17.5	17.50
Utilized hematite piece	1	41.8	41.80
	48	618.5	

130

Table 38.   Projectile Point Attributes

			Figure	
	32b	32a	32c	32d
Length(cm)	6.25	2.35	Unknown	Unknown
Blade Width(cm)	2.27	1.12	Unknown	Unknown
Stem Width(cm)	Unknown	0.49	0.53	1.96
Basal Width(cm)	1.53	0.71	0.49-0.19	2.12-0.51
Stem Length(cm)	ca.2.00	0.51	1.46	2.65
Max. Thickness(cm)	0.85	0.21	Unknown	Unknown
Weight(g)	11.80	0.70	4.50	7.60
Chert Type	Fosl.	Bur.	Dongola	Unknown
Chert Color	Gray-Pink	White	Bluish-gray	Yellow (10YR 7/6)

Key
Bur. = Burlington
Fosl. = Fossiliferous

Table 39.   Selected Lithic Tool Attributes

					Figure			
	N/I	32g	32e	32f	N/I	32i	32j	32h
Tool Type	Knife Frag.	Knife	Scraper	Biface	Core Frag.	Scraper	Scraper	Celt
Max. Length(cm)	3.28	5.22	2.29	6.80	6.59	7.66	6.89	8.50
Max. Width(cm)	2.51	2.64	2.63	4.65	5.97	5.31	10.61	3.85
Max. Thickness(cm)	0.90	0.93	1.31	1.75	2.76	2.73	ca. 3.86	2.89
Weight(g)	7.80	16.80	10.65	37.85	81.50	135.45	358.00	150.90
Rock/Chert Type	Bur.	Fosl.	Bur.	Fosl.	Bur.	Bur.	Bur.	Igneous
Chert Color	White	White	White	White	White	White	White	Dark Gray

Key
Bur. = Burlington
Fosl. = Fossiliferous
N/I = Not Illustrated

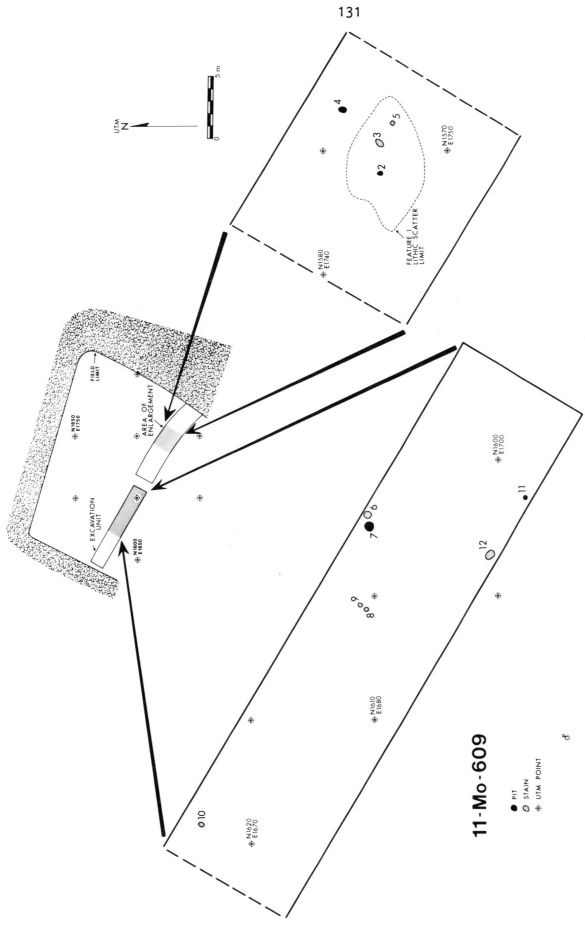

11-Mo-609

● PIT
∅ STAIN
⊕ UTM POINT

Figure 33. Distribution of Features at the Fiege Site

an oval scatter of chert flakes indicative of a lithic activity or chipping area. No diagnostic tools, however, were recovered from this scatter. In addition to these features, 7 stains (Features 3, 5, 6, 8, 9, 10, and 12) were observed. Many of these stains contained charcoal flecks and evidence of burned soil, but they were very shallow. These stains may represent surficial hearths.

Feature 1

Feature 1 was a large irregular-shaped surficial scatter of chert flake debris situated in the eastern portion of the right-of-way corridor. The scatter covered an area of ca. 90 m2 and had a maximum diameter of 11 cm. Pit Feature 2 was located in the center of this scatter as were two surficial stains, Features 3 and 5. Pit Feature 4 lay ca. 2 m northeast of the Feature 1 scatter. The scatter was found at the base of the plowzone, but it may have been partially disturbed by plowing.

The lithic material recovered from Feature 1 consisted primarily of local, nonutilized, white Burlington chert flakes (N=448), of which nearly 42% or 200 items evidenced some heat alteration. The occurrence of heat-altered flakes in an open lithic scatter indicates that those flakes were intentionally heat treated and not merely burned by accidental firing. Over 90% of the recovered chert materials from this feature consisted of small thinning flakes. Cores and large secondary flakes were not found in this feature. Four utilized flakes exhibiting unifacial retouch were recovered, but no other chert tools were present in this scatter. A total of 6 blocky chert pieces, 14 chert blades, 3 sandstone pieces, and 1 igneous rock fragment were also recovered from this scatter (Table 40).

Feature 1 is interpreted as a lithic activity area in which tool maintenance and tool resharpening activities were undertaken. Activities were probably of very short duration and probably involved the reduction or thinning of only a single tool or large chert piece.

133

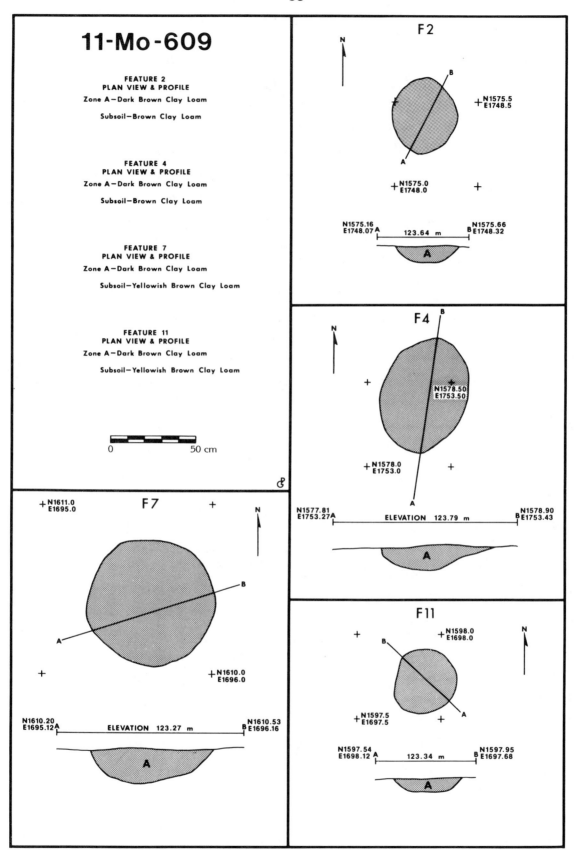

Figure 34. Plan and Profile Views of Pit Features

Table 40. Chert Flakes Recovered
from Feature 1

Chert Type	Thermally Altered		Not Thermally Altered	
	N	Wt(g)	N	Wt(g)
Burlington Glossy	201	129.5	290	326.7
Burlington Oolitic	-	-	2	0.6
Unknown/Cortex	-	-	15	10.4
Total	201	129.5	307	337.7

Table 41. Chert Flakes Recovered
from Feature 2

Chert Type	Thermally Altered		Not Thermally Altered	
	N	Wt(g)	N	Wt(g)
Burlington Glossy	25	5.4	154	49.5
Burlington Oolitic	-	-	4	2.6
Cortex	-	-	5	0.2
Total	25	5.4	163	52.3

Feature 2

Feature 2 was a small (45 cm x 40 cm), circular, shallow-basin pit, which was 11 cm deep and was located within the Feature 1 lithic scatter. This pit contained 187 small thinning flakes, of which only 16% were heat altered. In all probability these flakes were associated with the Feature 1 lithic scatter and are intrusive in this pit. A single chert blade was also recovered from this pit (Figure 34).

The function of Feature 2 is unknown. Faunal materials were not recovered although abundant charcoal flecks were observed in the pit fill. It is possible that Feature 2 represents a small fire pit associated with the heat treatment of lithic materials (Table 41).

Feature 4

Feature 4 was a medium (68 cm x 53 cm), oval, shallow basin pit (15 cm deep) which contained only 7 nonutilized, nonheat-altered Burlington chert flakes. This pit lay only 2 m northeast of Feature 1 and may have been associated with the lithic activities of that feature. Feature 4 contained abundant charcoal flecks and occasional burned clay fragments in its fill. Feature 4 is interpreted as a small fire pit (Figure 34).

Feature 7

Feature 7 was a medium (76 cm x 75 cm), circular, shallow-basin pit (21 cm deep) located in the central portion of the right-of-way corridor. A single sandstone fragment (1.9 g) was recovered from this pit. Feature 7 was found near a light scatter of Marion Thick sherds and, on this basis, it is tentatively associated with the Early Woodland component. Two fish scales and a rind fragment of squash (Cucurbita sp.) were recovered from this pit. The function of Feature 7 is presumably related to cooking and food processing activities (Figure 34).

Feature 11

Feature 11 was a small (40 cm x 38 cm), circular, shallow basin (11 cm deep) pit located ca. 15 m southeast of pit Feature 7. Feature 11 contained a single piece of sandstone (134.5 g). Several Marion Thick sherds were found less than 2 m from this pit and, on this basis, Feature 11 was assigned tentatively to the Early Woodland component. The function of Feature 11 is problematical although it probably served as a small cooking or processing pit (Figure 34).

SUBSISTENCE

Plant and animal remains were relatively scarce at the Fiege site. Two fish scales from Feature 7, and a single fragment of calcined bone from Feature 5, comprised the only faunal remains recovered from this occupation. Plant remains were slightly more abundant and were indicative of a Woodland floodplain extractive pattern. A number of wild plant resources were recovered from the pits (Features 2, 4, 7, and 11), and from surficial hearths (Features 3 and 5). Thick-shelled hickory nut fragments were most frequent, occuring in Features 2, 3, 4, and 5. A relatively low amount of wood remains from this site suggests that nutshells may have served as the primary fuel for fires in both the pits and hearths. A single persimmon seed and a single grape seed were recovered from Feature 2.

Of significance was the identification of a rind fragment of squash (Cucurbita sp.) in Feature 7. This was the only cultigen recognized at this site, and in fact, it is the first cultigen remain encountered in an Early Woodland occupation in the American Bottom. The occurrence of squash, grape, persimmon, hickory nut, and hazelnut, and the general absence of faunal materials indicate that the subsistence base for this occupation was derived primarily from plant resources in the inner channel ridge area, as well as from resources (nuts) acquired probably from the nearby uplands. Based on only one example, it is difficult to evaluate the relative importance of cultigens at the Fiege site occupation. Since the occupation appears to have been very short-term in nature, it is doubtful whether squash was actually grown in the vicinity of the occupation.

SITE SIGNIFICANCE

Overall, the amounts of material and occupational feature remains recovered from the Fiege site were relatively low. The excavated site area may represent only a portion of a larger occupation located both north and south of the channel corridor, within which these investigations were confined. Nevertheless, the remains recovered from this site have augmented the present data base concerning the Marion culture in the American Bottom.

The Fiege site is interpreted as a small, temporary, extractive settlement dating to the Early Woodland period. Tool maintenance activities, as well as plant and animal collecting and processing, occurred at this site. Broken ceramics from at least two Marion Thick jars lay scattered in the vicinity of the pits and hearths defining this occupation. The general paucity of remains, however, indicates that this was not a very intensive or long-term occupation. It is clear that Early Woodland groups, as identified at the Fiege and nearby Carbon Monoxide sites, utilized this particular inner channel ridge as a focus for activities involving predominantly wild plant and animal procurement and processing. Such settlements appear to have involved only a small number of individuals, probably nuclear families or procurement groups consisting of individuals from several families. Of significance, however, is the observation that such occupations differed remarkably from the preceding large, relatively permanent Late Archaic occupations known from this area. They differed not only in size and permanence, but also with regard to the organizational principles involved in the activities conducted at these sites. For example, occupations by Early Woodland Marion groups were spatially dispersed and apparently not organized around a single activity focus. On the other hand, tight pit-cluster groupings organized around open areas have been observed at the Late Archaic sites excavated in the American Bottom (McElrath and Fortier 1983; Fortier and Emerson 1984). Such groupings have not been observed at Early Woodland occupations in this area.

More examples are needed to elicit the complete range of settlement behavior for Early Woodland groups in the American Bottom. However, it is clear that in terms of general settlement and community organization in the floodplain, there presently exists enough information to suggest that the transition between the terminal Late Archaic and Early Woodland periods in this area was abrupt, and suggestive of a major cultural shift. The introduction of ceramics and early cultigens at this same time represent additional manifestations of this shift. Sites such as Fiege, therefore, constitute significant indicators of this shift and fill what has been, up until now, an extremely important gap in the prehistoric continuum of this area.

SUMMARY

The Fiege site was first discovered in 1976 by IDOT archaeological survey crews. Subsequent surveying and testing of this site in 1978 and 1979 indicated the possibility of a subsurface occupation, dating either to the Early or Middle Woodland period. Archaeological investigations by UIUC crews in 1979 were focused on a proposed rechannelization corridor extending across an area of the site, which had produced the densest concentration of surface materials. Machine excavations over ca. 70% of the corridor and subsequent shovel-scraping in this area produced a total of 12 features, consisting of 4 pits, 7 stains or hearths, and 1 lithic chipping area. The small amount of diagnostic material recovered from this site, including Marion Thick ceramics, suggested an Early Woodland date for this occupation. This occupation has been interpreted as a temporary Early Woodland extractive camp.

CHAPTER 4. EARLY MISSISSIPPIAN OCCUPATION AT THE TRUCK #4 SITE

by Andrew C. Fortier

This report presents the results obtained from archaeological
investigations at the Truck #4 (11-Mo-195) site conducted by the UIUC
from May through June 1979. The Truck #4 site was originally reported
during the 1971 Historic Sites Survey, but because it was identified
from only a light scatter of nondiagnostic material, a cultural
component could not be determined. The site was resurveyed in 1975 and
1976 by IDOT archaeological crews during survey of the proposed FAI-270
highway corridor. A possible "Late Bluff" (Emergent Mississippian)
component was indicated by the presence of limestone-tempered ceramics
and a single grog-tempered, dark-slipped sherd (Kelly et al. 1979:100).
The final survey of this site was undertaken in 1977 by UIUC
archaeological crews, and a "Late Bluff" (Emergent Mississippian)
component was confirmed. In addition, a possible "Early Bluff" (Late
Woodland) component was indicated by several ceramic fragments.
Subsurface test excavations were also conducted during 1977, which
revealed a shallow-basined pit which, however, lacked diagnostic
cultural materials.

On the basis of the results obtained from surface reconnaissance and
testing, recommendations were made to conduct further excavations at the
Truck #4 site. Subsequent investigations in 1979 uncovered 24 pit
features, representing a portion of an early Mississippian (Lohmann
phase) occupation. Surface materials indicated that the main part of
this occupation extended further to the east beyond the right-of-way
limits and toward the higher portion of the alluvial fan on which this
site was located. This occupation may have been similar in type to the
early Mississippian farmstead occupation excavated at the Carbon Dioxide
site, located ca. 300 m to the south (Finney and Fortier 1985).

The Truck #4 site excavations yielded significant information about
small, early Mississippian occupations in this portion of the American
Bottom, as well as information concerning the distribution and variation
among pit types found in such occupations. Very little occupational
debris was recovered from the pits at the Truck #4 site, and only a few
diagnostic artifacts could be associated with the occupation. The
general absence of materials in and around these small cooking and
processing pits, and the location of this occupation downslope from the
apex of the Hill Lake Creek alluvial fan, suggest that these pits
occupied the westernmost edge of a larger occupation probably situated
along the apex of the fan. The excavated area of the Truck #4 site must
have been a processing and/or cooking area, maintained at a distance
from the main living area located further east. Wood charcoal, nut
fragments, maize remains, and pieces of calcined burned bone were

recovered from the pits at this site. They indicate that the kinds of activities conducted on the fringes of this Mississippian occupation were focused primarily on processing and cooking wild plants and animals. The paucity of information obtained from these pits also suggests that such activities were probably conducted over a short period of time and did not involve an extensive amount of processed material.

SITE DESCRIPTION

The Truck #4 site is situated on an alluvial fan located just north of Hill Lake Creek, 125 m west of the creek's exit point from the adjacent bluffs. The fan is composed of silty loess deposits that extend outward from the bluffs in a northwest direction. Geomorphic coring at the site indicated that the fan deposits in the area of excavation extended to depths of just over 2 m (Bonnell and White 1981b:7). These deposits provide a cap over the eastern cut-bank surface of the Hill Lake meander scar. The uppermost portions of the fan have been eroded away in recent times. The early Mississippian occupation was situated just 10 cm to 15 cm below the present plowed surface of the alluvial fan and clearly was settled after the greater portion of the fan had been formed.

The Truck #4 site, as defined by the 1977 UIUC surveys, extended over an area of ca. 1.0 ha, 0.59 ha of which was to be impacted by the construction of FAI-270. Most of the surface materials lay east of the FAI-270 right-of-way. The southern end of the site had been disturbed by a field road and modern buildings. During survey, testing, and excavation, the site was defined within a plowed and cultivated vegetable truck farm (Figure 35).

The developmental history of the Hill Lake Creek fan is important in terms of understanding when certain physiographic features were available for occupation in this locality. Geomorphic studies indicate that this fan was an extremely dynamic entity and during certain periods was probably too unstable to support prehistoric occupation, particularly along its lower slopes. The following is a brief geomorphic history of the Hill Lake Creek fan based on the work of Bonnell and White (1981b).

Prior to fan deposition, and while the Hill Lake channel was still active in the floodplain, the cut-bank surface of the channel consisted of a stable, well-developed clay soil. This bank was exposed and cut by Hill Lake Creek, which emptied into the active channel. Any alluvial

141

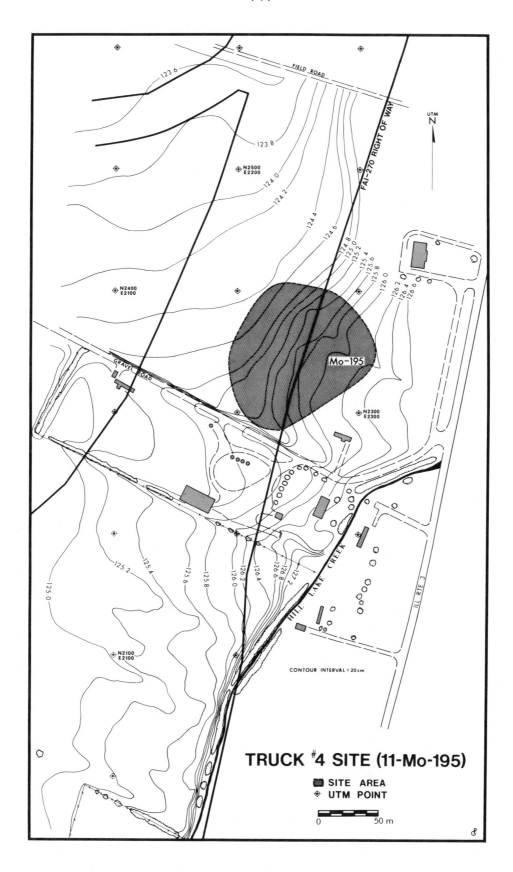

Figure 35.   Surface Extent of the Truck #4 Site

loess deposits carried down by Hill Lake Creek were essentially scoured away by the active Hill Lake channel. Some deposits probably covered the cut-bank surface in areas east of the channel edge.

By the Late Archaic and Early Woodland periods, the Hill Lake channel had been cut off and had begun to fill with fluvial and alluvial deposits. Bluff deposits carried down by Hill Lake Creek began to accumulate over the cut-bank surface. Indications are that the Hill Lake Creek channel may have shifted to the north from its southwestern orientation during this period as fan deposits accumulated in the channel area. This shift probably occurred sometime between the early Late Woodland and Middle Woodland periods. A Middle Woodland occupation at the Truck #7 site, located ca. 200 m northwest of the Hill Lake Creek outlet, apparently was buried by deposits from this fan. The shift northward of Hill Lake Creek apparently accelerated the development of fan deposits near the exit point of Hill Lake Creek from the bluffs. By early Mississippian times, fan deposits in this area had accumulated to a depth of 2 m to 3 m. Eventually Hill Lake Creek was deflected back to the south by these accumulated fan deposits. The early Mississippian occupation at the Truck #4 site was situated on the apex of the fan created by the Hill Lake Creek depositional activity.

At the time of the Mississippian occupation the Hill Lake meander channel probably consisted of small ponded areas. Fresh water could be obtained from Hill Lake Creek, located just south of the higher portions of the fan. South of the Hill Lake Creek fan and creek outlet, the Hill Lake meander cut-bank was open, i.e., had not been subject to alluvial deposition. An early Mississippian farmstead at the Carbon Dioxide site was found along this bank, indicating that the area directly south of the main fan had remained unaltered and stable during the buildup of fan deposits near the outlet of Hill Lake Creek. By Mississippian times, the fan was obviously stable enough to support occupation, although some minor deposition continued to occur through and after the occupation period. During the post-Mississippian period, the upper fan surface was also slowly eroded. Recent plowing served to accelerate the erosional process on this fan. At the time of excavation in 1979, erosion had removed all but 10 cm to 30 cm of silt cover overlying the early Mississippian occupation.

HISTORY OF SITE INVESTIGATIONS

The 1975 to 1976 surface reconnaissance at the Truck #4 site was conducted by IDOT survey crews, while the 1977 and 1979 investigations were accomplished by UIUC crews (Figure 36). The extent of the Truck #4 site within the right-of-way limits, as defined by the 1975 survey, was

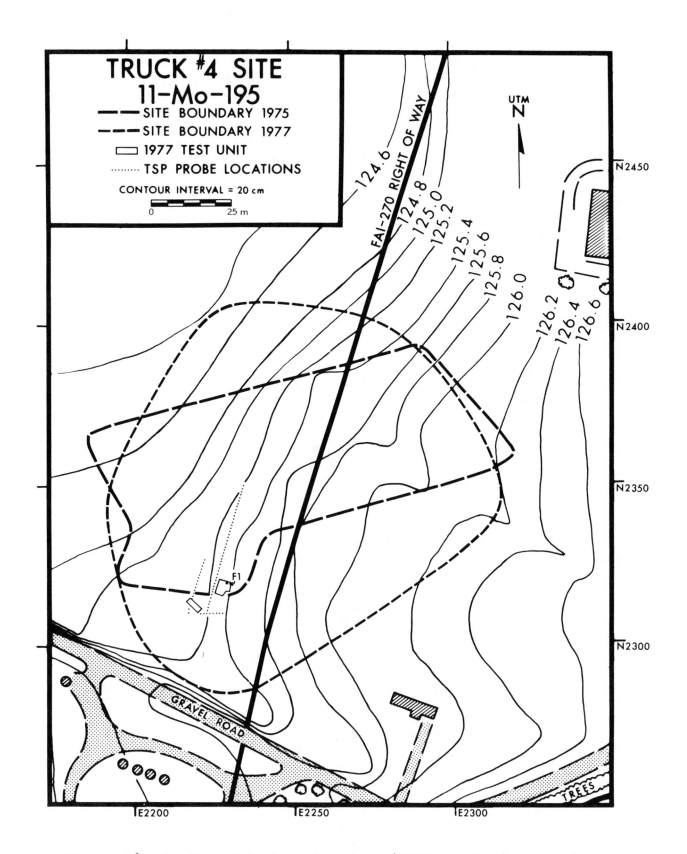

Figure 36. Limits of Surface Materials (1975 and 1977), Soil Probe Lines and Test Units (1977), and Location of Feature 1

0.59 ha, with a material density of 1 item per 69 m2. The site area was probed 45 times at 1 m intervals along three established grid transects with a 14" Oakfield Tube Sampler. "The purpose of probing was to search for subplowzone features without recourse to heavy equipment or shovel testing" (Bareis et al. 1977:30). Soil color, soil texture, and the presence or absence of cultural fill or materials were recorded at each probe interval. The utilization of the soil-probing technique at the Truck #4 site resulted in the discovery of a single subsurface pit feature (Feature 1). Charcoal flecks were observed in one soil probe. During 1977, the area around this probe (10 m2) was excavated, and an irregularly-shaped pit (97 cm x 75 cm), 16.5 cm deep, and basin-shaped in profile, was defined and excavated. Although charcoal flecking was observed in the pit fill, no cultural materials were recovered.

In 1977 a controlled surface collection was conducted at the Truck #4 site over an area of 0.38 ha. Fifty-three pieces of pottery were recovered from the surface, 75% of which were limestone tempered; 10% of these were red slipped, e.g., Monks Mound Red variety. Approximately 35% of the sherds consisted of plain, limestone-tempered items characteristic of the Pulcher Plain variety. The ceramics, despite the absence of diagnostic rims, were identical to materials found at early Mississippian sites in the area, and they were also similar to the Mississippian ceramics eventually excavated at the Carbon Dioxide site located several hundred meters to the south of the Truck #4 site (Tables 42 and 43).

Test excavations were conducted at the Truck #4 site following the controlled surface collection. A total of five 2 m x 2 m units were excavated. As previously mentioned, 10 m2 were excavated in the area, which produced evidence of subsurface charcoal flecking.

Additional test units were placed near an area of high surface density in the south-central portion of the right-of-way alignment. Several of these units were dry-screened through a 14" mesh screen. All of the units were excavated in 10 cm arbitrary levels except for the plowzone, which was excavated as a natural unit. Although 17 pieces of pottery were recovered while screening the plowzone, none were recovered from subplowzone contexts. Several nondiagnostic lithic items, however, were found in subplowzone contexts, including five pieces of sandstone in Test Unit 3 at a depth of 100 cm to 120 cm below the surface. The presence of cultural material at this depth suggested that a feature may have been present there, but due to the narrow confines of the test unit and the difficulty in recognizing cultural fill at this site, a difficulty that later became apparent during investigations in 1979, feature fill boundaries could not be determined.

Based on the surface collection and testing carried out at this site

145

Table 42. Surface Collection and Excavation Ceramic Material Inventory (1977)

Ceramics*	Surface Collection	Test Units (Nonfeature Context)	Total
Grog, plain	1	-	1
Grog, cordmarked	1	-	1
Grog, indeterminate	1	-	1
Grit, plain	1	-	1
Grit, cordmarked	2	-	2
Grit, indeterminate	3	-	3
Limestone, plain	18	1	19
Limestone, cordmarked	1	-	1
Limestone, indeterminate	12	-	12
Limestone, red slipped	5	-	5
Limestone, brown slipped ext. red slipped int.	2	-	2
Shell, plain	1	-	1
Indeterminate, cordmarked	1	-	1
Indeterminate, limestone red slipped int.	1	-	1
Indeterminate, indeterminate	2	-	2
Total	52	1	53

Adapted from Bareis et al. 1977:69

* Temper and exterior surface treatment

Table 43. Lithic Materials from Surface Collection (1977)
and Test Units (Nonfeature Context) from the Truck #4 Site

Materials	Surface Collection	Test Units (Nonfeature Context)	Total
Chert flakes and pieces	292	9	301
Utilized flakes	2	-	2
Hoe flakes	1	-	1
Bifaces	2	-	2
Chert cores	3	-	3
Ground stones	-	1	1
Limestone	20	-	20
Sandstone	25	5	30
Rough rock	9	-	9
Total	354	15	369

Adapted from Bareis et al. 1977:69

during 1975 and July 1977, it was recommended that the impact on the Truck #4 site be mitigated. Although it was apparent from the surface distribution that the major portion of the site lay outside of the right-of-way to the east and on the uppermost portion of the alluvial fan, the presence of a subsurface feature and materials indicated that at least a portion of a possible early Mississippian occupation might lie within the right-of-way area of the FAI-270 highway. Previous excavation of the Carbon Dioxide site, just south of this site, had revealed an occupation lying underneath a soil cover, which had produced little or no cultural material. Excavation during 1979 at the Truck #4 site focused, therefore, on the removal of plowzone overburden in areas that possessed both heavy and light surface material distributions.

EXCAVATION OBJECTIVES AND RESULTS

The proposed research design for the Truck #4 site focused on delineating the spatial limits of the indicated Mississippian occupation, at least within the right-of-way. The position of this site on an alluvial fan extending into a filled, or partially filled, Hill

Lake meander marsh, or lake, may be contrasted with the early Mississippian occupation at the Carbon Dioxide site, located ca. 300 m south of the Truck #4 site. The Carbon Dioxide site was located on the bank of the Hill Lake meander, with ready access to the resources of the lake. As a general Project research objective, it was hoped that subsistence variation could be determined for early Mississippian sites within definable physiographic localities in the American Bottom. The physiographic complexity of the Hill Lake locality was deemed ideal for examining possible variation at a number of different levels for small-scale extractive Mississippian settlements in this area.

Excavations were undertaken at the Truck #4 site during May and June 1979. The excavation block was initiated along the eastern right-of-way limits and extended ca. 70 m in a north-south direction. The block averaged 20 m to 30 m in width. Following machine removal of the plowzone, features were observed, mapped, and excavated. Additional shovel scraping was undertaken in areas producing obvious feature concentrations. A total of 252 work hours were expended on excavation activities.

Machine Excavation

The site limits within the right-of-way corridor comprised ca. 4500 m2 or 45% of the total site area as defined by the 1975-1977 surface surveys. During May 1979, a total of 1635 m2 of plowzone area were removed from an area adjacent to the eastern right-of-way limits that was coincident with an area of dense surface materials. The stripped area constituted just over 36% of the site area contained within the right-of-way limits, or just over 16% of the total Truck #4 site area (Figure 37).

Machine excavation was accomplished with a paddlewheel scraper during the course of one day. Approximately 5 cm to 20 cm of plowzone were stripped off the fan surface before definable features could be recognized. As expected, a relatively shallow plowzone was indicated here, since the site area had been utilized in recent years for vegetable cultivation and, thus, had been subjected only to shallow plowing. In addition, the fan surface in this locality had been greatly eroded so that prehistoric features would be expected to be apparent at a very shallow depth below the surface. The average surface contour elevation in the machine-excavated area was 125.30 m above mean sea level (amsl), and the average surface elevation for features was 125.20 m amsl, a difference of just 10 cm (Plate 9).

148

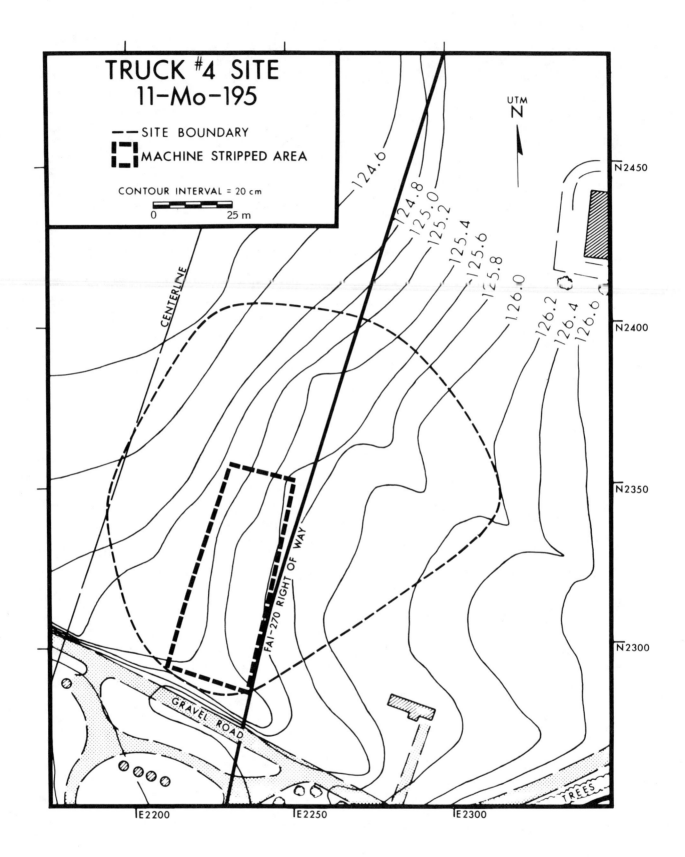

Figure 37. Limits of Machine Excavation at the Truck #4 Site

149

Plate 9. Excavation at the Truck #4 Site: upper left, view to the south prior to machine excavation; upper right, initial machine excavation, view to north; lower left, feature excavation, view to the north; lower right, feature excavation, view to the south

Materials Recovered

Machine scraping produced only a small quantity of material. The surface on which the features occurred was virtually sterile. This surface consisted of a silty loess redeposited soil, which was extremely hard and compact and which, when dry, resisted shovel scraping. Materials were collected while following heavy machinery and are presented in Table 44.

Ten lithic tools, including eight small utilized cores, were recovered, but none were diagnostic of a specific cultural period. Thirty-three additional chert items were also collected, as were numerous small pieces of sandstone, fossiliferous chert, and modern historic debris. Most of the cherts were local white and gray fossiliferous varieties. The occurrence of reddish, jasper-like cherts suggests that some chert resources were being taken out of the local Illinoian glacial tills, which are eroded off the nearby bluffs and specifically occur in the Hill Lake creek channel base. Only four ceramic items were found, including three limestone-tempered body sherds (two with red-slipped exterior surfaces) and one grit-tempered fragment. The recovered materials from the machine operations essentially duplicated the kinds of materials previously observed in the surface collection (Figure 38).

Table 44. Lithic and Ceramic Materials Recovered during Machine Excavation of Plowzone and Occupation Surface

Materials	N	Wt(g)	Mean	Comments
Nonutilized Chert Flakes	20	67.9	3.4	
Utilized Chert Flakes	2	19.3	9.7	
Chert Nodules/Pieces	11	682.8	62.1	
Fossiliferous Chert Pieces	3	95.7	31.9	
Sandstone	16	676.5	42.3	
Silicified Sediment	1	52.4	52.4	
Missouri River Clinker	2	8.5	4.3	
Body Sherds	2	5.9	–	Limestone-tempered, red-slipped (ext.)
	1	1.1	–	Limestone-tempered, plain (ext)
	1	4.2	–	Grit-tempered, indeterminate (ext.)
Total	59	1614.3		

151

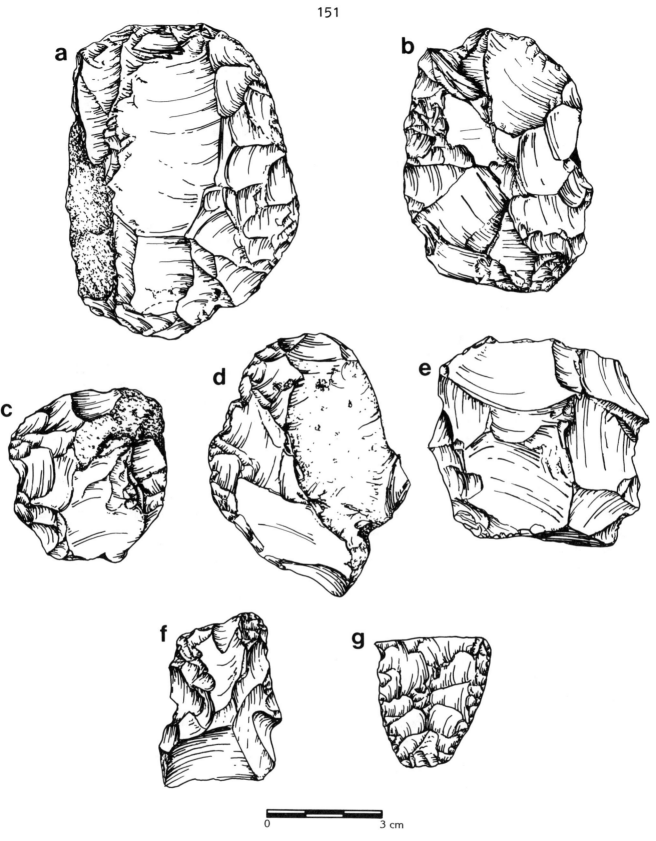

Figure 38. Chert Artifacts: a, g, from surface; b-f, from subplowzone contexts

FEATURES

A total of 27 features were initially defined following machine excavation. Four of these features (Features 10, 19, 23, and 28) were subsequently redefined as stains or surface disturbances. However, only Features 5, 20, 24 and 27 contained cultural material, and only Feature 20 could be assigned to a specific cultural component. The distribution of these features, with the primary concentration located along the eastern right-of-way limits, suggests that the main Truck #4 site occupation lies to the east, outside the FAI-270 right-of-way limits (Figure 39).

Feature clusters or specialized activity areas were not observed at this site although pit type variation could be recognized. With several exceptions, the pit fills were barely distinguishable from the surrounding subsoil. Fill matrices were usually distinguished from the subsoil by the presence of small, very poorly preserved charcoal flecks and occasional fragments of oxidized silt. Both seem to confirm the occurrence of burning in the pits. The surrounding subsoil contained abundant manganese-oxide mottles, which occurred in the pit fills but in lesser frequencies.

Five pit profile shapes were identified. Thirteen of the pits were basin shaped; one was conoidal; four pits had irregular basin shapes; five features had inslanting sides with flat bottoms; one pit had vertical sides and a slanted base. Table 45 summarizes the plan view and depth distribution of the pit features. The depth and size category ranges are arbitrary and are utilized here as they were established in the field.

Nearly 92% of the pit features at the Truck #4 site fall in the shallow depth category (0 cm to 25 cm). The mode for all features is 7 cm (21% of the pits), and the median is 9 cm. In fact, 58% of the pits have depths ranging from only 6 cm to 10 cm., and only two pits have depths greater than 25 cm. The extremely shallow depths of the Truck #4 site pit features may be attributed to erosion of the alluvial fan surface. Project geomorphologists have indicated that the upper portions of this fan have been gradually eroded downslope in recent times. It is believed, therefore, that the upper portions of the fills in this fan surface have also been eroded although the degree and rate of erosion is indeterminable.

The pits that contained cultural material are described in Table 46. Only Features 5, 20, 24 and 27 produced cultural remains.

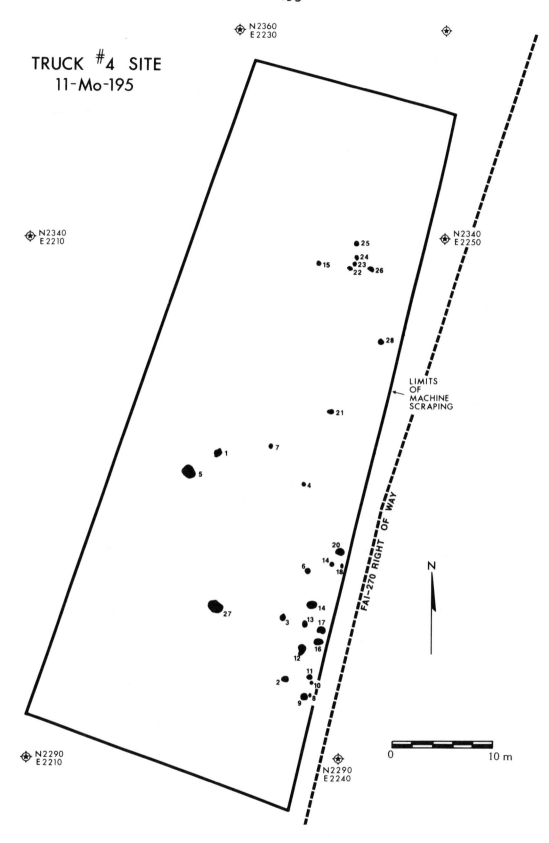

Figure 39. Distribution of Features at the Truck #4 Site

Table 45. Size and Depth Cataegories for Excavated Pit Features

Depth	Planview			Total
	Small (0-49 cm)	Medium (50-100 cm)	Large (101+ cm)	
Shallow (0-25 cm)	5	15	2	22
Medium (26-50 cm)	-	-	1	1
Deep (51+ cm)	-	-	1	1
Total	5	15	4	24

Table 46. Summary of Remains Recovered from Features

Feature	Material	N	Wt(g)	Comments
5	Chert Flakes	3	5.8	Nonutilized
	Chert Piece	1	31.4	
	Igneous Rock	1	68.2	Fragment
	Sandstone	4	1.0	
	Waterworn Pebble	1	0.4	
20	Chert Flake	1	0.3	Nonutilized
	Ceramics	10	80.2	Body Sherds
24	Chert Flakes	2	0.2	Nonutilized
	Sandstone	2	0.2	
	Silicified Sediment	2	0.1	
	Waterworn Pebble	1	0.4	
27	Chert Flakes	2	9.2	Cortical Flakes

Feature Descriptions

Four pit features (Features 5, 20, 24, and 27) are described in detail below. Generally, minimal amounts of cultural material were recovered from the four pits described below. Most of these pits exhibited evidence of burning, so presumably they functioned as either processing or cooking pits (Figures 40 and 41).

Feature 5

Feature 5 was a large (134 cm x 120 cm) oval, deep (157 cm), conoidal pit located at the western edge of the pit feature distribution exposed at this site. Feature 5 represents the only multi-zoned pit of this occupation, and it was the deepest pit at this site. Feature 5 contained very little cultural material: three nonutilized chert flakes (5.8 g), one chert piece (31.4 g), one igneous rock fragment (68.2 g), four pieces of sandstone (1.0 g), one waterworn pebble (0.4 g), four pieces of oxidized silt, and 125 pieces of calcined bone (0.3 g).

Three zones were recognized in this pit, including two upper fill zones (A1 and A2) and a lower fill zone (B). At the base of the A2 zone there were abundant charcoal flecks, small sandstone fragments (not recorded above), burned silt, and calcined bone (Figure 40). All of the chert materials, however, were found in the uppermost zone (A1). It appears that the pit may have served initially as a cooking or processing pit, as evidenced by the occurrence of charcoal, oxidized silt, and burned bone in the lower zones. The lithic materials recovered in the upper A1 zone may have been deposited into the pit as a result of natural pit filling processes related to the erosion of the alluvial fan.

Feature 20

Feature 20 was a medium (93 cm x 68 cm), oval, shallow (11 cm) pit with inslanting walls and an irregular bottom (Figure 40). It was located along the eastern right-of-way limits in the central portion of the excavation unit. Feature 20 contained only one zone, which included a dark silty clay matrix (10YR 4/1) that contained both charcoal flecks and cultural material. The cultural material included one nonutilized chert flake (0.3 g), one grit/grog tempered, thick-walled (8 mm to 10 mm) body sherd with exterior smoothed-over cordmarking and a plain interior (29.6 g), eight grit-tempered plain body sherds (50.1 g), and one limestone-tempered, plain body sherd (0.55 g). These sherds represent the only ceramics recovered from a pit context at the site.

156

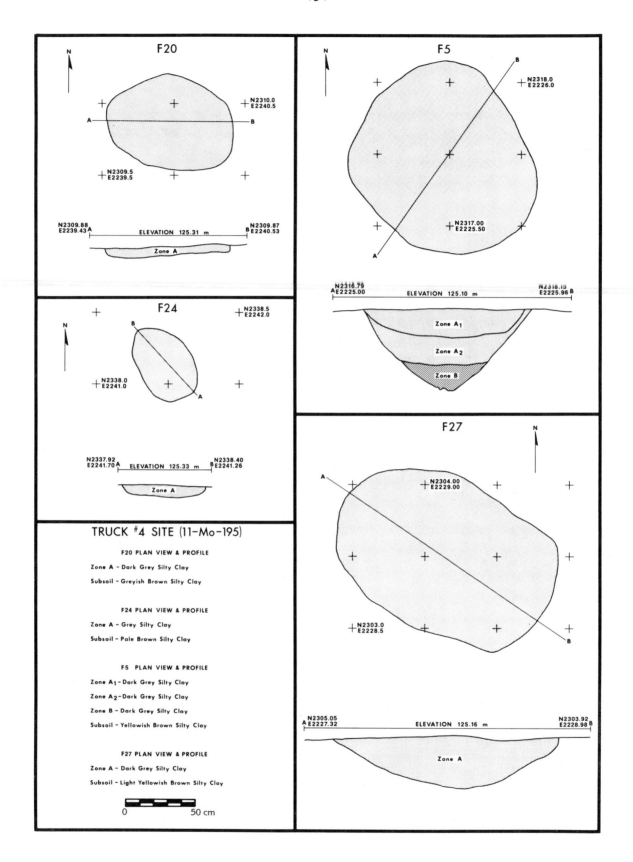

Figure 40. Plan and Profile Views of Pit Features

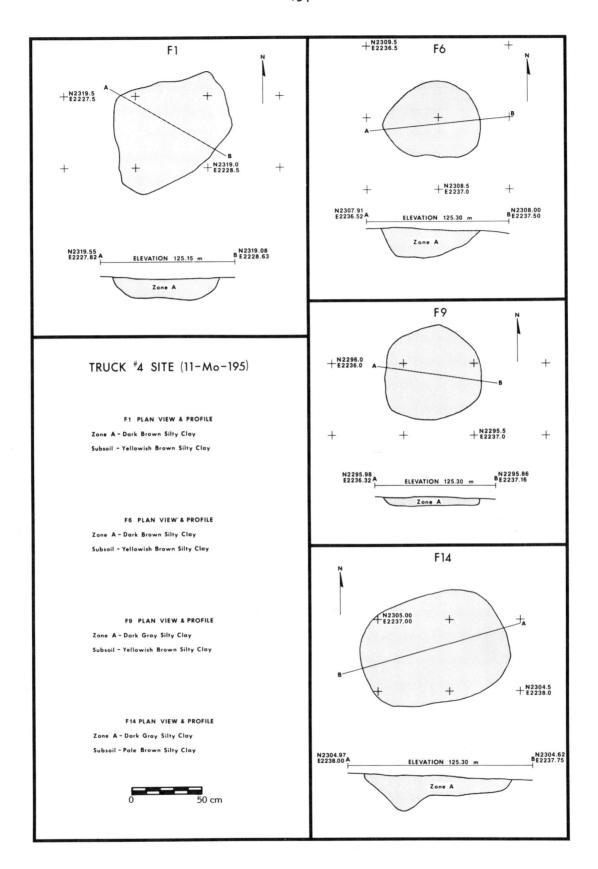

Figure 41. Plan and Profile Views of Pit Features

The function of Feature 20 is problematical although the occurrence of charcoal flecks in the fill indicates that the pit served as either a cooking or processing facility. A single cupule of maize was retrieved from this pit, which represents the only maize recovered at the Truck #4 site. The presence of maize and limestone-tempered pottery generally confirms the Mississippian affiliation proposed for this occupation.

Feature 24

Feature 24 was a medium (57 cm x 39 cm), oval, shallow (9 cm), basin-shaped pit located at the north end of the excavation unit. Feature 24 consisted of only one zone, which was marked by an absence of charcoal flecks. Cultural materials recovered from this feature consisted of two nonutilized chert flakes (0.25 g), two pieces of sandstone (0.2 g), two pieces of silicified sediment (0.15 g) and one waterworn pebble (0.4 g). This pit contained no diagnostic material. The function of Feature 24 is unknown (Figure 40).

Feature 27

Feature 27 was a large (157 cm x 108 cm), oval, 37 cm deep, basin-shaped pit located in the southern portion of the excavation unit. Feature 27 contained only one zone, which was comprised of abundant charcoal flecks. Only two cortical chert (9.2 g) flakes were recovered from this pit. Carbonized hickory (Carya sp.) and black walnut (Juglans nigra) shell were common. The function of Feature 27 is presumably related to cooking or some kind of specialized processing activity. The nut shell was probably utilized as fuel for the pit fire (Figure 40).

FAUNAL AND FLORAL REMAINS

A disappointingly small amount of plant and animal remains were recovered from the Truck #4 site. In fact, only 3.0 g of animal bone were found in the entire site, and of this amount, only 0.3 g were recovered from a pit (Feature 5). A single piece of unburned mammal bone was retrieved during machine scraping in subplowzone contexts. Nearly 125 extremely small pieces of calcined bone were recovered from Feature 5.

A total of 256 l of fill were processed from 15 pits for plant remains. Wood fragments, nut remains, seeds, and one maize cupule were identified. The scarcity of maize and seed remains (only four items were recovered) was striking, particularly for an early Mississippian occupation. Soil conditions were excellent for preservation, so it appears that the low frequency of remains was primarily a result of cultural, and not natural factors.

SITE INTERPRETATION

The Truck #4 site consisted of 23 pit features and 4 surficial disturbances distributed primarily along the easternmost portion of the FAI-270 right-of-way. Interpretation of the Truck #4 site is limited by the fact that the main occupation probably lies to the east outside of the right-of-way. The distribution of pits within the sampled corridor area, which represents only 16% of the site area as defined by the surface collection, formed no recognizable pattern. The anticipated Emergent Mississippian/Mississippian hamlet or farmstead community did not materialize within the excavated area, but it is believed that such an occupation does exist, probably on the higher portion of the alluvial fan.

A number of pits exhibited evidence of burning (Features 11, 5, 27, and 20) and presumably functioned as processing or cooking pits. Carbonized nut fragments in Feature 27 indicate that nuts were being utilized, probably as fuel for pit fires. In view of the small number of fragments recovered from flotation, it is assumed that this site was probably not a nut-processing station. Additional excavations east of the right-of-way limits will be necessary before making interpretative statements about activities carried on at this site.

It has been suggested that this site represents a portion of an early Mississippian occupation. This is based on the presence of Monks Mound Red-slipped, limestone-tempered pottery on the surface of the site, as well as on the occurrence of a single limestone-tempered sherd in Feature 20. No additional diagnostic cultural materials were recovered from Feature 20. The single maize remain is not conclusive but it generally supports the Mississippian date for the site.

The Truck #4 site may be part of a series of short term early Mississippian occupations distributed along the southernmost and eastern bank area of the Hill Lake locality. The surface materials correspond closely to materials excavated from the Carbon Dioxide (11-Mo-594) site, located just 300 m to 500 m to the south. An additional area between these two sites, which was not investigated, also contained cultural materials on the surface. In addition, early Mississippian materials were recovered from surface contexts at the Go-Kart South (11-Mo-552S) and Mund (11-S-435) sites, north of the Truck #4 site. This would indicate that the eastern bank of the Hill Lake scar served as an important focus for early Mississippian groups. Such sites appear to represent small, short-term occupations, perhaps associated with nearby centers, such as the Lunsford-Pulcher site located just 2 km to 4 km northwest and west of the Hill Lake locality. Such a pattern of dispersed settlements could have resulted from a single, nuclear family's periodic movements within the Hill Lake locality, or may have been produced over a shorter period of time by a community of family farmstead units spaced at regular intervals along the bank of this locality.

At the Truck #4 site, lithic manufacturing activities were indicated by the presence of core fragments, cortical flakes, large secondary decortification flakes, and by various heat-altered flakes and pieces. Virtually all of the chert types found at this site came from local sources, including white Burlington and gray to tan, fine-grained, fossiliferous varieties.

The Truck #4 site may be more significant because of its location in the Hill Lake locality than for its features and cultural materials. The Truck #4 site represents a significant site in terms of our understanding of geomorphic processes in the Hill Lake locality. As was mentioned, the Truck #4 site occupation is located on the upper portion of an already-formed alluvial fan. Project geomorphologists have suggested that this fan continued to build and erode long after it had formed. Nearly 2 m of loess deposition lies beneath the Truck #4 site occupation. Of considerable importance is the fact that the Truck #7 site, which contains a Middle Woodland occupation, is buried by the fan. This suggests that alluvial processes were particularly active between the end of the Middle Woodland and the beginning of the early Mississippian periods. A similar phenomenon was observed at the Mund site although, in that case, alluvial processes were particularly dynamic during the early Late Woodland period (Fortier et al. 1983).

SITE SIGNIFICANCE

Only a portion of the early Mississippian occupation at the Truck #4 site could be excavated due to the right-of-way limits, so the overall goal of delineating the complete Mississippian settlement at this site could not be attained. Nevertheless, the excavations at the Truck #4 site did succeed in exposing a portion of this settlement, and in determining its physiographic position within the Hill Lake locality. The settlement of higher fan or bank portions within the floodplain of the Hill Lake locality represents a Mississippian settlement pattern observed along the entire extent of this locality. This pattern is contrasted with the lower, inner channel occupations of the Early and Middle Woodland periods. This settlement shift occurred as a direct consequence of the deposition process, which filled the channel scar and which reduced significantly the amount of aquatic resources available in inner channel niches.

The pit features at the Truck #4 site constitute types (e.g., shallow basin) not found abundantly at other Mississippian sites in the American Bottom. The general scarcity of materials, particularly ceramics, in these pits is also atypical for this period. The significance of this is difficult to assess without knowing the complete settlement plan. These pits do not seem to represent the main activity or occupational focus of this site, which apparently lies to the east. These small, basin-shaped pits appear to represent shallow processing pits. It is, of course, possible that this occupation represents only a small Mississippian processing camp of very short duration. If so, occupations of this type would represent an unusual settlement type for the Mississippian period in the American Bottom.

SUMMARY

Archaeological excavations at the Truck #4 site were undertaken during May 1979 and revealed a portion of an early Mississippian (Lohmann phase) occupation, which consisted of 23 pits and 4 surficial disturbances. This occupational component appears to extend to the east, outside of the right-of-way limits. The exposed features represent the westernmost limits of the Mississippian occupation. The entire settlement was situated on the highest portion of an alluvial fan, extending out from the Hill Lake Creek ravine outlet. The nature and orientation of the occupation could not be established, although it may be similar to the early Mississippian farmstead community excavated at the Carbon Dioxide site.

The Truck #4 site represents one of several early Mississippian occupational components located along the eastern edge of the Hill Lake meander scar. This zone apparently constituted a settlement locus for small farmstead occupations from this period, ca. 975 A.C. to 1050 A.C. Although the Truck #4 site excavations were not extensive enough to establish the precise nature of the Mississippian occupation, they did, nonetheless, indicate the presence of a Mississippian occupation, and more specifically, its physiographic position in the Hill Lake locality. The Truck #4 site augments the data base specifically related to early Mississippian patterns of site locality selection in the American Bottom.

CHAPTER 5. MIDDLE WOODLAND OCCUPATIONS
AT THE TRUCK #7 AND GO-KART SOUTH SITES

by Andrew C. Fortier

This chapter presents the results obtained from archaeological
investigations at the Truck #7 (11-Mo-200) and Go-Kart South
(11-Mo-552S) sites conducted by the UIUC FAI-270 Archaeological
Mitigation Project during 1978 and 1979. The two site areas were
arbitrarily separated by a modern levee field road during the 1975 IDOT
survey. Following archaeological investigations, however, it was
decided that both sites should be combined in a single report.

Surface surveys indicated the presence of Emergent
Mississippian/Mississippian materials at both the Go-Kart South and
Truck #7 sites; additionally, Middle Woodland materials were recovered
from the Truck #7 site. On the basis of results obtained from testing
and surface reconnaissance, it was recommended that the impact on both
site areas be mitigated (Bareis et al. 1977:51-66). Subsequent
archaeological investigations during 1978 and 1979 uncovered 25
features, including a large, circular post structure dating to the Hill
Lake phase of the Middle Woodland period at the Truck #7 site, and a
single scraper cache feature at the Go-Kart South site, also dating to
the Middle Woodland period. Evidence for an Emergent Mississippian
subsurface occupation did not materialize at either site. Nonfeature
context Early Woodland materials were unexpectedly recovered at both the
Go-Kart South and Truck #7 sites.

The materials obtained from the Truck #7 and Go-Kart South sites
provide the first comprehensive occupational and subsistence information
on the Middle Woodland period in the American Bottom. The ceramics from
the Truck #7 site occupation were closely related to materials from the
Illinois River valley and eastern Missouri. Nevertheless, the
occupation at this site was locally adapted to American Bottom
resources, i.e., the majority of the recovered chert types were from
local sources, and the subsistence base was locally adapted. Also, the
predominance of grog tempering in the ceramic assemblage contrasted with
the more commonly encountered limestone-tempered Hopewell ceramics of
central Illinois.

This assemblage relates to the Hill Lake phase of the Middle
Woodland period in the American Bottom. The Hill Lake phase represents
an American Bottom variant of Pike-Hopewell and dates from ca. 100 A.C.
to 300 A.C. The Hill Lake phase occupation at the Truck #7 site dates
to about 160 A.C. The Truck #7 site represents the type site for the
Hill Lake phase in the American Bottom.

The Middle Woodland site(s) described in this report represents a unique, locally adapted occupation evidencing, however, external ties to both central and southern Illinois. Within the context of complex Mississippian developments that later characterized this area, Middle Woodland occupations in the American Bottom emphasize the fact that prehistoric populations, by Middle Woodland times, were already adapting themselves to locally available American Bottom resources. Hence, investigations of the Middle Woodland period in the American Bottom are clearly significant in terms of their contribution to understanding the increasingly complex, locally adapted cultural systems emergent in the American Bottom from 200 B.C. to 1300 A.C.

SITE DESCRIPTION

The Truck #7 site was located ca. 3 km northwest of Columbia, Illinois, in the southern portion of the FAI-270 alignment. This site was situated on a low inner channel sand bar within the now extinct Hill Lake meander channel. This sand bar deposit, which parallels the meander scar, is located at the foot of an alluvial fan originating at Hill Lake Creek, and it exits the bluffs at ca. 200 m southeast of the site. The site and inner channel ridge have been buried by a deposit of silty loess emanating from the Hill Lake Creek bluff outlet. The Truck #7 site occupation itself lies on a thin, silty, clay soil cap that overlies the sand bar deposit and underlies the loess overburden covering the site area (Bonnell and White 1981c).

As defined by the distribution of surface materials, the Truck #7 site occupied an area of ca. 1 ha, approximately 30% of which was to be impacted by the FAI-270 alignment and adjoining east-west frontage road. A narrow dirt field road represented the northern boundary of the Truck #7 site and arbitrarily separated this site from the Go-Kart South site.

The Go-Kart South site was situated directly north of the Truck #7 site, and it encompassed both the sandy inner channel ridge on which the Truck #7 site was located, and the lower inner channel fill area located east of the ridge. The Go-Kart South site extended northward to a horse corral area ca. 140 m north of the Truck #7 site. The Go-Kart South site encompassed an area of ca. 0.80 ha, 50% of which was to be impacted by the construction of the FAI-270 corridor.

HISTORY OF SITE INVESTIGATIONS

Truck #7 Site

The Truck #7 site was initially located in 1971 during the Historic Sites Survey of Monroe County conducted by James W. Porter (Kelly et al. 1979:101). A small collection of nondiagnostic chert and a single dentate-stamped body sherd were recovered. The multicolored chert (mostly Ste. Genevieve red varieties) present in this collection mirrored a similar chert assemblage collected at the Middle Woodland Dash Reeves site (11-Mo-80) located ca. 2 km south of the Truck #7 site. On the basis of the pottery and chert recovered during 1971, the Truck #7 site was designated as Middle Woodland.

During 1975, an IDOT FAI-270 survey was conducted at the Truck #7 site. An area of 0.42 ha, with a density of one item per 25 m2, was defined. The site area was defined by general surface collection techniques, so specific concentrations of material were not noted. In addition to an expanding-stemmed Middle Woodland point base, supplementing the previously recovered Historic Sites Survey Middle Woodland materials, three shell/grog-tempered body sherds were identified. These sherds indicated the presence of an Emergent Mississippian/Mississippian component at the Truck #7 site (Kelly et al. 1979:101) [Table 47].

Additional information was obtained by the UIUC Phase I survey and testing crews in 1977. A site contour map, a controlled surface collection, soil probing, and subsurface test excavations were all accomplished during the period from 15 to 17 August. The controlled surface collection, covering ca. 1 ha, confirmed the presence of Middle Woodland and Mississippian surface materials, expanded the original site limits to include an area of ca. 0.85 ha, and identified an extremely dense area of chert and ceramic debris in a 1600 m2 area within UTM grid coordinates E742160-742200 and N4262590-4262550 (Figure 42)

Preliminary testing (8 m2) and soil probing revealed the presence of subsurface materials and a single postmold. The subsurface materials were limited in number and generally not diagnostic, but the surface collection contained diagnostic Middle Woodland ceramics, including a "Hopewell" rocker-stamped rim, and numerous limestone-tempered and shell-tempered Mississippian sherds. Based on this information, it was expected that the Truck #7 site might contain both a small Mississippian farmstead and a Middle Woodland occupation (Bareis et al. 1977:63-66).

Approximately 30% of the areal extent of the Truck #7 site (2550 m2)

Table 47. Summary of Ceramic Materials Recovered from Pre-1978 Surface Collections at the Truck #7 Site*

Temper	Exterior Surface Treatment	Block 1	Block 2	Block 3	Block 4	Plowzone	Total
Grog	Plain	8	-	-	1	4	13
	Cordmarked	4	-	2	1	-	7
	Red-slipped	1	-	-	-	-	1
	With Lug	1	-	-	-	-	1
	Indeterminate	-	-	-	3	1	4
Grit	Plain	2	-	-	-	1	3
	Cordmarked	2	1	-	-	-	4
	Punctated	-	-	-	-	1	1
	With Notched Rim	1	-	-	-	-	1
	Indeterminate	-	-	-	4	3	7
Limestone	Plain	10	1	1	1	1	14
	Cordmarked	5	-	-	-	-	5
	Red-slipped	2	-	-	1	1	4
	Indeterminate	2	-	1	3	-	6
Shell	Plain	1	-	-	-	-	1
	Red-slipped	1	-	-	-	-	1
Indeterminate	Plain	1	-	-	-	-	1
	Indeterminate	14	1	-	5	2	22
Total		55	2	4	21	14	96

* Adapted from Bareis et al. 1977:65, Table 12.

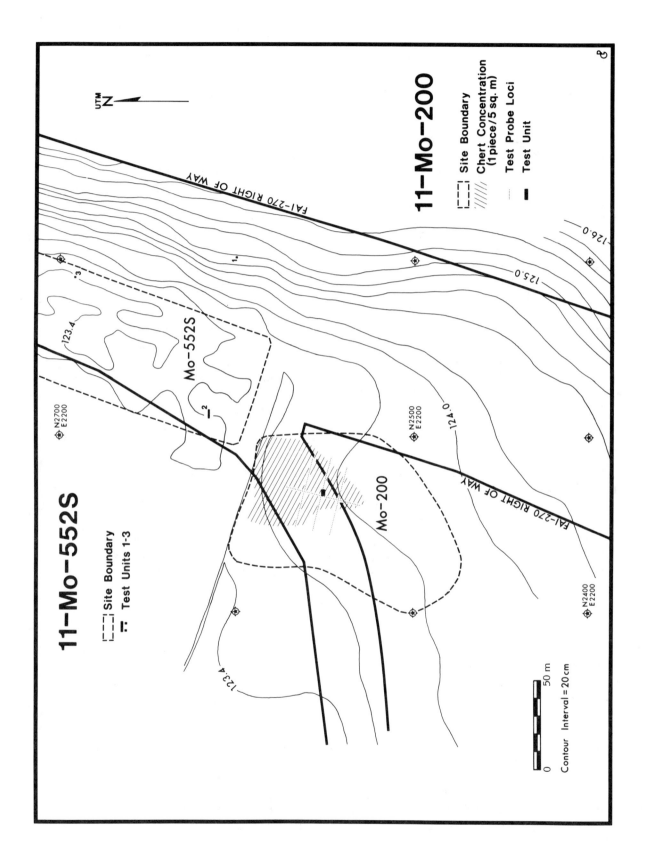

Figure 42. Concentration and Extent of Surface Materials and 1977 Soil
Probe Lines and Test Units

168

was to be impacted by both the mainline FAI-270 alignment and by a frontage road entering the mainline from the west. The frontage road was ca. 35 m wide and contained the greatest density of surface materials, as well as the excavated subsurface postmold. For this reason, it was decided that excavations would be focused in that area.

Archaeological excavations at the Truck #7 site were initiated in October 1978 following a cabbage harvest from that portion of the field, a harvest conducted by FAI-270 crew members. Excavations were continued up to December and then resumed and completed during May 1979. During this period, a total of 2348 m2 of plowzone were removed by heavy machinery in Blocks I through IV. Hence, the total area excavated within the right-of-way limits amounted to 92% of the site area impacted by highway construction. Eventually, a total of 25 features and 72 postmolds were defined and excavated. One thousand sixty work hours were expended in the field during the four-month excavation period.

Initially, a 10 m x 20 m block (Block I) was machine scraped in an area of dense chert debris (UTM E2160-2170, N2557-2577). Two Middle Woodland pit features were exposed and excavated following shovel scraping. Following excavation of those features, an additional 1913 m2 were exposed (Blocks II and III) by paddlewheel scraper in the same area, revealing a concentration of pit features and postmolds (Figure 43).

After shovel scraping the area of feature concentration (ca. 400 m2), a post pattern became apparent. This was designated as Feature 1, and it was identified as a large, circular post structure. Several pits were subsequently defined within the structure, as well as in the area immediately around the structure. During 1978, only the eastern half of the structure was defined and excavated. The remaining portion of the structure, as well as several pit features, were defined and excavated during the following spring (Plate 10).

An additional area (Block IV) was also excavated with a modified backhoe just east of Blocks I-III along the western limits of the FAI-270 mainline. This area coincided with the eastern extent of the site as defined by the surface distribution. A total of 235 m2 were removed from this area, but no features were observed.

During the course of the 1978 and 1979 seasons, all 25 features and 72 postmolds were defined, mapped, and excavated. These investigations revealed a small Hill Lake phase Middle Woodland occupation consisting of a large, single post, circular structure and associated pits. The pits and their contents, as well as the structure, represent unique data from this poorly known period in the American Bottom.

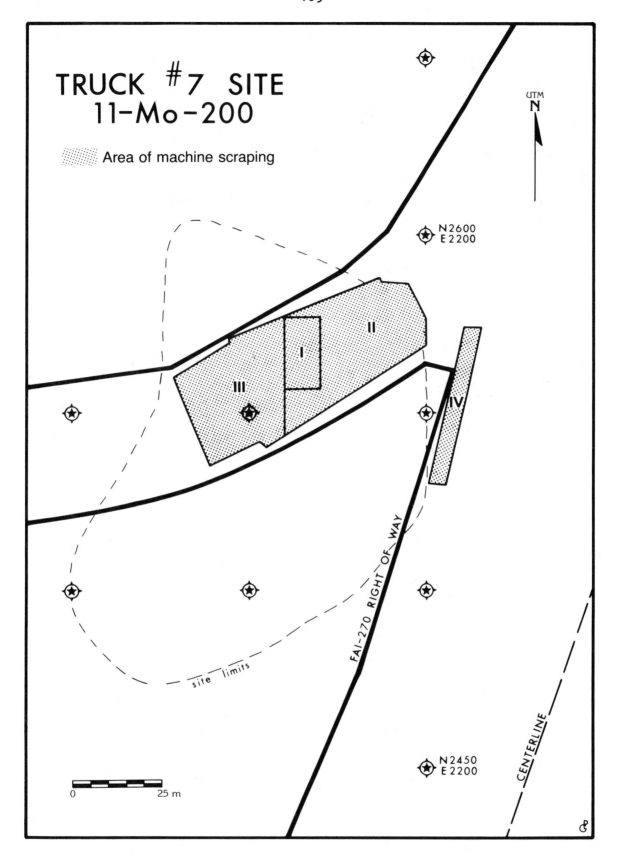

Figure 43. Machine Excavation Blocks I-IV at the Truck #7 Site

170

Plate 10. Excavation at the Truck #7 Site: upper left, aerial view of the Truck #7(a) and Go-Kart South(b) Sites; upper right, machine excavation at the Truck #7 site; lower left and right, excavation of Feature 1

Go-Kart South Site

The Go-Kart South site was originally included with the Go-Kart site, which was arbitrarily divided into three sectors: Go-Kart North, Central, and South. The northern sector of the Go-Kart site was eventually excavated, exposing an extensive subsurface late Archaic occupation consisting of numerous pits and lithic artifact concentrations (Fortier and Emerson 1984). The central sector produced only a limited quantity of surface materials (mixed with dense historic debris and modern structural disturbances) and did not warrant further investigation. The southern sector extended from a horse corral, marking the southern boundary of the central sector, to the slightly raised levee field road marking the northern boundary of the Truck #7 site. Thus, the Truck #7 and Go-Kart South sites were separated arbitrarily by a field road and not on the basis of archaeological materials recovered from the surface.

During the summer of 1976, IDOT FAI-270 survey crews conducted probe and phosphate tests in the southern sector of the Go-Kart site, and a contour map of the site area was made. A controlled surface collection was restricted to the northern sector. The site limits, as defined by the surface collection in the southern sector, encompassed an area of ca. 0.80 ha, approximately 60% of which was to be impacted by the proposed FAI-270 highway corridor (Figure 42).

Because of several high phosphate readings, test excavations were undertaken at the Go-Kart South site during 1976. Three test units were placed in various areas of the southern sector. Units 1 and 3, each 1 m x 1 m, contained a very dark to dark grayish brown (10YR 3/2) to black (10YR 2/1) clay gumbo subsoil. Subsurface cultural material consisted of sherds, chert, and limestone (Bareis et al. 1977:61). Excavation Unit 2 was a 1 m x 5 m unit, which also yielded subsurface materials. The recovered ceramics consisted primarily of plain, limestone-tempered body sherds similar to the Mississippian materials recovered from the adjacent Truck #7 site and were indicative of a possible Mississippian (Lohmann phase) occupation.

Based on the presence of subsurface materials, further investigation was recommended for the Go-Kart South sector. At that time, proposed excavation strategies were independently designed for the Truck #7, Go-Kart South, and Go-Kart North sites.

During September and October 1978, excavations in the Go-Kart South sector were initiated and completed, with the expenditure of only 444 man-hours. A total of 7688 m2 of plowzone were stripped by paddlewheel scraper in six block areas (Blocks A-F). Of this total,

4394 m2 of plowzone were removed within the site limit portions of the right-of-way, while 3294 m2 were removed east of the defined surface extent of the site. Over 90% of the determined site area within the right-of-way was examined. In addition to the archaeological work at this site, an extended east-west trench (103 m long, 2 m wide, and ca. 2 m deep) was excavated across the northern portion of the defined site area to aid in the geomorphological interpretation of the site (Bonnell and White 1981c) [Figure 44].

Machine excavation produced only one feature, a Middle Woodland tool cache consisting of a stacked pile of 33 flake scrapers, a projectile point, a hammerstone, and a piece of rubbed hematite. Various materials were recovered during the machine removal of the plowzone, including Early Woodland Marion Thick sherds; Mississippian (Lohmann phase) red-slipped, limestone-tempered ceramics; and numerous unidentified and heavily eroded sherds. The Early Woodland materials and the tool cache were located on the lower portion of a buried inner channel ridge, while the Lohmann phase materials were recovered within the fill of the old Hill Lake meander scar. The Lohmann phase ceramic material was associated with secondary alluvial fill deposits.

The recovered tool cache at the Go-Kart South site, presumably associated with the Middle Woodland occupation at the Truck #7 site, prompted the decision to produce a single site report covering both the Go-Kart South and Truck #7 site materials. Investigations at the Go-Kart South site were actually completed prior to the initiation of final excavations at the Truck #7 site. Machine excavation strategies differed at the two sites both because of differential sizes of the site areas involved (the Go-Kart South site encompassed a greater area than the Truck #7 site) and because the two site areas occupied slightly different geomorphic settings.

SURVEY AND TESTING

Surface surveys were conducted at various times at both the Truck #7 and Go-Kart South sites from 1971 to 1978. Subsequent testing produced a single postmold (Postmold 1), as well as nondiagnostic subsurface materials at the Truck #7 site. This postmold was not associated with the eventually excavated structure, which was located ca. 10 m north of the postmold. Testing at the Go-Kart south site did not reveal any subsurface features, although nondiagnostic subsurface materials were recovered.

The surface remains at the Truck #7 site indicated possible Middle

173

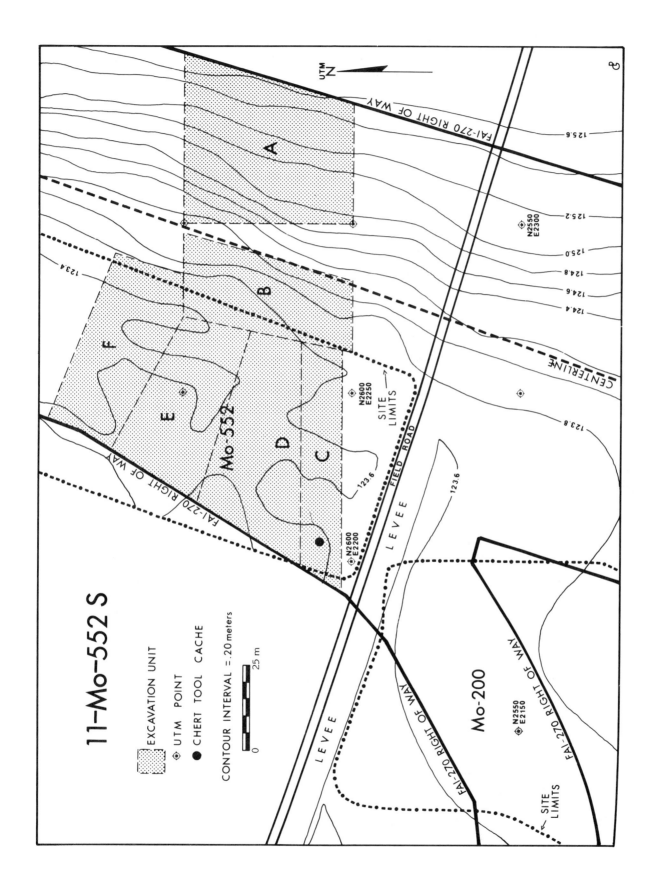

Figure 44. Machine Excavation Blocks A-F at the Go-Kart South Site

Woodland and Mississippian components. At the Go-Kart South site, only Mississippian remains were found on the surface. At the Go-Kart South site, the Mississippian materials had been secondarily deposited into the area by means of alluvial erosion. The single Mississippian feature (Feature 11) found at the Truck #7 site, however, indicates that an in situ occupation from this period may exist nearby. Concurrent with these erosional activities, modern plowing had recently disturbed the subsurface Middle Woodland occupation, resulting in a mixing of materials from both occupations.

The controlled surface collection conducted at the Truck #7 site during 1977 had produced a well-defined zone of concentrated chert and ceramic debris in an area of 1600 m2. When this zone was eventually excavated during 1978 and 1979, it was found to coincide with the subsurface location of the circular structure and its associated pits. Therefore, the relationship between the surface material density and the subsurface features was particularily close at the Truck #7 site. On the other hand, although the occurrence of the structure and its associated pits might have been predicted from the surface distribution, the outlying pits and miscellaneous postmolds that, together with the aforementioned features comprised the entire occupation, were only discovered as a result of wide-scale machine excavation over all available areas, regardless of their surface material densities.

Of interest at the Truck #7 site was a general scarcity of a purple variety of chert (Ste. Genevieve purple) in the surface collections. Less than 10% of the chert debris recovered from the surface of the site was associated with this chert type. On the other hand, the subsurface features eventually excavated in this same locality contained nearly 60% by weight and frequency of this chert type. This indicates that subsurface features and the floor midden of the structure itself may not have been significantly disturbed by plowing, for had materials been displaced by plowing an equal distribution of purple chert might be expected from surface and subsurface contexts.

The relationship of the Go-Kart South surface materials to the subsurface materials and to the single tool cache feature was not close. As previously suggested, the surface remains at this site were redeposited materials that were not associated with the Early Woodland or Middle Woodland subsurface remains. The cherts recovered from the surface consisted primarily of local and white Burlington types, which, although present in subsurface contexts, were not abundant. Because the nature and extent of subsurface materials at the Go-Kart South site could not be predicted accurately from the surface remains, wide-scale machine excavation was employed to strip off the redeposited overburden both from areas containing surface materials and from areas lacking surface indicators within the proposed right-of-way.

EXCAVATION RESULTS

The primary archaeological objective at the Truck #7 and associated Go-Kart South sites was to expose and excavate the postulated Middle Woodland encampment in order to obtain primary information concerning the nature of Middle Woodland occupations and adaptations in the American Bottom. It is not possible, of course, to resolve every question regarding an entire cultural period on the basis of the analysis of only a single occupation; however, the Truck #7 site investigations do provide a solid foundation for future Middle Woodland research in the area.

The Middle Woodland occupation at the Truck #7 site is unique with regard to the amount of data it provides, compared to the data provided thus far by other Middle Woodland sites in the American Bottom. Only a limited number of sites from the Hill Lake phase of the Middle Woodland period are known from the American Bottom (including tested sites, e.g., Dash Reeves), and none to date have produced either subsurface features or settlement plans. The Truck #7 site is, therefore, the first Hill Lake phase occupation to yield both subsurface features and a community plan. Prior to the Truck #7 site excavations, pit feature types from this period were unknown in the American Bottom. Additionally, the large, circular post structure uncovered at the Truck #7 site represents the first structure excavated from this time period in the American Bottom.

In addition to the discovery of new feature types and the delineation of unique ceramic and lithic assemblages at the Truck #7 site, the most important results of the Truck #7 site investigations have been the data relating to the settlement and subsistence systems at this site. The retrieval of these kinds of information was one of the primary research objectives established for the Hill lake locality site assemblage. The excavation and analysis of this Middle Woodland encampment, which occurred on an inner channel ridge of the Hill Lake meander scar and whose occupants exploited a broad spectrum of local plant resources, contributes significantly to our knowledge of Middle Woodland subsistence and site location strategies in the American Bottom.

To accomplish the research objectives of delineating the settlement plan and subsistence system at the Truck #7 site, a total site excavation strategy was adopted. The utilization of heavy machinery at this site, e.g., backhoe, paddlewheel scraper, and high-lift, was deemed more efficient and less costly than small-scale sampling. By stripping the plowzone and overburden from large areas within the right-of-way limits, feature concentrations were immediately visible. Hence, time was not lost excavating sterile areas. Given the cost and time constraints of the research environment, it is believed that the loss through machine operations of any surface/plowzone materials from above the occupation surface was more than offset by the recovery of an entire site plan and the subsistence data recovered from a variety of features within the entire occupation area.

The following sections present the results obtained from the 1978 to 1979 excavations at the Truck #7 and Go-Kart South sites. Both site designations are maintained in this report, since the two sites were excavated separately although both site areas should be combined. The primary focus in this report, however, is on the Truck #7 site, which exhibited the primary features associated with the Middle Woodland occupation.

Machine Excavations

Go-Kart South Site

During September 1978, investigations at the Go-Kart South site were initiated and completed. A total of 7688 m2 were machine stripped of plowzone within the defined FAI-270 right-of-way limits. Approximately 75% of the available area within the right-of-way and over 90% of the impacted site area were investigated. Cultural materials, including

Table 48. Surface and Machine Scraped Nontool
Material from the Go-Kart South Site

Material Type	N	Wt (g)	Mean Wt(g)
Chert Flakes	128	323.4	2.53
Chert Nodules	75	1540.1	20.53
Sandstone	318	5182.4	16.30
Limestone	15	132.8	8.85
Quartzite	3	158.4	52.80
Rough Rock	4	642.3	160.57
Modern Refuse*	4	47.1	11.78
Burned Clay	11	6.4	0.58
Missouri River Clinker	3	5.6	1.87
Total	561	8038.5	

* Modern refuse includes glass, plastic, metal, and a lead musket ball.

Table 49. Chert and Nonchert Tools Recovered from
Machine Excavation at the Go-Kart South Site

Chert Tools	Wt(g)	Chert Type	Provenience*
Core	225.7	Salem Creamy	Backdirt
Contracting-Stemmed Projectile Point	11.2	Gray Local	MS BPZ
Retouched Flake	48.6	Gray Local	MS PZ
Graver	27.4	Gray Local	MS PZ
Core	33.3	Ste. Gen. Red**	Surface
Biface Fragment	1.8	White Local	Surface
Hoe Fragment	13.4	Mill Creek	Backdirt
Utilized Flakes (N=8)	31.4	White Local	MS PZ

Nonchert Tools			
Grinding Stone	169.2	Igneous Rock	MS PZ
Metate Fragment	681.9	Sandstone	MS BPZ
Hammer/Grinding Stone Fragment	192.8	Igneous Rock	MS PZ

 * MS BPZ: Machine scraped below plowzone
   MS PZ: Machine scraped in plowzone
** Ste. Gen. Red: Sainte Genevieve Red

Table 50. Surface and Machine Scraped Ceramic Materials
from the Go-Kart South Site

Temper	Exterior Surface	N	Wt(g)	Comments
Grit	Cordmarked	44	231.4	2 Rim Sherds (30.4 g)
				1 Base Sherd (39.5 g)
	Indeterminate	22	29.0	
Grog	Cordmarked	17	28.3	
	Indeterminate	11	3.5	
Limestone	Plain	18	38.6	1 Rim Sherd (5.2 g)
	Cordmarked	12	8.4	
	Red-slipped	25	42.2	
	Indeterminate	4	1.9	
Shell	Plain	4	21.9	
	Cordmarked	14	20.9	
	Red-slipped	3	11.8	
Total		174	437.9	

Mississippian and Early Woodland ceramics, chert flakes, and sandstone appeared to be uniformly scattered over the entire machine-excavated area, with greater densities of materials occurring in the southwestern corner of Block C and along the western edge of the construction limits.

Six distinct machine-excavated blocks were placed so as to expose both the inner channel fill area and the inner channel ridge bank on the far western edge of the right-of-way limits. These blocks (A-F) included the following areas: A-2166 m2, B-1128 m2, C-920 m2, D-1303 m2, E-1064 m2, and F-1107 m2. Virtually all of the Mississsippian ceramics occurred within Blocks A and B and in the eastern portions of Blocks C-F. The Early Woodland Marion Thick pottery occurred primarily along the far western edge of the right-of-way on the slope of the eastern portion of the inner channel ridge. These Early Woodland materials were associated with a specific occupational surface, while the Mississippian materials were confined to the redeposited alluvium filling the inner channel area (Tables 48-50).

In addition to the archaeological investigations at Go-Kart South, an extended east-west geomorphic trench (103 m long, 2 m wide, and 2 m deep = 412 m3) was excavated across the northern portion of the defined site area. This trench was designed to aid in the geomorphological interpretation, not only of the Go-Kart South site area, but also of the greater Hill Lake meander scar locality. The trench revealed the nature of bank and channel-basin deposits at this site and demonstrated the relationship of subsurface topographic features to the distribution of cultural materials. As expected, the sandy deposits of the inner channel ridge were exposed in the westernmost portion of the trench.

Truck #7 Site

A preliminary surface survey conducted during October 1978 reconfirmed the presence of a dense scatter of materials located within the right-of-way portion of the proposed frontage road adjoining the main FAI-270 alignment. The area within the frontage road contained unharvested cabbage; therefore, in order to minimize crop damage, only a small excavation block (Excavation Block I) was opened in October. This was placed within an area of dense surface debris (Figure 43).

Excavation Block I consisted of a 20 m x 10 m block located in the center of the frontage road corridor. A flat-bladed high-lift was utilized to remove the plowzone overburden within this block. Although 200 m2 of plowzone were removed, only 50 m2 were shovel scraped in this area. High-lift scraping was terminated because of the irregular surface it created and the compaction of the soil it produced, both factors making shovel scraping extremely difficult. Pit Features 2 and 3 and Postmold 72 were identified along the eastern edge of Block I. They were excavated during the subsequent month.

The eastern edge of Excavation Block I actually overlapped the westernmost portion of the circular post structure later identified at the site. Features 2 and 3 represented interior pits within this structure. The structure outline, however, was not recognized at the time of the machine work because of the limited area that was opened, the poor late fall lighting, and the compaction of the soil by the high-lift scraper. It later became clear that the high-lift had not removed enough of the plowzone or alluvial overburden in this block to reveal the occupation subsequently defined in this area.

During December 1978, a paddlewheel scraper was employed to strip the plowzone from a larger area within the frontage road. A total of 1913 m2 were machine scraped within Blocks II and III, which were located east and west, respectively, of the original Block I area. An area of darker fill and associated cultural material was observed just east of Block I in Block II. Machine excavation was terminated in this area so that it could be more carefully shovel scraped. Although some cultural material was no doubt lost during the scraping operations, the machine blade never actually penetrated the alluvial overburden covering the subsurface occupation, which was eventually defined by shovel scraping (Tables 51 and 52).

Shovel scraping within the dense area of fill, defined above, produced the outlines of the circular post structure, as well as its internal pits. The soil within the structure and immediately around it was darker than the surrounding area, but this discoloration was the result of surficial staining rather than from any floor midden developed within the structure.

During 1979, additional machine scraping was accomplished in Blocks II and III, both of which were within the frontage road right-of-way. In addition, Block IV was opened near the junction of the frontage road and the mainline right-of-way limits. A total of 235 m2 were excavated with a modified flat backhoe blade. The purpose of this block was to expose an area still within the surficial limits of the site but away from the inner channel ridge. Block IV was scraped to a depth of ca. 45 cm below the surface, and although some isolated materials were found in this alluvial fill soil, no features were encountered. Further work in this area was, therefore, discontinued. The soil in this block was dark gray to black, indicating a highly organic soil, formed perhaps under marshlike conditions. Excavation of Block IV revealed, as did machine scraping in the eastern sectors of the

Table 51. Nonutilized Nonceramic Material
Recovered from Machine and Shovel Scraped
Contexts at the Truck #7 Site

Material Type	N	Wt (g)	Mean Wt(g)
Chert Flakes	916	1407.4	1.54
Chert Pieces	294	3065.5	10.43
Sandstone	112	1189.9	10.62
Limestone	120	1312.0	10.93
Rough Rock	9	19.8	2.20
Waterworn Rock	9	74.6	8.29
Modern Refuse*	28	115.3	4.18
Burned Clay	22	17.8	0.81
Hematite	3	24.1	8.03
Limonite	2	3.1	1.55
Silicified Sediment	3	2.6	0.87
Total	1518	7232.1	

* Modern Refuse includes cinder, glass, metal,
  ceramics, and gun shells.

Table 52. Ceramics Recovered from Machine and Shovel
Scraped Contexts at the Truck #7 Site

Temper	N	Wt(g)	Interior Treatment	Exterior Treatment	Decoration	Sherd Type
Grog	2	4.3	Indeterminate	Plain	None	Body
Grog	1	1.9	Indeterminate	Plain	None	Body
Grog	2	6.6	Plain	Plain	Rocker-Stamped	Rim
Grog	1	2.2	Plain	Plain	Rocker-Stamped	Body
Grog	2	2.6	Indeterminate	Indeterminate	None	Body
Limestone	1	1.2	Plain	Plain	None	Body
Limestone	1	1.0	Indeterminate	Indeterminate	None	Body
Limestone	1	0.4	Plain	Indeterminate	None	Body
Limestone	1	0.2	Indeterminate	Indeterminate	None	Body
Limestone	2	1.9	Indeterminate	Indeterminate	None	Body
Grit/Grog	1	0.9	Plain	Plain	None	Body
Grit	1	0.4	Indeterminate	Indeterminate	Rocker-Stamped	Body
Grit	2	1.0	Plain	Plain		
Grit	1	1.3	Plain	Plain	None	Body
Total	19	25.9				

Go-Kart South site, that the area just east of the inner channel ridge
and, therefore, east of the Middle Woodland occupation comprised the
easternmost portion of the Hill Lake Channel and most likely represented
a marsh environs adjacent to the inner channel ridge.

FEATURE DISTRIBUTION

The excavated Middle Woodland occupation at the Truck #7 and Go-Kart
South sites consisted of a large, circular post structure (Feature 1) in
association with 10 interior pits, 10 pits external to the structure, 4
surficial burned hearth areas (also outside of the structure), and a
single tool cache located ca. 40 m north of the structure. One of the
external pit features (Feature 11), located on the western periphery of
the occupation, was associated with a Mississippian (Lohmann phase)
component. All other features were associated with the Hill Lake Middle
Woodland occupation (Figure 45).

The small number of features comprising the Middle Woodland
occupation in this locality, the lack of superpositioning, the absence
of large midden areas, and the generally diffuse concentrations of
material between features suggests a relatively short-term, multifamily
dwelling in and around which various subsistence and lithic
manufacturing activities were performed. Most of the refuse recovered
from this occupation was found in pit features within the circular
structure. Virtually all of the seeds and nuts retrieved were also
recovered from pits inside the structure. A cluster of fired-soil areas
located ca. 10 m east of the structure, represented open hearths.
Specific hearth areas were absent inside the structure. Other pits
outside the structure characteristically exhibited evidence of burning
and a general absence of cultural and seed/nut materials. These
features were probably cooking pits.

The pits within the structure varied in both form and function. The
deeper pits, such as Features 14 and 19, contained the greatest variety
of cultural and ethnobotanical material. Features 10, 18, and 2 were
relatively small pits with abundant refuse. Each of these refuse pits
had dark fills clearly outlined against the yellowish brown, sandy silt
subsoil. They also exhibited evidence of burning. Several episodes of
filling were observed in Feature 14.

Feature 16 contained an extraordinary amount of lithic debris and
probably functioned as a depository for chert reduction and tool
preparation activities. Lithic activities were probably undertaken
directly over this pit. The only hammerstones recovered from this

182

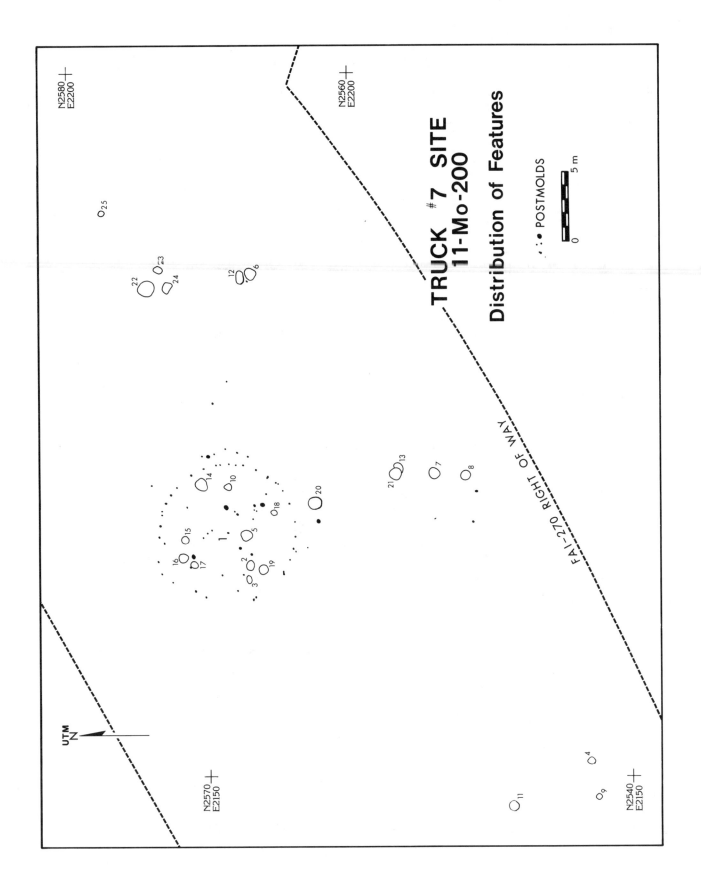

Figure 45. Middle Woodland Community Plan at the Truck #7 Site

occupation came from this pit. Feature 15, located adjacent to Feature 16, contained virtually no cultural material but yielded abundant seed remains. This pit is interpreted as a seed processing and/or storage facility.

The presence of core scraping tools in Features 14 and 16 and the presence of gouges in nonfeature contexts inside the structure floor area indicate possible meat and/or hide preparation activities carried out inside the structure. One adzelike tool may have functioned as a scraper or possibly as a woodworking tool. It is notable that very few utilized flakes occurred in the lithic assemblage despite the presence of abundant flake debitage. It appears that the specific objective of core reduction was the production of scraper tools.

There were a variety of activities carried out inside the structure, including seed and nut preparation and perhaps storage, refuse disposal, hide and/or meat preparation, and lithic manufacturing. The absence of these activites outside of the structure, except for cooking, suggests that the structure comprised a self-contained work area and probably sleeping unit. This represents inferential evidence for a late fall/winter occupation, since it is more likely that a greater variety of activities would be carried out inside the primary habitation unit rather than outside during the winter months.

Structure Feature 1

Feature 1 was circular in plan, with an interior diameter averaging from 9.5 m to 10.0 m (Figure 46). The structure consisted of a primary ring of 27 posts, with an average spacing between the posts of 1.14 m (measured from center to center of each post). Excluding the western portion of the ring, where some posts could not be recovered due to erosion, the distance between posts along the outer ring averaged 94 cm (Plate 11).

In plan view, the interior floor comprised an area of ca. 71 m2. The interior area did not contain definable floor fill, although the soil was darkly stained. Interior features and posts were defined several centimeters below this staining, which were easily visible against the background of a yellowish brown, sandy silt subsoil. Erosion of a possible floor and associated floor midden may have occurred although lithic tools and chert debris recovered on the same surface as the defined postmolds and pits suggest that floor erosion was minimal.

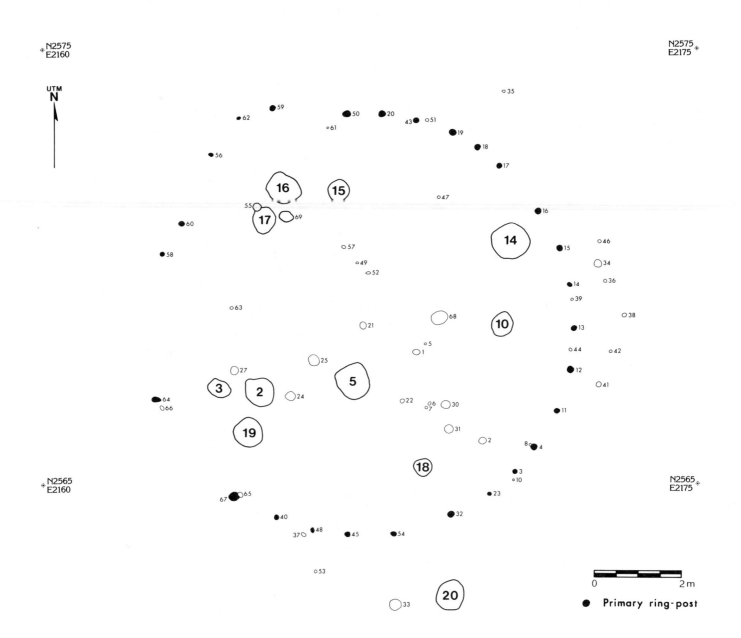

Figure 46. Middle Woodland Structure (Feature 1) and Associated Features

Plate 11. Feature 1, After Excavation: upper, view to the north with white plates marking excavated postmolds; lower, view to the south

The precise method of construction utilized to build this circular structure can only be conjectured. The structure was built directly onto a sterile sandy silt subsoil, which was more sandy in the western portion of the structure. The outer-ring posts were placed vertically and may have been bound together with horizontal posts, reeds, cord lashing, or a combination of these. Of course, only the bottom portions of the postmolds have been preserved, so it is difficult to know whether or not the posts were actually bent above their vertical placement.

Although the structure encompassed a relatively large area, the posts utilized in construction were not massive. In fact, the excavated postmolds were probably 30% to 50% larger than the original posts (Brose 1970:39; Fitting 1972:18). The structure, nevertheless, represented a relatively sturdy unit, and its construction was well planned. The evidence that exists in regard to its construction is ambiguous although some suggestions are presented below (Table 53).

One structural model consists of a circular arrangement of bent saplings bound together at the center to a center post whose function is not so much to provide actual support as to serve as a center guide for orienting the opposing saplings. This kind of structure has already been suggested in the archaeological literature (Faulkner and McCollough 1974). Although a central post is required for this kind of construction, interior support posts are not necessary. The central post in this type of construction need not be large, since stress is evenly distributed through the lashed, bent saplings.

Postmold 21 is interpreted as the central post of Feature 1. It may have served both as a support post for centrally lashed saplings and as an alignment guide for the placement of an outer ring of posts, as described above. However, it also functioned in this situation as an alignment post guiding the placement of several aligned pairs of internal support posts. The presence of these aligned, internal posts indicates that Feature 1 (described more completely below) was more elaborately constructed than suggested by the structural model proposed above.

Feature 1 contained a variety of internal posts (22), some of which may have functioned as partition posts, posts for hanging items, or posts utilized in hide processing. In addition, three paired posts, located in the northwestern (Postmolds 55 and 69), southwestern (Postmolds 27 and 72), and southeastern (Postmolds 31 and 2) sectors of the structure have been interpreted as interior post supports. They are related geometrically to the central post (Postmold 21). The relationship of this center post to these paired, internal posts and to the outer-ring posts is described below.

Table 53. Feature 1 Post Dimensions

Primary Ring Posts (N=27)

Postmold #	Diam.(cm)	Depth(cm)	Profile*	Base*
3	10.5	9.0	S	R
4	15.0	19.0	S	R
11	14.0	18.0	S	P
12	15.0	23.0	S	F
13	11.0	20.0	S	F
14	12.0	20.0	S	P
15	13.5	18.0	S	P
16	13.5	25.0	SL	R
17	12.5	22.0	S	R
18	13.5	20.0	SL	P
19	16.0	19.0	S	R
20	14.0	28.5	S	R
23	8.0	8.5	S	P
32	17.0	25.5	S	R
40	12.5	16.5	S	R
43	12.0	17.5	SL	R
45	12.0	25.0	S	R
48	15.5	18.5	S	R
50	18.0	23.5	S	R
54	12.0	17.0	S	R
56	12.0	8.0	SL	P
58	11.0	5.0	S	R
59	12.0	5.5	S	R
60	12.0	10.5	S	R
62	8.5	2.0	S	R
64	22.0	5.5	S	R
67	20.0	4.0	S	R
Mean	13.52	16.07		

Internal Posts (N=21)

Postmold #	Diam.(cm)	Depth(cm)	Profile*	Base*
1	14.0	10.0	S	R
2	17.0	8.0	S	R
5	6.0	11.5	SL	P
6	9.0	3.5	S	R
7	7.0	2.0	S	R
21	17.0	11.5	S	R
22	11.0	14.0	S	P
24	21.0	5.0	S	R
25	26.0	6.5	S	R
27	19.0	13.0	S	R
30	20.0	11.0	S	R
31	20.0	6.0	S	R
47	6.0	10.0	S	P
49	5.0	10.0	S	R
52	12.5	10.0	S	R
55	20.0	8.0	S	R
57	8.0	8.0	S	F
61	5.5	13.0	S	P
63	9.0	5.5	S	R
68	35.0	5.0	S	R
69	36.0	9.5	S	R
Mean	15.43	8.62		

Doorway Posts (N=6)

Postmold #	Diam.(cm)	Depth(cm)	Profile*	Base*
34	20.0	10.0	S	R
36	6.5	3.5	S	R
38	9.0	7.0	S	R
41	12.0	22.5	S	R
42	8.0	16.5	S	R
46	8.0	10.0	SL	F
Mean	10.58	11.58		

Secondary Wall Posts (N=7)

Postmold #	Diam.(cm)	Depth(cm)	Profile*	Base*
10	6.0	9.0	SL	F
37	10.0	12.5	S	F
39	5.0	6.0	S	P
44	8.0	11.0	S	F
51	8.0	12.5	S	P
65	13.0	5.5	S	R
66	7.0	10.5	S	R
Mean	8.14	8.07		

* S - straight, SL - slanted; R - rounded, F - flat, P - pointed

The central post in Feature 1, which measured 17 cm in diameter and 11.5 cm in depth, probably served as a reference guide for the placement of the outer ring posts, as well as for the internal-support posts. Such alignment posts have been recognized in Caddoan structures in the southern Plains where a temporary central post served as a guide for the even spacing of wall posts. When the structure was completed, the post was removed (Hoffman 1969:43). Although the structure from the Truck #7 site bears no relationship to Caddoan structural types, the principle of employing a center post for alignment is similar (Figure 47).

An arc initiated from the center post to the outer ring passes through virtually every post along the outer ring. The structure, therefore, represents a nearly perfect circle. In addition, many of the outer ring posts are aligned one to another through the center post (Figures 48 and 49). The east-west, outer ring post alignment could not be determined due to erosion of posts along the western arc. Complementary north-south outer ring posts include the following postmolds: Postmolds 20 and 45; Postmolds 43 and 48; Postmolds 32 and 59; Postmolds 19 and 40; Postmolds 17 and 67; Postmolds 15 and 64; and Postmolds 3 and 56. Since the spacing between these posts was not precise, the only way that they could have been perfectly opposed was through a central alignment point.

The interior support-post pairs were also aligned to the central post. An arc initiated at the central post passed through not only the interior-support posts furthest from the central post (e.g., Postmolds 2, 55, and 72) but also through those closest to the center post (e.g., Postmolds 27, 31, and 69) [Figure 48]. Only interior support Postmolds 2 and 55 fell along a line between two opposing outer ring posts. Hence, five posts fell along a single line extending from outer ring Postmold 56, through support-Postmold 55, through the center post, through support-Postmold 2, and to outer-ring Postmold 3. This alignment may represent one of the main structural support lines across the structure, linking the complementary outer-ring posts with complementary interior-support posts.

Another cross-structural alignment existed between outer-ring Postmold 64, inner-support Postmold 27, the center posts, and outer-ring Postmold 15. Internal support posts were not observed in the northeastern sector of the structure although the entire area was carefully shovel scraped several times. This northeast-southwest alignment differed somewhat from its intersecting northwest-southeast counterpart in that the inner-support Postmold 27 was part of the alignment. In the northwest-southeast line, the outer support posts (e.g., Postmolds 2 and 55) formed the alignment. The reason for this is unknown.

189

Figure 47. Partial Reconstruction of Feature 1 and Its Proposed Method
of Alignment from the Center Post

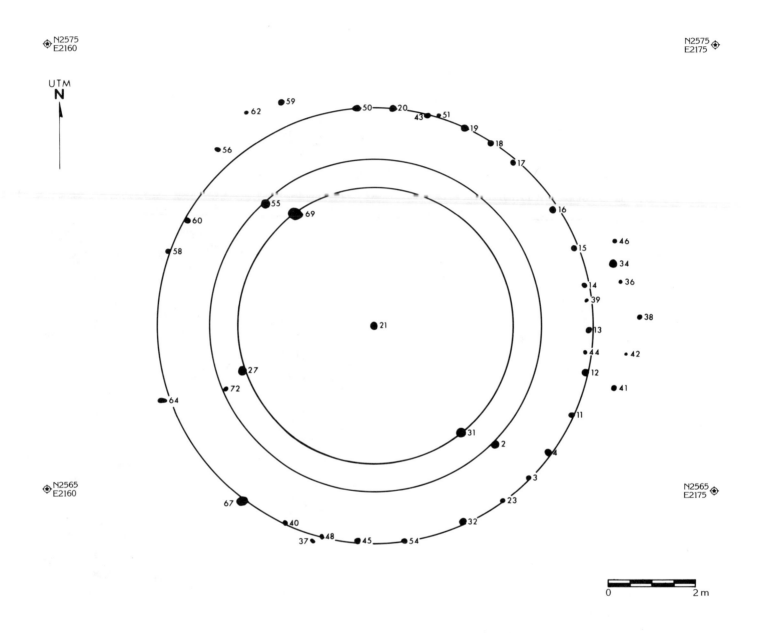

Figure 48. Concentric Alignment of Primary Wall Posts and Interior Support Posts of Feature 1, Utilizing the Center Post as the Midpoint

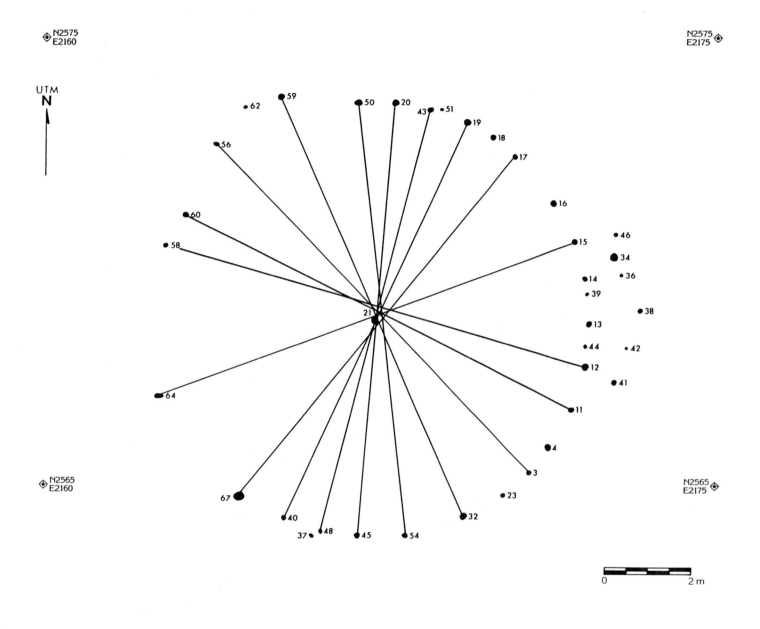

Figure 49. Opposition of Primary Wall Posts Through the Center Post (PM 21) of Feature 1

In each support-post pair, one post was slightly offset from the alignments mentioned above. Interior Postmolds 31, 69, and 72 were offset ca. 5 degrees from these alignments. The distance between the paired support posts in the southeastern and northwestern sectors was identical (i.e., 80 cm), while the distance between Postmolds 27 and 72 measured slightly less than 60 cm. The purpose of offsetting the internal support posts from the two intersecting cross-structural alignments is problematical.

There were no fallen beams inside the structure to suggest the precise arrangement or function of the roof or its relationship to the outer ring of posts comprising the wall. It is possible that because of the great size of the structure, internal supports were necessary to alleviate the stress accompanying a sapling bent nearly 5 m to the center post. A more reasonable alternative, however, is that this was not a bent sapling structure but one which consisted of some beams laid from the outer ring posts to the center of the structure, perhaps along the two major intersecting alignments. The beams probably extended from the outer ring posts to the center post with intervening support posts bracing the slanting roof beams. The beams may have been lashed or merely set within notches placed in the center support and/or ring posts. Hides, smaller branches, and, perhaps, reeds probably were utilized to fill the intervening roof and wall spaces. It is possible that a center post would not have been required once the beams were laid among the intervening support posts. The beams may have simply been lashed together at the center of this structure.

The selection of individual posts utilized in this structure was not random. The outer-ring posts differed significantly from the posts utilized in the interior of the structure. The mean diameters and depths of all interior and outer-ring posts were compared using Student's t-test for the comparison of means (Table 54) and a scattergram correlating the depths and diameters of these same posts (Figure 50). The postmold dimensions have been utilized for comparative purposes although it is realized that these dimensions are greater than the original post sizes.

The scattergram produced a distinct cluster of primary ring posts, while the interior post dimensions exhibited a broader range in postmold diameter. The postmold profiles were generally similar among the post classes, but the outer-ring postmolds were nearly twice as deep as the interior posts, while the interior postmolds were ca. twice as broad in diameter as the outer-ring posts.

These measurements indicate that the outer-ring posts were definitely a specialized post type different from the interior posts which exhibited a great deal of variability. The posts comprising the

193

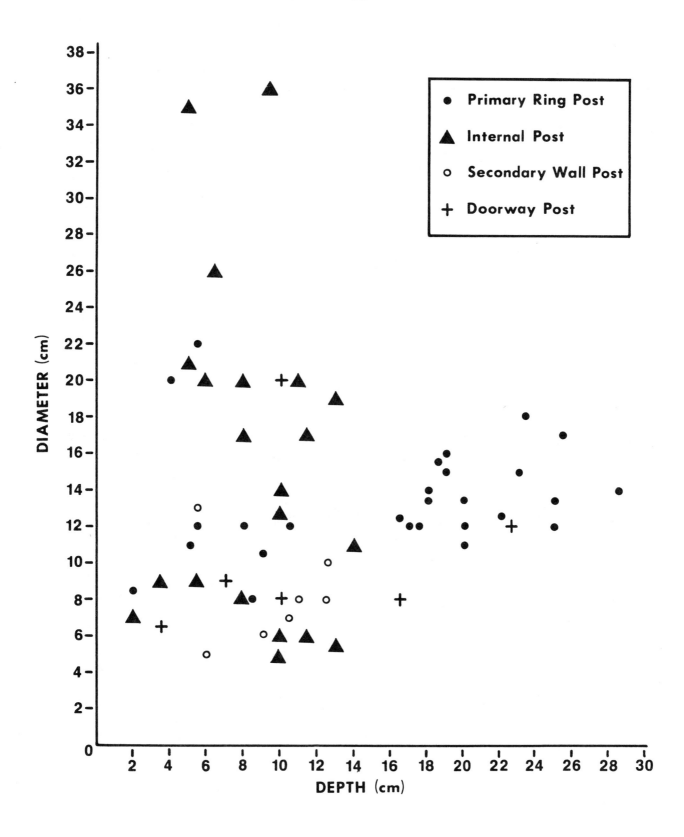

Figure 50. Comparative Scattergram of Various Post Type Diameters and Depths Associated with Feature 1

Table 54. Student's T-Test for Comparisons of Means of Ring and Interior Postmold Diameters and Depths in Feature 1

| | N | Mean Diameter (cm) | Standard Deviation | Standard Error | Pooled Variance Estimate | | |
					T Value	Degrees of Freedom	2-Tail Probability
Ring Postmolds	27	13.52	3.142	0.605			
					-1.02	46	0.314
Interior Postmolds	21	15.43	9.093	1.984			

| | N | Mean Depth (cm) | Standard Deviation | Standard Error | Pooled Variance stimate | | |
					T Value	Degrees of Freedom	2-Tail Probability
Ring Postmolds	27	16.07	7.65	1.489			
					4.18	46	0.000
Interior Postmolds	21	8.62	3.29	0.718			

Table 55. Cultural Material from Structure 1 Postmolds

| Postmold # | Chert | | | Ceramics | | | Other Material | | |
	Type	N	Wt(g)	Temper*	N	Wt(g)	Type	N	Wt(g)
12	Flake	6	3.2						
16	Piece	1	22.9						
17	Flake	1	0.5						
22	Flake	1	0.5				Burned Clay	2	2.9
25	Flake	1	0.5						
27	Flake	11	5.1	Grog	1	0.4			
30	Blade	10	13.8	Grog	1	2.2	Burned Clay	7	2.5
	Piece	1	2.6	LS/Grog	6	7.7			
32	Flake	2	88.0						
34	Piece	2	1.0						
	Flake	1	1.1						
37	Flake	1	0.6						
40	Flake	1	0.7						
41	Flake	6	2.6						
49	Flake	1	1.0						
50	Flake	1	0.6						
52	Flake	1	0.3						
	Piece	1	0.2						
54	Flake	1	0.3						
56	Flake	1	0.8						
69	Flake	12	4.4						
	Piece	1	20.6						

* LS indicates limestone.

outer ring were no doubt set deeper to alleviate the greater horizontal stress exerted on posts so widely spaced. The smaller dimensions of the outer posts situated along the western arc of the structure resulted from erosion. Although equal in elevation to the posts along the eastern arc, the soil in which the western arc was placed was sandier and probably more subject to erosion. Many of the postulated posts that did not materialize in this area had probably eroded away.

An arrangement of seven posts along the eastern exterior of the structure appears to represent a chambered area attached to the eastern wall. This attached area may have served as a covered entrance into the structure. No cultural materials were found in this chamber. The northernmost post in this arrangement was only 10 cm deep, but it was slanted in toward the primary ring. It probably represented a bent sapling, possibly attached to ring Postmold 15. The other posts were placed vertically. The two southernmost posts were relatively deep (Postmold 41: 22.5 cm, Postmold 42: 16.5 cm) and must have anchored the chambered entrance. Postmolds 36 and 38, situated in the center of the post pattern, were very shallow (3.5 cm and 7.0 cm deep) and small.

Directly adjacent to the doorway were two small postmolds (Postmolds 39 and 44), which occurred between Postmolds 12 and 13 and Postmolds 13 and 14, respectively, along the outer ring. These postmolds represented the only secondary posts positioned between posts of the primary ring. It is suggested that this was not coincidental but related to the proposed entrance way, these posts perhaps serving as doorway markers or small stakes buttressing the doorway in some manner.

A number of small postmolds were recognized along the outer ring, including Postmolds 10, 37, 51, 65, and 66. These small postmolds appeared to be associated with a single ring post and may have served to secondarily support, through lashing, the primary ring posts (Marshall 1969:168). Of interest were postmolds 37 and 51, which were associated with ring Postmolds 43 and 48. Postmolds 43 and 48 were aligned through center Postmold 21. Postmolds 37 and 51 were also aligned through the center post, and their post orientations were vertical. Postmold 51 was placed just east of the ring-centered post alignment, while Postmold 37 was placed west of the same alignment. The interior, paired, support posts were also aligned and offset in the same manner, so that the stake placement near the outer-ring posts (Postmolds 43 and 48) was probably not coincidental, but related in some way to support and/or strengthening of the outer ring posts (Figure 51).

Features 3 and 17 exhibited the only evidence of superpositioning in the structure. Neither feature, initially interpreted as a pit, contained significant amounts of cultural or faunal/floral remains. Both features were superimposed by one of the main, paired, support

196

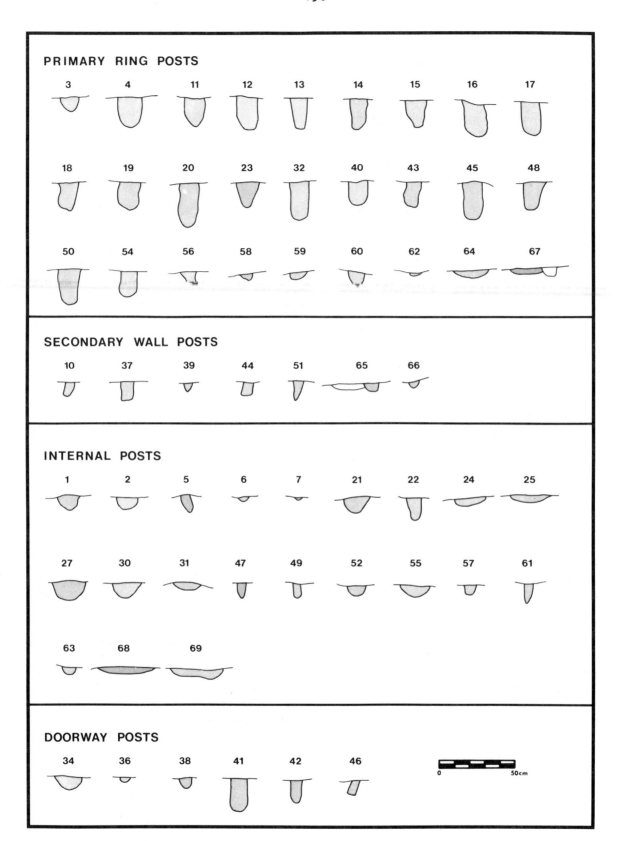

Figure 51. Feature 1 Postmold Profiles

posts. It is possible that these shallow-basin features were actually related to the placement of support Postmolds 55 and 72; hence, an alternative interpretation of these features as shallow, postpit depressions is also suggested.

The structure contained neither a hearth nor evidence of a central fireplace or cooking area. The presence of fired-soil zones several meters east of the structure indicates that hearths were probably established outside of the shelter. Nevertheless, the structure apparently was either accidentally or purposely destroyed by fire. Interior Postmolds 31 and 68 were obviously burned as evidenced by dark gray staining and large fragments of carbonized oak in both. A radiocarbon determination of 160 $\pm$ 75 A.C. was made from Postmold 31. In addition, many of the internal and outer-ring posts contained charcoal flecks indicating that they were also burned. A small amount of cultural material was recovered from eighteen of the postmold fills (Table 55).

The central post (Postmold 21) was also burned, although only a few flecks of charcoal were recovered in its fill. However, at the base of the postmold stain, an oxidized, orangish soil was observed. Similar soil oxidation, which is attributed to rather intensive burning, was not observed in any postmold inside the structure. It is possible that the fire that eventually burned the structure also destroyed the center post. The saplings or beams bound to this center support post may have prevented the center post from immediately collapsing and, for this reason, it was more intensely burned. Another explanation, following the Caddoan example, was that the center post was removed by burning after it had served its function as a construction guide, in which case the center post probably did not function as a support post in the structure but, rather, only as an orientation post utilized to establish construction alignment for support and wall posts.

Internal Pit Features

Excluding Features 3 and 17, which were interpreted as shallow post pits, there were eight pit features identified within the structure. These features consisted of refuse and processing pits, although some may have functioned as storage pits as well. All of the pits, with the exception of Feature 5, were situated on the periphery of the interior floor (Table 56; Figure 52).

Features 14 and 19 were relatively deep and contained the greatest variety of cultural materials. Features 12 and 18 were slightly belled

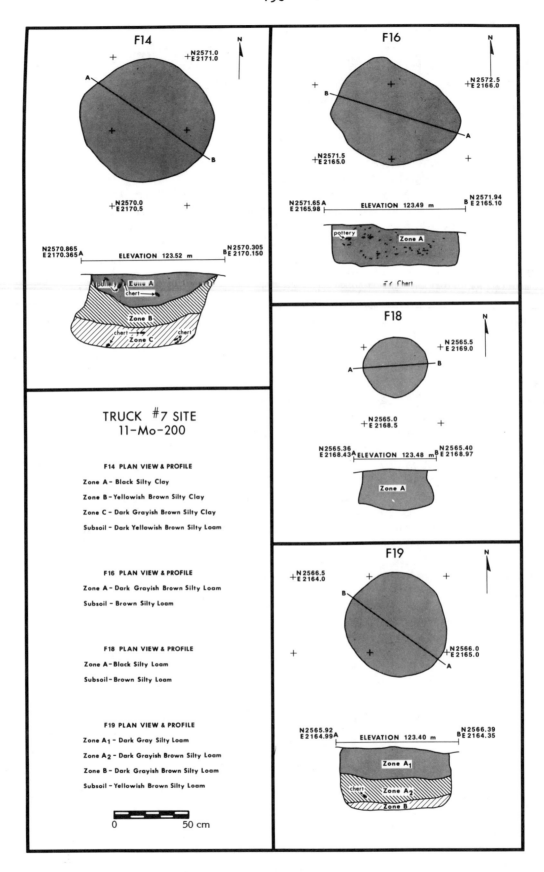

Figure 52. Plan and Profile Views of Pits found within Feature 1

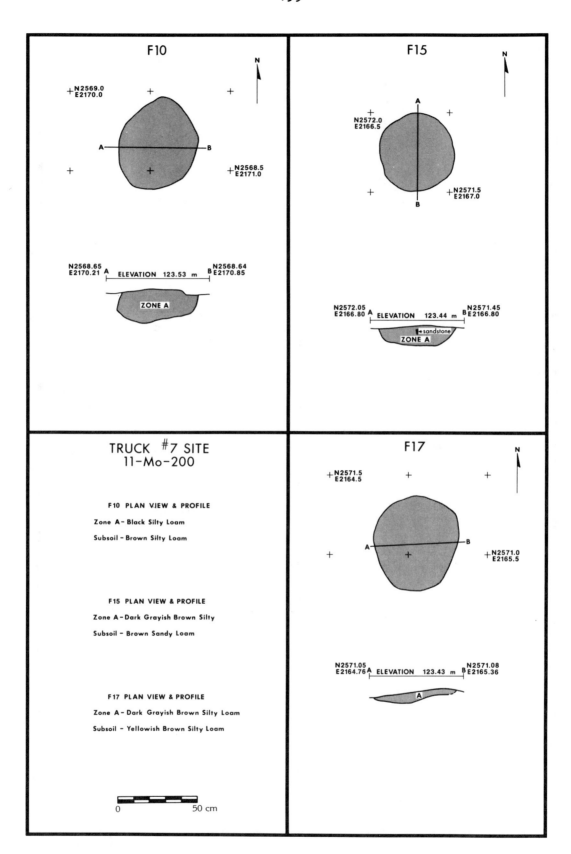

F10

N

+N2569.0
E2170.0
+

+

A━━━━━━━━B

+

+N2568.5
E2171.0

N2568.65
E2170.21 A ELEVATION 123.53 m B N2568.64
E2170.85

ZONE A

F15

N

+N2572.0
E2166.5

+

A

B

+

+N2571.5
E2167.0

N2572.05
E2166.80 A ELEVATION 123.44 m B N2571.45
E2166.80

←sandstone
ZONE A

TRUCK #7 SITE
11-Mo-200

F10 PLAN VIEW & PROFILE

Zone A - Black Silty Loam

Subsoil - Brown Silty Loam

F15 PLAN VIEW & PROFILE

Zone A - Dark Grayish Brown Silty

Subsoil - Brown Sandy Loam

F17 PLAN VIEW & PROFILE

Zone A - Dark Grayish Brown Silty Loam

Subsoil - Yellowish Brown Silty Loam

0   50 cm

F17

N

+N2571.5
E2164.5

+

+

A━━━━━━━━B

+

+N2571.0
E2165.5

N2571.05
E2164.76 A ELEVATION 123.43 m B N2571.08
E2165.36

A

Figure 52. continued

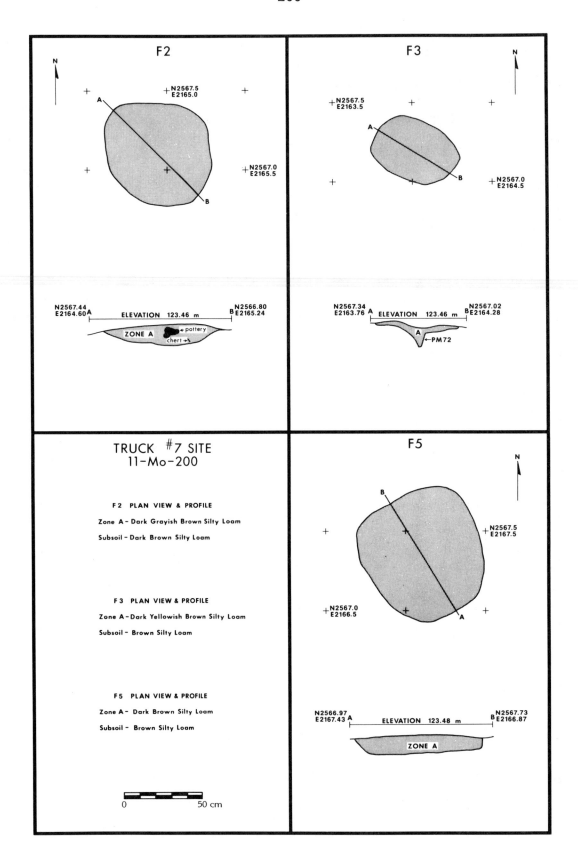

Figure 52. continued

Table 56. Feature Attributes

Feature	Plan Shape	Plan Dimensions (cm)	Maximum Depth (cm)	Elevation Range (mamsl)	Profile Shape
2*	Oval	76 X 66	14.5	123.43-123.29	Regular basin
3*	Oval	52 X 38	8.0	123.40-123.32	Irregular basin
4	Oval	53 X 47	15.5	123.28-123.13	Regular basin
5*	Circular	85 X 78	13.0	123.42-123.29	Irregular basin
6	Circular	87 X 80	18.0	123.28-123.10	Regular basin
7	Circular	82 X 75	16.5	123.34-123.17	Regular basin
8	Circular	72 X 70	19.5	123.37-123.17	Regular basin
9	Circular	44 X 41	15.0	123.27-123.12	Regular basin
10*	Oval	57 X 48	22.0	123.47-123.25	Irregular basin
11	Circular	74 X 70	40.5	123.29-122.89	Irregular basin
12	Oval	99 X 51	14.5	123.32-123.18	Regular basin
14*	Circular	88 X 82	50.0	123.45-122.95	Irregular basin
15*	Circular	48 X 48	14.5	123.43-123.28	Regular basin
16*	Oval	82 X 65	27.5	123.40-123.12	Straight-sided, Flat-bottomed
17*	Oval	61 X 52	11.0	123.36-123.25	Irregular basin
18*	Circular	42 X 40	30.0	123.43-123.13	Belled
19*	Circular	69 X 66	46.0	123.38-122.92	Straight-sided, Flat-bottomed
20	Oval	71 X 60	19.0	123.40-123.21	Regular basin
21	Oval	95 X 51	18.5	123.31-123.12	Regular basin

*Indicates features within Feature 1.

to one side. Feature 16 represents a depository for lithic debitage. The variety of flake types and the hammerstones recovered, and the general absence of other kinds of material suggest that core reduction and thinning were accomplished directly over this pit. The lithic debitage in this pit was so dense that the excavator found it difficult to prepare an even-profile wall. Nearly 3000 small thinning/shatter chert flakes were recovered from the flotation samples taken from this pit. Another 2000 items were recovered during the hand excavation (troweling) of this pit.

Feature 5 was the only feature to occur within the central area of the structure. The boundaries of this shallow depression were extremely diffuse, and only a small amount of cultural material was recovered. No wood, nuts, or seeds were found. The function of Feature 5 is problematic, although it may have been used for the processing of foods.

Feature 15 contained very little cultural material, but yielded the second highest amount of seeds of any feature in the structure, with Feature 10 yielding the most seeds. These pits probably represent seed processing or preparation pits.

There was a general tendency for the pits inside the structure to be paired. These pairs included Features 15 and 16 in the northwestern corner; Features 10 and 14 in the western sector; and Features 2 and 19 in the southwestern corner. Features 5 and 18 were isolated. There was no particular functional pattern to this distribution except that the lithic debitage pit (Feature 16) and seed preparation pit (Feature 15) in the northwestern corner occurred together, while the pits with more general refuse were paired in opposite quadrants of the structure. With the exception of Features 10 and 14, pits were located near the main support posts. The reason for this is unknown.

Preservation of faunal material was poor in these pit fills due to the high acidity of the soil and general scarcity of limestone in the fills. Ethnobotanical remains, however, were well preserved. Compared to the pits outside of the structure, nuts and seeds occurred in relatively high proportions to wood charcoal in pits inside the structure. Pits outside of the structure generally contained higher proportions of wood charcoal to nuts and seeds. This differential distribution of ethnobotanical remains may indicate that food processing and possibly storage occurred within, and not outside, the structure, as would be expected for a winter structure.

Feature 2

Feature 2 was a shallow (14.0 cm), basin-shaped pit located in the southwestern portion of the structure (Feature 1). The dark grayish brown, silty loam fill contained occasional small pieces of charcoal and some burned clay (58.6 g). Thirty-eight chert flakes with cortex (182.3 g) and 60 reduction percussion flakes (35.0 g) were recovered. The chert types present were Ste. Genevieve purple, Ste. Genevieve Red, and Salem Creamy, with a few Burlington Glossy and Burlington White Local flakes. One piece of rough rock (0.7 g) and 0.4 g of unidentifiable bone were also recovered. Fifty-four grog-tempered body sherds (119.9 g) were recovered from Feature 2. Feature 2 was probably used as a refuse and/or processing pit (Figure 52).

Feature 3

Feature 3 was a shallow (16.0 cm), irregularly-shaped pit located in the southwestern portion of the structure. One of the paired, internal support posts was identified in this pit; however, the postmold fill was not distinguishable from that of the pit. Feature 3 may, in fact, be a disturbance which occurred while the post was originally dug, with subsequent filling of debris from the structure floor. The dark yellowish-brown, silty loam fill contained some charcoal and burned bone (0.4 g). A total of 19 chert flakes with cortex (58.1 g), 34 reduction percussion flakes (11.7 g) and 33 thinning/shatter flakes (0.7 g) were recovered. The chert types included Ste. Genevieve Purple, Ste. Genevieve Red, and Salem Creamy and small amounts of Burlington Glossy and Burlington White Local flakes. Four grog-tempered body sherds (3.3 g) were recovered (Figure 52).

Feature 5

Feature 5 was a shallow (13.0 cm), basin-shaped pit located near the center of the structure. The dark brown, silty loam fill contained a few small pieces of oxidized burned soil. A total of four chert flakes with cortex (1.6 g) and six reduction percussion flakes (2.1 g) were recovered. The chert types present were Ste. Genevieve Purple, Ste. Genevieve Red, and Burlington White Local. Two pieces of sandstone (3.4 g) were also found. No ceramics were recovered from this feature. The function of Feature 5 is unknown (Figure 52).

Feature 10

Feature 10 was a shallow (22.0 cm), irregularly-sided, round-bottomed pit located in the eastern portion of the structure. Its black, silty loam fill contained some charcoal and burned clay (58.4 g). A total of 106 chert flakes with cortex (156.7 g), 254 reduction percussion flakes (66.9 g), 313 thinning/shatter flakes (3.9 g) and 14 block-fractured chert flakes (16.3 g) were recovered. The chert types included Ste. Genevieve Purple, Ste. Genevieve Red, and Salem Creamy, and small amounts of Burlington White Local flakes. Other material included two pieces of sandstone (33.4 g), five pieces of limonite (3.6 g) and one piece of daub (5.9 g). Two hundred forty-one mammal teeth fragments were recovered, probably deer, half of them being burned; 1.3 g of unidentifiable burned bone were also found. Thirteen grog-tempered body sherds (56.7 g) were recovered from Feature 10. A noded sherd from this feature was found to fit together with a similar noded sherd from Feature 18 (Figure 52).

Feature 10 contained the highest mean average of nuts and seeds of any pit feature at the site. This feature is interpreted as a processing and refuse pit contemporaneous with Feature 18.

Feature 14

Feature 14 was a bell-shaped round-bottomed pit of medium depth (50.0 cm) located in the northeastern portion of the structure. It was the deepest pit excavated at Truck #7 and contained three well-defined zones. Cultural material was recovered from all three zones (Zones A-C). The upper A zone contained mostly chert debris; Zone B contained the least amount of material, although it was the deepest zone; and Zone C contained the majority of the pottery, bone, and chert tools. A relatively large piece of unworked galena (50.7 g) originated from Zone C.

Zone C represents a refuse fill zone which apparently was burned subsequent to filling. The Zone B fill over this was secondarily deposited, perhaps to cover the original refuse fill. Cultural materials, as well as faunal and ethnobotanical remains, were present in Zone B, but occurred much less abundantly than in Zones A or C. Zone A represents a final refuse zone consisting primarily of lithic debris.

A total of 924 chert flakes with cortex (1076.3 g), 1179 reduction percussion flakes (431.2 g), 1855 thinning/shatter flakes (31.6 g) and 43 block fractures (685.2 g) were recovered from Feature 14. The chert types were predominantly Ste. Genevieve Purple and Red, with moderate amounts of Burlington White Local and Salem Creamy, as well as 2 Dongola and 2 Burlington Glossy flakes. In addition, 14 pieces of sandstone (202.6 g), 6 pieces of rough rock (508.1 g) and 185 pieces of bone (2.4 g) were recovered. The bone included 61 mammal (probably deer) teeth, 2 fish vertebrae and 3 unidentifiable fish elements, 1 unidentifiable snake vertebra, and small bone flecks. Several chert tools were recovered, including 6 retouched flakes (27.7 g), 2 biface fragments (9.9 g), 1 flake scraper (22.4 g) and 1 scraper made from a primary decortication flake (73.9 g).

Forty-seven sherds were recovered, with a total weight of 193.2 g. Two rims, one cross-hatched/plain and one cross-hatched/punctated, were included in the ceramic material from Feature 14. All of the sherds were grog and grog/limestone-tempered.

Feature 14 is interpreted as a refuse pit with at least two and possibly three filling episodes. It is possible that with its bell-shaped base, Feature 14 initially functioned as a storage pit; however, the evidence suggests that its primary function was for general refuse disposal (Figure 52).

Feature 15

Feature 15 was a shallow (14.5 cm), basin-shaped pit located in the northern portion of the structure. The dark grayish-brown, silty loam fill contained a fair amount of charcoal and a small amount of burned clay. A total of 18 chert flakes with cortex (21.6 g), 41 reduction percussion flakes (20.6 g), 2 thinning/shatter flakes (0.1 g), and 1 block fracture (0.6 g) were recovered. The chert types represented were Ste. Genevieve Purple, Ste. Genevieve Red, Salem Creamy, and Burlington White Local. In addition, 2 pieces of sandstone (209.7 g) and 5 unidentifiable bone fragments (0.1 g) were found. Only 1 sherd (0.9 g) was recovered. Feature 15 contained the second highest mean average of seeds at the site and may have been used for seed processing and/or refuse disposal (Figure 52).

Feature 16

Feature 16 was a basin-shaped pit of medium depth (27.5 cm), located in the northwestern portion of the structure. Its dark grayish-brown, silty loam fill contained some charcoal and burned clay (20.8 g). A total of 959 chert flakes with cortex (1617.8 g), 1938 reduction percussion flakes (780.2 g), 3359 thinning/shatter flakes (44.8 g), and 50 block fractures (573.6 g) were recovered. The majority of flakes were of the Ste. Genevieve Purple variety with moderate amounts of Ste. Genevieve Red, Salem Creamy, and Burlington White Local; one Dongola flake was also recovered. In addition, 9 pieces of sandstone (747.5 g), 5 mammal (deer) teeth fragments, 43 small unidentifiable bone fragments (2.8 g), 2 hammerstones (383.6 g), 1 grinding stone (520.8 g), 2 waterworn pebbles (0.7 g), and 10 pieces of red-stained clay (10.5 g) were found. Several chert tools were recovered, including 3 retouched flakes (17.7 g), 1 scraper (61.1 g), 1 preform (30.6 g), 1 denticulate (28.1 g), and 1 core (52.5 g). Feature 16 contained 53 body sherds, with a total weight of 255.6 g. The great quantity of lithic materials recovered from Feature 16, consisting of 3016 g of chert, 2 hammerstones, 1 preform, and the complete range of chert flake reduction types mentioned above, suggests that the pit functioned primarily as a container for processed chert which resulted from tool manufacturing activities (Plate 12). Feature 16 also functioned as a small refuse pit as evinced by the presence of other cultural materials (Figure 52).

Feature 17

Feature 17 was a shallow (11.0 cm), basin-shaped pit located in the northwestern portion of the structure. The dark grayish-brown, silty loam fill contained small amounts of charcoal. A total of 10 chert flakes with cortex (11.4 g), 18 reduction percussion flakes (3.5 g), and 74 thinning/shatter flakes (0.7 g) were recovered. Ste. Genevieve Purple and Red were the predominant chert types, although Salem Creamy and Burlington White Local were also represented. One piece of sandstone (3.0 g) was also found, but no ceramics were recovered. Postmold 55, one of the paired internal support posts, was superimposed on the northwest corner of Feature 17. This feature may have been similar to Feature 3 in its association with postmold excavation and secondary refuse disposal (Figure 52).

Feature 16
11– Mo – 200

0   5   10 cm

Plate 12. Lithics Recovered from Feature 16

Feature 18

Feature 18 was a bell-shaped pit of medium depth (20.0 cm), located in the southeastern portion of the structure. The black, silty loam fill contained some charcoal and burned clay (4.4 g). A total of 55 chert flakes with cortex (154.2 g), 194 reduction percussion flakes (57.2 g), 532 thinning/shatter flakes (7.7 g), and 7 block fractures (6.1 g) were recovered. Salem Creamy and Ste. Genevieve Red were the predominant chert types, with a moderate amount of Ste. Genevieve Purple and some Burlington White Local present. In addition, 3 pieces of sandstone (14.3 g) and a discoidal scraper (41.9 g) made from Ste. Genevieve Red chert were found. Feature 18 contained 49 mammal (deer) teeth, as well as 10 deciduous deer incisor fragments that were positively identified. Two hundred thirty-one small, unidentifiable bone fragments (4.1 g) were also recovered. A total of 27 grog-tempered sherds weighing 236.7 g, were identified, including 3 rims. There was a ceramic match between Feature 10 and Feature 18. Feature 18 contained the second highest mean average of nuts and seeds from the site, which, along with its belled shape, indicates a possible processing and storage pit for food with a secondary refuse disposal function (Figure 52).

Feature 19

Feature 19 was a straight-sided, flat-bottomed pit of medium depth (46.0 cm), located in the southwestern portion of the structure. It was situated immediately adjacent to pit Features 2 and 3. Its dark gray, silty loam fill matrix contained a slight amount of charcoal and burned clay (37.7 g). A total of 169 chert flakes with cortex (356.8 g), 346 reduction percussion flakes (282.8 g), 59 thinning/shatter flakes (0.8 g), and 23 block fractures (554.4 g) were recovered.

Other remains included 3 pieces of quartzite (5.7 g); 1 ground, smoothed, sandstone metate fragment (198.8 g); 25 pieces of ochre-stained clay (111.5 g); 1 retouched flake (9.8 g); and 71 small, unidentifiable bone fragments (3.0 g), 61 of which were burned. Eighty-three grog or grog/limestone-tempered body sherds (396.2 g) with plain and dentate rocker stamped, brushed (Baehr) and cordmarked decorations were recovered. One large, plain, rocker-stamped sherd was recovered that contained two drilled holes.

A possible fired-clay figurine fragment, weighing 5.3 g, was also recovered from Feature 19. The fragment represented a possible head portion of a figurine. It consisted of a pinched head with a long burnished nose bridge and a single incised eye slit on the left side of the face. The back of this fragment contained a vertical, hollow channel, as if a small dowel had been utilized, perhaps to connect the head with the upper torso. Unfortunately, the fragment was too small to reveal other features, or to be positively identified as a human figure. The fragment was 3.9 cm long and ca. 1.6 cm wide. Its side-to-side thickness measured 1.7 cm. The fragment was fired, and it appeared to be tempered with finely crushed grog.

Feature 19 is interpreted as a refuse pit, but it may also have functioned as a storage pit. The pit contained ca. equal but minimal quantities of burned nuts, seeds, and wood. The pit contained three zones, the upper two of which were clearly delineated from the lower zone. Virtually all of the recovered material originated from the upper two zones, which both exhibited signs of burning. Much of the chert from the upper zones had been burned, especially the Ste. Genevieve Red variety, which exhibited multiple potlid fractures on many of the flakes. The chert was probably burned unintentionally as a result of a general refuse fire. Charcoal was particularly common in the uppermost zone (Figure 52).

Pits External to the Structure

Feature 4

Feature 4 was a shallow (15.5 cm), basin-shaped pit located in the southwestern corner of the site near Feature 9. Its dark brown, silty loam fill contained a small amount of charcoal. No material was recovered from this feature. This feature is interpreted as a processing and/or cooking pit (Figure 53).

Feature 6

Feature 6 was a shallow (18.0 cm), basin-shaped pit located adjacent to Feature 12 in the eastern portion of the site. Its dark grayish-brown, silty clay fill was divided into two zones, both containing charcoal. The lower, "B", zone had a heavy amount of burned (oxidized and reduced) soil. A total of 32 chert flakes with cortex (42.8 g), 29 reduction percussion flakes (29.4 g), and 3 chert block fractures (1.7 g) were recovered. The chert types present were mainly Ste. Genevieve Purple and Red with small amounts of Salem Creamy and Burlington White Local flakes also present. Other materials present included 3 pieces of sandstone (115.2 g), burned clay (9.1 g), 8 pieces of daub (6.3 g), and 0.7 g of unidentifiable burned bone. Twelve grog-tempered, plain rocker-stamped sherds (199.7 g) were found. The sherds from Feature 6 fit with a similar sherd from the adjacent

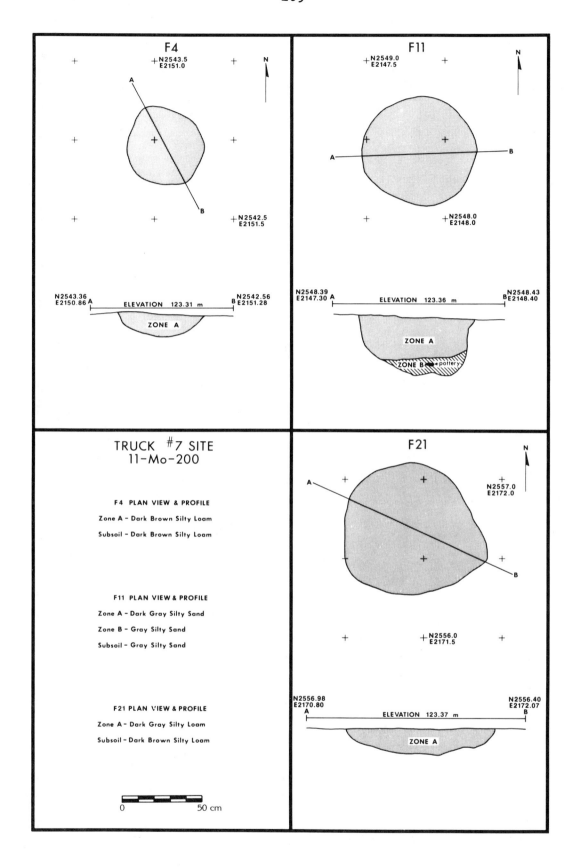

Figure 53. Plan and Profile Views of Pits found outside Feature 1

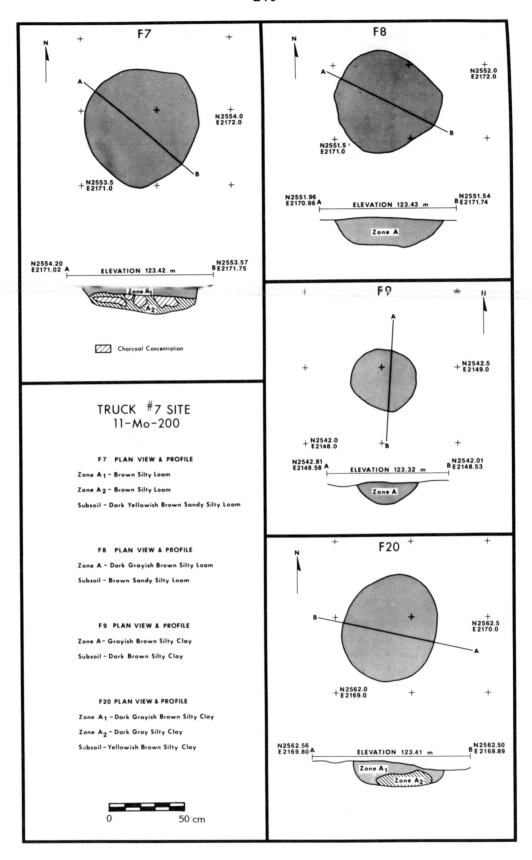

Figure 53. continued

Feature 12, and, therefore, the pits may have been coeval. The function of this pit may have been for refuse disposal (Figure 54).

Feature 7

Feature 7 was a shallow (16.5 cm), basin-shaped pit located in the south-central portion of the site. The pit contained two zones, the lowermost of which contained three major charcoal concentrations, demonstrating burning within the fill. The only material present consisted of three pieces of fired sandstone (3.7 g). The highest mean average of wood charcoal retrieved from pits at Truck #7 was recovered from Feature 7. On this basis, this feature is interpreted as a cooking and/or processing pit (Figure 53).

Feature 8

Feature 8 was a shallow (19.5 cm), basin-shaped pit located in the south central portion of the site. Its dark grayish-brown, silty loam fill contained moderate amounts of charcoal and burned clay. No other material was recovered from this feature. Feature 8 was similar in function to Feature 7, i.e., a cooking and/or processing pit (Figure 53).

Feature 9

Feature 9 was a shallow (15.0 cm) basin located in the southwestern corner of the site near Feature 4. The fill was a dark grayish-brown, silty clay. Feature 9 contained no material, and its function is indeterminate (Figure 53).

Feature 12

Feature 12 was a shallow (14.5 cm) basin located in the eastern portion of the site adjacent to Feature 6. Its dark grayish-brown, silty clay fill contained moderate amounts of charcoal and small amounts of burned clay. Twelve chert flakes with cortex (51.1 g) and 16 reduction percussion flakes (10.8 g) were recovered. The chert types represented were Ste. Genevieve Purple, Ste. Genevieve Red, and Salem Creamy. In addition, 97 pieces of unidentifiable bone (4.4 g) and 3 grog-tempered, plain rocked sherds (24.6 g) were found. The sherds from Feature 12 fit with sherds from Feature 6, implying that the two pits were coeval. This pit is interpreted as having a processing or refuse disposal function (Figure 54).

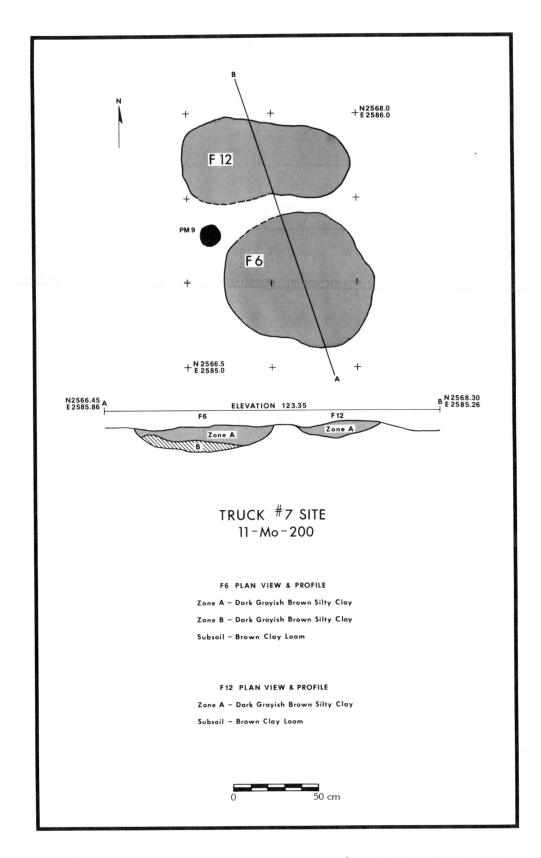

Figure 54. Plan and Profiles of Features 6 and 12 and Plan View of Postmold 9

Feature 20

Feature 20 was a shallow (19.0 cm), basin-shaped pit located only 1.5 m south of the structure. Two zones were recognized. Initially, this feature was recognized during shovel scraping adjacent to the structure. It was observed as a large, black stain abundant with burned clay and charcoal flecks on the surface. A single, Marion Thick sherd (7.8 g), subsequently broken into three pieces, was found directly on top of the feature. Excavation of this feature, however, failed to produce a single cultural item. A decomposed organic zone (dark gray, silty clay, 10YR 3/1) lay at the base of this feature. No seed, nut, or wood material, however, was identified from this pit, probably due to poor preservation.

The function of Feature 20 is problematical, although it is believed to have been associated with the Middle Woodland occupation at the Truck #7 site due to its proximity to the structure. A large post (Postmold 33), 27 cm in diameter and 10 cm in depth, was located near this feature and may be related to it. The post and pit may represent a specialized processing area. Isolated posts were also found near Features 6 and 12, and also near Feature 8, which was outside of the structure. It is suggested that the isolated, Marion Thick sherd was intrusive (Figure 53).

Feature 21

Feature 21 was a shallow (18.5 cm), basin-shaped pit located in the south-central portion of the site. Its dark gray, silty loam fill contained heavy amounts of charcoal and some burned clay (0.8 g). The only material recovered consisted of three pieces of silicified sediment (1.9 g). Another pit (Feature 13) was originally mapped adjacent to Feature 21, but that pit was later determined to be a stain. Feature 21 was possibly a processing and/or cooking pit (Figure 53).

Non-structural Postmolds

Eight postmolds occurred at the site which were not associated with the structure. They were located to the south and east of the structure (except for Postmold 35, which was 1 m north of the structure), all within a 20 m radius of the central post of Feature 1. Postmold 9 was located adjacent to Features 6 and 12, and may have been associated with them. These external, isolated posts were probably used for various processing activites at the site such as hide stretching or food drying (Table 57).

Table 57. Nonstructural Postmold Attributes

Postmold #	Diameter (cm)	Depth (cm)	Profile Shape+ Side	Bottom	UTM Location
9	12.0	20.5	S	R	E2185.08-2185.20, N2567.22-2567.34
26*	16.0	6.0	S	R	E2167.94-2168.10, N2551.15-2551.31
28	17.5	5.5	S	R	E2176.42-2176.56, N2569.76-2569.89
29	22.0	9.5	S	R	E2170.00-2170.28, N2550.84 2551.09
33	27.0	10.0	S	R	E2167.97-2168.23, N2562.07-2562.32
35	7.5	24.5	SL	R	E2170.56-2170.63, N2573.99-2574.06
53	9.0	13.0	S	F	E2166.20-2166.28, N2562.92-2563.01
70	16.0	11.5	S	R	E2177.99-2178.16, N2568.61-2568.77

+ Profile Shapes: S = straight; SL = slanted; R = round; F = flat

* Postmold 26 was originally found in the 1977 testing of the site and was then
called "Feature 1", but was later assigned a postmold number in 1978.

Table 58. Surficial Fired Areas

Feature	Length (cm)	Width (cm)	UTM Location
22	124	100	E2184.09-2185.23, N2573.84-2574.99
23	69	64	E2185.66-2186.31, N2573.27-2573.96
24	89	72	E2184.21-2185.10, N2572.54-2573.26
25	44	41	E2189.87-2190.28, N2577.34-2577.77

215

Fire-stained Areas

In the eastern portion of the site, ca. 10 m from the structure, there was a large area of diffuse burning. Four "features" were mapped and excavated within this area and eventually designated as fire-stained areas. These areas contained concentrated patches of charcoal, burned clay, and burned soil, had no definite shape either horizontally or vertically, and contained no artifacts. It would appear that this area was used as a large, open hearth or hearths, purposely set away from the living area of the site to lessen the chance of igniting the structure (Table 58).

Non-Middle Woodland Pit

Feature 11

Feature 11 was an irregular, basin-shaped pit of medium depth (40.5 cm), located ca. 25 m southwest of the Middle Woodland, circular structure. This is a multizoned pit, with an upper, loosely packed, gray, silty sand fill, 30 cm thick, and a lower, compacted, gray silty sand fill with evidence of burning. Both zones contained cultural material. A total of three flakes with partial cortex (9.0 g), nine reduction percussion flakes (4.0 g), and four block fracture chert pieces (2.5 g) were retrieved. The chert types included Ste. Genevieve Red and Purple varieties, Salem Creamy, and Burlington White Local and Glossy. In addition, three pieces of sandstone (144.8 g), four pieces of limestone (365.7 g), one biface fragment (8.1 g), and nine pieces of silicified sediment (4.3 g) were found.

Feature 11 contained the only Mississippian ceramic material recovered from a feature context at the Truck #7 site. These remains included nine shell-tempered (5.9 g), plain body sherds and eight limestone-tempered (8.6 g), plain body sherds. The shell-tempered and limestone-tempered pottery occurred only in the lower burned zone. In addition, three grog-tempered (1.5 g), plain body fragments were identified. The grog-tempered sherds could not be associated definitely with the Mississippian component and may represent intrusive Middle Woodland ceramics from the nearby Middle Woodland occupation. In that regard, the chert types found in this pit were identical to those types recovered in the Middle Woodland assemblage. These were also probably intrusive to the pit, which was heavily disturbed by rodent activity.

Feature 11 was the only pit at the Truck #7 site that contained maize remains. Carbonized kernels, cupules, and glumes were recovered from both zones, although they were more frequent in the lower burned zone. Feature 11 is interpreted as a cooking and/or maize processing pit associated with a Mississippian component (probably Lohmann phase). This component is probably located in the immediate vicinity but outside of the right-of-way limits (Figure 53).

CERAMIC ASSEMBLAGE

The ceramic materials recovered from the Truck #7 and Go-Kart South sites included types associated with the Early Woodland, Middle Woodland, Late Woodland, and Mississippian periods. The occupation at the Truck #7 site was characterized by the presence of decorated Middle Woodland sherds in feature contexts and by occasional, isolated occurrences of Early Woodland Marion Thick ceramics. Feature 11 contained plain, shell-tempered and limestone-tempered Mississippian body sherds, as well as three grog-tempered, plain sherds which may be associated with the Middle Woodland component. At the Go-Kart South site, the ceramics consisted of Early Woodland, Late Woodland, and Mississippian varieties. The latter varieties were recovered only in the alluvial overburden covering the inner channel ridge and inner channel scar east of the ridge.

The ceramics recovered from the previous surface collections and testing activities at these sites have already been reported (Kelly et al. 1979; Bareis et al. 1977). This section presents only those ceramics recovered by archaeological investigations during 1978-1979.

Truck #7 Site

The ceramic assemblage from the Truck #7 site represents the first excavated ceramic assemblage from the Hill Lake phase of the Middle Woodland period in the American Bottom. Although ceramic materials from this period had been observed in this area, the decorative varieties which typify this period had never been found associated together in feature contexts.

While the Truck #7 assemblage is unique in the American Bottom, it is similar to the Pike-Hopewell assemblages known from the classic Havana/Hopewell period in the Illinois River valley and from Missouri (Chapman 1980:21-77). The Truck #7 assemblage was small, but the decorative modes utilized at this site included plain and dentate rocker stamping, punctating, incising, cross-hatching, bar stamping, gouging, brushing, and cordmarking. In fact, only 10% of the total ceramic sample was plain or indeterminate. The assemblage decorative types clearly relate to the Pike-Baehr series defined in the Illinois River valley (Griffin 1952; Struever 1968b). It is interesting to note, however, that the Pike-Baehr ceramics of that area were exclusively limestone-tempered while those from the Truck #7 site and other Hill Lake phase sites in the American Bottom were predominantly grog-tempered. The use of limestone in combination with grog as temper was, however, also observed in the Truck #7 assemblage.

Eighty-four percent of the Truck #7 site sherds, by weight, came from 9 of the 10 pits found inside the structure. Middle Woodland ceramics were also present in 2 features (Features 6 and 12) situated outside the structure. A total of only 5 vessels could be distinguished, based on rim portions. All of the vessels represent jar forms. Two vessels each came from Features 14 and 18, inside the structure.

The plain, rocker-stamped body sherds and the bar-stamped, plain rocker-stamped rims (Vessel 1) accounted for 75% of the decorated ceramic assemblage by weight. The second most prevalent (8%) mode of decoration by weight was brushing. The interiors of all sherds were plain and, occasionally, smoothed by burnishing. The five jars from Truck #7 were grog-tempered; 15 body sherds from Feature 14, however, exhibited a combination of limestone and grog tempering (Plate 13).

The interior and exterior surfaces of many of the decorated sherds exhibited a thin coating of burnished clay as if a slip had been applied. This "slip" was cracked and peeled in many places, exposing a rougher vessel surface beneath the coating. The following is a description of each vessel found at the Truck #7 site (Figures 55-58; Tables 59-61).

Vessel 1

Vessel 1 came from Feature 18 and was represented by two decorated, grog-tempered rim sections weighing 184.9 g. The decoration consisted of three horizontal rows of stamped, vertical, bar-shaped impressions, below which were placed two rows of overlapping, plain rocker stamping. The lip was rounded, but bevelled inward. The bevelled portion was ca. 12 mm wide. Vessel 1 represents a large jar, with an orifice diameter of 38-39 cm, based on only 7% of the orifice. The vessel walls were 13-41 mm thick. The interior surface was plain and smoothed, although not burnished. Several fine indentations were observed on the interior

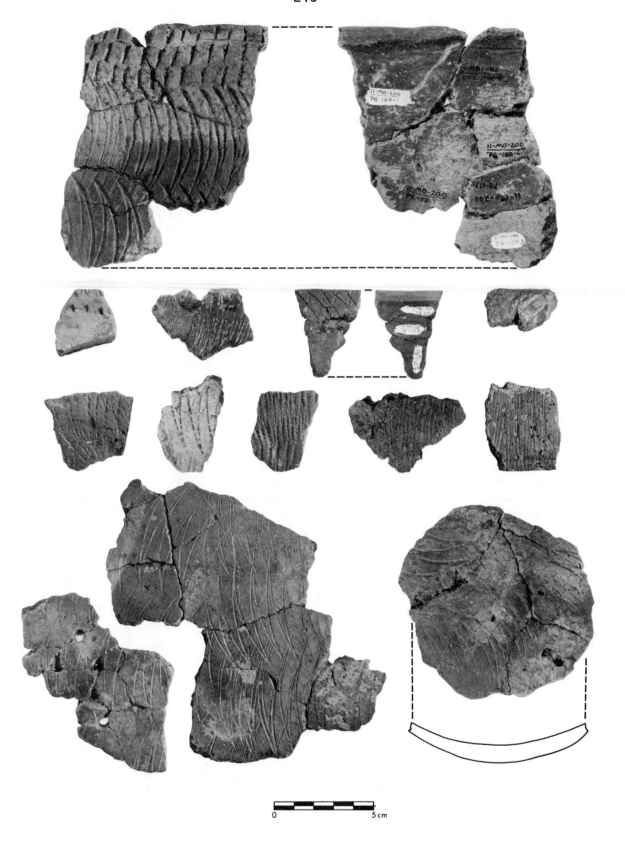

Plate 13.   Hill Lake Phase Ceramics Recovered from the Truck #7 Site

surface, especially at the base of the bevelled lip. The interior
surface was dark gray (10YR 4/1) and pale brown (10YR 6/3) (Figure 55a).

The rocker impressions were linked and completely filled the area
below the bar stamps. The impressions were relatively deep and wide
(ca. 1-2 mm). A total of 10 rocker impressions in the upper row were
counted, which ran horizontally in an area of 0.1 cm on one of the
sherds. The rocker stamps averaged from 4.5-5.0 cm in height. The
second row of rocker stamping overlapped the upper row, with the second
row of impressions cutting through the first row.

The bar stamps were ca. 1-2 mm deep, ca. 10 mm long, and 2-3 mm
wide. The upper portions were squared-off and wide, while the lower and
central portions were tapered and narrow. These impressions were
probably made with a hollow, rectangular-ended object, such as the end
of a reed or cut bone. The upper row of bar stamps was situated
directly below the lip, and the upper portions of each bar were covered
by excess clay from the lip.

Vessel 2

Vessel 2 represents a small, decorated, grog-tempered jar rim (5% of
the orifice), weighing 9.7 g, which was found in Feature 14. The
orifice diameter ranged from 20-22 cm. The decoration consisted of an
unlinked and linked cross-hatch design located directly below the
exterior lip and extending down 16 mm below the lip. The remaining
portion of the sherd was plain and smoothed. The vessel wall thickness
varied from 5-7 mm. The lip was bevelled inward and was highly
burnished. As with Vessel 1, excess clay was apparently added to the
lip and subsequently burnished. The bevelled lip portion was ca. 9 mm
wide. The interior surface was plain, smoothed, and dark gray in color
(10YR 4/1). The exterior surface color varied from dark gray to
grayish-brown (10YR 5/2) and pale brown (10YR6/3). Cross-hatching below
the lip is a type marker for the classic Hopewell and Pike-Baehr phases
of the Middle Woodland sequence in the Illinois River valley and also
appears in the Creve Coeur Hopewell assemblage in eastern Missouri
(Chapman 1980:50) [Figure 56b].

Vessel 3

Vessel 3 was found in Feature 18 and represents a small,
grog-tempered rim fragment, which weighed only 2.1 g. The exterior
surface was covered with extremely fine cross-hatching which extended up
to the lip. The lip was flattened and burnished. The lip was 5 mm wide
and, as with Vessels 1 and 2, additional clay had been added to the lip

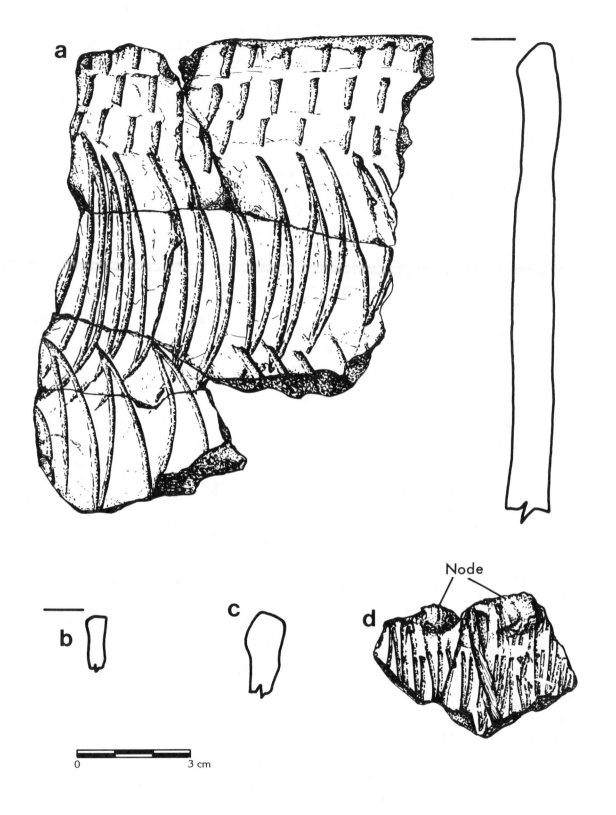

Figure 55. Ceramics Recovered from Feature 19; a, Vessel 1 (bar-stamped); . b, Vessel 6; c, Vessel 5; d, noded, rocker-stamped body sherd

221

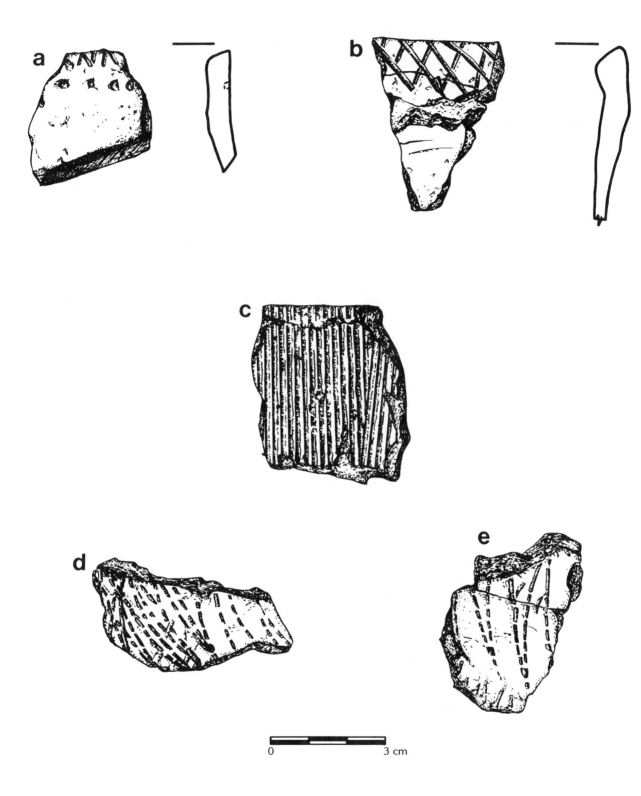

Figure 56. Decorated Ceramics from Feature 14: a, Vessel 4, cross-hatched, gouged; b, Vessel 2, cross-hatched; c, Baehr brushed; d-e, dentate rocker-stamped

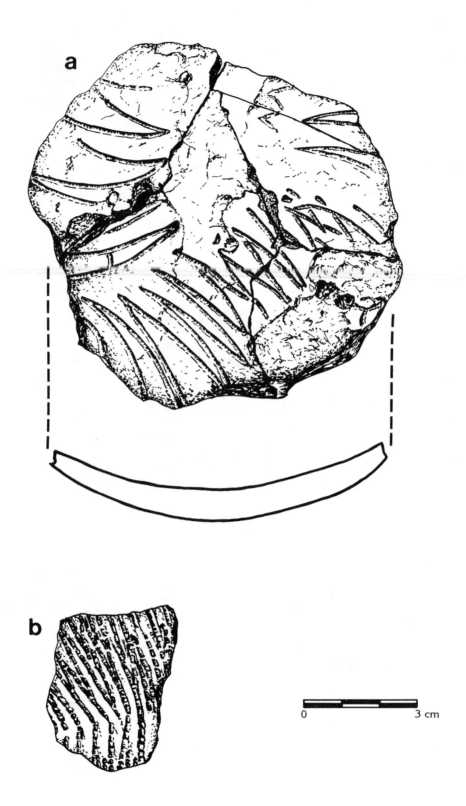

Figure 57. Rocker-Stamped Base from Feature 6 (a) and Dentate Rocker-Stamped Body Sherd from Feature 12 (b)

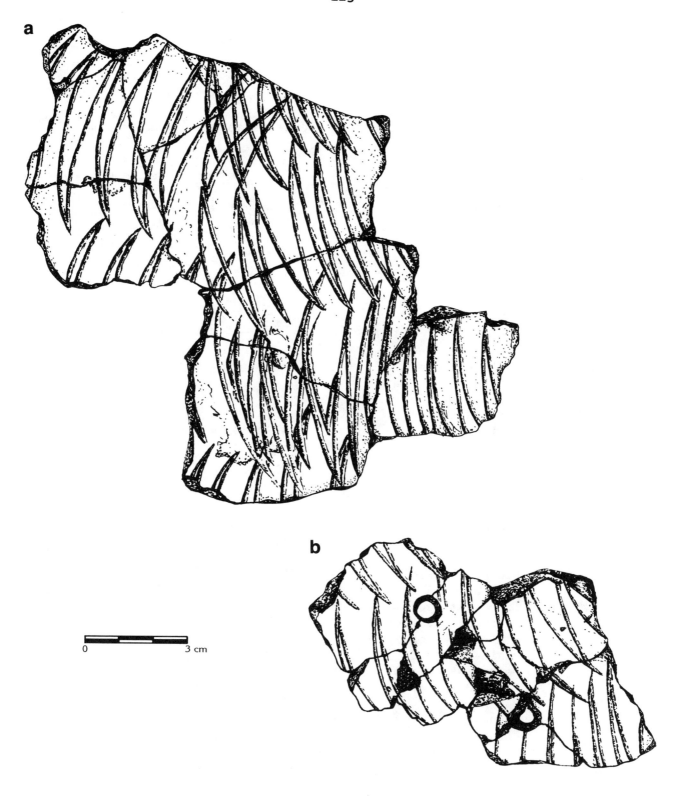

Figure 58. Rocker-Stamped Body Sherds from One Vessel Recovered from Feature 19 (Note drilled holes in b)

Table 59. Ceramics from Feature Contexts at the Truck #7 Site

Feature	Exterior Surface	N	Wt(g)	Temper	Comments
2*	Plain-Rockered	26	81.8	Grog	
	Brushed	8	19.8	Grog	
	Plain	8	9.6	Grog	
	Unknown	12	8.7	Grog	
Total		54	119.9		
3*	Brushed	3	2.8	Grog	
	Unknown	1	0.5	Grog	
Total		4	3.3		
6	Plain-Rockered	12	199.7	Grog	3 Base Sherds= 103.0 g
10*	Plain-Rockered	1	6.1	Grog	Exterior Nodes
	Plain-Rockered	4	24.3	Grog	
	Brushed	8	26.3	Grog	
Total		13	56.7		
11	Unknown	3	1.5	Grog	
	Plain	9	5.6	Shell	
	Plain	8	8.6	Limestone	
Total		20	15.7		
12	Plain-Rockered	3	24.6	Grog	
14*	Cross-hatched/Plain	1	9.7	Grog	Rim
	Cross-hatched/Punct.	1	6.7	Grog	Rim
	Plain-Rockered	4	38.3	Grog	
	Plain-Rockered	3	13.3	LS/Grog	
	Dentate-Rockered	6	39.3	Grog	
	Brushed	8	42.9	LS/Grog	
	Plain	4	17.0	Grog	
	Unknown	4	4.2	LS/Grog	
	Unknown	16	21.8	Grog	
Total		47	193.2		

* Inside of Feature 1

Table 59. continued

Feature	Exterior Surface	N	Wt(g)	Temper	Comments
15*	Unknown	1	0.9	Grog	
18*	Bar-Stamped/Plain				
	Rockered	8	184.9	Grog	Rim (2) Sherds
	Plain-Rockered	1	3.3	Grog	Exterior Node
	Plain-Rockered	5	35.1	Grog	
	Dentate-Rockered	1	1.5	Grog	
	Brushed	1	0.8	Grog	
	Plain	1	2.8	Grog	
	Unknown	9	6.2	Grog	
	Cross-hatched/Plain	1	2.1	Grog	Rim Sherd
Total		27	236.7		
19*	Plain-Rockered	45	316.3	Grog	(2 Drilled Holes)
	Dentate-Rockered	1	0.5	Grog	
	Brushed	6	21.1	Grog	
	Cordmarked (?)	25	49.1	LS/Grog	
	Unknown	6	9.2	Grog	
Total		83	396.2		
20	Unknown	3	7.8	Grit	Marion Thick
1	Plain-Rockered	1	2.2	Grog	PM 30
	Plain-Rockered	6	7.7	LS/Grog	
	Plain	1	0.4	Grog	PM 27
Total		8	10.3		
16*	Plain-Rockered	31	175.4	Grog	
	Plain-Rockered	2	6.7	LS/Grog	
	Dentate-Rockered	3	13.0	Grog	
	Plain	10	51.2	Grog	
	Indeterminate	7	9.3	Grog	
Total		53	255.6		

* Inside of Feature 1

Table 60. Summary of the Ceramic Materials Recovered
from Feature Contexts at the Truck #7 Site

| | Total Ceramics | | Non-Middle Woodland Ceramics | | |
Feature	N	Wt(g)	N	Wt(g)	Component
1	8	10.3	-	-	
2	54	119.9	-	-	
3	4	3.3	-	-	
6	12	199.7	-	-	
10	13	56.7	-	-	
11	20	15.7	17	14.2	Mississippian
12	3	24.6	-	-	
14	47	193.2	-	-	
15	1	0.9	-	-	
16	53	255.6	-	-	
18	27	236.7	-	-	
19	83	396.2	-	-	
20	3	7.8	3	7.8	Early Woodland
Total	328	1520.6	20	22.0	

Table 61. Ceramic Vessels from the Truck #7 and Go-Kart South Sites

Vessel #	Form	Orifice Diameter (cm)	%	Wt(g)	Exterior Surface	Feature	Temper
1	Jar	38-39	7	184.9	Bar-Stamped/ Plain-Rockered	18	Grog
2	Jar	20-22	5	9.7	Cross-Hatched/ Plain	14	Grog
3	Jar	-	-	2.1	Cross-Hatched/ Plain	18	Grog
4	Jar	-	-	6.7	Cross-Hatched/ Punctated	14	Grog
5	Jar	-	-	6.6	Incised	-	Grog/LS
6	Jar	-	-	5.2	Plain	-	LS
7	Jar/ Bowl	-	-	30.4	Cordmarked	-	Grit

Note: Vessels 1-5 are from Truck #7, and Vessels 6-7 are from Go-Kart South.
Vessel 6 is a Mississippian jar. Vessel 7 is an Early Woodland, Marion Thick jar
or bowl form.

prior to burnishing. The interior surface was plain, smoothed and dark gray (10YR 4/1) in color. The exterior surface of this fragment was completely decorated and was grayish-brown (10YR 5/2) in color.

Vessel 4

Vessel 4 was recovered from Feature 14. It represents a small, decorated, grog-tempered jar rim fragment, weighing 6.7 g. The rim was decorated with short cross-hatching on the exterior lip below which appeared a single, horizontal row of crescent-shaped gouges. The cross-hatches were only 4 mm in height. The crescent gouges averaged 3 mm in height and 2 mm in width. The vessel walls were 10-11 mm wide. The lip was flat and slightly bevelled inward. It had not been smoothed or burnished. The interior surface was plain, smoothed, and dark gray (10YR 4/1) in color. The exterior surface was smooth and very pale brown (10YR 7/3) in color (Figure 56a).

Vessel 5

Vessel 5 was a small, decorated, grog-tempered rim fragment, which was recovered during machine scraping in Block II. The decoration consisted of parallel incised lines running obliquely (4-6 mm apart) down from the lip. The sherd was small (6.6 g) and heavily eroded on the exterior surface. The lip was rounded and irregularly thickened (8-11 mm).

The interior surface was plain, smooth, and gray (10YR 5/1). The exterior surface was light gray (10YR 7/2) or ash colored, which may have resulted from burning. Although primarily grog-tempered, small inclusions of limestone also occurred.

The ceramic assemblage from the Truck #7 site was relatively small, consisting of only 328 sherds (1520.6 g) from 13 features. Only 5 rims were recovered. As mentioned previously, the remaining body sherds were mostly decorated. Plain rocker stamping was the most frequent form of decoration on the body sherds (Figure 55c).

Decoration

Plain and Dentate Rocker Stamping

Plain and dentate rocker stamping were common at the Truck #7 site.

These decorative forms parallel Griffin's Hopewell Rocker plain and dentate types in the Illinois River valley. According to Griffin, this is a rare form of decoration typical of the later period of Hopewell development, and it is often associated with cross-hatched rim decoration (Griffin 1952:118). It also appears at the Creve Coeur site in eastern Missouri where it is called Creve Coeur Rocker-Marked, and at the Renner site in western Missouri, the type site for the Kansas City Middle Woodland focus. There, as at Creve Coeur, cross-hatched rims are associated with plain rocker stamping (Chapman 1980:29).

The plain rocker-stamped decoration at the Truck #7 site could only be associated with bar-stamped decoration, although it is possible that the cross-hatched rims found at Truck #7 were related to the plain rocker-stamped body sherds. Rocker stamping or marking occurred over the entire body, as far as could be determined from the sherds at the Truck #7 site. One conical base sherd from Feature 6 contained rocker stamping over the entire basal portion (Figure 57a). The rocker stamps were rowed. One body sherd from Feature 19 exhibited at least four consecutive rows of rocker stamping (Figure 58). Two drilled holes were present on one sherd of this vessel indicating that a portion of this broken vessel may have been secondarily utilized as a pendant. In this case, and most others where rowed rocker stamping was utilized, the rocker-stamped rows overlapped one another. In some cases, the rocker stamping appeared to have been haphazardly placed, with widely-spaced marks (8-10 mm apart) overlapping more narrowly spaced marks (3-4 mm apart). The height and width of the rocker-stamped decoration varied from sherd to sherd, but the average height was ca. 4.5 cm and the average width was 4-6 mm. The depth of the marks also varied but was usually less than 1 mm (Table 62).

The dentate rocker-stamped decoration was more rare at the Truck #7 site and was represented by only 11 small body sherds from feature contexts. The stamps were generally shorter than the plain rocker stamps, averaging only 3 cm in height. The spacing between the stamps was also narrower than that of the plain rocker marks. The implement utilized for both the dentate rocker-stamped and plain rocker-stamped pottery at the Truck #7 site is unknown, although the curved edge of a shell (notched for dentate stamping) could have produced this type of decoration (Figure 56d-e).

Brushing

Brushing occurred on pottery in six features (Features 2, 3, 10, 14, 18, and 19). This brushing is referred to as "Baehr Brushed" in this report, following Illinois River valley terminology (Griffin 1952:120). By weight, this type of decoration accounted for 8% of the decorative modes found at the Truck #7 site. The brush marks were extremely

Table 62. Summary of the Exterior Surface Treatments on Middle Woodland
Ceramics Recovered from Feature Contexts

Surface Treatment	N	Wt(g)	Comments
Plain-Rockered	144	934.8	Features 1, 2, 6, 10, 12, 14, 16, 18, 19
Dentate-Rockered	11	54.3	Features 14, 16, 18, 19
Brushed	34	113.7	Features 2, 3, 10, 14, 18, 19
Plain	24	81.0	Features 1, 2, 14, 16, 18
Cordmarked (?)	25	49.1	Feature 19
Indeterminate	79	84.3	Features 2, 3, 11, 14, 15, 16 18, 19
Cross-hatched/Plain	2	11.8	Vessels 2 (Feature 14) and 3 (Feature 18)
Cross-hatched/Punctated	1	6.7	Vessel 4 (Feature 14)
Bar-stamped/Plain-Rockered	8	184.9	Vessel 1 (Feature 18)
Total	328	1520.6	

shallow and probably represent brush strokes rather than incisions,
since very fine striations could be observed within the channels. The
channels were placed side by side, were narrow, usually less than 1 mm
wide, and occasionally overlapped (Figure 56c).

Other Forms of Decoration

Other decorative types appeared at the Truck #7 site, but were rare.
These types included cordmarking (25 sherds from Feature 19),
cross-hatching, and punctating (only one sherd from Feature 14). A
noded sherd with plain rocker stamping over the nodes also occurred
(Figure 55d). Pieces of this sherd were found in Features 10 and 18 and
represent the only sherd pieced together from separate pits at the site.
Both features occurred within the structure. The cordmarked sherds were
heavily eroded and possibly smoothed over. The cordmarks were unevenly
spaced and narrow.

Discussion

The Truck #7 site ceramic collection, although small, comprised a distinct assemblage of decorative types representing the Pike-Hopewell phases in Illinois. The use of grog tempering at the Truck #7 site, however, contrasted with the general use of limestone tempering in Central Illinois. Grog-tempered ceramics have also been observed at the Dash Reeves site (11-Mo-80), a site located ca. 2 km south of the Truck #7 site. Ceramics from the Dash Reeves site consisted primarily of rocker stamped varieties but fabric-impressed sherds also occurred at this site. The presence of grog tempering in ceramics from Middle Woodland sites in the American Bottom probably represents a local ceramic tradition which may be derived from Middle Woodland Crab Orchard influences. In that regard, the presence of southern Illinois Dongola chert in the Truck #7 site lithic assemblage and a galena piece traced to the Pitosi Formation of southeastern Missouri (Walthall 1981:54), provide additional evidence that the Truck #7 site occupants had contact with the southern Illinois area or perhaps even originated from that area. Ceramic variability within the Hill Lake phase is still too poorly known to resolve problems concerning areal ceramic interaction, but it is apparent that the American Bottom may be an important area (because of geographical positioning between the Illinois River valley and southern Illinois) for delineating the nature and extent of interaction during the Middle Woodland period in Illinois.

Go-Kart South Site

All of the ceramic materials from the Go-Kart South site were recovered during machine scraping. Early Woodland, Late Woodland, and Mississippian ceramics were identified. No Middle Woodland ceramics were observed. The majority of the ceramics, and all of the Early Woodland ceramics, were recovered in the southwest portion of Block C, which was located adjacent to the western edge of the FAI-270 right-of-way.

All of the Mississippian ceramics occurred within the silty alluvial overburden covering the inner channel ridge and depression. It is likely, therefore, that this entire ceramic assemblage represents redeposited materials from one of three places: 1) they may be eroded into this area from the nearby bluffs or bluff base; 2) they may originate from the alluvial fan which extended into this area from Hill Lake Creek and which passed through the Mississippian component at Truck #4 and/or 3) they may emanate from the upper portions of the unexposed, inner channel ridge located west of the excavation area and outside of the right-of-way.

Sixty percent of the ceramics (by weight) recovered from the Go-Kart
South site represent Early Woodland Marion Thick vessels. A rim section
recovered from one Marion Thick jar (Vessel 7) was cordmarked on both
interior and exterior surfaces and was coarsely grit-tempered with
crushed, igneous rocks. The orifice diameter of this vessel could not
be determined. A portion of a vessel base was found in the same
vicinity as the rim, i.e., the western end of Block C. Broken pieces of
sandstone were also observed in this area and were probably associated
with the Early Woodland sherds. Regular, circumscribed scatters of
Early Woodland materials recognized, e.g., at the Carbon Monoxide site,
were not observed at the the Go-Kart South site. The Early Woodland
pottery was extremely fragmented and crumbly and was embedded in the
silty clay soil covering the sand bar. It was located along the east
sloping portion of the inner channel ridge.

The Late Woodland component was represented by cordmarked,
grog-tempered sherds. Only 7% of the ceramic materials by weight were
associated with this component. These materials were recovered in the
silty alluvium covering the ridge and depression area.

The limestone-tempered and shell-tempered sherds recovered from the
Go-Kart South site were related to an early Mississippian component. A
limestone-tempered, plain jar rim (Vessel 6, Table 61), and twenty-five
red-slipped, limestone-tempered body sherds were recovered. Other
ceramics included plain, cordmarked, and red-slipped, shell-tempered
sherds as well as cordmarked, limestone-tempered body sherds. The
Mississippian sherds constituted 33% by weight of the total Go-Kart
South site ceramic assemblage.

The absence of Middle Woodland sherds in the Go-Kart South site is
notable, since the Middle Woodland occupation at the Truck #7 site lay
only 40 m south of the southern limit of the exposed area at the Go-Kart
South site. In addition, the Middle Woodland tool cache found at the
Go-Kart South site lay within the concentrated area of debris in Block
C. This indicates that the northwestern limits of the Middle Woodland
occupation fell within the machine scraped area at the Truck #7 site.

LITHIC ASSEMBLAGE

Chert Types

All chert recovered from feature contexts at the Truck #7 and
Go-Kart South sites was grouped into chert source type categories.

Curiously only a small collection of chert tools was recovered during the surface reconnaissance and machine excavation of the Truck #7 site (Figure 59). The identification of precise local sources for this chert is beyond the scope of this report. In some cases, general geologic information can now be suggested, but the precise locality has not been determined. The following source categories are based primarily on examination of color variations, the presence and absence of fossiliferous inclusions, and graininess (i.e., fine- or coarse-grained).

Ste. Genevieve (Red and Purple Varieties)

The Ste. Genevieve category was derived from the occurrence of red chert nodules with purple [actually, reddish-gray (10YR 6/1, 5/1) to dark gray (2.5YR 4/0)] interiors in a Ste. Genevieve formation outcrop located at the mouth of Carr Creek, Monroe County, Illinois (John Kelly, personal communication).

Red Variety

This chert type was the second most abundant type found in features at the Truck #7 site, e.g., 21.1% by number and 21.3% by weight. A total of 2001 pieces, weighing 1573.8 g, were recovered. This was the most abundant chert type by weight in Features 5, 10, and 15. A single, steeply-retouched discoidal scraper from Feature 18 was also of this variety. This type, along with a white local chert variety, represented the predominant chert types recovered from the surface of the Truck #7 site.

Ste. Genevieve Red variety chert was fine-grained to moderately coarse-grained and exhibited a wide range of color, from light red (2.5YR 6/6) to reddish-brown (2.5YR 5/4). Fossil inclusions were common. Another variant of this chert type was very pale brown (10YR 8/3), with numerous distinct light red inclusions (2.5YR 6/8). The cortex on this chert varied from reddish-brown (2.5YR 6/6) to white (10YR 8/1) and was highly weathered.

Purple Variety

The purple variety of Ste. Genevieve chert ranged in color from a reddish-gray (10R 6/1, 5/1) to dark gray (2.5YR 4/0). It was usually fine-grained with some cloudy white quartz inclusions. Heat-altered flakes ranged in color from pale, weak red (10R 6/2, 6/4, and 10R 5/2, 5/3) to dusky red (10R 3/2). The cortex consisted of weathered, chalky,

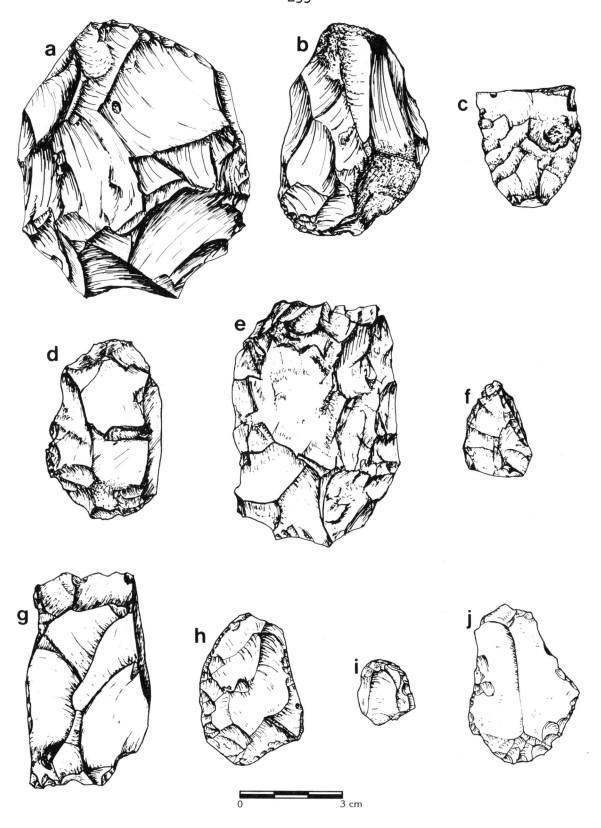

Figure 59. Miscellaneous Worked Core and Flake Scrapers Recovered During Machine Excavation of Block II at the Truck #7 Site

white limestone with occasional fossils. The assignment of this chert type to the Ste. Genevieve formation is tentative, based only on the presence of the purple chert at Carr Creek.

The purple variety was the most abundant chert found in feature contexts at the Truck #7 site, e.g., 56.3% by number and 58.8% by weight. It was the most abundant chert by weight in Features 2, 6, 11, 12, 14, 16, 17, and 18. The total number of pieces recovered from features was 5339, with a weight of 4331.1 g. Interestingly, this chert type was only rarely recovered during the surface collections made at the Truck #7 site.

Salem (Creamy and Local Oolitic)

The Salem limestone, chert-yielding formation precedes both the St. Louis and Ste. Genevieve formations and commonly outcrops along the bluff edges near the Hill Lake locality. The chert types found in this formation exhibit a great deal of variation, but mostly include local oolitic varieties commonly found at most Hill Lake sites investigated thus far. It may also include a fine-grained, tan-colored, creamy variety, although a specific source has not yet been identified. The creamy variety is occasionally banded.

The Salem creamy chert variety was the third most abundant type at the Truck #7 site, accounting for 14.5% by frequency and 13.7% by weight. A total of 1378 pieces, weighing 1006.8 g, were recovered. It was the most abundant chert in Features 3 and 19 and was also recovered from the surface of the site.

Salem creamy was a fine-grained to coarse-grained chert ranging in color from light gray (10YR 7/2) and very pale brown (10YR 7/3, 7/4) to pale brown (10YR 6/3). The fossiliferous cortex ranged in color from white (10YR 8/1) to yellow (10YR 8/6) to light reddish-brown (2.5YR 6/6).

The Salem local oolitic variety was represented in features by only 78 pieces, weighing 101.5 g. This chert was fine-grained and ranged in color from pale red (10YR 6/2) to light red (2.5YR 6/6). These colors were the result of heat alteration from an original oolitic chert, which was light gray to tan-colored.

Burlington (White Glossy; White to Gray Oolitic)

Only seven pieces of Burlington white glossy chert, weighing 2.8 g, were recovered in feature contexts. These flakes were very fine-grained and appeared lustrous. All of the flakes of this type were a uniform white (10YR 8/1) color.

The white oolitic variety occurred more frequently (437 pieces, weighing 166.66 g) in features at the Truck #7 site than did the glossy variant. It was the most abundant chert found on the surface of the Truck #7 site. Twelve tools, all found on the surface or in the plowzone were of this chert variety. A projectile point, an adze and a knife made from this chert were recovered in the interior portion of the structure at the Truck #7 site during shovel scraping.

The white to gray, oolitic variety was coarse to moderately grained and exhibited a wide range of colors, including white (10YR 8/1) and light gray (10YR 7/2). This chert was heavily fossiliferous. Heat-altered varieties were light red (2.5YR 6/8) in color.

Dongola

Dongola is a nonlocal chert common to southern Illinois. It represents the only exotic or imported chert at the Truck #7 or the Go-Kart South sites. Only three pieces of Dongola chert were recovered at the Truck #7 site, from Features 14 and 16 (6.7 g). However, the Go-Kart South site tool cache, which consisted of various scrapers and a projectile point, consisted predominantly of Dongola chert. In addition, some of the numerous small, thinning flakes from Features 14 and 16 which could not be identified because of their small size may have been derived from Dongola chert. This chert was fine-grained and ranged in color from gray (10YR 5/1) to grayish-brown (10YR 6/1).

Indeterminate Source

Most of the indeterminate chert was a very grainy, dark gray variety which may have derived from either the Salem or the St. Louis formations in this area. There were 145 indeterminate pieces recovered from feature contexts, weighing 143.1 g.

Cortical

All pieces of chert that consisted of only cortex or that did not possess enough of an interior to be identified were placed in the cortical category. There were 84 cortical pieces, weighing only 28.7 g.

Truck #7 Site Lithics

The Middle Woodland lithic assemblage at the Truck #7 site consisted of chipped chert artifacts, chert debitage, and miscellaneous nonchert stone tools. Since lithic assemblages in feature contexts are unique for the Middle Woodland period in this region, particular attention was directed towards categorizing not only the chert source type distribution but also the various morphological classes of lithic debris found at this site (Tables 63-67).

Approximately 50% by weight and 20% by count of all chert debris recovered from features at the Truck #7 site contained cortex. The larger cortical pieces were angular and block-shaped with relatively thick cortical crusts (ca. 0.4-1.0 cm). Virtually all of the chert was derived from local sources and apparently was transported unprepared to the site.

The entire range of core reduction debris was recovered from feature contexts inside the structure at the Truck #7 site. Included were block- fractured core fragments, secondary noncortical flakes, and small thinning and shatter flakes. Worked tools and preforms produced from core-reduction activities were also retrieved from pits inside the structure. Although nearly 12,000 pieces of chert were recovered within the structure, a relatively low density of tools, including utilized and retouched debitage flakes, was encountered.

The Truck #7 site is conspicuous for its lack of a blade technology, a facet of lithic technology normally observed at Middle Woodland occupations in the Illinois River valley. Small lamellar flakes did occur at the Truck #7 site but the expected corresponding blade cores did not. These lamellar flakes appeared to have been unintentionally manufactured during secondary core reduction and rarely exhibited evidence of utilization or intentional retouching. Most of these flakes have been grouped within the category of small thinning or shatter flakes.

Table 63. Distribution of Chert Types from Feature Contexts at the Truck #7 Site

Feature	Ste. Genevieve Purple N	Wt(g)	Ste. Genevieve Red N	Wt(g)	Ste. Genevieve Orange Speckled N	Wt(g)	Salem Creamy N	Wt(g)	Salem Local Oolitic N	Wt(g)
2	44	155.1	26	42.5	-	-	21	18.4	-	-
3	16	2.6	19	14.5	-	-	42	47.3	-	-
5	1	0.1	7	3.2	-	-	-	-	-	-
6	27	35.6	22	26.7	-	-	4	5.6	-	-
10	172	50.1	137	85.9	2	0.3	352	84.7	2	1.5
11	1	6.4	5	4.7	-	-	2	1.1	-	-
12	8	38.0	12	20.5	-	-	4	1.9	-	-
14	2893	1605.3	621	433.3	6	3.1	156	63.3	19	2.6
15	25	12.8	19	16.2	-	-	9	3.8	3	1.0
16*	1826	2006.4	600	506.9	5	5.0	232	232.8	54	96.4
17	53	9.2	32	1.7	-	-	5	0.3	-	-
19	120	303.6	229	359.1	1	0.9	221	507.6	-	-
Total	5339	4331.1	2001	1573.8	14	9.3	1378	1006.8	78	101.5
Mean Wt(g)		0.81		0.79		0.66		0.73		1.30

Feature	Burlington White Local N	Wt(g)	Burlington Glossy N	Wt(g)	Dongola N	Wt(g)	Indeterminate N	Wt(g)	Cortical N	Wt(g)
2	2	0.1	1	0.1	-	-	4	1.1	-	-
3	4	0.6	2	0.6	-	-	1	0.1	2	4.8
5	1	0.1	-	-	-	-	1	0.3	-	-
6	5	3.7	-	-	-	-	5	2.2	1	0.1
10	13	0.8	-	-	-	-	9	19.9	-	-
11	2	0.6	2	0.2	-	-	4	2.5	-	-
12	1	0.1	-	-	-	-	2	1.0	1	0.4
14	202	57.7	2	1.9	2	6.5	69	47.3	31	3.3
15	6	9.1	-	-	-	-	-	-	-	-
16*	151	65.0	-	-	1	0.2	33	39.6	45	19.3
17	7	0.3	-	-	-	-	3	4.0	2	0.1
18	28	18.3	-	-	-	-	3	1.7	2	0.7
19	15	10.2	-	-	-	-	11	23.4	-	-
Total	437	166.6	7	2.8	3	6.7	145	143.1	84	28.7
Mean Wt(g)		0.38		0.40		2.23		0.99		0.34

* Feature 16 thinning/shatter flakes were not separated according to chert type and are not included in the counts.

Table 64. Percentages of Chert Types by Feature

Feature		Ste. Genevieve Purple	Ste. Genevieve Red	Ste. Genevieve Orange Speckled	Salem Creamy	Salem Local Oolitic	Bur- lington Glossy	Bur- lington White Local	Dongola	Indeter- minate	Cortical
2	% N	44.9	26.5	-	21.4	-	1.0	2.0	-	4.1	-
	% Wt	71.3	19.5	-	8.5	-	<0.1	<0.1	-	0.5	-
3	% N	18.6	22.1	-	48.8	-	2.3	4.6	-	1.2	2.3
	% Wt	3.7	20.6	-	67.1	-	0.8	-	-	0.1	0.0
5	% N	10.0	70.0	-	-	-	-	10.0	-	10.0	-
	% Wt	2.7	86.5	-	-	-	-	2.7	-	8.1	-
6	% N	42.2	34.4	-	6.2	-	-	7.8	-	7.8	1.6
	% Wt	48.2	36.1	-	7.6	-	-	5.0	-	3.0	0.1
10	% N	25.0	19.9	0.3	51.2	0.3	-	1.9	-	1.3	-
	% Wt	20.5	34.9	0.1	34.7	0.6	-	0.3	-	8.2	-
11	% N	6.2	31.2	-	12.5	-	12.5	12.5	-	25.0	-
	% Wt	41.3	30.3	-	7.0	-	1.3	3.9	-	16.1	-
12	% N	28.6	42.8	-	14.3	-	-	3.6	-	7.1	3.6
	% Wt	61.4	33.1	-	3.1	-	-	0.2	-	1.6	0.6
14	% N	72.3	15.5	0.1	3.9	0.1	<0.1	5.0	0.1	1.7	0.7
	% Wt	72.2	19.5	0.1	2.8	0.1	<0.1	2.6	0.3	2.1	0.1
15	% N	40.3	30.6	-	14.5	-	-	9.7	-	-	-
	% Wt	29.8	37.8	-	8.8	-	-	21.2	-	-	-
*16	% N	62.0	20.3	0.2	7.9	0.2	-	5.1	<0.1	1.1	1.5
	% Wt	67.5	17.0	0.2	7.8	0.2	-	2.8	<0.1	1.3	0.6
17	% N	52.0	31.4	-	4.9	-	-	6.9	-	2.9	2.0
	% Wt	59.0	10.9	-	1.9	-	-	1.9	-	25.6	0.6
18	% N	19.4	34.5	-	41.9	-	-	3.5	-	0.4	0.2
	% Wt	47.0	26.0	-	17.8	-	-	8.1	-	0.7	0.3
19	% N	20.1	38.3	0.2	37.0	0.2	-	2.5	-	1.8	-
	% Wt	25.2	29.8	0.1	42.1	0.1	-	0.8	-	1.9	-
Total	% N	56.3	21.1	0.1	14.5	0.1	0.1	4.6	<0.1	1.5	0.9
	% Wt	58.8	21.3	0.1	13.7	0.1	<0.1	2.2	0.1	1.9	0.4

*Feature 16 thinning/shatter flakes were not separated according to chert type.

Table 65. Distribution of Flake Type Categories from Feature Contexts
at the Truck #7 Site

Feature	Primary Decortication		Secondary Decortication		Reduction Percussion		Thinning/ Shatter (2-4 mm)		Thinning/ Shatter (<2 mm)		Block Fracture With Cortex		Block Fracture Without Cortex	
	N	Wt(g)	N	Wt(g)	N	Wt(g)	N	Wt(g)	N	Wt(g)	N	Wt(g)	N	Wt(g)
2	13	151.7	25	30.6	60	35.0	-	-	-	-	-	-	-	-
3	7	51.1	12	7.0	34	11.7	6	0.3	27	0.4	-	-	-	-
5	1	0.4	3	1.2	6	2.1	-	-	-	-	-	-	-	-
6	6	10.5	26	32.3	29	29.4	-	-	-	-	2	0.7	1	1.0
10	21	93.1	85	63.6	254	66.9	102	2.4	211	1.5	7	8.8	7	7.5
11	1	6.4	2	2.6	9	4.0	-	-	-	-	3	2.4	1	0.1
12	5	46.2	7	4.9	16	10.8	-	-	-	-	-	-	-	-
14	183	451.0	741	625.3	1179	431.2	573	16.6	1282	15.0	37	627.9	6	57.3
15	5	11.3	13	10.3	41	20.6	-	-	2	0.1	1	0.6	-	-
16	253	757.1	706	860.7	1938	780.2	761	22.8	2598	22.0	33	543.3	17	30.3
17	4	6.3	6	5.1	18	3.5	6	0.3	68	0.4	-	-	-	-
18	12	73.9	43	80.3	194	57.2	152	4.6	380	3.1	4	3.8	3	2.3
19	41	122.5	128	234.3	346	292.8	30	0.5	29	0.3	19	546.4	4	8.0
Total	552	1781.5	1797	1958.2	4124	1745.4	1630	47.5	4597	42.8	106	1733.9	39	106.5
Mean Wt(g)		3.23		1.09		0.42		0.03		0.01		16.36		2.73

Table 66. Percentages of Flake Type Categories by Feature at the Truck #7 Site

Feature		Primary Decortication	Secondary Decortication	Reduction Percussion	Thinning/ Shatter (2-4 mm)	Thinning/ Shatter (<2 mm)	Block Frac. w/ Cortex	Block Frac. w/o Cortex
2	% N	13.3	25.5	61.2	-	-	-	-
	% Wt	69.8	14.1	16.1	-	-	-	-
3	% N	8.1	13.9	39.5	7.0	31.4	-	-
	% Wt	72.5	9.9	16.6	0.4	0.6	-	-
5	% N	10.0	30.0	60.0	-	-	-	-
	% Wt	10.8	32.4	56.7	-	-	-	-
6	% N	9.4	40.6	45.3	-	-	3.1	1.6
	% Wt	14.2	43.7	39.8	-	-	0.9	1.3
10	% N	3.0	12.4	37.0	14.8	30.7	1.0	1.0
	% Wt	38.2	26.1	27.4	1.0	0.6	3.6	3.1
11	% N	6.2	12.5	56.2	-	-	18.7	6.2
	% Wt	41.3	16.8	25.8	-	-	15.5	0.6
12	% N	17.8	25.0	57.1	-	-	-	-
	% Wt	74.6	7.9	17.4	-	-	-	-
14	% N	4.6	18.5	29.5	14.3	32.0	0.9	0.1
	% Wt	20.3	28.1	19.4	0.7	0.7	28.2	2.6
15	% N	8.1	21.0	66.1	-	3.2	1.6	-
	% Wt	26.3	24.0	48.0	-	0.2	1.4	-
16	% N	4.0	11.2	30.7	12.1	41.2	0.5	0.3
	% Wt	25.1	28.5	25.9	0.7	0.7	19.0	1.0
17	% N	4.0	5.9	17.6	5.9	66.7	-	-
	% Wt	40.4	32.7	22.4	1.9	2.7	-	-
18	% N	1.5	5.4	24.6	19.3	48.2	0.5	0.4
	% Wt	32.8	35.6	25.4	2.0	1.4	1.7	1.0
19	% N	7.2	22.6	61.0	5.3	5.1	3.3	0.7
	% Wt	11.7	22.5	28.1	<0.1	<0.1	52.4	0.8
Total	% N	4.3	14.0	32.1	12.7	35.8	0.8	0.3
	% Wt	24.0	26.4	23.5	0.6	0.6	23.4	1.4

Table 67. Frequency and Percentile Distribution of Flake Types by Chert Type from Feature Contexts

Chert Type		Primary Decortication	Secondary Decortication	Reduction Percussion	Thinning Shatter (2-4 mm)	Thinning Shatter (<2 mm)	Block Frac. w/Cortex	Block Frac. w/o Cortex
Ste. Genevieve Purple	N	265	1117	2317	481	1092	48	19
	Wt(g)	1118.10	1275.10	928.20	13.60	12.40	922.80	80.70
	Mean	4.22	1.14	0.40	0.03	0.01	19.22	4.25
	% by N	5.00	20.90	43.40	9.00	20.40	0.90	0.30
	% by Wt	25.80	29.40	21.40	0.30	0.30	21.30	1.90
Ste. Genevieve Red	N	120	393	902	174	365	36	11
	Wt(g)	418.90	366.00	368.50	5.20	3.70	397.70	14.80
	Mean	3.49	0.93	0.41	0.03	0.01	11.05	1.34
	% by N	6.00	19.60	45.10	8.70	18.20	1.80	0.50
	% by Wt	26.60	23.20	23.40	0.30	0.20	25.30	0.90
Salem Creamy	N	62	168	532	148	449	15	4
	Wt(g)	155.50	202.40	264.30	3.80	3.60	371.40	5.80
	Mean	2.51	1.20	0.50	0.02	0.01	24.76	1.45
	% by N	4.50	12.20	38.60	10.70	32.60	1.10	0.30
	% by Wt	15.40	20.10	26.20	0.40	0.40	36.90	0.60
All Other Chert Types	N	21	118	382	66	93	7	4
	Wt(g)	60.30	110.50	188.70	2.20	1.50	61.80	5.10
	Mean	2.87	0.78	0.49	0.03	0.02	8.83	1.27
	% by N	3.00	17.10	55.30	9.50	13.40	1.00	0.60
	% by Wt	13.40	24.60	41.90	0.50	0.30	13.70	1.10

Flake Type Morphology and Distribution

Various chert flake types, exhibiting the full range of core reduction, were recovered from the Truck #7 site. The following morphological categories were devised to aid in the description and tabulation of the lithic debris retrieved at this site: primary decortication flakes; secondary decortication flakes; reduction/ percussion flakes; thinning/shatter flakes; and block fractures with and without cortex. These categories and their distributions are described below. Only flakes recovered from feature contexts were categorized in this manner.

Primary Decortication Flakes

Primary decortication flakes are the first pieces removed from a chert core nodule or block. At the Truck #7 site, any piece of chert with a flake surface and two or more surfaces covered with cortex, or with a single surface, more than 50% of which was covered with cortex, was assigned to this category. There were several chert tools that had been made from primary decortication flakes at the site. Primary decortication flakes accounted for 4.3% of the total number of chert pieces from the site and 24.0% of the total weight. The average weight per flake was 3.23 g.

Secondary Decortication Flakes

Secondary decortication flakes are pieces removed from primary decortication flakes or broken nodules, preparatory for final reduction. All chert flakes from the site that had cortex on only one surface, and had a recognizable striking platform, were categorized as secondary decortication flakes. These flakes accounted for 14.0% of the total number of pieces of chert at the site and 26.4% of the total weight. The average weight per flake was 1.09 g.

Reduction/Percussion Flakes

Reduction/percussion flakes comprised a large category containing all chert flakes that 1) exhibited flake characteristics, 2) had no cortex, and 3) were larger than 4 mm (would not fit through a 4 mm screen). The range of variation in size and shape within this category was great. Reduction/percussion flakes are the direct result of reducing a piece or core into a desired shape for tool use or into a preform before final edge flaking. Reduction/percussion flakes accounted for 32.1% of the total number of chert pieces at the site and 23.5% of the total weight. The average weight per flake was 0.42 g.

Thinning/Shatter Flakes

Thinning/shatter flakes are the result of 1) intentional reduction
or retouching of a tool or preform and 2) unintentional shattering of
chert during percussion. At the site, many of these flakes had no bulbs
of percussion. Over 5000 small, thinning/shatter flakes were recovered
from this site, and it was believed that categorizing this number of
flakes would be too time consuming. Therefore, this category of flakes
was grouped according to size by passing the flakes through 4 mm and
2 mm screens (5 and 10 mesh). The screen size was selected
arbitrarily and served only to subdivide this class of flakes into two
gross, measurable, size classes. There was a tendency for the flakes
that were 2-4 mm in size to have recognizable bulbs of percussion, while
the flakes less than 2 mm in size usually lacked bulbs. This tendency
was not statistically established. The majority of chert that was less
than 2 mm in size came from floated material.

Five pits contained a high percentage (by number) of
thinning/shatter flakes: Feature 10 (45.5%), Feature 14 (46.3%),
Feature 16 (53.3%), Feature 17 (72.6%), and Feature 18 (67.5%). It is
proposed that these pits were specifically used for the processing and
disposal of chert debris. Thinning/shatter flakes accounted for 48.5%
of the total amount of flakes at the site by number but only 1.2% of the
total by weight. The average weight per flake was 0.03 g for the 2-4 mm
sized flakes and 0.01 g for the flakes less than 2 mm in size.

Block Fractures

Block fractures occur during the initial fracture of chert nodules,
and they are blocky and angular (square and rectangular) in shape. They
do not exhibit usual flake characteristics such as bulbs of percussion
or hinges. The block-fractured chert at the site usually included
pieces containing thick cortex on one or both ends of the block.
However, sometimes no cortex was observed, suggesting that such pieces
were the products of secondary reduction.

Block fractures accounted for 1.1% of the total amount of chert
found at the site and 24.8% of the total weight. The average weight per
piece was 16.36 g for pieces with cortex and 2.73 g for pieces without
cortex.

Chert Tools

Twenty-six chert tools were recovered from features at the Truck #7 site (Table 68). Thirteen were made from Ste. Genevieve purple variety chert. The tools included 10 retouched flakes, 6 scrapers, 2 biface fragments, 1 denticulate, 2 knives, 1 adze, 1 gouge, 1 projectile point fragment, and 2 preforms. For the most part, this tool assemblage was dominated by scraping and small cutting tools (Figures 60-62).

Scrapers

The scraper category included three scraper types found in surface/plowzone contexts, in subsurface features, and between subsurface features (both interior and exterior to the structure) at the Truck #7 site. These types included a) flake scrapers; b) discoidal, plano-convex scrapers; and c) core scrapers with steep end retouching.

Flake scrapers are characteristically flat, angular flakes with retouching on the dorsal surface (Figure 60b). One scraper, found during machine scraping several meters east of the structure at the Truck #7 site, exhibited steep retouching on its distal end and was categorized as an end scraper (Figure 59j). This item exhibited the characteristics of the Category C (steeply retouched end) scrapers found in the tool cache at the Go-Kart South site.

Discoidal scrapers are oval-shaped and thick, with steeply retouched edges. They are plano-convex in cross-section. Only one discoidal scraper was found at the Truck #7 site, in Feature 18 (Figure 60f). This type of scraper is associated with Category B (steeply retouched flakes) in the tool cache at the Go-Kart South site.

The most commonly occurring scraper at the Truck #7 site was a core scraper (Figure 60c-d). The scrapers that occurred in Features 14 and 16 were typified by steep retouching of a single end of a primary decortication flake (Figure 61c). All of these tools were blocky, angular, and very thick. One of these core scrapers was bifacially worked at one end and retouched on one side at the opposite end. These kinds of scrapers were not found in the tool cache at the Go-Kart South site.

Some of the scraping tools found at the Truck #7 site paralleled those found in the tool cache at the Go-Kart South site, both in form and in the steep retouching found along the dorsal edge. Discoidal scrapers and end scrapers with steep retouching occurred within the

Table 68. Lithic Tools from Feature and Nonfeature Contexts at the Truck #7 Site

Figure	Provenience	Chert Tool Type	Wt(g)	Chert Type	Comments
59e	MS Block II	Preform	87.3	Burlington White Local	
59a	MS Block II	Scraper	86.2	Ste. Genevieve Purple	Made from primary decortication flake
59h	MS Block II	Retouched Flake	9.3	Burlington White Local	
59i	MS Block II	Retouched Flake	1.0	Burlington White Local	Heat altered
59j	MS Block II	Flake Scraper	9.0	Burlington Glossy	
62g	Fea.1	Knife	12.6	Burlington White Local	
N/I	MS Block II	Discoidal Core Tool	184.0	Burlington White Local	
62a	Fea. 1	Adze	193.0	Salem Local Oolitic	
N/I	Gen. Surf. Col.	Retouched Flake	9.5	Burlington White Local	
59c	MS Block II	Retouched Flake	8.0	Ste. Genevieve Orange Speckled	Heat altered
59g	MS Block II	Core Fragment	47.5	Salem Local Oolitic	
59d	MS Block II	Scraper	32.6	Ste. Genevieve Purple	Made from primary decortication flake
59f	MS Block II	Biface Fragment	5.5	Burlington White Local	
62f	Fea. 1	Flake Scraper	27.6	Burlington White Local	
62e	Fea. 1	Bifacial Preform	19.5	Ste. Genevieve Purple	
62b	Fea. 1	Gouge	78.6	Ste. Genevieve Purple	
62d	Fea. 1	Projectile Point	15.5	Burlington White Local	Contracting stem
N/I	Gen. Surf. Col.	Projectile Point	3.1	Indeterminate	Base, only, expanding stem
N/I	Fea. 11	Biface Fragment	8.1	Indeterminate	Heat altered
N/I	Fea. 14	Retouched Flake	13.9	Ste. Genevieve Purple	
N/I	Fea. 14	Retouched Flake	2.1	Salem Creamy	
60c	Fea. 14	Core Scraper	73.9	Ste. Genevieve Purple	Bifacially worked at one end
60a	Fea. 14	Flake Knife	7.1	Ste. Genevieve Purple	Retouched on only one lateral edge
N/I	Fea. 14	Biface Fragment	2.8	Ste. Genevieve Purple	Tip fragment
N/I	Fea. 14	Retouched Flake	4.5	Ste. Genevieve Orange Speckled	
N/I	Fea. 14	Retouched Flake	0.7	Ste. Genevieve Purple	
60b	Fea. 14	Flake Scraper	22.4	Ste. Genevieve Purple	
N/I	Fea. 14	Retouched Flake	4.2	Dongola	
N/I	Fea. 14	Retouched Flake	2.3	Dongola	
61c	Fea. 16	Core Scraper	61.1	Ste. Genevieve Purple	
61a	Fea. 16	Preform	30.6	Ste. Genevieve Purple	
N/I	Fea. 16	Retouched Flake	13.3	Ste. Genevieve Purple	
61d	Fea. 16	Denticulate	28.1	Salem Creamy	
61b	Fea. 16	Core	52.5	Salem Creamy	
N/I	Fea. 16	Retouched Flake	2.9	Ste. Genevieve Purple	Heat altered
N/I	Fea. 16	Retouched Flake	1.5	Ste. Genevieve Purple	Heat altered
60f	Fea. 18	Discoidal Scraper	41.9	Ste. Genevieve Red	
60e	Fea. 19	Retouched Flake	9.8	Ste. Genevieve Orange Speckled	

	Provenience	Nonchert Tool Type	Wt(g)	Source Material	Comments
N/I	Fea. 16	Hammerstone	227.0	Igneous Cobble	
N/I	Fea. 16	Hammerstone	156.6	Igneous Cobble	
N/I	Fea. 16	Grinding Stone	520.8	Igneous Cobble	Possible anvil
N/I	Fea. 19	Metate Fragment	198.8	Sandstone	

MS: Machine scraped
N/I: Not illustrated

246

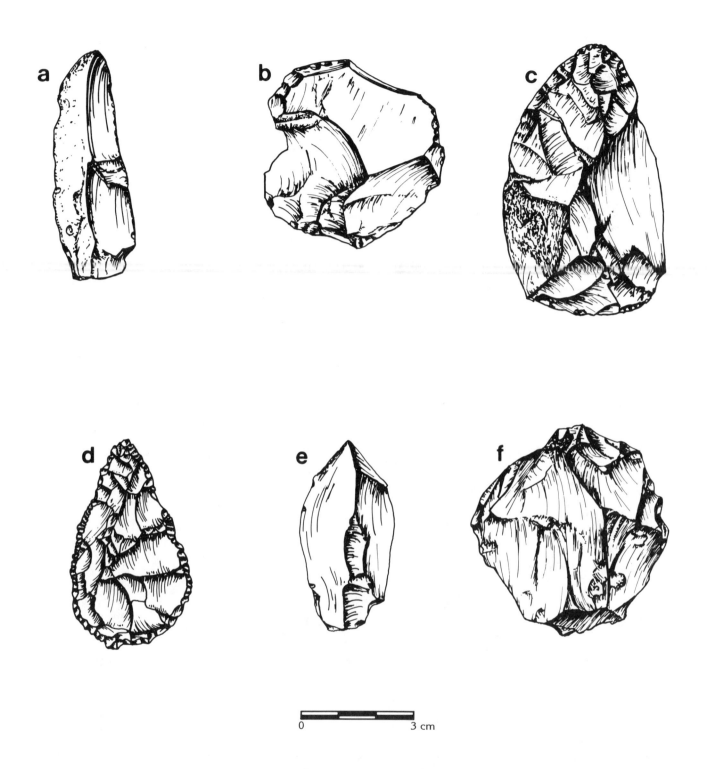

Figure 60. Chert Artifacts: a-d, from Feature 14; e, from Feature 19; f, from Feature 18

247

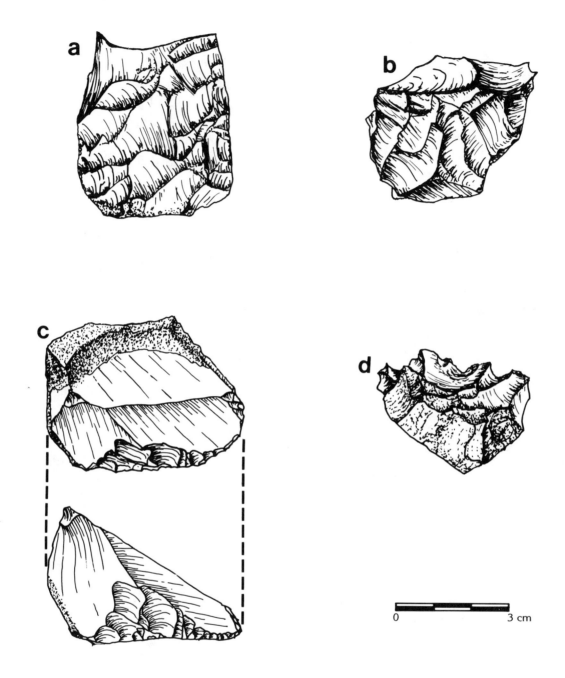

Figure 61. Chert Artifacts from Feature 16: a, preform; b, retouched flake; c, steeped core scraper; d, denticulate core scraper (top view)

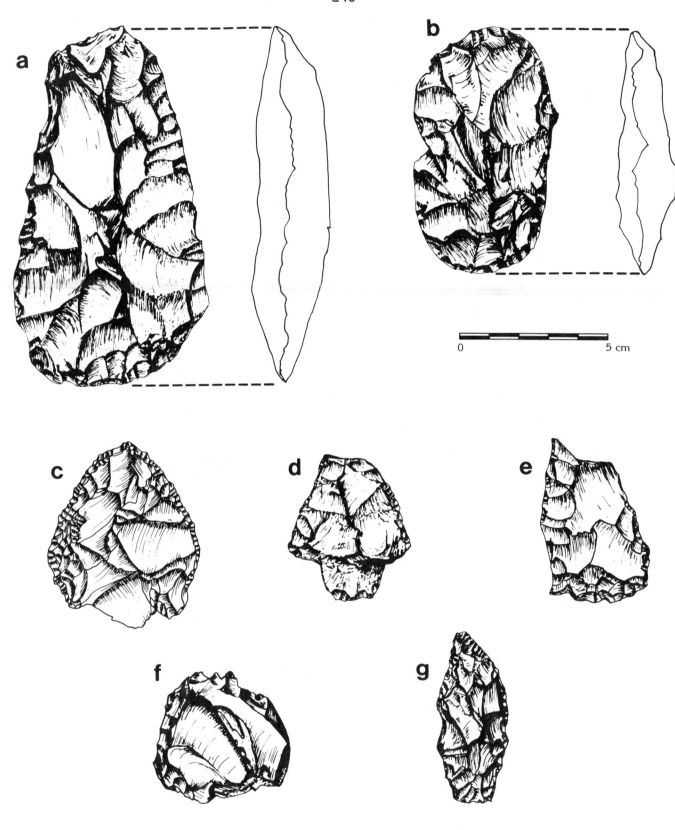

Figure 62. Chert Artifacts found on or near the Floor of Feature 1

Truck #7 site structure and within the tool cache. This lends support
to the suggestion that the isolated tool cache at the Go-Kart South site
should be associated with the Middle Woodland occupation at the Truck #7
site.

Denticulates

Only one denticulate was found at the Truck #7 site.   It was
recovered from Feature 16 and was made of Salem creamy chert. It was
made on a cortical fragment; the tool consisted of ca. 60% cortex.   The
tool was characterized by a series of denticulate edges with deep, wide
notching along one edge and fine retouching within the notches.   The
function of this tool is problematical, but its serrated edge indicates
a cutting or shearing function (Figure 61d).

Blade and Flake Knives

One blade/flake knife was recovered, from Feature 14.   It was an
elongated, blade-like, cortical flake that was finely retouched along
the noncortical lateral edge. The cutting edge was extremely thin and
sharp.   It was one of only several flakes at the Truck #7 site that
could be designated as blades and the only one of those which had been
utilized as a tool (Figure 60a).

Gouges and Adzes

A gouge and an adze were recovered from the interior of the
structure during shovel scraping in that area. The gouge, of purple
chert, was manufactured from an elongated, plano-convex core
(Figure 62b).   It was bifacially worked on the two bevelled ends of the
dorsal surface. The flaking was broad, erratic, and multidirectional
except at the utilized ends, which were finely retouched. An adze was
also recovered inside the structure. This tool was of local, white,
oolitic chert and manufactured from a plano-convex core (Figure 62a).
The broad, utilized end was bevelled, and the midportion of the tool was
humped.   The flaking was multidirectional but oriented towards the
tapered ends and lateral edge. Unlike the gouge, only the broad end was
utilized.   The tool was bifacially worked. The term "adze" is purely
descriptive, since the function of this tool is problematical.   This
tool is differentiated from the gouge previously described on the basis
of its greater length, greater width of its worked, bevelled end, and by
its greater weight (see Table 68).

Projectile Points

Four Middle Woodland projectile points were recovered from the Truck #7 site and the Go-Kart South sites. One of these, a Manker-like point found in the tool cache at the Go-Kart South site, is described elsewhere. Two projectile points were found at the Truck #7 site, while another was recovered from Block C at the Go-Kart South site. None of the points were found in pit feature contexts, although a contracting-stemmed point from the Truck #7 site was found in the disturbed soil immediately above the Feature 1 structure and was associated with the structure (Figure 62d). An expanding-stemmed, basal fragment found at the Truck #7 site was recovered during the IDOT surface collection of that site.

The projectile points were all broken, with the exception of the Manker-like point in the tool cache. Although broken, they clearly represent common Middle Woodland point types. For this reason, they were assigned to the Middle Woodland occupation in this locality. Three of these points are described below.

A. Contracting-stemmed Point

A contracting-stemmed projectile point was recovered that was made of an off-white, local, coarse-grained, oolitic chert. The tip was broken, the base was contracting, and the width between barbs was relatively wide. Flaking was broad and the blade edges were not finely retouched. A specific point type was not assigned, although the contracting-stemmed base indicated a Middle Woodland affiliation. It was found in the western portion of the circular structure, but in mixed alluvium (Figure 62d).

The maximum length of this point was 5.2 cm; the width between barbs was 4.4 cm; the stem length was 1.3 cm; the stem width was 2.2 cm; the stem base width was 1.7 cm; the thickness was 1.3 cm; and its weight was 15.5 g.

B. Expanding-stemmed, Basal Fragment

An expanding-stemmed basal fragment of a projectile point/hafted scraper (?) was recovered from the surface of the Truck #7 site. Only the base and lower stem portion remained. The basal portion was expanded, and the point appeared to have been corner-notched, although the notching was only partially represented on one side. This fragment was made of Ste. Genevieve red chert, and it was thermally altered, probably intentionally. This point was identified as a possible Snyder's Affinis type. Only the stem base width (2.30 cm) could be measured; the specimen weighed 3.1 g.

C. Contracting-stemmed Point

A contracting-stemmed point was found during machine scraping in the western end of Block C at the Go-Kart South site. It was found in the clay subsoil associated with the inner channel ridge. The basal portion was contracting. The point was broken at the midsection portion of the blade. It was very crudely chipped and was made of a coarse-grained, local, light gray, oolitic chert. It was identified as a possible Waubesa or Dickson contracting-stemmed point, and it was, therefore, associated with the Middle Woodland occupation at this site (Figure 63c).

The maximum length of this point was 7.40 cm; the width between barbs was 3.34 cm; the stem length was ca. 2.30 cm; the stem width was 2.45 cm; the blade thickness was 1.75 cm; and the weight was 11.10 g.

Nonchert Tools

Only a limited number of nonchert tools were recovered from the Truck #7 site. These included two igneous, cobble hammerstones, one of which was fired and cracked. Both hammerstones exhibited battering and pecking fractures on various portions of the cobble. They were both found in Feature 16, which was a depository for a large quantity of lithic debitage. Also found in Feature 16 was a grinding stone made of igneous rock. One side was extremely polished from grinding and was fire-cracked. The other side was partially smoothed and flat but exhibited pecking marks. It is suggested that this tool may have also served as an anvil stone for core reduction activities, especially since it was associated with the Feature 16 debitage depository.

A fragment of a ground, sandstone metate was recovered from Feature 19. It contained several ground, circular concavities and was burned and fire-cracked. This tool, along with the grinding stone from Feature 16, provided good evidence for grinding activities at the site.

Discussion of Truck #7 Lithic Assemblage

The lithics recovered from the Truck #7 site represented a relatively uniform assemblage of chert debris and tools, mostly

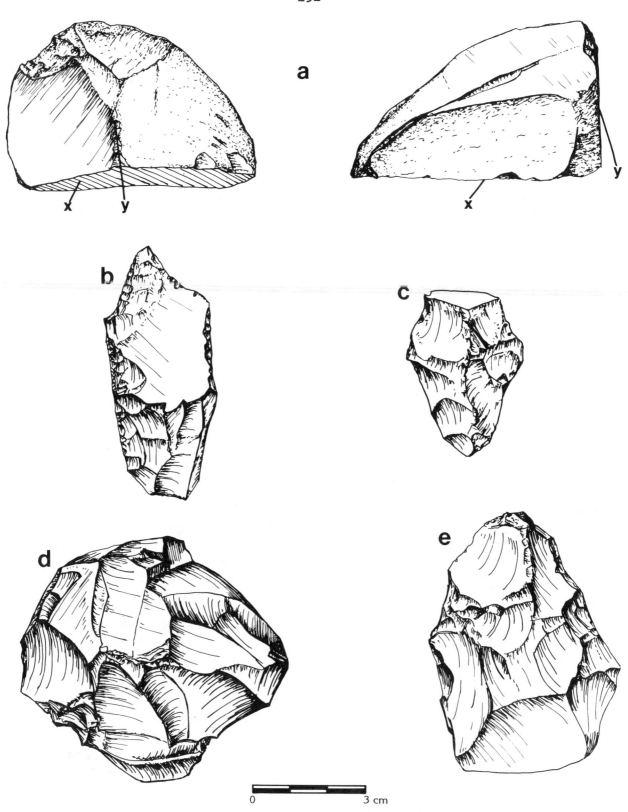

Figure 63. Miscellaneous Core and Bifacial Tools Recovered During Machine Excavation at the Go-Kart South Site

concentrated within Feature 1 (structure) and specifically distributed within the pit features in that structure (Plate 14). Very little debitage was recovered between features inside or outside the structure, suggesting that manufacturing and/or reduction activities were focused primarily in the structure and over or near specific pits. Feature 16 contained two hammerstones, a possible anvil stone, over 5000 chert flakes, including 3000+ small (2-4 mm) thinning/shatter flakes, a preform, and several chert scraper tools. It was suggested that this pit served as the primary depository of lithic debitage within the structure.

Considering the density of chert debris in the pits within the structure, the general scarcity of secondary retouched or utilized flakes in this assemblage was surprising. It would appear that the lithic chipping activites were directed toward the manufacture of larger tools such as gouges and scrapers. In fact, only a few prepared cores were recovered at this site, suggesting that most of the original core nodules had been reduced considerably prior to their having been brought to the site.

The lithic tools within the structure were not abundant but were evenly distributed throughout the pits. They consisted almost entirely of crude, core scraping tools, in contrast to the more finely worked scrapers in the tool cache from the Go-Kart South site. A knife, gouge, and adze were found in the northeast sector of the structure just north of Feature 14. This may have been a work or processing area, possibly for hide or meat preparation. Two ground stone fragments were recovered from Features 16 and 19. These tools were presumably utilized for grinding plant products such as nuts or seeds. A specific location for such grinding activities within the structure could not be determined. A galena nodule from Feature 14 represents the only exotic nonchert item recovered from inside the structure. Its use as a pigment is inferred. As mentioned previously this particular nodule has been traced to the Potusi formation of southeastern Missouri (Walthall 1981:54).

The distribution of the various flake types by feature and by chert source has been presented in Tables 63-67. These tables were prepared to quantify the range of reduction activity accomplished in the interior portion of the structure. The absence of lamellar blades at the Truck #7 site, often present at Hopewell sites in the Illinois River valley, was noteworthy.

254

Plate 14. Selected Chert Artifacts Recovered from Feature 1 at the Truck #7 site: a-c, projectile points and fragments; d, knife; e, small flake scraper; f, adze; g-h, core scrapers; i, preform; j, gouge

Go-Kart South Site Lithics

Description

Except for the tool cache, all of the lithic tools from the the Go-Kart South site were recovered from surface contexts, from alluvial overburden, or from nonfeature subsurface contexts. The assemblage in the alluvial overburden was composed of two components, Mississippian and Middle Woodland. The subsurface material consisted primarily of Middle and Early Woodland materials. For the most part, it was impossible to subdivide these assemblages because of their mixed nature.

The majority of the subsurface tools were found below the alluvial overburden in the inner channel ridge occupational surface. They were particularly concentrated in Excavation Block C, which was adjacent to the Truck #7 site occupation area. The Middle Woodland tool cache was also found at the western end of Block C. The relationship of the surrounding chert debris in Block C to the Middle Woodland occupation at the Truck #7 site is problematical (Figure 63).

The distribution of chert types at the Go-Kart South site generally paralleled the assemblage from the Truck #7 site. As at the Truck #7 site, the surface collections and the materials collected during machine scraping contained only a few examples of the Ste. Genevieve purple chert variety. All of the chert types found at the Truck #7 site, however, were also found in Block C at the Go-Kart South site. On this basis, along with the tool cache, this section of Go-Kart South site has been associated with the Truck #7 Middle Woodland occupation area. As was explained previously, only a modern dirt field road separates these two occupational areas.

Tool Cache (Feature 1)

During the late fall of 1978, while machine stripping the western portion of Block C at the Go-Kart South site, a unique lithic tool cache was exposed. This cache was assigned a feature number (1) and it was excavated by hand over a two day period. It consisted primarily of a stacked pile of 33 worked scraper tools, but also contained a Manker corner-notched projectile point; a chipped hammerstone; a small, worked piece of hematite; a bifacially worked tool; a small, utilized flake; and two nonutilized flakes. The projectile point and the hammerstone had been found at the base of the stacked tool cache.

The tools were stacked vertically 10.5 cm high and occupied an area of 27 x 25 cm. The cache was situated in silty clay (10YR 3/2) soil that was undisturbed by plowing. No evidence of fill was found around the cache. Approximately 70% of the worked scrapers were lying with their ventral surfaces up. Ten scrapers were lying horizontal to the surface, while five were oriented vertically to the surface. The remaining 18 scrapers were slightly angled either downward or upward to the surface (mean=21.7 degrees). The total weight of the cache, including the hammerstone and hematite, was 787 g (Plates 15 and 16).

Of the 36 chert tools found in the cache, including the projectile point, 31 were made of nonlocal Dongola chert; 3 were made of local, Ste. Genevieve red chert; and 2 were made of local Fern Glen chert. The consistency in texture and color of the Dongola tools suggests that they had been made from either a single core or from cores that derived from a single outcrop. None of the tools in the cache had been heat-treated.

The hammerstone had been fashioned from a small, ovate, quartzite cobble which had battering marks on one end. Presumably the hammerstone was utilized in manufacturing the other cache tools. The hammerstone was lying at the base of the cache at about a 20 degree angle to the basal surface. It was 6.0 cm long, 4.4 cm wide, and was 1.9 cm thick.

One small, red, soft hematite piece was associated with the cache. It had been rubbed down in several places from use. It weighed only 2.6 g and obviously was approaching the end of its usefulness as a red pigment source.

The projectile point found in this cache was categorized as a Manker corner-notched point. It was made from Dongola chert and was found lying horizontally at the base of the cache. The metric attributes of this point are presented in Figure 64. The dimensions of this point fell within the Manker attribute range calculated by White (1968:68) for Illinois River valley points of this type, although the base of the example from the Go-Kart South site was slightly broader.

The scraping tools, which made up the main tool category in this cache, were divided, for purposes of description, into three primary categories. These included A) retouched flakes, B) steeply retouched flake scrapers, and C) steeply retouched end scrapers. All three categories were also observed in the Middle Woodland lithic assemblage at the Truck #7 site. The descriptions of these categories and their metric attributes are presented in Tables 69-71.

The categories were arbitrarily created on the basis of general morphology and location of retouching. However, six attributes were

257

Plate 15. Excavation at the Go-Kart South Site: upper, view to southwest; lower left and right, Feature 1 tool cache

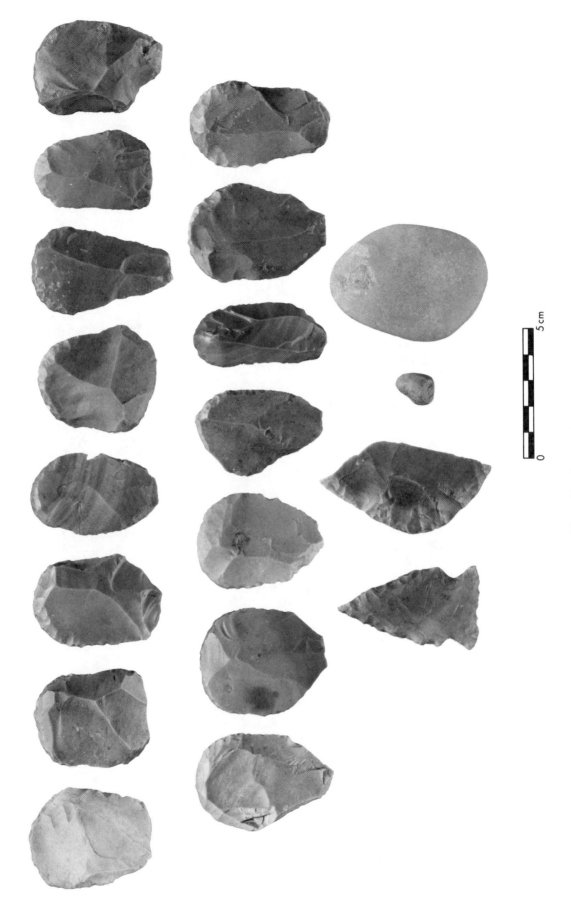

Plate 16. Feature 1 Tool Cache

Table 69. Attributes of Tool Cache from the Go-Kart South Site

				Scrapers				
Item	Tool Category*	Length (cm)	Width (cm)	Circum. (cm)	% Worked	Thickness (cm)	Weight (g)	Chert Type
4	B	5.5	5.0	16.8	100	1.6	52.1	Dongola
5	B	5.1	3.4	13.7	100	1.0	21.4	Dongola
6	A	4.3	3.3	12.9	75	0.6	6.2	Dongola
7	C	5.1	2.4	12.9	88	1.0	12.2	Dongola
8	C	4.9	3.5	14.0	82	0.9	19.5	Dongola
9	A	4.0	3.4	13.2	83	0.6	8.7	Dongola
10	C	4.8	3.9	14.2	72	1.2	21.9	Ste. Genevieve Red
11	A	4.6	4.1	14.5	88	0.9	18.6	Fern Glen
13	C	5.5	4.3	14.5	88	0.8	13.2	Dongola
15	C	5.4	3.8	14.0	71	0.8	19.2	Dongola
16	C	5.1	3.6	14.5	77	1.2	20.7	Dongola
17	C	4.8	3.7	13.7	80	1.0	17.2	Ste. Genevieve Red
18	C	4.9	3.3	12.9	88	0.9	13.7	Dongola
19	C	5.3	3.7	14.7	85	0.7	15.7	Dongola
20	C	5.0	3.2	13.1	88	0.5	10.0	Dongola
21	B	6.0	5.4	18.6	84	1.4	59.2	Dongola
22	A	6.4	3.8	15.6	94	0.6	11.6	Dongola
23	C	5.4	3.4	14.1	83	0.9	17.4	Dongola
24	B	5.0	4.3	14.4	88	1.7	39.1	Ste. Genevieve Red
25	B	4.5	4.4	14.1	82	1.3	30.5	Dongola
26	B	5.5	3.6	15.1	100	1.3	29.0	Dongola
27	A	5.8	3.6	15.2	100	0.9	18.2	Dongola
28	C	4.6	3.1	12.7	76	0.8	11.3	Dongola
29	A	4.8	3.0	12.1	87	0.6	7.1	Dongola
30	A	5.2	2.9	13.7	77	0.6	8.9	Fern Glen
31	B	5.1	4.2	14.4	88	1.0	21.8	Dongola
32	A	4.0	4.0	12.6	57	0.9	15.5	Dongola
33	A	4.7	3.2	13.1	80	0.6	9.9	Dongola
34	C	4.3	3.7	13.7	81	0.8	16.8	Dongola
35	C	4.8	4.2	14.5	90	1.0	21.1	Dongola
36	A	3.8	2.8	10.9	51	0.6	7.2	Dongola
PP31	C	4.7	4.4	14.1	82	1.1	18.8	Dongola
PP10	B	6.0	5.1	17.5	100	1.6	61.3	Dongola

Total N of Scrapers = 33; Total Weight = 675.0 g; Mean Weight = 20.45 g

	Additional Tool Cache Material		
Item	Material Category	Wt(g)	Raw Material Type
12	Biface	21.7	Dongola chert
14	Projectile Point	14.0	Dongola chert
PP8	Utilized Flake	2.9	Dongola chert
PP38	Flake	0.4	Indeterminate chert
PP39	Flake	0.6	White Local chert
37	Hammerstone	69.8	Quartzite
PP15	Worked Hematite	2.6	Hematite

* A - Retouched Flakes; B - Steeply Retouched Flake Scrapers;
  C - Steeply Retouched End Scrapers

Table 70. Worked Areas on Scrapers and Retouched Flakes
from the Tool Cache at the Go-Kart South Site

Item	Tool Category*	Side Worked		End or Edge Worked			Ventral Side
		Dorsal	Ventral	Lateral	Proximal	Distal	Edge Worked
4	B	X	–	X	X	X	
5	B	X	X	X	X	X	Lateral
6	A	X	X	X	–	X	Lateral
7	C	X	X	X	–	X	Lateral
8	C	X	X	X	–	X	Lateral
9	A	X	X	X	–	X	Lateral
10	C	X	–	X	–	X	
11	A	X	–	X	–	X	
13	C	X	X	X	–	X	Lateral
15	C	X	–	X	–	X	
16	C	X	–	X	–	X	
17	C	X	X	X	–	X	Lateral
18	C	X	–	X	–	X	
19	C	X	X	X	–	X	Lateral
20	C	X	–	X	–	X	
21	B	X	–	X	–	X	
22	A	X	X	X	X	X	Lateral
23	C	X	–	X	–	X	
24	B	X	–	X	X	X	
25	B	X	–	X	–	X	
26	B	X	X	X	X	X	Lateral and Distal
27	A	X	–	X	–	X	
28	C	X	–	X	–	X	
29	A	X	–	X	X	X	
30	A	X	X	X	X	X	Lateral
31	B	X	–	X	–	X	
32	A	X	X	X	–	X	Lateral
33	A	X	–	X	X	–	
34	C	X	–	X	–	X	
35	C	X	–	X	–	X	
36	A	X	–	X	–	X	
PP10	B	X	X	X	X	X	Lateral and Proximal
PP31	C	X	–	X	X	X	
		33	13	33	10	32	

* See Table 69 for key to Tool Category.

Table 71. Mean Metric Attributes within Tool
Categories A-C of the Tool Cache

Category A: Retouched Flakes (N=10)

Attribute	Mean	Standard Deviation	Standard Error
Length (cm)	4.760	0.836	0.264
Width (cm)	3.410	0.456	0.144
Edge Circumference (cm)	13.380	1.427	0.451
Percent of Edge Worked	79.200	15.332	4.848
Thickness (cm)	0.690	0.145	0.046
Weight (g)	11.190	4.636	1.466

Category B: Steeply Retouched Flake Scrapers (N=8)

Attribute	Mean	Standard Deviation	Standard Error
Length (cm)	5.337	0.515	0.182
Width (cm)	4.425	0.711	0.251
Edge Circumference (cm)	15.575	1.814	0.641
Percent of Edge Worked	92.750	7.996	2.827
Thickness (cm)	1.362	0.267	0.094
Weight (g)	39.300	16.275	5.754

Category C: Steeply Retouched End Scrapers (N=15)

Attribute	Mean	Standard Deviation	Standard Error
Length (cm)	4.973	0.333	0.086
Width (cm)	3.613	0.510	0.132
Edge Circumference (cm)	13.840	0.656	0.169
Percent of Edge Worked	82.067	6.006	1.551
Thickness (cm)	0.907	0.187	0.048
Weight (g)	16.580	3.761	0.971

Total of Means for Categories A-C

Attribute	Category A	Category B	Category C
Length (cm)	4.760	5.337	4.973
Width (cm)	3.410	4.425	3.613
Edge Circumference (cm)	13.380	15.575	13.840
Percent of Edge Worked	79.200	92.750	82.067
Thickness (cm)	0.690	1.362	0.907
Weight (g)	11.190	39.300	16.580

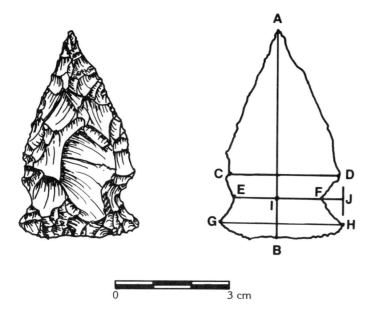

A-B	Length	5.4 cm
C-D	Maximum blade width	3.0 cm
E-F	Stem width	2.4 cm
G-H	Basal width	3.2 cm
I-B	Stem length	1.4 cm
D-H	Notch opening	1.3 cm
F-J	Notch depth	0.4 cm
	Thickness	0.8 cm
	Weight	14.0 g

0   3 cm

Figure 64. Manker Point Associated with the Go-Kart South Site Tool Cache

Table 72. Significant Variance (Student's T-Test) between
Attribute Means in Tool Categories A-C

Categories Compared	N	Attributes	T Value	Degrees of Freedom	2-Tailed Probability
A-Retouched Flakes	10	Width	3.68	16	0.002
B-Steeply Retouched Flakes	8	Edge Circumference	2.88	16	0.011
		Thickness	6.84	16	0.000
		Weight	5.24	16	0.000
B-Steeply Retouched Flakes	8	Width	3.17	21	0.005
C-Steeply Retouched End Scrapers	15	Edge Circumference	3.37	21	0.003
		% of Worked Edge	3.62	21	0.002
		Thickness	4.80	21	0.000
		Weight	5.25	21	0.000
A-Retouched Flakes	10	Thickness	3.09	23	0.005
C-Steeply Retouched End Scrapers	15	Weight	3.20	23	0.004

selected so that the main categories could be quantitatively compared. These attributes included length, width, edge circumference, percent of edge worked/retouched, thickness, and weight. It would have been useful to calculate the angle of retouch, since steepness of retouch was one of the criteria used to distinguish Category B from Category C. This, however, was not attempted in this analysis.

Although the general tool categories differed from one another, the same comparative attributes could be utilized because all of the tools were made from flakes with clearly defined ventral and dorsal sides, and distal and proximal ends. Length, for example, was measured from the proximal end (bulb of percussion) to the distal end (hinge) of the flake. Width was the maximum right angle distance across the length axis. Circumference edge was simply the distance around the edge of the worked and unworked portions of the tool.

The means calculated for each attribute category are presented in Table 71, and generally support the originally established intuitive categories. While some of the means were similar, others clearly demarcated the categories; Table 72 presents a t-test comparison of means between each of the three tool categories. For example, Category A (retouched flakes) and Category B (steeply retouched flake scrapers) differed significantly in four of six metric categories, including width, edge circumference, thickness, and weight. The greatest difference occurred between Category B and Category C (steeply retouched end scrapers) where five categories differed significantly, in terms of width, edge circumference, percent of worked edge, thickness, and weight. Categories A and C were more similar, differing significantly only in regard to thickness and weight.

The categories discussed above are as follows:

Category A: Retouched Flakes (Figure 65, Items 6, 9, 11, 22, 27, 29, 30, 32, 33, and 36)

Category A was characterized by thin (mean=0.69 cm), angular flakes with flat retouching along both the lateral and/or distal ends of the ventral and/or dorsal flake surfaces. The mean weight for this category was 11.19 g, the lowest of any of the categories.

Category B: Steeply Retouched Flake Scrapers (Figure 66, Items 4, 5, 21, 24, 25, 26, 31, and PP 10)

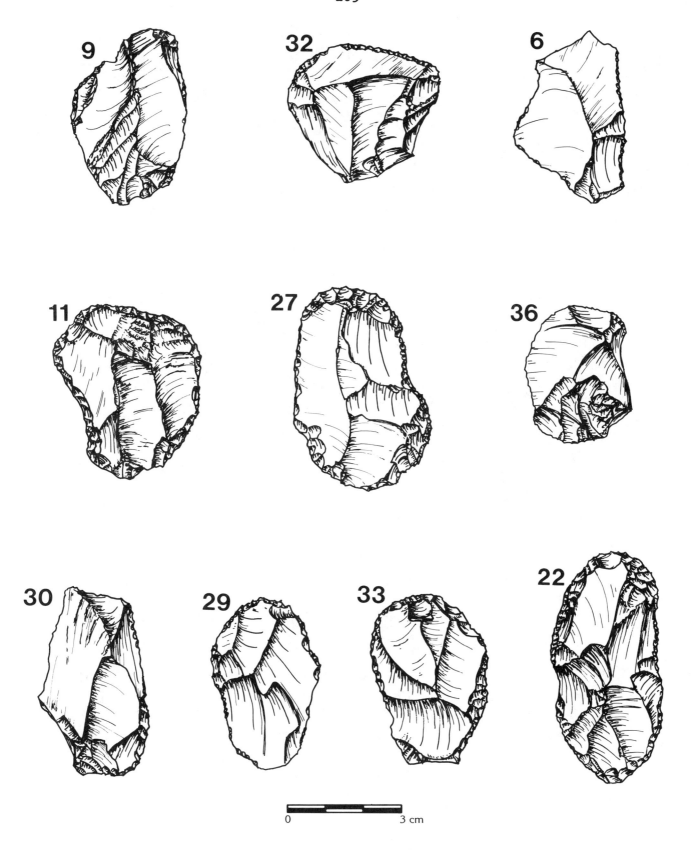

Figure 65. Retouched Flakes (Category A) from the Go-Kart South Site Tool Cache

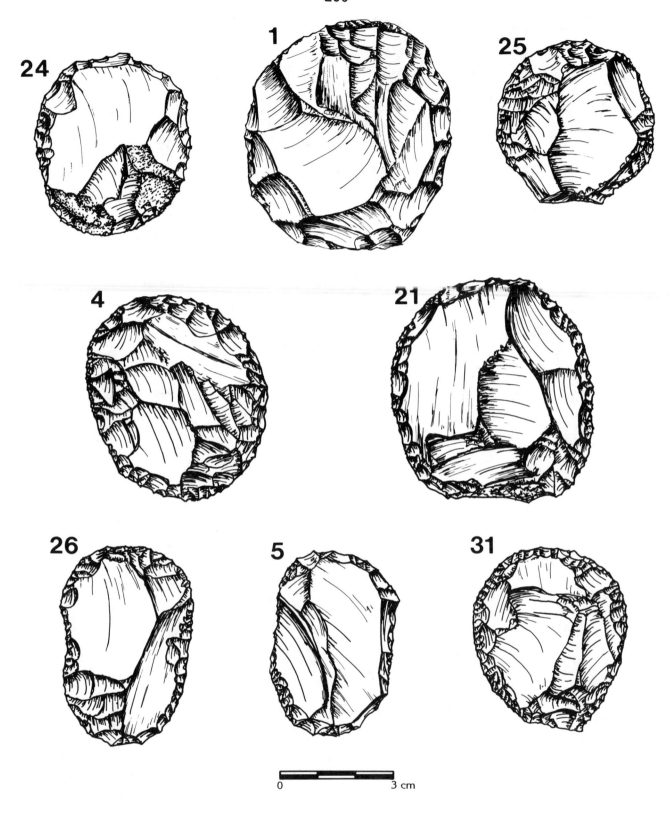

Figure 66. Steeply Retouched Flake Scrapers (Category B) from the Go-Kart South Site Tool Cache

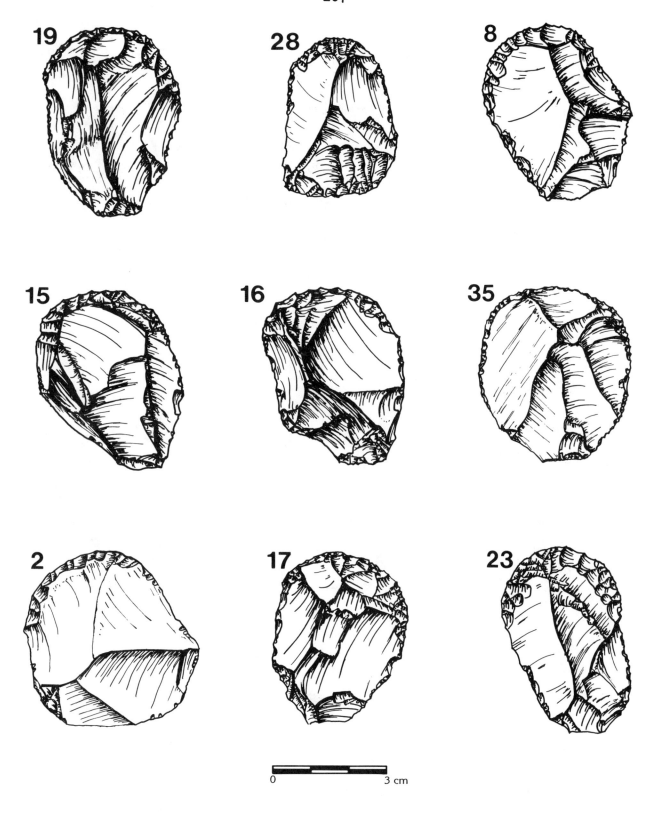

Figure 67. Steeply Retouched End Scrapers (Category C) from the Go-Kart South Site Tool Cache

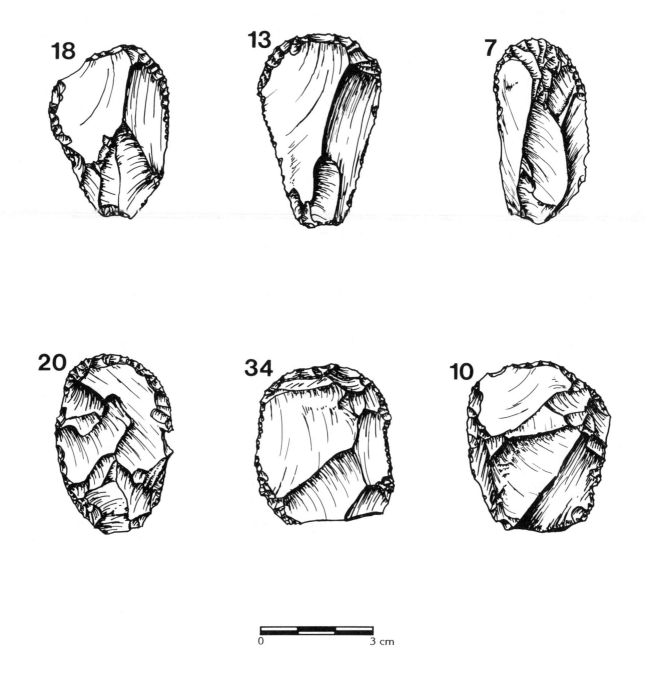

Figure 67. continued

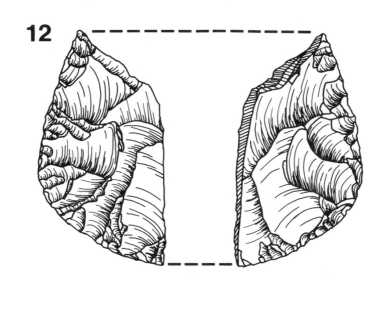

12

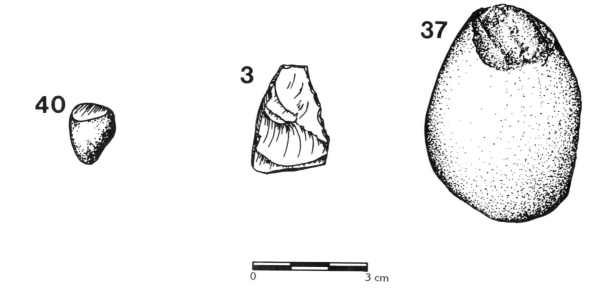

40

3

37

0   3 cm

Figure 68. Miscellaneous Items from the Go-Kart South Site Tool Cache:
12, biface; 40, worked hematite; 3, utilized flake; 37, quartzitic
hammerstone

Category B was typified by relatively thick (mean=1.36 cm), oval to circular flakes with steep retouching around the entire circumference of the dorsal portion of the flake. These are generally referred to as discoidal scrapers. The mean weight for this category was 39.30 g, the highest of any category in the cache.

Category C: Steeply Retouched End Scrapers (Figure 67, Items 7, 8, 13, 15, 16, 17, 18, 19, 20, 23, 28, 34, 35, and PP 31)

Category C was characterized by a variety of angular to oval, moderately thick (mean-0.91 cm) flakes with steep retouching on the distal, dorsal portion of the flake, and flat retouching along the lateral, dorsal edges nearest the distal steeply retouched end. The mean weight for this category was 16.58 g.

Category D: Bifacially Worked Tool (Figure 68, Item 12)

Category D, an angular flake tool, was characterized by flat, bifacial flaking on its dorsal and ventral surfaces. The function of this tool is unknown, although it may represent a preform.

Category E: Projectile Point (Item 14)

Category E was assigned to a side-notched, expanding-stemmed, Manker-like projectile point. Its metric attributes are described in Figure 64.

Category F: Additional Material Found in Tool Cache (Figure 68)

Hematite: Utilized, one ground end, 2.6 g; Hammerstone: made from waterworn cobble 69.8 g; Retouched Flake: fragment, from Dongola chert, 2.9 g; Flake: white local oolitic chert, 0.6 g; Flake: indeterminate chert, 0.4 g.

Discussion of the Go-Kart South Site Tool Cache

The Go-Kart South site tool cache is thought to be a discarded tool kit. No evidence exists that would relate this cache to a burial or specialized activity area. It is suggested that the tools were stacked within a closed container, probably a leather pouch, and purposely discarded or simply lost. The tools were not stacked in any particular order or according to any particular tool category. The miscellaneous nonutilized flakes, the rubbed hematite, the pecked hammerstone, and the broken, bifacially worked tools indicate that this was a utilized tool kit and not one containing nonutilized tools for ceremonial purposes. The consistency in flaking techniques and the similarities in category attributes suggest that the tools were made by a single individual.

The tool cache at the Go-Kart South site was probably associated with the Middle Woodland occupation at the Truck #7 site. The tools and projectile point represent Middle Woodland tool types. The cache is unique for its variety of tool forms, and should not be considered equivalent to the Hopewell preform caches reported elsewhere in the Midwest. Additional wear analysis should be performed on this cache to determine possible functions and evidence of use (White 1968:31-49).

RADIOCARBON DETERMINATIONS

Four radiocarbon dates were obtained for the Middle Woodland occupation at the Truck #7 site. These dates were determined by the radiocarbon dating laboratory of the Illinois State Geological Survey located at the UIUC. All of the samples were taken from features located inside the structure. Two pits were dated, and one burned post was dated twice. The two dates obtained from the burned post (Post 31) inside the structure were widely divergent, the two samples yielding dates of 160 $\pm$ 75 A.C. and 445 $\pm$ 75 A.C. It is suggested that the higher date be disregarded, since it falls outside of the range of the Middle Woodland period in the American Bottom and also outside of the other two dates obtained from Features 14 and 18, which were 90 $\pm$ 75 A.C. and 230 $\pm$ 75 A.C., respectively. Disregarding the 445 A.C. date, the remaining three dates averaged 160 A.C. Table 73 presents the dates obtained from the Truck #7 site.

FAUNAL REMAINS

Faunal remains were recovered from 11 pit features and 1 postmold at the Truck #7 site, and did not occur at the Go-Kart South site. Identifications of recovered faunal remains were provided by Lucretia Kelly. The quantity of material recovered from these features was relatively sparse due to poor preservation, which resulted both from high soil acidity at the site and the absence of limestone in pit fills. The bone was mostly burned and in extremely fragmentary condition. Only features inside the structure, i.e., Features 10, 14, 16, and 18,

Table 73. Radiocarbon Determinations from the Truck #7 Site

Feature Type	Feature	Material Dated	Date B.P.	Date A.C.	ISGS #
Pit	14	Wood Charcoal	1860 ± 75	90 ± 75	ISGS-600
Pit	18	Nutshell Frags.	1720 ± 75	230 ± 75	ISGS-703
Post	31	Wood Charcoal (Quercus, Red)	1790 ± 75	160 ± 75	ISGS-634
Post	31	Wood Charcoal (Quercus, Red)	1505 ± 75	445 ± 75	ISGS-636

Table 74. Animal Bone Unidentifiable to Class by Feature
from the Truck #7 Site

Feature	Burned Bone		Unburned Bone		Total N	Total Wt(g)
	N	Wt(g)	N	Wt(g)		
2	4	0.20	1	0.20	5	0.40
3	32+	0.45	-	-	32+	0.45
6	18	0.70	-	-	18	0.70
10	58	1.30	-	-	58	1.30
11	1	0.10	-	-	1	0.10
12	97	4.40	-	-	97	4.40
14	118	2.40	-	-	118	2.40
15	5	0.15	-	-	5	0.15
16	40	2.65	3	0.20	43	2.85
18	164	3.60	67	0.55	231	4.15
19	61	2.90	10	0.10	71	3.00
PM32	10	0.30	-	-	10	0.30
Total	608	19.15	81	1.05	689	20.20

+ Fragments were too small to count.

produced materials identifiable to a specific class of fauna. These remains mostly consisted of fragments of deer teeth, including 241 fragments from Feature 10, 61 fragments from Feature 14, 5 fragments from Feature 16, and 49 fragments from Feature 18. Feature 18 also yielded 10 deciduous deer incisor fragments, suggesting the presence of a small deer, one year of age or younger. It was impossible to determine a minimum number of individuals, although one individual per pit suggests a maximum number of four deer. Feature 14 also produced 2 vertebrae and 3 unidentifiable fish elements, as well as a single, unidentifiable snake vertebra.

A total of 689 unidentifiable bone fragments, weighing only 20.2 g, were also recovered from the 11 pit features and single postmold. Nearly 95% of this bone by weight was burned. Table 74 presents this information.

Based on this poorly preserved sample, it is impossible to assess the importance or even range of animal resources procured by the Middle Woodland occupants of the Truck #7 site. Both deer and fish contributed to the subsistence base at this occupation. The presence of deer teeth in four pits inside the structure suggests that nonedible portions of captured deer were taken into the structure interior. This may indicate that both meat processing and probably hide preparation were carried out within the structure, an idea also supported by the various scraping tools found discarded in pits and within the structure.

Limited faunal information has also typified Middle Woodland sites located within the inner channel areas of the American Bottom. This, no doubt, is partly due to acidic soil conditions, and the absence of limestone in pits into which refuse was discarded, but it is also the product of the short-term nature of these occupations, which did not permit the procurement of great numbers of animals. The occupation of a low, inner channel area, such as the Truck #7 site may have been structured primarily around the exploitation of marshland plant resources. Fishing and hunting probably only supplemented the diet of these occupants during plant procurement trips to specialized physiographic localities.

SITE INTERPRETATION

The preceding sections have presented the results obtained from archaeological excavations carried out during 1978 and 1979 at the Truck #7 and the Go-Kart South sites. These investigations have revealed a relatively small but significant Middle Woodland occupation located on a presently buried, inner channel ridge within the Hill Lake meander scar. This occupation has been buried by an alluvial fan extending out from Hill Lake Creek. The inner channel ridge is only slightly buried, but the adjacent channel scar has been completely filled in by the alluvial deposits. The early Mississippian (Lohmann phase) remains found on the surface and in the alluvial deposits covering the Truck #7 site and the Go-Kart South site areas represent secondarily deposited materials (except Feature 11).

Excavations were confined to the right-of-way areas associated with the main FAI-270 corridor and an adjacent frontage road entering the corridor from the west. The frontage road contained all of the Middle Woodland features found at the Truck #7 site. The tool cache from the Go-Kart South site was also associated with the Middle Woodland occupation. It is very likely that the Middle Woodland occupation extends outside of the right-of-way, probably to the northwest on the remaining portion of the inner channel ridge. Surface materials in that area indicate the possibility of a more extensive occupation than defined in this report. Approximately 90% of the originally defined surface site limits within the right-of-way was excavated at both the Truck #7 and the Go-Kart South sites.

Component Distribution

Early Woodland, Middle Woodland, and early Mississippian materials were recovered from the Truck #7 site and the Go-Kart South site areas. At the Truck #7 site, Early Woodland Marion Thick sherds were rare and occurred on the same surface as the Middle Woodland occupation. A fragmented Marion Thick sherd was found on the surface of Feature 20, but this is interpreted as an intrusive item. Other Marion Thick sherds were found at the far western end of Excavation Block III at the Truck #7 site. These were isolated finds located on a lower sandy portion of the inner channel ridge.

At the Go-Kart South site, Marion Thick sherds were found at the western end of Excavation Block C on the downward sloping edge of the inner channel ridge. These materials were embedded in the silty clay soil covering the sandy ridge. The kinds of circumscribed scatters of Marion Thick pottery and sandstone identified at the Carbon Monoxide site (this volume) were not observed here, although sandstone pieces and lithic debris were found in the same area. Further investigations along the apex of the ridge, located west of this area and outside of the right-of-way, would probably reveal an Early Woodland community plan similar to that which was exposed at the Carbon Monoxide site. The presence of Early Woodland materials on low, isolated inner channel

275

ridges fits the Early Woodland settlement pattern already observed at
several sites in the American Bottom.

The Middle Woodland occupation described in this report was located
primarily within the Truck #7 site area. The tool kit cache comprised
the only Middle Woodland remains found at the Go-Kart South site. The
Middle Woodland component is associated with the Hill Lake phase in the
American Bottom. This assessment is based primarily on the ceramic
assemblage, which was characterized by rowed plain and dentate rocker
stamping, brushing, cross-hatched rims, and cross-hatched rims with
crescent reed punctates. One vessel (Vessel 1) contained both plain
rocker stamping and rows of bar stamping. Most of the lips were thick,
smoothed over and bevelled inward, typical traits of the Pike-Hopewell
phase in central Illinois. The radiocarbon determinations obtained from
the Truck #7 site indicate an occupation date of 90 A.C. to 230 A.C.,
which falls within the expected range for the Hill Lake phase in this
area, i.e., ca. 100 A.C. to 300 A.C.

As previously mentioned, the early Mississippian component at both
the Truck #7 and the Go-Kart South sites was identified primarily on the
basis of redeposited materials found within the alluvial fill deposits
covering the channel and inner channel ridge. However, a single feature
(Feature 11) with early Mississippian (Lohmann phase) sherds and maize
remains was excavated at the Truck #7 site. It is probable, therefore,
that an early Mississippian occupation of undefined extent and nature
existed in proximity to the area exposed during 1978-1979. The most
likely location for this occupation would have been along the apex of
the inner channel ridge situated outside of the right-of-way limits
northwest of the exposed the Truck #7 site occupation.

Community Plan

The structure and feature types excavated at the Truck #7 site
represent a rare example of a Middle Woodland community plan in the
American Bottom. The focus of this occupation was obviously Feature 1,
with its associated internal and external pit features. The occupation
was conspicuous in its lack of refuse middens, a feature characteristic
of Middle Woodland sites in the Illinois River valley. Although various
materials were recovered from the refuse pits inside the structure, they
were not abundant. Less than 10 ceramic vessels and only a limited
number of discarded lithic tools were recovered from this occupation.
Hence, it is suggested that the Truck #7 site occupation represents a
relatively small but intensive short-term settlement, occupied minimally
during the late fall and probably into the winter. Although evidence
for winter occupation at this site is largely conjectural, it seems

probable based on the large size and construction of the circular
structure and the distribution of refuse and activity debris within, as
opposed to outside, the structure.

The circular structure represented the primary activity focus of the
occupation. Lithic manufacture, nut and seed storage and preparation,
and hide preparation were probably carried out within the structure.
Pits located outside of the structure contained little lithic or ceramic
material, with the exception of Features 6 and 12. These external pits
appear to have functioned primarily as cooking and/or processing pits.
The external pits lacked seeds and nuts, but contained greater amounts
of wood charcoal than did pits found inside the structure. The fired
areas located east of the structure also indicate that activities,
including burning or firing, were generally conducted outside of the
structure. The primary refuse pits, however, were located inside of the
structure.

The alignment of posts comprising the structure indicated a
sophistication of construction techniques not usually attributed to
groups associated with this time period in Illinois. The use of a
center alignment post, which also may have served as a center support
post, as well as the aligned, interior, support post pattern, has
revealed that house construction was planned and carried out in a
carefully measured and geometrically ordered manner. There is no
conclusive evidence that this structure was ceremonial in nature or was
otherwise exceptional. It appears to have represented a large, seasonal
habitational unit, perhaps for an extended or multifamily unit. The
wide variety of activities undertaken within the structure, particularly
those associated with lithic tool manufacture, food preparation, and
cooking indicates habitation rather than ceremony. A number of similar
structures are known from the Illinois River valley (McGregor 1958;
Marshall 1969) and from Tennessee (Faulkner and McCollough 1974),
suggesting that oval and circular post structures were common house
forms during this period in the Midwest and Southeast. Although the
investigators did not make this observation, a recently excavated
circular structure from the Duck River valley in Tennessee appears to be
similar in complexity to the Truck #7 site structure, particularly in
regard to the use of paired, geometrically symmetrical interior posts
and cross-aligned wall posts. The use of a central alignment post may
also be evidenced there (Kline et al. 1982:27).

Subsistence

One of the original research objectives at the Truck #7 site was a determination of the subsistence base through the retrieval of both faunal and floral remains. To a certain extent, the realization of this objective was limited by poor bone preservation at the site due to high soil acidity and scarcity of limestone in pits. Preservation factors no doubt also affected the ethnobotanical assemblage, although in that case the materials were abundant enough to permit some general statements.

The diversity of plant remains recovered at this site, including 5 nut, 14 seed, and 14 wood types, indicates a rather broad-spectrum exploitation of marsh and nearby bluff resources. The presence of pokeweed and paw-paw suggests a late fall occupation. Both fruits decay rapidly and ripen during September and October. The starchy seed complex, emergent during the Middle Woodland period in Illinois, was also represented at the Truck #7 site, indicating that seed cultivation represented an important part of the subsistence system at this site. In addition, nut collection and processing were also carried out, although it is interesting that hazelnut, a variety predominant in Middle Woodland assemblages elsewhere in the Midwest, occurred only rarely at the Truck #7 site.

The faunal evidence was minimal, consisting only of deer teeth fragments, nondiagnostic fish bone, and a single snake vertebra. Deciduous deer teeth fragments, found in Feature 18, inside the structure, indicate that a small deer, one year of age or less, was procured. This evidence suggests that both hunting and fishing were an integral part of the subsistence system.

Ceramic and Lithic Assemblages

Lithic manufacturing activities were carried out within the structure, the results of which constituted a major portion of the material remains of the Middle Woodland occupation. Chert cores, with their original cortex, were brought into the structure and reduced directly into pits. Only a limited number of lithic tools were recovered from this occupation, and they consisted primarily of various scraper and gouge types, perhaps used for hide preparation and woodworking activities. The total amount of materials recovered from feature contexts at the Truck #7 site was 13,630 items weighing 11,700 grams. Of this amount chert constituted 94 and 63 percent of the assemblage by number and weight, respectively, while ceramic items comprised only 2 and 12 percent of the assemblage by number and weight, respectively (Table 75).

Table 75. Total Material* Recovered from Pit Features
at the Truck #7 Site

Feature	Chert N	Chert Wt(g)	Ceramics N	Ceramics Wt(g)	Sandstone N	Sandstone Wt(g)	Burned Clay N	Burned Clay Wt(g)	Bone N	Bone Wt(g)	Rough Rock N	Rough Rock Wt(g)	Other Material N	Other Material Wt(g)	Other Material Type
2	98	217.3	54	119.9	-	-	160	58.6	5	0.4	1	0.7	30	7.2	Pottery Grog
3	86	70.5	4	3.3	-	-	-	-	32	0.4	-	-	-	-	-
4	-	-	-	-	-	-	-	-	-	-	-	-	-	-	-
5	10	3.7	-	-	2	3.4	-	-	-	-	-	-	-	-	-
6	64	73.9	12	199.7	3	115.2	29	9.1	18	0.7	-	-	8	6.3	Daub
7	-	-	-	-	3	3.7	-	-	-	-	-	-	-	-	-
8	-	-	-	-	-	-	-	-	-	-	-	-	-	-	-
9	-	-	-	-	-	-	-	-	-	-	-	-	-	-	-
10	687	243.8	13	56.7	2	33.4	52	58.4	299	1.3	-	-	1	5.9	Daub
													5	3.6	Limonite
													4	365.7	Limestone
													9	4.3	Silicified Sediment
11	16	15.5	20	15.7	3	144.8	-	-	1	0.1	-	-	-	-	-
12	28	61.9	3	24.6	-	-	-	-	97	4.4	6	508.1	1	50.7	Galena
14	4001	2224.3	47	193.2	14	202.6	19	17.4	185	2.4	-	-	2	0.7	Waterworn Pebble
													10	10.5	Red Stained Clay
15	62	42.9	1	0.9	2	209.7	-	-	5	0.1	-	-	-	-	-
16	6306	3016.4	53	255.6	9	747.5	15	20.8	48	2.8	-	-	-	-	-
17	102	15.6	-	-	1	3.0	5	4.4	290	4.1	-	-	3	5.7	Quartzite
18	788	225.2	27	236.7	3	14.3	32	37.7	71	3.0	-	-	1	1.2	Coal
													1	5.3	Figurine Fragment
19	597	1204.8	83	296.2	-	-	-	-	-	-	-	-	25	111.5	Red Stained Clay
20	-	-	3	7.8	-	-	1	0.8	-	-	-	-	-	-	-
21	-	-	-	-	-	-	-	-	-	-	-	-	3	1.9	Silicified Sediment
Total	12845	7415.8	320	1510.3	42	1477.6	313	207.2	1051	19.5	7	508.8	103	580.5	
Mean Wt(g)		0.58		4.72		35.18		0.66		0.02		72.68			

*excluding lithic tools

Most of the chert types found at this occupation could have been obtained from local sources, including the distinctive red and purple varieties which have been associated with the Mississippian-age Ste. Genevieve Formation. Dongola chert, comprising the majority of artifacts in the tool cache from the Go-Kart South site, does not occur locally but could have been derived from sources in southern Illinois. A few Dongola chert flakes were found in features inside the structure but not in sufficient quantity to indicate that the tool cache was made inside the structure. It is likely that this cache was manufactured elsewhere and that the Dongola artifacts were imported into the site.

The ceramic assemblage consisted of fewer than 10 vessels, all in extremely fragmentary condition. All of the sherds recovered from this occupation represent decorated jars. Despite the decoration, however, these jars are interpreted as utilitarian vessels used probably for storage and/or cooking. Most of the ceramics found in this occupation were tempered with crushed pottery (grog), although in a few instances, uneroded limestone fragments were observed with the grog temper. The decorative techniques found in this assemblage were commonly utilized towards the end of the Middle Woodland period in Illinois. Vessel walls were relatively thin, and only a few Hopewell traits, such as cross-hatched lips, were apparent. There was no evidence for zoning at this site. It is probable, therefore, that this occupation post-dates the classic Hopewell period in this area.

Significance of Investigations

This report represents the first detailed description of an excavated Middle Woodland, Hill Lake phase occupation in the American Bottom. The feature types, the circular post structure, the lithic and ceramic assemblages found in feature contexts, and the floral and faunal remains each represent a unique data set which should serve as a valuable base for future Middle Woodland investigations in the American Bottom. Prior to the excavations at the Truck #7 site, feature types from this period were unknown in this area as were the engineering principles involved in structure construction. The structure, with its associated pits, also provided interesting insights into the organization of activites undertaken inside and outside the dwelling. Based on only this example in the American Bottom, it is difficult to evaluate how typical this occupation may have been, but it does serve as a valuable model for investigating other Middle Woodland occupations in this area.

SUMMARY

    Archaeological investigations at the Truck #7 site and the Go-Kart
South sites revealed a small but intensive occupation, consisting of
only 26 features, that dated to the Hill Lake phase of the Middle
Woodland period. The occupation was situated on an inner channel sand
bar of the Hill Lake meander, presumably to exploit the low-lying
aquatic resources of this locality. Seed and nut processing, hunting,
meat and hide preparation, and lithic manufacturing activities were all
in evidence at this site. The ethnobotanical evidence suggests that the
site was occupied minimally during the late fall. The presence of a
large, well-planned, circular, probably multifamily structure, would
also suggest that the occupation may have extended into the winter. A
wide variety of activities carried out within, not generally outside,
the structure supports this contention.

CHAPTER 6. PLANT REMAINS

by Sissel Johannessen

One of the stated objectives of the research design for
investigation of archaeological sites in the Hill Lake locality was the
determination of subsistence practices associated with each cultural
component at each site with a view toward interpreting the various
functions of settlements within the Hill Lake meander scar. One route
of inquiry into the question of subsistence was the systematic recovery
and analysis of plant remains. The results of this investigation are
presented in this chapter.

The analysis of plant remains from the sites in the Hill Lake
locality was part of a wider paleoethnobotanical investigation of all
sites excavated by the FAI-270 Project in the American Bottom and
adjacent uplands. One objective of the overall investigation was to
determine the spatial and temporal variability in the patterns of
man-plant relationships across the 4000 years of occupation represented
by the sites investigated. Analysis of the sites in the Hill Lake
locality provides an opportunity to recover evidence of the changing use
of one small area of the American Bottom through time.

FLORAL SETTING

The physiographic features of the Hill Lake locality include a
former channel of the Mississippi River near the bluff foot, which may
have been active up until about 3300 B.P. An upland stream, Hill Lake
Creek, flows down from the uplands here and has formed an alluvial fan
extending onto the floodplain.

The following description of the floral resources that would have
been available to the prehistoric inhabitants of the Hill Lake locality
is taken from Gregg (1975), Hus (1908), Telford (1927), Welch (1975),
and Zawacki and Hausfater (1969). The floral descriptions by Gregg,
Welch, and Zawacki and Hausfater were reconstructed from original U.S.
government land survey notes (made in about 1820), and from other
studies of the local flora. The Gregg and Welch studies concern the
American Bottom, and the Zawacki and Hausfater study concerns the lower
Illinois valley, a similar environment to that of the American Bottom,
located some 60 miles to the north. Telford's work is a survey of
forest types in Illinois, and Hus reports on a direct observation of the
American Bottom in the beginning of the twentieth century.

The low area of the Hill Lake meander scar was probably either an oxbow lake or a slough during the prehistoric occupation of the locality, depending on the rate of deposition of sediment in the channel scar. Oxbow lakes near the bluff foot are described by Hus (1908) as supporting a rich flora. A woody growth included willows and cottonwoods, maple, elms, ash, honey locust, mulberry, oaks, and river birch. Shrubs would have included elder, buttonbush, grapes, and brambles. The still waters of the lake may have supported beds of waterlilies, American lotus, and pondweed, while arrowhead, cattails, rushes, and sedges lined the bank.

Sloughs would have been bordered by herbs and a few trees and shrubs: clumps of willows, water-locust, Kentucky coffee tree, river birch, buttonbush, and rows of cattails on the bank as well as arrowhead, knotweeds, and waterplantain.

The talus slopes of the bluff supported a rich and varied flora. Zawacki and Hausfater report 36 woody and 14 herbaceous plants from this zone that are ethnographically documented as having been used. Welch reports that oak, elm, and ash were the dominant witness trees in this zone, but a great variety of other useful species were also present, including sugar maple, black walnut, hackberry, butternut, persimmon, and pawpaw. Herb growth is well developed in this association. Typical of the slope floor would have been mayapple, bloodroot, wild ginger, spring beauty, waterleaf, trillium, Solomon's seal, and Jack-in-the-pulpit.

This rich flora extends back into the bluffs along the slopes of the secondary stream drainage, which is also the favored habitat of black walnut. The valley of the stream drainage would have allowed easy access through the steep bluffs into the upland forests, in which oak and hickory dominate. Within a few kilometers of the bluff edge such special habitats as hill prairies, sinkholes, and limestone glades, where plants such as prickly pear, yucca, and prairie clover grew, would also have been found.

The prehistoric inhabitants of the Hill Lake locality undoubtedly used many of these plants from all zones for fuel, food, shelter, tools, medicine, and ritual. Yarnell (1964) has listed almost 400 taxa that were used by the Indians of the Upper Great Lakes region in early historic times. The full range of plant taxa used prehistorically is not represented in the carbonized remains recovered through flotation from an archaeological site. Differential conditions of deposition, preservation, and recovery create a small and biased sample. In examining the plant remains from a single assemblage, these factors make it difficult to assess the relative importance of the various classes of plant remains present. The emphasis on a particular class of plants can best be seen by contrast with other assemblages. For example, at the Late Archaic Go-Kart North site on the American Bottom in the Hill Lake locality nutshell was very abundant (eight times as abundant as wood charcoal) but seeds were scarce (0.4 seeds per 10 l). The Middle Woodland Truck #7 site assemblage contrasted sharply; nutshell was only half as abundant as wood, while seeds were 17 times more frequent than at the Late Archaic site. These contrasting patterns of debris presumably reflect different patterns of behavior regarding plants by the inhabitants of the two sites, i.e., the early emphasis on nuts was supplanted by a greater use of seeds. As Asch and Asch (1978:329) have argued, "variation in the percentages of different plants between archaeological assemblages can indicate changes in utilization".

The five sites in the Hill Lake locality contained components which spanned about 1000 years - from Early Woodland through early Mississippian times. The patterns of plant remains characterizing each of the components are described below, and, in a summary section, are compared for evidence of variation in man-plant interactions throughout this time span.

METHODS

During excavation of the sites under consideration, flotation samples of known volume (usually 10 liters) were taken routinely from each natural stratum of every feature excavated. In addition, charcoal samples were collected directly into aluminum foil when the excavator observed a charcoal concentration.

All flotation samples were water-floated according to the IDOT system (Wagner 1976), a method of tub flotation using wooden boxes lined with a #40 mesh (0.42 mm) screen.

For analysis of the plant remains, sampling was necessary. The sampling procedures used were designed to result in a sample which would come as close as possible to 1) representing all variation present within a particular component, and 2) being sufficiently systematic to allow comparison of results between components. Therefore, analysis was not limited to "special" features (e.g., those with abundant charred plant remains), but encompassed all feature types within a component.

The sampling procedure was begun by assigning each feature from a site (or from a component if the site was multicomponent) to a particular morphological and/or functional feature category at the discretion of the site director. These categories might include, for example, structures, shallow basin pits within structures, bell-shaped pits, stains, ceramic concentrations, etc. Features lacking firm component associations, or exhibiting excessive disturbance from rodents or superpositioning, were generally discarded from consideration. Then, from each of the established categories, features were selected at random to make up a sample of at least 40% of the total features at the site or component. At least one 10 l flotation sample was then selected from each natural stratum of each of the selected features.

The processing of the selected flotation samples then proceeded as follows. If the heavy fraction of a sample still contained large amounts of soil residue, making hand-sorting of the botanical material excessively time consuming, the fractions were further cleaned by chemical flotation (Bodner and Rowlett 1980, Struever 1968a). The technique for this process, which was developed in the FAI-270 laboratory utilizes a gravitational flow of the material onto a fine cloth screen, which results in increased recovery and less mechanical breakage of the delicate plant parts than does the conventional scoop-and-dump technique.

The cleaned and dried samples were then passed through a 2 mm sieve. Each fraction was sorted by hand under low magnification (10X-30X). All material greater than 2 mm in size was sorted into categories (e.g., wood, nutshell, maize); each category was weighed, and the fragments were counted. The less than 2 mm portion of the samples was scanned carefully and all seeds, seed fragments, and remains of cultivated plants were removed. Sample weights and the counts of wood and nut fragments are based on the greater than 2 mm material only. Seeds were not weighed.

Since plant material decomposes quickly in the damp soils of the river bottom, only charred materials were considered to be of archaeological origin.

Identification was attempted of all seeds, all nut fragments, cultivated plants, and of the first 20 randomly selected wood fragments from each sample. Identifications were made with the aid of standard texts (Martin and Barkley 1961, Montgomery 1977, Panshin and de Zeeuw 1970), and, ultimately, by a one-to-one comparison to specimens in a modern reference collection, which were charred for greater comparability. Identifications were made to the genus level where possible. Specific identifications were made only when 1) only one species of a genus exists in the area (e.g., Diospyros virginiana), or 2) all other possible species have been eliminated on the basis of comparative morphology (e.g., Polygonum erectum). Generous help in identification was given by the following people: Nancy and David Asch

(Northwestern University Archaeobotanical Laboratory), Frances B. King (Illinois State Museum), Gail Wagner and Leonard Blake (Washington University at St. Louis), the Forest Products Laboratory (University of Missouri at Columbia), Dr. Dunn (Herbarium Curator, University of Missouri at Columbia), Drs. Harlan, Hilu, and DeWet (Crop Evolution Laboratory, UIUC), and Dr. D´arcy (Missouri Botanical Garden).

RESULTS

Fiege Site

The Fiege site consisted of 12 features (4 pits, 7 stains, and 1 lithic concentration), situated on a buried inner channel ridge of the former Hill Lake channel. Although diagnostic materials were not recovered from feature contexts, the lithic and ceramic materials recovered from surface and nonfeature subsurface contexts indicated an Early Woodland occupation of the site.

A total of 150 l of fill from seven of the 12 features were analyzed (Features 2, 3, 4, 5, 6, 7, and 11). Charred plant remains were very sparse; only 2.9 g were recovered in all. The majority of these were nutshell remains. Scattered wood fragments, a few seeds, and one squash rind fragment, were also recovered (Table 76).

Nut

Samples from three of the seven features analyzed yielded no nutshell, and a total of 174 fragments were recovered from the remaining four features. The majority of these remains were thick-shelled hickory, and a few fragments of hazelnut were also identified.

Seeds

The samples yielded a total of only seven seeds. The two identifiable seeds were both from fleshy fruits, a persimmon and a grape.

Table 76. Flotation-recovered Plant Remains from the Fiege Site (11-Mo-609)

	Feature							
	2	3	4	5	6	7	11	Total
total wt. charcoal (g)	1.3	0.3	0.1	0.8	<0.1	0.3	0.1	2.9
total vol. flot. analyzed (l)	20	10	30	10	10	50	20	150
NUT (total frags.)	98	30	3	43	–	–	–	174
thick-shelled hickory								
Carya sp.	43	15	1	30	–	–	–	89
hazelnut								
Corylus americana	2	1	–	1	–	–	–	4
hickory and walnut								
Juglandaceae	53	14	2	12	–	–	–	81
SEED (total)	3	–	1	–	–	1	2	7
persimmon								
Diospyros virginiana	1	–	–	–	–	–	–	1
grape								
Vitis sp.	1	–	–	–	–	–	–	1
unknown	1	–	1	–	–	–	–	2
unidentifiable	–	–	–	–	–	1	2	3
TROPICAL CULTIGENS								
squash								
Cucurbita sp.								
(N of rind frags.)	–	–	–	–	–	1	–	1
WOOD (total frags.)	–	2	–	3	4	32	5	46
Kentucky coffee-tree								
Gymnocladus dioica	–	–	–	–	–	2	–	2
coffee-tree/honey locust								
Gymnocladus/Gleditsia	–	–	–	–	–	5,5?	–	5,5?
bark	–	–	–	–	–	–	4	4
diffuse-porous	–	–	–	2	–	3	–	5
ring-porous	–	–	–	–	–	6	–	6
unidentified	–	2	–	1	4	11	1	19

Mesoamerican Cultigens

One small fragment of squash rind (<u>Cucurbita</u> sp.) was recovered from Feature 7. An Early Woodland origin of this squash is possible, but it remains uncertain in view of the lack of a positive cultural affiliation for this feature. Cucurbit remains dating to the Early Woodland period have not been recovered in west central Illinois (Asch, Farnsworth, and Asch 1979:82), but squash and gourd from Early Woodland and earlier contexts have been recovered in Kentucky (Yarnell 1969), Tennessee (Chapman and Shea 1977), and Missouri (Chomko and Crawford 1978; Kay, King, and Robinson 1980).

Wood

The samples yielded very little wood charcoal, only 46 fragments, or 3 fragments per 10 l of fill. Kentucky coffee tree and honey locust were the only taxa identified. Both species prefer floodplain environments.

Carbon Monoxide Site

The Carbon Monoxide site represents Early Woodland Marion phase and late Early Woodland (Columbia Complex) occupations of a ridge within the Hill Lake meander scar. The ridge may have been relatively recently exposed in the channel at the time of the Marion phase occupation, while the Columbia Complex occupation was based on a more well-developed humus horizon of the established ridge. The Marion phase component consisted of a dispersed scatter of seven features: four well-defined scatters of Marion Thick pottery, two shallow pits, and one postmold. The later, more restricted Columbia Complex component was made up of 18 features: 1 structure, 11 pits, and 6 activity areas. There were also 24 pits and stains of unknown association, and two historic features.

Of the 49 features making up the Carbon Monoxide site, 21 (or 42%) were selected for analysis of their floral contents. Five of the 21 belonged to the Marion component (Features 5, 17, 18, 20, and 47), eight belonged to the Columbia Complex component (Features 4, 6, 13, 15, 19, 21, 22, and 27), and eight were of unknown affiliation (Features 11, 31, 32, 33, 35, 37, 38, and 39). A total of 710 l of fill from these 21 features was examined, resulting in the recovery of 24.4 g of charred botanical material. Table 77 presents the data, and shows that the material was unevenly distributed, being much more abundant in the Columbia Complex features than in the Marion features. Seeds were quite

Table 77. Flotation-recovered Plant Remains for the Carbon Monoxide Site (11-Mo-593)

| | Marion Phase Feature | | | | | |
	5	17	18	20	47	Subtotal
total wt. charcoal (g)	0.0	<0.1	0.1	<0.1	0.1	0.4
total vol. flot. analyzed (l)	10	20	20	40	20	110
NUT (total frags.)	-	-	-	-	-	0
thick-shelled hickory						
Carya sp.	-	-	-	-	-	-
pecan/bitternut						
C. illinoensis/C. cordiformis	-	-	-	-	-	-
hazelnut						
Corylus americana	-	-	-	-	-	-
hickory and walnut						
Juglandaceae	-	-	-	-	-	-
butternut						
Juglans cinerea	-	-	-	-	-	-
black walnut						
J. nigra	-	-	-	-	-	-
SEEDS (total)	-	2	11	2	-	15
goosefoot						
Chenopodium sp.	-	-	1	-	-	1
grasses						
Gramineae	-	-	-	-	-	-
American lotus						
Nelumbo lutea						
(N of shell frags.)*	-	-	(4)	(17)	-	2
knotweed						
Polygonum sp.	-	-	1	-	-	1
dock						
Rumex sp.	-	1	-	-	-	1
unknown	-	-	-	1	-	1
unidentifiable	-	1	8	-	-	9
WOOD (total frags. recovered)	-	5	21	4	24	54
(total frags. identified)	-	5	21	4	24	54
birch						
Betula sp.	-	-	-	-	-	-
hickory						
Carya sp.	-	-	-	-	-	-
persimmon						
Diospyros virginiana	-	-	-	-	-	-
ash						
Fraxinus sp.	-	-	-	-	10	10
honey locust/mulberry						
Gleditsia/Morus	-	-	-	-	-	-
sycamore						
Platanus occidentalis	-	-	2	-	-	2
oak						
Quercus sp.	-	-	-	-	-	-
elm and hackberry						
Ulmaceae	-	-	-	-	-	-
grape-vine						
Vitis sp.	-	-	-	-	-	-
diffuse-porous	-	-	-	-	-	-
ring-porous	-	-	-	-	-	-
unidentifiable	-	5	19	4	14	42

*all fragments from one feature counted as one seed

Table 77. continued

	4	6	13	15	19	21	22	27	Subtotal
					Columbia Complex Feature				
total wt. charcoal (g)	5.3	0.0	2.6	2.2	4.7	0.3	1.6	3.8	20.5
total vol. flot. analyzed (1)	100	40	40	30	40	30	20	40	340
NUT (total frags.)	370	-	132	141	321	21	109	227	1321
thick-shelled hickory									
Carya sp.	138	-	91	32	120	5	21	92	499
pecan/bitternut									
C. illinoensis/C. cordiformis	8	-	1	21	-	1	14	-	45
hazelnut									
Corylus americana	-	-	-	-	-	-	-	-	-
hickory and walnut									
Juglandanceae	204	-	40	74	195	15	74	127	729
butternut									
Juglans cinerea	8	-	-	14	6	-	-	8	36
black walnut									
J. nigra	12	-	-	-	-	-	-	-	12
SEEDS (total)	7	7	2	1	2	25	1	32	77
goosefoot									
Chenopodium sp.	-	-	-	-	-	-	-	-	-
grasses									
Gramineae	1?	-	-	-	-	25	-	-	26
American lotus									
Nelumbo lutea									
(N of shell frags.)*	(2)	-	-	-	-	-	-	(10)	2
knotweed									
Polygonum sp.	-	-	-	-	-	-	-	-	-
dock									
Rumex sp.	-	-	-	-	-	-	-	-	-
unknown	-	2	-	1	-	-	1	-	4
unidentifiable	5	5	2	-	2	-	-	31	45
WOOD (total frags. recovered)	80	-	65	23	40	1	11	17	237
(total frags. identified)	80	-	54	23	40	1	11	17	226
birch									
Betula sp.	-	-	-	-	-	-	-	-	-
hickory									
Carya sp.	-	-	1	-	1	-	-	-	2
persimmon									
Diospyros virginiana	1	-	-	-	-	-	-	-	1
ash									
Fraxinus sp.	-	-	-	-	-	-	-	-	-
honey locust/mulberry									
Gleditsia/Morus	17	-	-	21	3	-	-	3	44
sycamore									
Platanus occidentalis	-	-	-	-	-	-	-	-	-
oak									
Quercus sp.	-	-	9	-	2	-	-	-	11
elm and hackberry									
Ulmaceae	6	-	-	-	-	-	-	2	8
grape-vine									
Vitis sp.	-	-	-	-	3	-	-	-	3
diffuse-porous	-	-	1	1	-	-	-	-	2
ring-porous	21	-	7	-	-	-	1	2	31
unidentifiable	35	-	36	1	31	1	10	10	124

*all fragments from one feature counted as one seed

Table 77. continued

	11	31	32	33	35	37	38	39	Subtotal	Total
Unknown Phase Feature										
total wt. charcoal (g)	<0.1	2.6	<0.1	<0.1	0.6	0.1	0.0	0.1	3.5	24.4
total vol. flot. analyzed (1)	20	30	40	30	60	40	20	20	260	710
NUT (total frags.)	-	160	-	-	43	-	-	13	216	1537
thick-shelled hickory										
Carya sp.	-	7	-	-	-	-	-	-	7	506
pecan/bitternut										
C. illinoensis/C. cordiformis	-	-	-	-	-	-	-	-	-	45
hazelnut										
Corylus americana	-	42	-	-	43	-	-	10	95	95
hickory and walnut										
Juglandaceae		77							77	805
butternut										
Juglans cinerea	-	-	-	-	-	-	-	-	-	36
black walnut										
J. nigra	-	34	-	-	-	-	-	3	37	49
SEEDS (total)	-	5	-	-	1	1	-	-	7	99
goosefoot										
Chenopodium sp.	-	-	-	-	-	-	-	-	-	1
grasses										
Gramineae	-	-	-	-	-	-	-	-	-	26
American lotus										
Nelumbo lutea										
(N of shell frags.)*	-	-	-	-	-	-	-	-	-	4
knotweed										
Polygonum sp.	-	3	-	-	-	-	-	-	3	4
dock										
Rumex sp.	-	-	-	-	-	-	-	-	-	1
unknown	-	2	-	-	1	-	-	-	3	8
unidentifiable	-	-	-	-	-	1	-	-	1	55
WOOD (total frags. recovered)	1	10	4	2	6	8	-	-	31	322
(total frags. identified)	1	10	4	2	6	8	-	-	31	311
birch										
Betula sp.	-	-	-	-	-	4	-	-	4	4
hickory										
Carya sp.	-	-	-	-	-	-	-	-	-	2
persimmon										
Diospyros virginiana	-	-	-	-	-	-	-	-	-	1
ash										
Fraxinus sp.	-	-	-	-	-	1	-	-	1	11
honey locust/mulberry										
Gleditsia/Morus	-	-	-	-	-	-	-	-	-	44
sycamore										
Platanus occidentalis	-	-	-	-	-	-	-	-	-	2
oak										
Quercus sp.	-	4	-	-	2	-	-	-	6	17
elm and hackberry										
Ulmaceae	-	-	-	-	-	3	-	-	3	11
grape-vine										
Vitis sp.	-	-	-	-	-	-	-	-	-	3
diffuse-porous	-	-	2	-	-	-	-	-	2	4
ring-porous	-	1	-	1	1	-	-	-	3	34
unidentifiable	1	5	2	1	3	-	-	-	12	178

*all fragments from one feature counted as one seed

scarce in both components, and no remains of Mesoamerican cultigens were
recovered from either component.

Nut

Samples from the five Marion phase features analyzed (110 l of fill)
were completely devoid of nutshell. In contrast, all Columbia Complex
features with the exception of Feature 6 (a structure) yielded abundant
nut remains, an average of 36 fragments per 10 l. Of the nut remains,
93% were thick-shelled hickories, 3% were pecan hickories, 3% butternut
and 1% black walnut. Of the eight features of unknown association,
three contained nutshell. Fragments of hazelnut shell were recovered
from these three features, in addition to the taxa mentioned above.

All the nut types identified would have been available in the
American Bottom, although their favorite habitats vary; pecans, for
example, are limited to the main river bottoms, since they require
protracted periods of inundation (Telford 1927:16), and hazelnuts are
most abundant at the boundary of the upland forest and prairie (Asch and
Asch 1980:155).

Seeds

Seeds were not well represented in the samples from either component
at the Carbon Monoxide site; only 77 were recovered in all. Of the 32
identifiable seeds, the Marion samples yielded single specimens of
goosefoot, dock, and knotweed (not _Polygonum_ _erectum_), and the Columbia
Complex sample yielded a few grass seeds. The remains of nut-like
American lotus seeds were identified from both Early Woodland
components. American lotus occurs in "oxbow lakes and ponds in river
floodlands, upland sinkhole ponds, artificial lakes and ponds, and
sloughs, and is commonest and in greatest abundance in the floodplain of
the Mississippi and Missouri rivers and their tributaries..."
(Steyermark 1963:668). The rootstocks, young leaves, and seeds of the
plant are edible. The seeds ripen in September and October, and the
rootstocks, although they can be dug in the spring, are at their best in
late autumn. Numerous ethnographic accounts have recorded the use of
this plant for food, including its drying and storage (Pease and Werner
1934:346-347, Smith 1928:262).

Mesoamerican Cultigens

No remains of Mesoamerican cultigens were recovered from the
samples. Of course, this does not necessarily mean that they were not

used by the prehistoric inhabitants of the Carbon Monoxide site. Squash and gourd remains have been documented from Archaic contexts in Missouri (King 1980) and from Early Woodland times in Kentucky. Watson and Yarnell (1969:76) have argued that the inhabitants of Salts Cave were horticulturalists, growing squash and gourd as well as several indigenous plant taxa (Iva, Helianthus, and possibly Phalaris Chenopodium). The presence of a lone squash remain at the nearby Fiege site represents the earliest evidence of this cultigen in the American Bottom. An Early Woodland association has been suggested for this remain. In west-central Illinois all these cultivated taxa are virtually absent in assemblages dating to both Late Archaic and Early Woodland times (Asch, Farnsworth, and Asch 1979).

By Middle Woodland times in west-central Illinois, however, remains of both cucurbits and of indigenous cultivated plants become common. At the early Middle Woodland components of the Dickson Camp and Pond sites in central Illinois, for example, (see Cantwell 1980:147), squash and gourd remains, as well as specimens of the indigenous seed complex, were recovered, which led Asch and Asch (1980:158) to infer cultivation at the sites. The total absence of remains of cultivated plants in the samples from the Carbon Monoxide site, therefore, seems anomalous.

Wood

The frequency of wood charcoal was very low in the Carbon Monoxide samples, although wood charcoal was more evenly distributed among the features than was nutshell. The average frequencies of wood fragments in both the Marion and Columbia Complex samples were similar (7 and 5 fragments per 10 l, respectively).

The wood taxa represented were typical of the lowland and bluff slope forests that probably grew nearest the site. Represented were, in descending order of abundance: honey locust and mulberry, oaks, ash, elm and hackberry, birch, sycamore, hickory, and persimmon. A few fragments of grape vine were also identified. The small number of identifiable fragments from the Marion samples precluded a comparison of the wood composition between the two components.

Summary

Botanical materials from 21 features at the Carbon Monoxide site were analyzed. Nut remains were dominant in the Columbia Complex features, but were absent from the features assigned to the Marion component. Overall, wood charcoal was scarce, and the taxa represented were characteristic of bottomland and slope forests nearest the site. A

few wild seed remains were recovered, including American lotus, an
inhabitant of floodplain lakes. Remains of cultivated plants of either
exotic or North American origin were lacking.

Truck #7 Site

The Truck #7 site represents a Middle Woodland occupation (ca. 100
A.C. to 300 A.C.) within the Hill Lake meander scar, and near the
valley in the bluff through which Hill Lake Creek flows onto the
floodplain. The site consisted of the remains of a large circular
structure, with ten pits within its circumference, and ten pits and four
surficial burned areas scattered around its southern and eastern sides.
Seven of the pits inside the structure (Features 3, 10, 14, 15, 16, 18,
and 19), and five external pits (Features 6, 7, 8, 11, and 21), as well
as eight postmolds, were randomly selected for analysis of their floral
contents.

The processing of 726.5 l of fill from the 12 selected pit features
resulted in the recovery of 48.3 g of charred plant remains
(Tables 78 and 79). Overall, fragments of wood charcoal were about
twice as frequent as nutshell fragments. Small seeds were common,
especially in several of the pits inside the structure.

No remains of Mesoamerican cultigens were associated with the Middle
Woodland component at the Truck #7 site, although maize was recovered
from one feature that was associated with an early Mississippian
component at the site.

Nuts

A total of 1137 fragments of nutshell were recovered from the 12
pits, at an average frequency of 15.6 fragments per 10 l of fill. The
condition of the nutshell was generally poor; the fragments were small
and eroded, possibly a reflection of the general conditions of
preservation at the site (Table 80).

The majority of the nutshell fragments (62.4% of the identifiable
fragments) were assigned to the taxon, Juglandaceae (hickory and
walnut), since the fragments were too small to distinguish the two
genera.   In addition, the sample yielded thick-shelled hickories
(12.4%), pecan hickories (5.1%), walnuts (2.9%), hazelnut (1.2%), and
acorn (0.4%). Unidentifiable fragments made up 16.1% of the total.

Table 78. Flotation-recovered Plant Remains from the Truck #7 site (11-Mo-200)

| | Interior Pit Feature | | | | | | | |
	3	10	14	15	16	18	19	Subtotal
total wt. charcoal (g)	0.1	5.8	16.0	0.4	1.1	14.1	2.2	39.7
total vol. flot. analyzed (l)	31.5	39	167	30	60	115	120	562.5
NUT (total frags.)	4	330	196	3	36	516	46	1131
hickory								
Carya sp.	–	25	30	1	3	68	13	140
pecan/bitternut								
C. illinoensis/C. cordiformis	–	23	15	–	–	20		58
hazelnut								
Corylus americana	–	–	1	–	2	9	–	12
hickory and walnut								
Juglandaceae	–	226	83	1	17	356	20	703
walnut								
Juglans spp.	–	–	21	–	1	8	2	32
acorn								
Quercus sp.	–	2	–	–	2	–	–	4
unidentifiable	4	54	46	1	11	55	11	182
SEEDS (total)	–	143	8	60	6	146	126	489
paw-paw								
Asimina triloba								
(N of frags.)*	–	–	–	–	–	(19)	–	1
pink								
cf. Caryophyllaceae	–	1	–	–	–	–	–	1
goosefoot								
Chenopodium sp.	–	74	3	6	3	100	6	192
grasses								
Gramineae	–	–	1	–	–	1	8	10
Gramineae Type 6 L	–	8	–	31	–	1	2	42
marsh elder								
Iva sp.	–	–	–	–	–	1	–	1
legume								
Leguminoseae	–	1?	–	–	–	1	–	1,1?
maygrass								
Phalaris caroliniana	–	44	–	–	–	10	62	116
pokeweed								
Phytolacca americana	–	3	–	–	–	2	–	5
knotweeds								
Polygonum spp.	–	2	–	–	–	2	1	5
erect knotweed								
P. erectum	–	–	1	–	–	–	2	3
sumac								
Rhus sp.	–	–	–	–	–	1	–	1
nightshades								
Solanaceae	–	–	–	–	–	1	1	2
wild bean								
Strophostyles sp.	–	–	–	–	–	1?	3	3,1?
unknown	–	7	–	23	3	2	10	45
unidentifiable	–	3	3	–	–	22	31	59

*all fragments from one feature counted as one seed

Table 78. continued

| | Exterior Pit Feature | | | | | | |
	6	7	8	11	21	Subtotal	Total
total wt. charcoal (g)	0.2	4.8	1.3	0.4	1.9	8.6	48.3
total vol. flot. analyzed (l)	30	40	40	34	20	164	726.5
NUT (total frags.)	-	2	-	4	-	6	1137
hickory							
Carya sp.	-	-	-	1	-	1	141
pecan/bitternut							
C. illinoensis/C. cordiformis	-	-	-	-	-	-	58
hazelnut							
Corylus americana	-	2	-	-	-	2	14
hickory and walnut							
Juglandaceae	-	-	-	2	-	2	705
walnut							
Juglans spp.	-	-	-	1?	-	1?	32,1?
acorn							
Quercus sp.	-	-	-	-	-	-	4
unidentifiable	-	-	-	-	-	-	182
SEEDS (total)	5	-	-	2	-	7	496
paw-paw							
Asimina triloba							
(N of frags.)*	-	-	-	-	-	-	1
pink							
cf. Caryophyllaceae	-	-	-	-	-	-	1
goosefoot							
Chenopodium sp.	-	-	-	1	-	1	193
grasses							
Gramineae	1?	-	-	-	-	1?	10,1?
Gramineae Type 6 L	-	-	-	1	-	1	43
marsh elder							
Iva sp.	-	-	-	-	-	-	1
legume							
Leguminoseae	-	-	-	-	-	-	1,1?
maygrass							
Phalaris caroliniana	-	-	-	-	-	-	116
pokeweed							
Phytolacca americana	-	-	-	-	-	-	5
knotweeds							
Polygonum spp.	1	-	-	-	-	1	6
erect knotweed							
P. erectum	1?	-	-	-	-	1?	3,1?
sumac							
Rhus sp.	-	-	-	-	-	-	1
nightshades							
Solanaceae	-	-	-	-	-	-	2
wild bean							
Strophostyles sp.	-	-	-	-	-	-	3,1?
unknown	1	-	-	-	-	1	46
unidentifiable	1	-	-	-	-	1	60

*all fragments from one feature counted as one seed

Table 78. continued

| | Interior Pit Feature | | | | | | | |
	3	10	14	15	16	18	19	Subtotal
TROPICAL CULTIGENS								
maize (N of frags.)								
Zea mays	-	-	-	-	-	-	-	-
WOOD (total frags. recovered)	3	118	1033	25	77	500	132	1887
(total frags. identified)	3	77	264	25	71	230	132	802
maple								
Acer sp.	-	-	-	-	-	16?	-	16?
horse chestnut								
cf. _Aesculus_ sp.	-	-	-	-	-	1?	-	1?
birch								
cf. _Betula_ sp.	-	-	-	-	-	2?	-	2?
hickory								
Carya sp.	2	-	26	-	1	22	3	54
pecan/bitternut								
C. illinoensis/C. cordiformis	-	-	23	-	-	2,2?	-	25,2?
persimmon								
Diospyros virginiana	-	-	2?	3,9?	-	5	2	10,11?
ash								
Fraxinus sp.	-	-	1?	-	3?	1	3	4,4?
locust/coffee-tree/mulberry								
Gleditsia/Gymnocladus/Morus	-	-	4	2	-	2	-	8
walnut								
Juglans sp.	-	-	3	-	-	1?	-	3,1?
mulberry								
Morus sp.	-	2?	-	-	-	2?	2	2,4?
oak								
Quercus sp.	1?	34	84	-	20	30	36	204,1?
Quercus (red group)	-	-	18	-	-	1	16	35
cottonwood/willow								
Salicaceae	-	-	9	-	-	1	3	13
basswood or tuliptree								
Titlia or _Liriodendron_ sp.	-	-	-	-	-	-	-	-
elm and hackberry								
Ulmaceae	-	4	1	-	-	11	5	21
unknown	-	-	-	-	-	-	-	-
bark	-	1	4	-	5	13	-	23
diffuse-porous	-	-	3	-	-	11	2	16
ring-porous	-	3	43	3	10	35	18	112
unidentified	-	33	43	8	32	72	42	230

Table 78. continued

	Exterior Pit Feature						
	6	7	8	11	21	Subtotal	Total
TROPICAL CULTIGENS							
maize (N of frags.)							
Zea mays	-	-	-	33	-	33	33
WOOD (total frags. recovered)	24	440	83	21	193	761	2648
(total frags. identified)	24	56	45	21	40	186	988
maple							
Acer sp.	-	-	-	-	-	-	16?
horse chestnut							
cf. Aesculus sp.	-	-	-	-	-	-	1?
birch							
cf. Betula sp.	-	-	-	-	-	-	2?
hickory							
Carya sp.	1	-	-	1	-	2	56
pecan/bitternut							
C. illinoensis/C. cordiformis	-	-	-	-	-	-	25,2?
persimmon							
Diospyros virginiana	-	-	-	-	-	-	10,11?
ash							
Fraxinus sp.	-	3,3?	-	-	-	3,3?	7,7?
locust/coffee-tree/mulberry							
Gleditsia/Gymnocladus/Morus	-	-	-	-	10	10	18
walnut							
Juglans sp.	-	-	-	-	-	-	3,1?
mulberry							
Morus sp.	-	-	-	-	-	-	2,4?
oak							
Quercus sp.	2	-	18?	-	-	2,18?	206,19?
Quercus (red group)	-	1?	-	-	-	1?	35,1?
cottonwood/willow							
Salicaceae	-	-	-	-	-	-	13
basswood or tuliptree							
Titlia or Liriodendron sp.	-	-	-	-	7	7	7
elm and hackberry							
Ulmaceae	-	-	-	-	-	-	21
unknown	-	49	27	-	-	76	76
bark	-	-	-	2	12	14	37
diffuse-porous	2	-	-	-	2	4	20
ring-porous	8	-	-	9	-	17	129
unidentified	11	-	-	9	9	29	259

Table 79. Nonflotation-recovered Identified Charcoal Samples
from the Truck #7 Site

Taxon	Feature 14	Feature 16	Feature 19	Postmold 31
NUT				
hickory Carya sp.	X	-	-	-
WOOD				
hickory Carya sp.	-	X	-	-
oak Quercus sp.	X	-	-	X
red oak Quercus (red group)	X	-	-	X
white oak Quercus (white group)	X	-	X	-

Note: X indicates presence of species

Table 80. Nutshell from the Truck #7 Site

Taxon	% of Total Fragments
hickory or walnut Juglandaceae	62.4
thick-shelled hickory Carya sp.	12.5
pecan or butternut C. illinoensis or C. cordiformis	5.1
black walnut or butternut Juglans spp.	2.8
hazelnut Corylus americana	1.2
acorn Quercus sp.	0.2
unidentifiable	16.1

N = 1129 fragments

Seeds

A total of 496 seeds were recovered, an average of 6.8 seeds per 10 l of feature fill. This frequency contrasted with those of earlier assemblages; for example, at three Late Archaic sites in the American Bottom (Go-Kart North, Missouri Pacific #2, and Dyroff), the average numbers of seeds per 10 l were 0.4, 0.7, and 0.5, respectively. The overall frequency of seeds at the Middle Woodland Truck #7 site was about 12 times higher than at the Late Archaic sites.

The majority of the Truck #7 seeds were goosefoot and maygrass. These seed types are members of a complex of small starchy seeds that first appear in the area in quantity in Middle Woodland assemblages, and continue to dominate the archaeological seed spectra through Mississippian times, making up an average of 75% of all identifiable seeds from Middle Woodland times onward (Asch, Farnsworth, and Asch 1979:83). It has been proposed that this complex of seeds was cultivated. This hypothesis is based on field studies of the three species that make up the complex (Phalaris caroliniana, Chenopodium bushianum, and Polygonum erectum), which indicate that they do not grow densely enough in nature in the area (and in the case of maygrass not at all, since its modern range stops south of the study area) to account for their striking ubiquity and abundance in archaeological contexts (Asch and Asch 1980; Asch, Farnsworth and Asch 1979; Cowan 1978). At the Truck #7 site, the starchy seed complex made up 73% of the total identifiable seeds. This was similar to percentages at other Middle Woodland assemblages in Illinois; for example, at the Archie, Crane, Loy, and Massey sites in the Illinois River drainage, the starchy seeds made up ca. 77% of the identifiable seeds (Asch and Asch 1978:333).

Other seeds recovered from the Truck #7 site were grasses, knotweeds, nightshades, pokeweed, wild bean, and sumac. One feature also contained a number of fragments of pawpaw seed. All these seeds represent potential food plants, with the possible exception of pokeweed. The young leaves of pokeweed are edible, but the mature leaves, roots, and seeds, contain phytolaccatoxin as well as mitogens that can cause serious blood disturbances (Lewis and Elvin-Lewis 1977:90, 278). However, pokeweed seeds are not uncommon in archaeological contexts, and it is likely that they had some economic or possibly medicinal importance.

The presence of the seeds of such fleshy, quickly-decaying fruits as pokeweed and pawpaw suggests that some deposition of feature fill occurred during their ripening months of September and October, since they would have been unlikely candidates for long term storage.

Mesoamerican Cultigens

No remains of squash or gourd rind were recovered from the Truck #7 site, although cucurbit rind is a common constituent of samples from Middle Woodland assemblages in the Illinois River drainage (Asch, Farnsworth, and Asch 1979:83).

An anomalous occurrence at the site was the presence of maize in Feature 11, a pit feature on the southwest periphery of the site. Four 10 l flotation samples were analyzed from the two strata of the pit, and all four contained fragments of maize kernels and cupules. The presence of Mississippian pottery in this pit, however, suggests that the maize should be associated with that time period.

Wood

Wood charcoal was the most abundant class of charcoal recovered from the Truck #7 site. Every pit feature analyzed yielded wood charcoal, with an average frequency of 36 fragments per 10 l of fill.

The majority of the flotation-recovered wood charcoal was oak (45.0% of the total identifiable fragments) and true hickory (9.7%). Represented in smaller quantities were honey locust, Kentucky coffee tree or mulberry, elm/hackberry, cottonwood/willow, pecan, maple, persimmon, basswood, walnut, ash, birch (?), and horse chestnut (?).

Table 81 compares the percentage frequencies of the archaeological wood types (flotation-recovered material) to those of the nearby forest zones: floodplain, hillside-talus slope, and upland, as reconstructed by Zawacki and Hausfater (1969). A basic correspondence is evident. However, if the inhabitants of the Truck #7 site were gathering firewood indiscriminately from the forest zones nearest the site (i.e., the floodplain forest and hillside talus slopes), then oak and hickory, which together make up 59.4% of the archaeological wood, seem overrepresented. The percentages of oak and hickory (45.0% and 14.4%, respectively) are closer to those of the upland forest (56% and 19%) than to those of the floodplain and talus slope forests. Either most of the wood was gathered in the upland forest, or oaks and hickories were selected wherever they occurred. A selection for oak and hickory seems logical in view of the fact that the comparative heat values (a ton of wood compared to a ton of coal) of these genera are among the highest (Carya spp. 93-98%, Quercus spp. 83-92%) [Zawacki and Hausfater 1969:32-35].

Table 81.   Comparison Between Wood Taxa from the Truck #7 Site
and Reconstructed Forest Zones

Wood Taxa from Truck #7	Identifiable Frags. (%)	Taxa in Reconstructed Forest Zones* (%)		
		Floodplain Forest*	Hillside-Talus Slope*	Upland Forest*
oaks				
Quercus spp.	45.0	19.7	17.9	56.1
hickory				
Carya spp.	14.4	3.3	7.4	19.1
locust, Kentucky coffee-tree or mulberry+				
Gleditsia, Gymnocladus or Morus	4.1	2.0	-	0.2
ash				
Fraxinus sp.	2.4	12.5	7.5	1.1
elm or hackberry				
Ulmaceae	3.6	-	4.7	0.9
cottonwood or willow				
Salicaceae	2.2	-	-	-
maple				
Acer sp.	2.8	13.8	10.4	0.4
persimmon				
Diospyros virginiana	3.6	0.7	-	-
basswood or tuliptree+				
Tilia or Liriodendron	1.2	-	4.7***	0.6***
walnut				
Juglans sp.	0.7	-	11.3	1.2
birch?				
cf. Betula sp.**	0.3	-	-	-
buckeye?				
cf. Aesculus sp.**	0.2	-	-	-

N = 580 fragments identified

+ The condition of fragments precludes distinction of genera.
* See Zawacki and Haustater 1969:22-25, 32-35, 42-45
** These identifications are tentative.
*** Tilia

Table 82. Flotation-recovered Plant Remains for Postmolds at the Truck #7 Site

	Postmold							
	2	3	4	11	12	16	30	69
total wt. charcoal (g)	-	-	<0.1	<0.1	<0.1	0.1	0.4	<0.1
total vol. flot. analyzed (l)	10	1.5	3.5	1.5	1.5	5.0	8.5	10.0
NUT (total frags.)	-	-	-	-	-	3	3	-
hazelnut Corylus sp.	-	-	-	-	-	3	2	-
hickory and walnut Juglandanceae	-	-	-	-	-	-	1	-
WOOD (total frags.)	-	-	2	4	2	17	33	1
hickory Carya sp.	-	-	-	-	-	1	1	1
honey locust/coffee-tree Gleditsia/Gymnocladus	-	-	-	-	-	-	2	-
oak Quercus sp.	-	-	-	-	-	-	3	-
red oak Quercus (red group)	-	-	-	-	-	-	1	-
white oak Quercus (white group)	-	-	-	-	-	-	1	-
ring-porous	-	-	2	2	1	9	12	-
unidentifiable	-	-	-	2	1	7	13	-
SEEDS (total)	-	-	-	-	-	-	-	2
goosefoot Chenopodium sp.	-	-	-	-	-	-	-	1
grape Vitis sp.	-	-	-	-	-	-	-	1
OTHER (total frags.)	-	-	1	-	-	-	-	1
coal	-	-	1	-	-	-	-	1

Samples from the eight postmolds analyzed contained little botanical material (Table 82). Samples from two of the postmolds were completely devoid of material, six contained small amounts of wood charcoal (oak, hickory, and locust or Kentucky coffee tree), and two contained a few nutshell fragments (hickory and hazelnut). One postmold yielded two seeds (chenopod and grape).

A comparison of the contents of the pit features inside the structure to those outside showed differences in the proportions of the plant types they contained. The contents of the pit features inside the structure yielded a much higher ratio of plant food remains (e.g., nuts and seeds) than did the external pit features. Although the average frequency of wood charcoal fragments was about the same in both feature categories, the internal pits yielded 45 times more nutshell and about 16 times more seeds (relative to the amount of wood charcoal) as the external features (Table 83). That the main activities of storage and/or processing of plant foods took place inside the structure seems a plausible explanation for this contrast. Also, the uneven distribution of the seeds between the two feature categories strengthens the argument for their economic importance. As Minnis (1981) has argued, the distribution of seed types (e.g., in dense concentrations, or associated with particular feature types) can differentiate seeds resulting from direct resource use from those resulting from natural seed rain.

Table 83. Relative Frequencies of Categories of Plant Remains
in Internal vs. External Pits at the Truck #7 Site

Plant Category	Internal Pits (7 Features Analyzed)	External Pits (5 Features Analyzed)
Wood Charcoal (mean N of frags.)	30.4	44.7
Nutshell (mean N of frags.)	18.1	0.4
Seeds (mean N of seed)	6.8	0.4

Notes: Counts represent an average number of fragments or seeds per 10 l sample for each feature category. Counts were derived by adding all nut fragments, wood fragments or seeds from all samples analyzed from each of the two feature categories, and dividing by the total number of 10 l samples analyzed from that feature category.

Summary

The pattern of plant remains from the Truck #7 site included a spectrum of wood taxa which was relatively broad but with a focus on oak and hickory. Nut remains differed from the pattern found further north in this time period in being primarily hickory, rather than hazelnut. The majority of the seeds recovered are representative of a complex of indigenous plants that were probably encouraged, i.e., cultivated. The pit features inside the structure were found to contain a much higher proportion of food plant remains than those outside.

Truck #4 Site

The excavated portion of the Truck #4 site consisted of 27 features, which were part of a larger site, much of which lies outside the right-of-way. The site is situated to the north of the Hill Lake Creek ravine opening on the alluvial fan, which extends onto the floodplain.

The site has been assigned a Mississippian (Lohmann phase) affiliation, although only one feature yielded artifacts diagnostic of that cultural period.

A total of 256 l of fill from the following 15 features were examined for plant remains: Features 2, 3, 4, 5, 7, 8, 11, 12, 13, 14, 16, 20, 21, 25, and 27. Despite the volume of fill processed, almost no charred botanical material was recovered. The total amount weighed 1.7 g, and consisted of a few wood fragments, nut remains, seeds, and one maize cupule (Table 84).

Nut

Most of the features analyzed yielded no nut remains, and most of the 44 total fragments recovered came from Feature 27. Thick-shelled hickory and black walnut were identified.

Seeds

It is unusual that samples associated with this cultural period contained so few seeds. Only four seeds were recovered (average frequency = 0.2 seeds per 10 l of feature fill). A knotweed and a grass seed were identified.

Table 84. Flotation-recovered Plant Remains from the Truck #4 Site (11-Mo-195)

	Feature															Total
	2	3	4	5	7	8	11	12	13	14	16	20	21	25	27	
total wt. charcoal (g)	-	<0.1	-	<0.1	-	-	0.2	-	-	0.6	-	0.4	-	-	0.4	1.7
total vol. flot. analyzed (1)	12	10	10	30	6	10	30	20	10	18	20	20	10	20	30	256
NUTS (total frags.)	-	1	-	-	-	-	-	1	-	-	-	1	-	-	42	44
thick-shelled hickory Carya sp.	-	-	-	-	-	-	-	-	-	-	-	-	-	-	7	7
hickory and walnut Juglandaceae	-	1	-	-	-	-	-	-	-	-	-	1	-	-	27	29
black walnut Juglans nigra	-	-	-	-	-	-	-	-	-	-	-	-	-	-	8	8
SEEDS (total)	-	-	1	3	-	-	-	-	-	-	-	-	-	-	-	4
grass gramineae	-	-	1	-	-	-	-	-	-	-	-	-	-	-	-	1
knotweed Polygonum sp.	-	-	-	1	-	-	-	-	-	-	-	-	-	-	-	1
unidentifiable	-	-	-	2	-	-	-	-	-	-	-	-	-	-	-	2
TROPICAL CULTIGENS																
maize cupule Zea mays	-	-	-	-	-	-	-	-	-	-	-	1	-	-	-	1
WOOD (total frags. recovered)	-	-	-	1	-	-	19	-	-	50	-	10	-	-	1	81
(total frags. examined)	-	-	-	1	-	-	19	-	-	24	-	10	-	-	1	55
hickory Carya sp.	-	-	-	-	-	-	-	-	-	-	-	4	-	-	-	4
coffee-tree/honey locust Gymnocladus/Gleditsia	-	-	-	-	-	-	-	-	-	24	-	-	-	-	-	24
basswood? cf. Tilia sp.	-	-	-	-	-	-	1	-	-	-	-	-	-	-	-	1
bark	-	-	-	-	-	-	-	-	-	-	-	2	-	-	-	2
ring-porous	-	-	-	-	-	-	4	-	-	-	-	2	-	-	1	7
unidentifiable	-	-	-	1	-	-	14	-	-	-	-	2	-	-	-	17

Mesoamerican Cultigens

The only trace of Mesoamerican cultigens at the Truck #4 site was one maize cupule recovered from Feature 20. The presence of maize is expected for an early Mississippian assemblage; in fact, the overall scarcity of maize remains in the Truck #4 samples is unusual.

Wood

A very low average frequency of three wood fragments per 10 l of fill characterized the samples. The taxa identified were honey locust or Kentucky coffee tree, hickory, and basswood (?).

SUMMARY

A summary of data from the plant remains from the various components can be seen in Table 85. Several of the components, especially the Early Woodland Marion components at Fiege and Carbon Monoxide, the Columbia Complex component at Carbon Monoxide, and the Mississippian component at the Truck #4 site, were small and yielded such sparse plant remains that little basis for comparison exists. Nevertheless, several trends in the plant remains are evident which suggest changing patterns of plant exploitation by the inhabitants of the Hill Lake locality.

The inhabitants of the locality in all time periods appear to have preferred the same nut types; thick-shelled hickories were dominant in all assemblages although small percentages of black walnut, acorn, and hazelnut were also often present. The overall quantity of nut remains, however, declines through time (when viewed in relation to the amount of wood charcoal). The Early Woodland Fiege site and the Columbia Complex Carbon Monoxide component yielded four to five times as much nutshell as wood charcoal, while all the later components yielded less nutshell than wood. The Carbon Monoxide site Marion component was very unusual in yielding no nutshell at all, but this may be a factor of the small size of the sample and the nature of the features, which consisted mostly of small circumscribed, surficial activity scatters. Conceivably this decline reflects a decrease in the use of nuts through time. This decrease is strongly evidenced in the larger context of the American Bottom (Johannessen 1982) as well as in west central Illinois as a whole (Asch, Farnsworth, and Asch 1979).

A corresponding trend in the data was an increase in the frequency

Table 85. Summary Data for Hill Lake Sites

| | Early Woodland | | | Middle Woodland | Mississippian |
| | Marion Phase | | Columbia Complex | Hill Lake Phase | Lohmann Phase |
	11-Mo-609	11-Mo-593	11-Mo-593	11-Mo-200	11-Mo-195
seeds per 10 l	0.47	1.36	2.76	6.8	0.15
nut frags. per 10 l	11.06	-	38.82	15.6	1.69
wood frags. per 10 l	3.10	0.10	6.97	36.2	3.12
nut:wood ratio	3.78	-	5.57	0.43	0.5
seed:wood ratio	0.15	0.28	0.40	0.19	0.05
starchy seeds* (%)	-	16.7	-	71.7	-
features with maize (%)	-	-	-	-	6.7
features with cucurbits (%)	14.3	-	-	-	-
hickory and walnut Juglandaceae (%)	97.7	-	93.0	74.9	81.8
hazelnut Corylus (%)	2.3	-	-	1.2	-
oak Quercus (%)	-	-	-	0.4	-
black walnut Juglans nigra (%)	-	-	0.9	2.8	18.2

*Phalaris caroliniana + Chenopodium sp. + Polygonum erectum, % of identifiable seeds

of seeds, and, especially, increasing proportions of a complex of starchy seeds. The starchy seed plants were almost certainly cultivated, and formed part of a widespread gardening complex that included squash and gourd, and the oily-seeded plants, sunflower and marsh elder (Ford 1981).

Squash remains were almost non-existent in samples from these Hill Lake locality sites; only one rind fragment was recovered (from an Early Woodland context at the Fiege site). Maize remains were recovered only from the Mississippian components.

The plant debris from the series of small settlements in the Hill Lake locality has yielded evidence that the relationships of the prehistoric inhabitants to the land and resources changed through time. The general trend was towards an intensification in methods of plant food production. A primary dependence on wild plant foods (especially nuts), which requires a relatively large supporting territory, was replaced by more intensive use of a smaller area; i.e., plant cultivation. The late Middle Woodland inhabitants of the locality appear to have cultivated a complex of small-seeded cereal plants, and by Mississippian times further intensification was indicated by the addition of maize to the crop complex.

The trajectory of intensification evidenced at the Hill Lake sites is by no means a local phenomenon, but rather a manifestation of widespread changes in man-plant relationships that occurred with variations throughout the American Bottom, Illinois, and eastern North America.

CHAPTER 7. CONCLUSIONS

by Andrew C. Fortier

The preceding chapters have presented the results obtained from archaeological investigations at five sites located in the southern portion of the Hill Lake locality of the American Bottom. The excavations produced remains dating from the Early Woodland through Historic periods. Many of these sites contained evidence of multicomponent occupations although none were extensive in size or of long duration. For the most part, each of the site reports represents a detailed account of the data recovered, the spatial distribution of artifacts, and, where possible, their function. The following sections will attempt to make some general observations and conclusions based on the data bases presented in the preceding reports.

CHRONOLOGICAL FRAMEWORK

The archaeological resources of the Hill Lake locality involve at least 3000 years of prehistoric occupation. Virtually every bank portion and inner-channel ridge of this locality exhibited some evidence of prehistoric occupation. It is obvious, therefore, that the Hill Lake locality served as an important focus for prehistoric populations.

An extensive Late Archaic, Titterington occupation dating to 2100 B.C. was exposed at the Go-Kart North site (Fortier and Emerson 1984) located approximately 500 m north of the Truck #7 and Go-Kart South sites. Materials from this Archaic phase or from subsequent terminal Late Archaic phases were not found in the southern portion of the Hill Lake locality. The absence of Late Archaic remains here may be due to the fact that the Hill Lake meander was still an active channel up until about 1500 B.C., and the inner-channel ridges were not fully exposed until about 600 B.C. Many of the bank portions of the meander scar may have been too unstable to support occupation during the period from 1500 B.C. to 600 B.C.

The first identifiable cultural remains in the southern Hill Lake meander locality were associated with the Early Woodland Marion phase, as defined by Munson (1966). Coarsely tempered, flat-bottomed, thick-walled vessels, with interior-exterior cordmarking (e.g., Marion Thick), and Kramer projectile points, represent the type markers for Early Woodland Marion occupations in the American Bottom (Kelly et al. 1979: 23-24, Linder 1974). Of the five sites investigated in the Hill

Lake locality, only the Truck #4 site failed to produce Marion Thick pottery. None of the components with this pottery produced diagnostic projectile point forms. Occupations associated with these remains consisted of small, isolated, but discrete scatters of ceramic and lithic materials, located almost exclusively along low, inner-channel sand bars or lower bank portions of the meander scar. The Carbon Monoxide site produced the most extensive occupational evidence yet exposed for the Marion phase in the American Bottom. Other sites such as Fiege and Truck #7 yielded only isolated ceramic fragments. Unfortunately, no radiocarbon dates could be determined for any of the Marion components in this locality. It is assumed that the Early Woodland period in the American Bottom probably was of short duration, extending from ca. 600 B.C. to 200 B.C. Radiocarbon dates from elsewhere in the Midwest suggest an even more restricted range, from 600 B.C. to 400 B.C. (Munson and Hall 1966).

A late Early Woodland occupation designated as the Columbia Complex was defined at the Carbon Monoxide site. A Middle Woodland occupation was recovered at the Truck #7 and Go-Kart South site. Each occupation was situated on an inner-channel sandy ridge, located within the Hill Lake meander. At the Carbon Monoxide site, late Early Woodland (Columbia Complex) features and remains were found in superimposed position above an Early Woodland, Marion occupation. The ceramic remains, as well as the radiocarbon dates, of 170 B.C. and 10 B.C., indicate that the Columbia Complex occupation dates to a terminal phase of the Early Woodland period in the American Bottom, and is tentatively associated with the Florence phase (Emerson et al. 1983). Because the Columbia Complex assemblage is so small and possesses so few analogs in the area, it has been designated as a complex rather than a phase.

The Middle Woodland occupation at the Truck #7 site dates to between 90 A.C. and 230 A.C., and falls within the Hill Lake phase. The ceramic materials recovered from this occupation are most closely analogous to the Pike-Hopewell phase of the Illinois River valley. Some Hopewell ceramic decorative traits such as cross-hatched and gouged upper-rim areas appear in this assemblage. Middle Woodland ceramics were associated primarily with the Truck #7 site, but were also found at the adjacent Go-Kart South site. On this basis, it was felt that the two sites actually comprised a single Middle Woodland occupation area.

Late Woodland remains occurred infrequently at sites in this portion of the Hill Lake locality. The Carbon Dixoide site, however, did contain a small occupation, with several components dating to an early phase (Rosewood) of the Late Woodland period. This occupation was radiocarbon dated at 250 A.C. - 320 A.C. The pit cluster units recognized at this site represent the first occupational evidence from this phase yet recovered in the American Bottom floodplain (Finney and Fortier 1985). A more extensive Late Woodland Mund phase occupation was uncovered at the Mund site located at the northern end of the Hill Lake locality. These sites have been described in other reports (Fortier et al. 1983, Finney and Fortier 1985).

There was no evidence for Emergent Mississippian occupation in the Hill Lake locality, although during survey and testing some remains were generally categorized as "Late Bluff-Mississippian". Early Mississippian (Lohmann phase) materials, however, were recovered from every site in this locality. The most significant occupational data was derived from the Carbon Dioxide site, which contained two Lohmann phase household clusters and associated pits. These clusters, which formed a clear community plan, were occupied sometime between 975 A.C. and 1050 A.C. (Finney and Fortier 1985). Other sites in the Hill Lake locality, such as the Truck #4 and #7 sites, produced scatters of pits or isolated pits with Lohmann phase ceramics. The remaining sites contained only isolated occurrences of ceramics dating to this phase.

Considering the proximity of the Lunsford-Pulcher site, situated approximately 2 km to the west, which contains evidence of intensive Mississippian settlement, the discovery of Mississippian farmsteads and other remains in the Hill Lake locality was not unexpected. It is assumed that a close relationship existed between the Lunsford-Pulcher site and the Mississippian sites of the Hill Lake locality.

SETTLEMENT DISTRIBUTION, DURATION, AND FUNCTION

Each of the occupations in this volume was located in a spatially discrete portion of the Hill Lake locality. Occupations representative of the Early and Middle Woodland time periods occurred within the abandoned channel on inner- channel ridges, while Late Woodland and Mississippian occupations were found primarily along the meander cut-bank or on alluvial fan deposits directly overlying bank edges. Terminal Late Archaic (1000 B.C. - 500 B.C.) occupations were not recovered here, but an earlier Titterington, Late Archaic community was exposed and excavated on the meander bank just north of these sites (Fortier and Emerson 1984).

The settlement history of the Hill Lake locality can be summarized as follows. The first inhabitants were Late Archaic groups associated with the Titterington phase, ca. 2100 B.C. Isolated remains from earlier phases of the Archaic period were also recovered here, but specific occupations were not identified. A single Late Archaic, Titterington settlement was exposed and excavated at the Go-Kart North site (Fortier and Emerson 1984). The community plan consisted of nine distinct work or living areas distributed in a linear pattern along the east cut-bank of the then active Hill Lake channel. This settlement was relatively intensive and may have been occupied over a period of several seasons. The selection of high, stable clay banks along meander scars has already been recognized as typical of the Late Archaic settlement strategy on the floodplain of the American Bottom (Fortier and Emerson 1984; McElrath and Fortier 1983).

Sometime between 1000 B.C. and 600 B.C. the Hill Lake channel was apparently cut off from the Mississippi River. This was a particularly dynamic geomorphic period in that 1) the channel was no longer free flowing; 2) portions of the channel scar were subjected to fluvial and alluvial filling; 3) lakes, ponds, and marshes were forming in the channel scar; and 4) numerous point bars and ridges were formed and exposed in the inner-channel scar. No evidence of Late Archaic occupation after 2100 B.C. has been recovered in this locality, so presumably this area was too dynamic from a geomorphic standpoint to support occupation.

Occupations associated with various Early and Middle Woodland groups were distributed throughout the Hill Lake locality from ca. 600 B.C. to 300 A.C., but they were situated almost exclusively on the low, inner-channel ridges of the meander scar or, in the case of the Early Woodland components, were also situated along the lower portions of the old meander cut-bank. Settlement of the inner-channel areas of the floodplain, particularly during the Early Woodland and early Middle Woodland periods, represents a settlement pattern occurring throughout the American Bottom. Many of the inner-channel ridges and lower cut-banks of the American Bottom have been subjected to deep alluvial and fluvial burial. As a result, the distributional patterns, as well as the numbers of Early and Middle Woodland settlements in this area, can only be conjectured. The FAI-270 project excavations in the Hill Lake locality have revealed the existence of such buried resources in the American Bottom.

The Early and Middle Woodland occupations of the Hill Lake locality represent relatively small work-and-living areas. Although the length of occupation is problematical for each component, none of the occupations can be regarded as resulting from multiyear or even multiseasonal settlements. All of the Early and Middle Woodland occupational components appear to represent short-term extractive camps for procuring and processing wild plant and animal resources from the aquatic environment of the cut-off Hill Lake meander. Permanent settlement may also have been incompatible with Early and Middle Woodland hunting and collecting systems, geared apparently more to seasonal mobility and circulation within areas than to permanent occupation of a specific locality. Also, exploitable plant and animal resources may have been irregular due to fluctuating water levels and perhaps erosional fill episodes.

During the subsequent Late Woodland and Mississippian periods settlements occurred only on the higher bank portions of the Hill Lake meander scar or on the higher portions of alluvial fans projecting onto the scar. It is probable that by Late Woodland times a significant portion of the scar had already been filled by alluvial deposits, thus shrinking the potential aquatic resources in the inner-channel areas. Late Woodland and Mississippian occupations were instead situated in close proximity to the locality's major creeks, i.e., Hill Lake and Hill Creeks, which flowed out of the adjacent bluffs.

Geomorphic data from the Hill Lake locality indicate that a major erosional episode or series of major erosional episodes occurred between 300 A.C. and 500 A.C. The precise cause of these fill episodes is unknown, but the effect was to create two major alluvial fans. One extended from Cement Hollow at the north end of this locality, which was associated with Hill Creek; the other projected from the Hill Lake Creek outlet. Both fans had Late Woodland or Mississippian occupations distributed over their upper surfaces. Both fans had also buried earlier Middle Woodland components. Once these fans were formed, the Hill Lake locality exhibited a long period of relative geomorphic stability that extended from the early Mississippian to the modern period. Early Mississippian (Lohmann phase) settlement marks the final stage of prehistoric occupation here.

It is clear from the FAI-270 transect through the Hill Lake locality that prehistoric settlement was not continuous, nor generally permanent, particularly at the southern end of the locality. Most of the site components in this volume represent temporary, seasonal encampments to exploit aquatic resources from the meander channel and subsequent marsh. The relative positioning of settlements appears to have been directly related to the geomorphic history of this locality. Geomorphic instability significantly reduced the possibilities for permanent occupation here. Cultural remains excavated from various contexts have allowed us to reconstruct the geomorphic sequence of this locality. In turn, a geomorphic context developed through which the shifting settlement patterns could be better understood.

ANIMAL AND PLANT RESOURCES

A variety of plant and animal resources were available to the prehistoric groups occupying the Hill Lake locality. It is suggested that most Hill Lake settlements were scheduled in accordance with the availability of specific resources in the channel aquatic environs. The Hill Lake locality also was close to upland resources, so presumably these occupants had ready access to both floodplain and upland flora and fauna.

Variation in faunal-resource procurement through time was far less significant than the changes observed in plant utilization. Fish, bird, turtle, and deer represent the primary animal resources recovered from the excavated sites of this locality. The amount of faunal material generally increased through time, for example, between Early and Middle Woodland components and later Mississippian occupations. However, faunal materials were much more poorly preserved at the earlier components, probably due to their location in the lower, wetter, inner-channel zones of this locality. Notably absent from all sites were remains of fresh water mussels. This is probably due to the fact that the Hill Lake channel represented a dying meander incapable of maintaining stable water levels or aquatic conditions suitable for mussel populations.

One of the more important reasons for settlement in the inner-channel portions of the Hill Lake locality must have been accessibility to aquatic plant resources not available in the uplands. In this volume Johannesson has already detailed the major trends of plant selection in the cultural continuum here and in the American Bottom generally. The high proportions of wild plant food and the scarcity of cultigens during pre-Mississippian times and the corresponding shift to cultigens during the Mississippian period marks the most significant trend at these sites.

Generally, plant procurement from the Early Woodland to Mississippian periods was characterized by certain key plants being utilized in increasing quantities. Introduced cultigens such as squash and corn were added to the diet to supplement the subsistence base. This process was documented by the occurrence of the starchy seed complex (goosefoot, knotweed, and maygrass) at the Middle Woodland Truck #7 site, which Johannessen in this volume and Asch and Asch (1978, 1980) have argued represents evidence for seed cultivation. Isolated occurrences of these seeds occur prior to the Middle Woodland period, but they were not intensely utilized until the later phases. This seed complex was also maintained through the subsequent Late Woodland and Mississippian periods, even while maize was being added to the subsistence base during the early Mississippian period.

The occurrence of maize in the Hill Lake locality is actually documented for the first time in the Mund phase Late Woodland component at the Mund site, dated at ca. 500 A.C. However, it is not until the Lohmann phase of the early Mississippian period that it appears as a major resource. Maize was recovered from Mississippian pits at the Truck #4, Truck #7, and Carbon Dioxide sites in the Hill Lake locality. It was completely absent at the Middle Woodland Truck #7 occupation despite excellent preservation conditions for floral materials inside the structure.

Another trend was the gradual decline in the nut resources following the Middle Woodland period. The reason for this decline is unknown and poorly documented in the American Bottom. However, it may be related to the growing reliance on the starchy seed complex and to the emergence of maize during the period 200 A.D. - 1000 A.D.

The procurement of subsistence resources during any period here represents only a small segment of subsistence systems in the entire American Bottom and adjacent uplands. Therefore, the subsistence data from prehistoric occupations in the Hill Lake locality cannot totally represent that of any specific cultural group. However, the broad range of local resources recovered from the sites suggests that complex subsistence systems, which were adapted primarily to these local resources, existed in this area. More significantly, a local familiarity with the entire spectrum of regional plant and animal resources was one of the primary ingredients in the settlement process that eventually precipitated more complex social and economic systems in the American Bottom.

MATERIAL ASSEMBLAGE VARIATION AND FUNCTIONAL IMPLICATIONS

Each of the occupational components in the Hill Lake locality contained a distinct material assemblage consisting of lithic and/or ceramic remains, as well as structural and/or pit features that usually marked the most intensely occupied portions of the habitation areas. The significance of these data lies in the fact that, for the first time in this locality, assemblages can be placed in the context of specific and often clearly delineated settlement plans. Remains can, at the very minimum, be associated with specific kinds of features, and arguments concerning community and material function can now be based on good contextual information.

The earliest material assemblage in this volume dates to the Early Woodland period (ca. 500 B.C. - 200 B.C.) and is best represented at the Carbon Monoxide site. This assemblage consisted of well-defined and isolated scatters of broken ceramic vessels interspersed with fragments of burned sandstone, red ochre, chert flakes, and burned clay. The type marker for this assemblage is a thick-walled, coarsely-tempered vessel type known commonly as Marion Thick. This vessel type was also recovered in lesser quantities from the Fiege, Truck #7, Carbon Dioxide, and Go-Kart South sites. The discrete scatters of material found at the Carbon Monoxide site were interpreted as habitation foci, demarcating activites carried out within the confines of temporary structures or lean-tos. Ground sandstone metate pieces and burned clay, sandstone, and bone fragments indicate that plant processing and cooking were carried out here. The variation in material frequency from scatter to scatter was marked, suggesting that some functional differentiation may have occurred within the Early Woodland occupation. Ceramic variation, for example, in terms of lip treatment, cordmarking, and temper type occurred on a scatter by scatter basis but also within a single scatter (Feature 1). The material assemblages within these scatters appear to represent the products of small social units, probably nuclear families.

A late Early Woodland assemblage was also identified at the Carbon Monoxide site. This Carbon Monoxide assemblage has been dated to the late Early Woodland period (ca. 170 B.C. - 10 B.C.), and it consisted of discrete lithic and ceramic scatters, as well as processing/cooking and refuse pits. A possible basin structure was also associated with this occupation. The lithic tool inventory was comprised primarily of small scrapers, utilized flakes, bifacial knives, and numerous small reduction flakes, the latter apparently resulting from tool maintenance. Large cores and cortical flakes were absent, which suggested that primary core reduction activities were undertaken elsewhere. These ceramics are atypical and difficult to categorize but appear related to undecorated Florence phase ceramics. The material assemblage suggests that a variety of activities, mostly associated with plant processing and animal butchering, were undertaken here. The occupation has been interpreted as a short-term seasonal extractive camp consisting probably of an extended family or several nuclear families.

The occupation at the Truck #7 site was dated to the Middle Woodland period and, on the basis of ceramics, was associated with the Hill Lake phase of the American Bottom. The Truck #7 occupation, which consisted of a large circular post structure with associated pits, appears to have been of longer duration than the Early Woodland occupations at the Carbon Monoxide site. Most of the material assemblage was recovered from pits located inside the structure. It appears that most activities associated with this occupation were carried out within the structure, including seed grinding, food processing, cooking, lithic manufacturing, and probably animal butchering. The post structure clearly formed the central focus of this occupation, although pits and a light scatter of material outside of the structure indicate that some activities, probably asociated with food preparation, were also undertaken outside.

The location of most of the lithic, ceramic, and subsistence remains and the related diversity of activities inside the structure has led to the interpretation of this occupation as a late fall through winter habitation. The size and complexity of construction of the structure also tends to support this hypothesis.

Late Woodland remains were only sparsely represented in the southern portion of the Hill Lake locality. Occupational evidence in the form of pits organized into distinct groups occurred only at the Carbon Dioxide site. These Late Woodland occupations, dating between 250 A.C. and 350 A.C., have been interpreted by Finney in another volume as seasonal extractive camps (Finney and Fortier 1985). The pit groupings were differentiated primarily on the basis of the materials found in 23 pits, as well as by their spatial clustering patterns. Small groups of discrete pits were utilized by nuclear family units to process and cook plant and animal materials. The varying frequencies of material occurrence in these pit groups reflect differential activity intensities as well as functional variation.

Finally, Mississippian occupations were identified at the Carbon Dioxide, Truck #4, and Truck #7 sites. The Truck #4 site consisted of 24 pits while the Truck #7 Mississippian occupation had only one pit. The Carbon Dioxide site, however, produced a well-defined early Mississippian farmstead community consisting of four structures, six pits, and one lithic scatter. The Carbon Dioxide site, as well as the Truck #4 and Truck #7 components, dated to the Lohmann phase of the Mississippian period (ca. 975 A.C. - 1050 A.C.).

The relationship of the Carbon Dioxide farmstead to the other Early Mississippian occupations at the the Truck #4 and Truck #7 sites is problematical as is the association of all these occupations with the Mississippian center at Lunsford-Pulcher. The three Lohmann phase occupations here possessed red-slipped, limestone-tempered pottery, as well as evidence of maize, but further analogs were absent. It is possible that these small occupations functioned as outlying settlements attached to the Lunsford-Pulcher center. However, the settlement at Lunsford-Pulcher is so poorly known that relationships can only be hypothetically proposed.

The types of raw materials comprising the lithic assemblages of Hill Lake sites, particularly the chert resources, appear to have been extracted primarily from local sources. The following observations can be made concerning chert source and type selection through time. During the Early Woodland period the predominant chert type was a white variety derived from local Keokuk-Burlington formations. However, since these formations do not occur in the immediate site vicinity, the chert had to be transported into the sites.

A variety of chert types were present in the post-Marion phase occupations at the Carbon Monoxide and Truck #7 sites, but the types of chert utilized were radically different. For example, at the Carbon Monoxide site, a dark-and-light banded, gray-colored local (Salem formation) chert comprised the predominant chert type. This chert was probably obtained from either stream-bed sources in the adjacent uplands above the locality or from nearby formations, e.g., near Cement Hollow. The cherts from the Truck #7 site consisted of red, orange, and purple varieties probably derived from local Ste. Genevieve formations, outcrops of which have been located at the mouth of Carr Creek, which is situated 3 km south of this site (Kelly 1984). Local Burlington white varieties also occurred as did some Dongola chert, an imported chert from southern Illinois. Multicolored Ste. Genevieve cherts were also recovered from the Dash Reeves site, a Middle Woodland occupation located ca. 2 km to 3 km south of the Truck #7 site. The preferential selection of these kinds of cherts occurs almost exclusively during this time period in the Hill Lake locality area and appears to represent a useful material marker for the latter phases of the Middle Woodland period in this area.

Chert samples from the Late Woodland occupation at the Carbon Dioxide site indicated a selection for local Salem types of chert as well as white Burlington varieties. The red and purple Ste. Genevieve varieties were absent although a related reddish-brown glossy chert, termed "Root Beer", was present. So-called Root Beer chert may represent a lustreous variety of Ste. Genevieve Red (Kelly 1984). Exotic or imported cherts did not occur at the Carbon Dioxide site.

During the Mississippian period local cherts continued to be exploited from the uplands above the Hill Lake locality. Nonlocal cherts (Mill Creek and Dongola) were present at the Carbon Dioxide site. White Burlington varieties were also common at most of the Mississippian sites in this locality.

Apparently, Hill Lake Mississippian peoples no longer relied strictly on local chert sources but, in fact, preferred imported types, especially for certain types of tools, such as hoes (e.g., Mill Creek chert). The preference for these kinds of cherts may reflect expanded exchange systems and/or wider circulation patterns operating during the Mississippian period in the American Bottom (Porter 1969, 1974; Kelly 1980).

The material assemblages recovered from sites in the Hill Lake locality are not assumed to be necessarily typical, but they do reflect changes in certain raw material preferences within the context of a single locality. The extraction of local cherts was, for example, common throughout the prehistoric period although it varied according to specific cultural periods. Apparently, it was more important during the early Middle Woodland and Late Woodland periods than during the late Middle Woodland (Havana/Hopewell) and Mississippian periods when more imported cherts were selected. It has been traditionally argued that these latter periods maintained expanded exchange networks and undertook a broader range of regional and cross-regional interaction. If this is so, the material assemblages from Hill Lake sites, although small in size, tend to corroborate this hypothesis.

SIGNIFICANCE OF THE INVESTIGATIONS

In the introductory chapter, six major research goals were proposed for Hill Lake locality sites. The significance of the archeological investigations conducted here is directly related to these goals. These goals are, therefore, repeated briefly, with a summary of the recovered data bearing on them.

Goal 1.   The determination of the nature and extent of all occupations and their relationship to local physiographic features and geomorphic processes.

This goal was addressed and essentially resolved at every site in the study area. Geomorphic coring and/or trenching was accomplished at each site, and particular attention was paid to physiographic features during the course of machine excavation. The only limiting factor in determining the nature and extent of subsurface occupations was the right-of-way corridor. The Fiege, Truck #4, and Go-Kart South sites produced only partial occupational information due to their positions within the proposed alignment. Otherwise, more or less complete occupations were delineated at the Carbon Monoxide and Truck #7 sites. Excavation was comprehensive enough to produce evidence for multicomponent occurrences even if this meant the recognition of an isolated component based only on the recovery of a few diagnostic sherds. This kind of recognition could only have been accomplished by maximizing the subsurface exposure of a site, something that was systematically accomplished at all sites through the use of extensive machine excavation.

One of the most significant accomplishments of this approach was the eventual delineation of settlement shifts which occurred in accordance with major geomorphic trends and episodes.

Goal 2.   The determination of the chronological and and cultural affiliation of components and their placement within the American Bottom cultural continuum.

The chronological affiliation of the components often proved to be more difficult to establish than the cultural affiliations. For example, while it was recognized that a portion of the Carbon Monoxide site was affiliated with the Marion phase in this area, an absolute date for this phase could not be determined. The Columbia Complex dates of 170 B.C. and 10 B.C. from this same site, derived from a late Early Woodland occupation directly overlying the Marion phase occupation, suggest only that the Marion component at this particular site probably falls in the expected time range for this cultural period or minimally predates 170 B.C. to 10 B.C.

There were no major unresolved components at sites in this locality, although it is again reiterated that virtually every cultural component excavated in this group represents a rare data set for this area. Each of the sites has filled important gaps in the prehistoric continuum being established for the American Bottom. Although these components had been previously recognized in surface surveys, many of them had never been excavated as a unit assemblage. This alone may represent the single most significant accomplishment of the excavations carried out in the Hill Lake locality.

Goal 3.   The determination of temporal and spatial relationships between cultural components at individual sites.

This goal is related to the previous one, except that it deals more specifically with internal site component associations, particularly in relationship to the distribution of these components within or on similar physiographic features. It became obvious at an early stage in the excavations that most of the Hill Lake physiographic units capable of supporting habitation produced not one but several occupations. At the Carbon Monoxide site, a late Early Woodland occupation was superimposed over a Marion phase Early Woodland component. To establish this stratigraphic positioning, all excavated materials (not in pits) were piece-plotted vertically and horizontally. By this rather time-consuming technique, the cultural stratigraphy was revealed and the spatial configuration of distinct activity areas became apparent.

Other multicomponent situations were delineated simply by thoroughly shovel scraping an area following machine excavation. In several cases, such as at the Truck #7 site, additional components were found around the periphery of the main component occupation, and they were discovered through systematic attempts to expose not only an area with major concentrations of cultural material but also surrounding units containing less material. This excavation strategy resulted both in the delineation of internal occupation boundaries for the main occupations and the exposure of unexpected secondary components situated along the main occupation edges.

Goal 4.   Determination of site and feature functions.

Most of the Hill Lake sites produced enough information to provide a basis for determining site function and the function of specific features within an occupation. Such determinations would not have been possible without wide-scale exposure of subplowzone areas. The sites of this volume have been interpreted as short-term, probably seasonal, habitations focused primarily on the extraction of the aquatic resources available in the Hill Lake channel. The short-term nature of these occupations was usually indicated by a small number of features, an absence of thick midden deposits, and a general absence of functional tool and feature complexity at sites. Subsistence resources recovered from features indicated that both aquatic and upland resources were exploited.

Feature functions were not always determinable, but attempts were made to distinguish storage from cooking pits, and efforts were made to define all potential activity areas, as represented by distinct subsurface scatters of lithics and ceramics. Such activity areas were defined at the Carbon Monoxide and Fiege sites. These kinds of features were, prior to the FAI-270 Project, virtually unknown and often ignored in the American Bottom. This was due primarily to their not being distinguishable in small test units and to biases that researchers have had toward the larger, more obvious features at sites. Excavations at Hill Lake sites, however, have shown that such scatters represent common and perhaps even typical feature forms, especially for the smaller, extractive camps so prevalent in this area.

Functional variation within the sites was difficult to establish at every site, but several sites provided significant insights about functional complexity within occupation units. The Middle Woodland structure at the Truck #7 site, for example, contained ten internal pits that varied in size, form, and material contents. One pit contained only seed remains, while another served as a depository for lithic rejectage. Other pits functioned as cooking and/or processing units with secondary refuse deposition occurring. The features excavated with this structure, therefore, have enabled us to reconstruct a set of activities carried out within the structure, including seed processing,

322

lithic manufacturing and tool maintenance, cooking, and meat processing. This constitutes the first such data for this time period in the American Bottom and should provide future researchers with a useful model for depicting the kinds of conjunctive activities being carried out at sites from this poorly known Middle Woodland period.

Variation in post size was also observed at the Truck #7 site structure, and this variation was interpreted as being functional in nature and related to a specific manner of constructing houses. Middle Woodland house types and their principles of construction could only be conjectured before the excavation and analysis of features at the Truck #7 site. The proposed utilization of a central post to align both exterior wall and interior support posts was heretofore undocumented in the Midwest for this period.

Goals 5 and 6. Determination of subsistence resources for
each occupation and the delination of major
subsistence shifts through time.

This formed a primary goal of excavations in the Hill Lake locality, and, as was suggested previously, the data recovered from these excavations have afforded the opportunity for developing a subsistence data base where none before existed in this area. Most features excavated in this locality, except lithic and ceramic activity areas, were sampled for subsistence information. This process included the recovery of various quantities of fill, which was then carefully water-screened and floated. The retrieved remains were then sorted and identified by Project faunal and floral specialists. The most important results have already been summarized elsewhere in this chapter. The appearance of the starchy seed complex during the Middle Woodland period and the initial occurrence of maize during the early Mississippian period mark the two most important ethnobotanical events of this locality. The significance of these occurrences at the Hill Lake sites is that 1) they document previously recorded floral shifts in this area, and 2) they indicate that the sites along the Hill Lake locality were not isolated cultural units, but participants in broader changes occurring throughout this area during any given time period.

The exploitation of aquatic and upland resources at sites such as Carbon Monoxide and Truck #7 indicates the existence of generalized subsistence systems, and perhaps more significantly, systems focused on and adapted to local resources. Occupational shifts within the Hill Lake locality and between various upland and floodplain localities apparently operated throughout the prehistoric period. These systems appear to have resulted primarily from the existence of numerous resource-rich microzones throughout the American Bottom, most of which could not apparently support long-term, permanent occupation, due perhaps to geomorphic instability in the floodplain, but which could satisfy the seasonal needs of communities in optimal locations, such as inner-channel ridges and bank edges. The small occupations of short duration identified in the Hill Lake locality lend significant support to this proposed settlement model.

No discussion is offered here concerning a possible upland-lowland settlement system. Because of borrow pit excavations carried out in the uplands overlooking the Hill Lake locality, numerous large and small occupations are known. Many of the floodplain and upland assemblages are nearly identical, suggesting that they may be the products of a single community moving back and forth between these very different resource zones. In the future a more thorough study should be made of this settlement system, and it should be apparent that locality settlement strategies are part of a much more complex and dynamic settlement system.

SUMMARY

The sites in this portion of the Hill Lake locality formed a contiguous unit represented by discrete occupations of variable size, and consisted of several different components ranging in time from the Early Woodland to Historic periods. Each of the sites, regardless of size, has supplemented significantly the data base for a cultural period in the American Bottom. They represent, however, only portions of the entire prehistoric continuum of this area and only part of a much greater data base excavated by the FAI-270 project during the past five years. Therefore, the real significance of the Hill Lake data will become more apparent in the context of a broader areal synthesis incorporating the entire data base, including additional sites excavated in the Hill Lake locality, but included in other volumes [e.g., the Go-Kart North (Fortier and Emerson 1984); the Carbon Dioxide (Finney and Fortier 1985); and the Mund sites (Fortier et al. 1983)].

Excavation of subsurface prehistoric resources in this floodplain environment proved to be a difficult task even with the relatively comprehensive testing program utilized initially by this project. Most of the occupations were deeply buried under as much as 1 m of alluvium, and surface materials, in retrospect, did not always prove to be good indicators of where the main occupations lay beneath the surface. Since a primary objective of the FAI-270 Project was the discovery and excavation of prehistoric community plans, heavy machinery was utilized to more efficiently and more rapidly remove the overburdens covering the various subsurface occupations. The loss of some plowzone cultural material was inevitable, but the choice between recovering an occasional projectile point or rim sherd in dubious context, and delineating an entire community, seemed an obvious one, especially in the context of highway construction deadlines and in the context of genuine anthropological significance. The occupation units exposed by these techniques will provide, for years to come, invaluable models for the excavation of similar habitations in the American Bottom, especially in situations where time and money have not been so generously provided.

REFERENCES

Asch, David L., and Nancy B. Asch
1978   The economic potential of _Iva annua_ and its prehistoric importance in the lower Illinois valley. In The nature and status of ethnobotany, edited by Richard I. Ford, pp. 301-341. Museum of Anthropology, University of Michigan, Anthropological Papers 67.

Asch, David L., Kenneth B. Farnsworth and Nancy B. Asch
1979   Woodland subsistence and settlement in west central Illinois. In Hopewell archaeology: the Chillicothe conference, edited by David S. Brose and N'omi Greber, pp. 80-85. Kent State University Press, Kent Ohio.

Asch, Nancy B., and David L. Asch
1980   The Dickson Camp and Pond sites: Middle Woodland archaeobotany in Illinois. In Dickson Camp and Pond: two early Havana tradition sites in the central Illinois valley, by Anne Marie Cantwell, Appendix B, pp. 152-160. Illinois State Museum Reports of Investigations 36.

Bareis, Charles J. and James W. Porter
1984   Research Design. In American Bottom Archaeology: A Summary of the FAI-270 Project Contribution to the Culture History of the Mississippi River Valley, edited by Charles J. Bareis and James W. Porter, pp. 1-14. University of Illinois Press, Urbana and Chicago.

Bareis, Charles J., James W. Porter, and John E. Kelly
1977   Report of investigations and proposed mitigation for the Hill Lake meander scar: St. Clair and Monroe counties, Illinois. Department of Anthropology, University of Illinois at Urbana-Champaign, FAI-270 Archaeological Mitigation Project .

Bodner, Constance and Ralph Rowlett
1980   Separation of bone, charcoal, and seeds by chemical flotation. American Antiquity 45:110-116.

Bonnell, Linda M., and William P. White
  1981a Geomorphic investigations at the Carbon Monoxide site (11-Mo-593). _Department of Anthropology, University of Illinois at Urbana-Champaign, FAI-270 Archaeological Mitigation Project Geomorphological Report_ 2.

  1981b Geomporphic investigations at the Truck #4 site (11-Mo-195). _Department of Anthropology, University of Illinois at Urbana-Champaign, FAI-270 Archaeological Mitigation Project Geomorphological Report_ 3.

  1981c Geomorphic investigations at the Go-Kart South site (11-Mo-552S) and Truck #7 site (11-Mo-200). _Department of Anthropology, University of Illinois at Urbana-Champaign, FAI-270 Archaeological Mitigation Project Geomorphological Report_ 4.

Brose, David
  1970 The archaeology of Summer Island: changing settlement systems in northern Lake Michigan. _Museum of Anthropology, University of Michigan, Anthropological Papers_ 41.

Cantwell, Anne-Marie
  1980 Dickson Camp and Pond: two early Havana tradition sites in the central Illinois valley. _Illinois State Museum, Reports of Investigation_ 6.

Chapman, Carl H.
  1980 _The archaeology of Missouri, II._ University of Missouri Press, Columbia.

Chapman, Jefferson and Andrea Brewer Shea
  1977 Paleoecological and cultural interpretations of plant remains recovered from Archaic period sites in the lower Little Tennessee River valley. Paper presented at the 34th Annual Meeting of the Southeastern Archaeological Conference.

Chomko, Stephen A., and Gary W. Crawford
  1978 Plant husbandry in prehistoric eastern North America: new evidence for its development. _American Antiquity_ 43:405-405.

327

Coulter, Samuel M.
    1904   An ecological comparison of some typical swamp areas. <u>Missouri Botanical Garden, Fifteenth Annual Report</u>: 39-71.

Cowan, C. Wesley
    1978   The prehistoric use and distribution of maygrass in eastern North America: cultural and phytogeographic implications. In The nature and status of ethnobotany, edited by Richard I. Ford, pp. 263-288. <u>Museum of Anthropology, University of Michigan, Anthropological Papers</u> 67.

Emerson, Thomas E., George R. Milner, and Douglas K. Jackson
    1983   The Florence Street site. <u>American Bottom Archaeology FAI-270 Site Reports</u>, Volume 2, edited by Charles J. Bareis and James W. Porter. University of Illinois Press, Urbana and Chicago.

Faulkner, Charles H., and Major C. R. McCollough
    1974   Excavations and testing, Normandy Reservoir Salvage Project: 1972 season. <u>Department of Anthropology, University of Tennessee, Normandy Archaeological Project, Volume 2, Report of Investigations</u> 12.

Finney, Fred A. and Andrew C. Fortier
    1985   The Carbon Dioxide site, by Fred A. Finney and The Robert Schneider site, by Andrew C. Fortier. <u>American Bottom Archaeology FAI-270 Site Reports</u>, Volume 11, edited by Charles J. Bareis and James W. Porter. University of Illinois Press, Urbana and Chicago.

Fitting, James E. (editor)
    1972   The Schultz site at Green Point. a stratified occupation area in the Saginaw valley of Michigan. <u>Museum of Anthropology, University of Michigan, Memoirs</u>, 4.

Ford, Richard I.
    1981   Gardening and farming before A. D. 1000: patterns of prehistoric cultivation north of Mexico. <u>Journal of Ethnobiology</u> 1:6-27.

Fortier, Andrew C. and Thomas E. Emerson
    1984   The Go-Kart North site, by Andrew C. Fortier and The Dyroff
            and Levin sites, by Thomas E. Emerson. American Bottom
            Archaeology FAI-270 Site Reports, Volume 9, edited by
            Charles J. Bareis and James W. Porter, University of
            Illinois Press, Urbana and Chicago.

Fortier, Andrew C., Fred A. Finney, and Richard B. Lacampagne
    1983   The Mund site. American Bottom Archaeology FAI-270 Site
            Reports, Volume 5, edited by Charles J. Bareis and James
            W. Porter. University of Illinois Press, Urbana and
            Chicago.

Greenup, William C.
    1838   Documents relative to the drainage of Illinois lands.
            United States Senate Document 2:1-5. Twenty-fifth Congress,
            Third Session.

Gregg, Michael L.
    1975   Settlement morphology and production specialization: the
            Horseshoe Lake site, a case study. Unpublished Ph.D.
            dissertation, Department of Anthropology, University of
            Wisconsin, Milwaukee.

Griffin, James B.
    1952   Some Early and Middle Woodland pottery types in Illinois.
            In Hopewellian communities in Illinois, edited by Thorne
            Deuel, pp. 93-129. Illinois State Museum, Scientific Papers
            5.

Helm, Edwin G.
    1905   The levee and drainage problem of the American Bottoms.
            Association of Engineering Societies 35:91-116.

Hoffman, Michael P.
    1969   Prehistoric development in southwestern Arkansas. Arkansas
            Archaeologist 10:37-49.

Hus, Henri
    1908   An ecological cross section of the Mississippi River in the
            region of St. Louis, Missouri. Missouri Botanical Garden,
            Annual Report 19:127-258.

Johannessen, Sissel
    1982   Paleoethnobotanical trends in the American Bottom: Late Archaic through Mississippian. Paper presented at the 47th annual meeting, Society for American Archaeology, April 14-17, 1982. Minneapolis, Minnesota.

Kay, Marvin, Francis B. King, and Christine Robinson
    1980   Cucurbits from Phillips Spring: new evidence and interpretations. American Antiquity 45:806-822.

Kelly, John E.
    1980   Formative developments at Cahokia and the adjacent American Bottom: a Merrell Tract perspective. Unpublished Ph.D. dissertation. Department of Anthropology, University of Wisconsin, Madison.

    1984   Late Bluff chert utilization on The Merrell Tract, Cahokia. In Prehistoric chert exploitation: studies from the midcontinent, edited by B. M. Butler and E. E. May, Center for Archaeological Investigations Occasional Paper 2:23-44.

Kelly, John E., and Andrew C. Fortier
    1983   The Range site (11-S-47): The Archaic, Early Woodland, and Middle Woodland components. Department of Anthropology, University of Illinois at Urbana-Champaign, FAI-270 Archaeological Mitigation Project Report 60.

Kelly, John E., Jean R. Linder, and Theresa J. Cartmell
    1979   The archaeological intensive survey of the proposed FAI-270 alignment in the American Bottom region of southern Illinois. Illinois Transportation Archaeology Scientific Reports 1.

King, Frances B.
    1980   Plant remains from Phillips Spring, a multicomponent site in the western Ozark highland of Missouri. Plains Anthropologist 25:217-227.

Kline, Gerald W., Gary D. Crites, and Charles H. Faulkner
    1982   The McFarland Project: early Middle Woodland settlement and subsistence in the Upper Back River valley in Tennessee. Tennessee Anthropological Association, Miscellaneous Paper Number 8.

330

Lewis, Walter H., and Memory P.F. Elvin-Lewis
    1977   Medical botany: plants affecting man's health. John Wiley and Sons, New York.

Linder, Jean R.
    1974   The Jean Rita site: an Early Woodland occupation in Monroe county, Illinois. The Wisconsin Archeologist 55:99-162.

Marshall, James A.
    1969   Engineering principles and the study of prehistoric structures: a substantive example. American Antiquity 34:166-171.

Martin, Alexander C., and William D. Barkley
    1961   Seed identification manual. University of California Press, Berkeley.

McElrath, Dale L. and Andrew C. Fortier
    1983   The Missouri Pacific #2 site. American Bottom Archaeology FAI-270 Site Reports, Volume 3, edited by Charles J. Bareis and James W. Porter. University of Illinois Press, Urbana and Chicago.

McGregor, John C.
    1958   The Pool and Irving villages: a study of Hopewell occupation in the Illinois River valley. University of Illinois Press, Urbana-Champaign.

Minnis, Paul E.
    1981   Seeds in archaeological sites: sources and some interpretative problems. American Antiquity 46:143-152.

Montgomery, Frederick H.
    1977   Seeds and fruits of plants of Eastern Canada and northeastern United States. University of Toronto Press, Toronto.

Munson, Patrick J.
    1966   The Sheets site: a Late Archaic-Early Woodland occupation in west-central Illinois. Michigan Archaeologist 12:111-120.

1982   Marion, Black Sand, Morton, and Havana relationship: an Illinois Valley perspective. The Wisconsin Archeologist 63:1-17.

Munson, Patrick J., and Robert Hall
    1966   An Early Woodland radiocarbon date from Illinois. The Michigan Archaeologist 12:85-87.

Panshin, A., J., and Carl De Zeeuw
    1970   Textbook of wood technology Volume 1, (Third edition). McGraw-Hill, New York.

Parmalee, Paul W., Andreas A. Paloumpis, and Nancy Wilson
    1972   Animals utilized by Woodland peoples occupying the Apple Creek site, Illinois. Illinois State Museum, Reports of Investigations 23.

Pease, Theodore Calvin, and Raymond C. Werner (editors)
    1934   The French foundations: 1680-1693. Collections of the Illinois State Historical Library, Volume 23.

Porter, James W.
    1969   The Mitchell site and prehistoric exchange systems at Cahokia: A.D. 1000 +300. In Explorations into Cahokia archaeology, edited by Melvin L. Fowler, pp. 137-164. Illinois Archaeological Survey Bulletin 7. University of Illinois, Urbana.

    1971   An archaeological survey of the Mississippi valley in St. Clair, Monroe, and Randolph counties. In Preliminary report of 1971 historic sites survey: archaeological reconnaissance of selected areas in the State of Illinois, Part 1, Summary Section A, pp. 28-32. Illinois Archaeological Survey, Urbana.

    1974   Cahokia archaeology as viewed from the Mitchell site: a satellite community at A.D. 1150-1200. Unpublished Ph.D. dissertation, Department of Anthropology, Universtiy of Wisconsin, Madison.

1980   Introduction, In Annual Report of 1979 Investigations, pp. 1-17. Department of Anthropology, University of Illinois at Urbana-Champaign, FAI-270 Archaeological Mitigation Project Annual Report.

Smith, Huron H.
1928   Ethnobotany of the Meskwaki Indians. Milwaukee Public Museum, Bulletin 4:175-326.

Steyermark, Julian A.
1963   Flora of Missouri. Iowa State University Press, Ames.

Struever, Stuart
1968a   Flotation techniques for the recovery of small-scale archaeological remains. American Antiquity 33:353-362.

1968b   A re-examination of Hopewell in Eastern North America. Unpublished Ph. D. dissertation. University of Chicago, Chicago.

Telford, Clarence J.
1927   Third report on a forest survey of Illinois. Bulletin of the Illinois State Natural History Survey, Volume 16.

Wagner, Gail E.
1976   IDOT flotation procedure manual. Ms. on file, Illinois Department of Transportation, District 8, Fairview Heights.

Walthall, John A.
1981   Galena and aboriginal trade in eastern North America. Illinois State Museum, Scientific Papers 17. Springfield.

Watson, Patty Jo, and Richard A. Yarnell
1969   Conclusions: the prehistoric utilization of Salts Cave. In The prehistory of Salts Cave, Kentucky, by Patty Jo Watson, pp. 71-78. Illinois State Museum, Reports of Investigations 16.

Welch, David
1975   Wood utilization at Cahokia: identification of wood charcoal
        from the Merrell Tract. Unpublished M.A. thesis, Department
        of Anthropology, University of Wisconsin, Madison.

White, Ante M.
1968   The lithic industries of the Illinois valley in the Early
        and Middle Woodland period. Museum of Anthropology,
        University of Michigan, Anthropological Papers 35.

Williams, Joyce and Richard Lacampagne
1982   Final report on archaeological investigations at the Adler
        site (11-S-64). Department of Anthropology, University of
        Illinois at Urbana-Champaign, FAI-270 Archaeological
        Mitigation Project Report 43.

Yarnell, Richard A.
1964   Aboriginal relationships between culture and plant life in
        the upper Great Lakes region. Museum of Anthropology,
        University of Michigan, Anthropological Papers 23.

1969   Contents of human paleofeces. In The prehistory of Salts
        Cave, by Patty Jo Watson, pp. 41-54. Illinois State Museum,
        Reports of Investigations 16.

Zawacki, April A., and Glenn Hausfater
1969   Early vegetation of the lower Illinois valley. Illinois
        State Museum, Reports of Investigations 17.